Order Ethics or Moral Surplus

Order Ethics or Moral Surplus

What Holds a Society Together?

Christoph Luetge

LEXINGTON BOOKS
Lanham • Boulder • New York • London

Published by Lexington Books
An imprint of The Rowman & Littlefield Publishing Group, Inc.
4501 Forbes Boulevard, Suite 200, Lanham, Maryland 20706
www.rowman.com

Unit A, Whitacre Mews, 26-34 Stannary Street, London SE11 4AB

Copyright © 2015 by Lexington Books

All rights reserved. No part of this book may be reproduced in any form or by any electronic or mechanical means, including information storage and retrieval systems, without written permission from the publisher, except by a reviewer who may quote passages in a review.

British Library Cataloguing in Publication Information Available

Library of Congress Cataloging-in-Publication Data

Luetge, Christoph, 1969-
Order ethics or moral surplus : what holds a society together? / Christoph Luetge.
pages cm
Includes bibliographical references and index.
ISBN 978-0-7391-9867-4 (cloth : alk. paper) -- ISBN 978-0-7391-9868-1 (electronic)
1. Social ethics. 2. Political science--Philosophy I. Title.
HM665.L84 2015
170--dc23
2014048576

∞ ™ The paper used in this publication meets the minimum requirements of American National Standard for Information Sciences Permanence of Paper for Printed Library Materials, ANSI/NISO Z39.48-1992.

Printed in the United States of America

To Lt. Walter Papendick (1896–1918)
of the Second Royal Prussian Foot Guards,
who died for the old order

Contents

Preface ... ix

1. Introduction: The Challenge of Globalization to Philosophy ... 1
2. Normativity under Conditions of Globalization: The Conception of Order Ethics ... 21
3. Society Requires Capacities of the Individual ... 69
4. Society Requires a Sense of Justice ... 143
5. Society Requires Incentives and Rules ... 165
6. Conclusion: Normativity ex nihilo? ... 209

Outlook ... 225

Bibliography ... 227

Index ... 241

About the Author ... 251

Preface

In 1994, when attending the European Forum Alpbach, I asked Nobel laureate James M. Buchanan (1919–2013), whether he found it sufficient that the citizens of a society simply stuck to the rules. He hesitated for a moment, and then gave the terse reply: "No."

This answer, it seemed to me, required further elaboration. It consequently led me to the primary concern of the present work, which may be formulated as follows: What skills or traits do the members of a modern society require in the era of globalization in order for their society to remain stable?

Some further explanation is necessary here. To begin with, I make the assumption that no demands are necessary for the individual's systemic compliance with the institutionally anchored, sanction-based rules of a society. This is already ensured by the individuals' self-interest. By contrast, however, many theorists believe that members of society not only need to maintain the rules, but meet other preconditions as well or what I call *moral surpluses*. I doubt, however, on the one hand, that these surplus values are necessary for social stability and, on the other, that they can be presupposed systematically under the conditions of globalization.

Chapter 1 first deals with the phenomenon of globalization from a philosophical point of view based on the approaches of Otfried Höffe and John Rawls. Both already hint at the basic theme of this book, as each assumes that there are anthropological conditions of social stability—even under conditions of globalization—that must be normatively stipulated.

Chapter 2 lays out the systematic foundations of my ethical conception: Under conditions of globalization, the approach of order ethics appears to be promising, because it is based on the logic of advantages and incentives rather than anthropological preconditions. I deduce order ethics in a novel way with the help of a thought experiment. This concept is explicated, defended against some standard objections, and elaborated in greater methodological detail.

Chapters 3 to 5 form the book's main part. Here, I examine eight proposed candidates for moral surplus values. I start with strong precondition-based requirements and conclude with approaches that make increasingly fewer and weaker demands on the actors.

Chapter 6 offers a summary and defines its own approach. Since none of the recommended surplus values appear to be viable, the question of alternatives must be raised. The proposed alternative of order ethics is not based on anthropological findings, features, or surplus values, but rather on the preconditions of situations. Three minimum preconditions can be identified that are required to provide sufficient stability for a modern society under the conditions of globalization: sociality, an ability to communicate, and an ability to invest. These three conditions have the decisive advantage over the discussed candidates insofar as they do not need or expect individuals to break with the logic of advantages and incentives.

I would like to thank James M. Buchanan, Ken Binmore, David Gauthier, Jürgen Habermas, and Karl Homann for their encouragement and for the works that inspired much of this book. Christopher Reid has done an excellent job translating the manuscript. Many thanks go to Jana Hodges-Kluck, Natalie Mandziuk, and Kari Waters at Lexington Books as well as to an anonymous reviewer for their work and valuable comments. In preparing the final version, Benjamin Großmann-Hensel, Christian Hamann, and Wally Eichler have been very helpful.

Chapter One

Introduction

The Challenge of Globalization to Philosophy

This book aims to discover the normative foundations of modern societies under the conditions of globalization. This line of inquiry has multiple aspects, which must be addressed separately.

First, it is necessary to explain what is to be understood by a society's *normative foundations*. For our purposes, this includes the capabilities and/or qualities of the citizens belonging to these societies. In the theoretical approaches that will be discussed, these capabilities and/or qualities are taken to be necessary for allowing a society to become *and to remain* stable. Thus these capabilities and/or qualities are typically *required* in a normative sense, independent of their actual existence or efficacy.[1] It is the primary claim of these approaches that if the normative foundations of a society are not present or have been eroded through social processes, the stability of the society in question will find itself at considerable risk. If the foundations cannot be re-established for an extended period, the collapse or decline of the respective society must be expected.[2]

Second, this book will center on *modern* societies. These kinds of societies are categorically distinct in their structure from pre-modern societies.[3] Modern societies are anonymous societies, characterized by a high degree of pluralism, and do not "play" zero-sum games. The general focus is on modern societies that have *democratic* forms of governance. This implies that the effective political control of the government—closely following John Rawls (1999, §2)—is through elections. According to Karl Popper (1945/1950), it is the fundamental achievement of democracy that governments can be replaced without bloodshed. To ensure this, certain supporting democratic institutions are essential, whose existence and, to a large degree, efficacy are required for the "normal operation" of the democratic societies presented in the theories of this book. This normal operation in any case already makes the question about normative foundations, *without* the additional problems associated with the processes of globalization, highly contentious.

The effects of the *processes of globalization* are the second element to the book's basic question. Under globalization, I understand with Otfried Höffe (1999/2002, 13) the "increase and intensification of worldwide social relations," which furthermore have a far-reaching impact on society, economy, politics, and culture. These effects are discussed in many disciplines, especially in sociology, economics, political science, social psychology, and cultural studies.[4] Does philosophy have anything to contribute here? In my view, philosophy cannot afford to ignore the impact of globalization processes, or dismiss them as incidental developments.

There have, in fact, not been very many prominent philosophical opinions expressed on the topic of globalization. Two of the few volumes that I would like to discuss in this introduction are exemplary in showing the problems that emerge for philosophy when it tries to interpret novel phenomena with previous schemata and categories. The two approaches are found in the works entitled *Demokratie im Zeitalter der Globalisierung* ("Democracy in the Era of Globalization") by Höffe (1999/2002) and *The Law of Peoples* by Rawls (1999). An account of these essays at this point will broaden the scope somewhat and elucidate the differences and similarities in the treatment of the phenomenon of globalization. As an introduction to the primary focus of this book, it will be essential to work out what requirements both authors anticipate for the members of societies under the conditions of globalization.

First, a few words on methodology. In this book, I will continually draw on the methods and findings of individual disciplines. At the same time, I have tried throughout to keep such recourse methodologically consistent. By this I mean that the methods and results from different individual disciplines are used *only for certain problems* for which the concerned discipline can claim authority. An effort was made to avoid falling back on a specific area of study in the context of problems for which its tools are not suitable or relying on an eclectic mixture of different disciplines, without specifying the relationship they have to each other or the relevant philosophical questions. It will be up to the reader to decide whether I have succeeded in doing this.

PHILOSOPHY AND GLOBALIZATION I: OTFRIED HÖFFE

I will begin with Höffe's remarks on globalization. His starting point is a sketch of the effects of globalization and its associated phenomena and processes. Höffe tries to relativize the importance of globalization processes, which he in no way views as a "sign of our times" (Höffe 1999/2002, 20). He downplays the theory of the gradual disempowerment of the state ("genuinely global tasks" [ibid. 14] cannot be solved regionally) and simultaneously stresses the role of counter-movements and the historical dimension. There have already been globalization processes in other periods of history, for instance, around 1800 and 1492 (see ibid. 21ff.), and even during antiquity (see ibid. 234). Moreover, what we now call globalization is just a "trend" (ibid. 25), yet still not an outcome. It is therefore not justified to refer to this trend as *the* defining phenomenon of our time.

Just the same, Höffe sees "social reality pushing powerfully beyond the individual democracies" (ibid. 9). As a consequence, the idea has emerged of a "global community" or a "world republic" (ibid.). Höffe suggests that the manifestation of this world republic may neither be left entirely to the forces of the market, nor those of an unchecked social evolution, but must rather be supported by a democratic responsibility framework. This would ensure that a "democracy committed to principles of justice" (ibid. 10, 37ff.), whose elements Höffe already describes at the level of the nation state (cf. Höffe 1987), would also come to bear at the global level. The most important of these elements are indicated here:

1. The coercive powers of government institutions are bound by rules that would ultimately be legitimized by the consensus of the citizens. In the Kantian tradition, Höffe understands the individual as an end in itself, who must be regarded as the final point in the legitimation chain. Her consent to government rules proceeds from a weighing of advantages, implying a contract-theoretical justification of democracy. Höffe's ideas, however, are distinguished from other comparable contract-theoretical notions (such as James M. Buchanan's)[5] insofar as he uses the concept of "transcendental exchange" (ibid. 53ff.). An exchange then must satisfy certain conditions to be fair. The subjective (or rather "subject-based") precondition is the *actual* freedom of consent. The objective (or rather: the "object-side") preconditions include at least the approximate equivalence of barter items and certain minimal transcendental anthropological requirements, rather than those that are of an all-encompassing biological-philosophical type. A "minimal anthropology," which defines the "initial conditions of the [human] capacity for action" (ibid. 56), is indispensable. In turn, it becomes clear that, according to Höffe, the criteria for a fair exchange are themselves not defined in contract-theoretical terms. It is therefore not a comprehensive contract theory that is at issue, but rather a state and legal theory with contract-theoretical elements.
2. The principles of justice in a democracy are also substantively determined. Accordingly, there are, for instance, negative liberties (defensive rights) and positive liberties (which justify the welfare state).[6]

Here, Höffe formulates in detail[7] fairly extensive social rights that may, however, be immediately derived from his contract-theoretical concept. There are also other fundamental principles such as the one of proto-justice, according to which all involved individuals recognize each other reciprocally (and "originally") as legal subjects as well as a universal legal mandate. Generally speaking, the principles of justice are "largely undisputed" (ibid. 227).[8]

3. Public authorities are required to adhere to the foundational principles such as the separation of powers. Höffe points out that the concept of separation of powers is not of modern origin, but can already be found among the Greeks or the Iroquois Indians of the nineteenth century. The further principles of subsidiarity, difference (whereby communities have a right to be different), and federalism may also be ascribed to historical models.

4. Höffe's contract-theoretical concept, however, places demands not only on the institutions of a modern society, but also on its citizens. The citizens must be able to avail themselves of a functioning "morality" (ibid. 193). In particular, they must orient their behavior in terms of four civic virtues:

> a. *Sense of legality*: a citizen's legal sense demands that she comply with the law. The reasons for why the individual may be law-abiding are irrelevant. Höffe relegates civic courage that goes beyond legal compliance to the authoritarian state. By contrast, in a democracy, civic courage and the supposed right to resistance raises serious problems.
> b. *Sense of justice*: the citizens of a democracy should be able to use their sense of justice[9] to recognize cases of partisanship such as in government and administration. At the same time, this sense should reinforce and heighten their moral self-esteem (see ibid. 202), for example, in a tolerant attitude.
> c. *Sense of citizenship*: through their sense of citizenship, citizens must also feel called upon to take responsibility for their own communities (ibid. 209).
> d. *Sense of public spirit*: lastly, the sense of public spirit demands—in practical terms—that people take on charitable tasks and develop an understanding of their own culture. The sense of public spirit, however, also requires that citizens, as regards a theory of virtue, adopt a general attitude of prudence in opposition to the "tendency toward insatiability" (ibid. 217), which is a threat to everyone. The *pleonexia*—Höffe once again takes up this concept from antiqui-

ty of wanting more (see also ibid. 93)—represents a substantial risk in all spheres of life for a democracy based on principles of justice.

Proceeding from this sketch of a national, principle-based democracy, Höffe conceptualizes a "subsidiary and federal world republic" (ibid. 227ff.) that is supposed to implement at the global level the principles previously found to be just. Once he describes in detail the historical dimension of the theory of international law,[10] Höffe (ibid. 267ff.) then considers possible arguments that have been used to dispute the need and/or possibility of a world state.

First, in terms of world policy, a purely strategic point of view maintains that a world government would not be possible because the individual states would perceive all supranational organizations and agencies only as instruments of their own power politics.[11] Höffe does not consider this political-realistic point of view to be convincing. It ignores the growing international interdependence of states, and above all does not take into account that a system of international treaties that is only based on mutual deterrence cannot be permanently stable.[12]

Second, Höffe rejects the "neo-institutional position" (see ibid. 276ff.), which sees non-state actors taking on many of the tasks previously handled by national governments. This position is "certainly justified" (ibid. 277), but overestimates the role of non-governmental organizations. Moreover organizations do not fulfill Höffe's justice-related requirements, for they are neither impartial (see ibid. 280) nor democratically controlled (ibid. 282).

Third, Höffe does not find the path to a gradual democratization of the world of states to be practicable. Following Immanuel Kant's hypothesis in *Perpetual Peace*,[13] such a position supposedly holds that conflicts between states will disappear and a peaceful coexistence will take hold along with the worldwide realization of democracy. In Höffe's view, this basic assumption of other aspects of political theory[14] is by no means empirically grounded, and a number of counter examples could also be found.[15] Beyond this, however, even if the representatives of the Kantian position can claim a certain degree of plausibility, a world state would have responsibilities such as peacekeeping, which, even in a world with a growing number of democracies, cannot be fulfilled in any other way.

After challenging his opponents' arguments, Höffe presents the concept of a complementary world republic based on contract theory. At the heart of the model is a *twofold global social contract*. This contract should be settled, on the one hand, between the individual states and, on the other, between all the (world) citizens. In the first case, the individual states agree to peacefully resolve their disputes in a manner consistent with international law. In the second case, the citizens agree to refrain from vigilantism, as in the national social contract, in order to free themselves from the state of nature. In both cases, the parties would give their consent out of a sense of their respective "distributive-collective advantage" (ibid. 308).

According to Höffe, a simple global social contract would not be adequate, for it would necessarily preserve the nation-state level. Collectives would pursue their own interests, which would not be reducible to the overall interests of their members (ibid. 309). In any event, it would not be possible to conceive of the direct access from the level of particular individuals to the level of the world state in a sensible way. The world-state legislature must therefore contain *two* chambers, with one representing the states and the other their citizens.

Höffe makes clear that the world republic could only assume strictly limited powers lest it mutate into a "Leviathan." The areas of responsibility should only be extended with a great deal of caution. A world republic must also justify itself to an international public, which, indeed, has not yet been formed. However, even the latter could not guarantee that the diverse interests would receive at least approximately the same amount of attention (ibid. 322). This reflects a major problem for current international organizations such as the UN, which are not actually democratic, but rather oligarchic in nature (consider the UN Security Council). A world republic would therefore have to be fundamentally different from the UN.

But, even at the global level, the conditions are not only to be fulfilled institutionally. The world's citizens would have to do their part to "establish the necessary institutions and fill them with life" (ibid. 335). A world republic is not possible without "a cosmopolitan motivation, rooted in habits and character traits" (ibid.). This motivation is expressed in four virtues, which are opposed to an overvaluation of institutions. They also correspond to those that would be required at the national level:

1. *Sense of global rights*: the global citizen's sense of world rights should lead her to accept on her own current legally binding arrangements. She should also recognize laws free of *coercion* (see ibid. 341). This must be required or else there is a risk of "free riding" (ibid. 342).[16]
2. *Sense of global justice*: the sense of justice should above all come to bear at the global level in the two chambers of the world parliament and in the media. Höffe divides this sense into three sub-senses, which should a) facilitate the global legal order through mutual recognition of the parties as equals, b) make sure that this global legal order remains independent of shifts of power, and c) guarantee an equal evaluation of injustice throughout the world. In addition, world citizens with a sense of global justice would not take advantage of legal loopholes, even if it would not contradict the letter, but indeed the spirit, of the law (ibid. 344).

3. *Sense of global citizenship*: the world citizen must have a sense of global citizenship. Nonetheless, this would not require the same type of political commitment as the sense of national citizenship, given that the relevant political arena would be much larger and more complex. Certainly, world citizenship could very well demand participation in elections and other democratic institutions such as NGOs or "Doctors without Borders." According to Höffe, world politics should not be left to career politicians.
4. *Sense of global public spirit*: much like the global citizen, the citizen of the global society is characterized by a sense of global public spirit. This sense of public spirit is intended, on the one hand, to promote social engagement such as in the form of exchange-partnerships and the establishment of democracies in developing countries. On the other hand, the sense of public spirit has a cultural component that is supposed to be responsible, for example, for the cultivation of language, literature, art, and music. Höffe maintains that it is not contradictory to demand a sense of public spirit on the global level, even if there are no objective commonalities, as in the case of smaller communities. The "contemplation of shared human reason" (ibid. 348) could be helpful here.

How useful is it to stipulate such anthropological requirements on a global scale? Höffe remarks that, undoubtedly, "the complexities of civic virtues increase on a global scale" (339). In any case, these four virtues, which already present problems on the national level, should be present in the citizens of the global society. Only with their help would it be possible to address the following individual tasks of a world republic that Höffe identifies:

a. Peace and justice: discussed here, among other things, are problems of global jurisdiction, international crime, the interstate monopoly of power to be transferred to the world republic, and the right of asylum.
b. Self-determination of peoples, the right to secession (see ibid. 379ff.), and humanitarian interventions, which should only be permitted in cases of *serious* human rights violations (ibid. 393ff.).
c. A social and ecological world market: the world republic should also establish and implement international competitive regulations with the help of institutions such as a world office of fair trade. Not only should a global commercial law be developed, but also an "ethics of world-market regulations" (ibid. 402). In cases of market failure, this relies on global justice as the "moral corrective" (ibid. 407). It establishes, among other things, global social standards based on human rights.

On the whole, Höffe's conception of a world republic is full of preconditions. A remark on Höffe's method—which the author himself designates as being based on "moral law" (ibid. 11, also 28 and 83ff.)—is also germane: it is supposed to "deal with" (*befassen*) material laws and empirical constraints, as in economics, politics, and so on (see ibid. 11). It is set against a preference-based method (ibid. 99), which apparently means an economic method in the broadest sense.[17] It also has normative implications. Thus, according to Höffe, the global civic virtues are not primarily preference-based or economic in nature, but are supposedly necessitated by the "moral law" (ibid. 337). It is unclear, however, how this is to be understood from a methodological standpoint. In particular, it is not apparent in my view how empirical requirements and material laws are to interact with normative statements. The term "to deal with" is highly ambiguous. But, precisely because it does *not* concern a method relating to a single discipline, particularly not economics, it is only possible to conclude that philosophy takes the lead with regard to the moral-legal point of view. Whether it is possible to meaningfully draw on the individual disciplines with such an approach is at least uncertain. The suspicion arises that moral-legal mandates finally confront material laws in a manner that, again, is unmediated.

In summary, Höffe endorses the concept of the world state with moral-legalistic and contract-theoretical arguments. The conception of John Rawls—which I turn to now—has its origin in a similar, although not identical, theoretical foundation. While Rawls (1999) begins with observations that resemble Höffe's, he ultimately arrives at starkly different conclusions.

PHILOSOPHY AND GLOBALIZATION II: JOHN RAWLS'S "LAW OF PEOPLES"

Even though Rawls, in his "Law of Peoples" (1999), does not mention globalization as a phenomenon by name, his approach is clearly tailored to the changes in the world situation due to globalization processes.[18] This is indicated, for instance, by his aim to establish principles for the—permanent and not just temporary—social cooperation of liberal and non-liberal peoples of various kinds. Such social cooperation emerges as a particularly urgent problem under the conditions of globalization.

As with Höffe, Rawls attempts to transfer his own conception of the state, which is developed for the nation state, to the global level. Without explaining in detail the concept of justice as fairness (for more elaboration on this, see chapter 4), two important points are worth mentioning. According to Rawls (1971 and 1993), the institutions of a society can determine their compatibility with the notion of justice as fairness on the basis of the model of the *original position*. In the *original position*, the actors establish two principles of justice under constraints that must be met by the institutions of a society: first, public offices must in general be open to everyone in the same manner; second, social and economic inequalities must have a favorable effect on the least advantaged. A society whose citizens grow up with institutions that satisfy these two principles of justice can be designated as liberal. This is the basic idea of the Rawlsian conception *before* the "Law of Peoples," that is, in reference to the nation state.

What, then, is the objective of a "law of peoples"? It should first be noted that Rawls is guided by the Kantian principle of *foedus pacificum* (see Kant [1976ff., vol. 11]) and—unlike Höffe—explicitly rejects the idea of a *world state* as being neither desirable nor possible. In his view, a world state can only either lead to despotism or a fragile structure with very little enforcement power (cf. Rawls 1999, 36). Rawls also obviously holds the world state to be unrealistic, because he assumes that liberal peoples will always have to live together with non-liberal peoples (ibid. 59ff.).

Since the idea of a world state can be excluded, the only goal remaining is some kind of community of nations, which, in turn, must be organized in accordance with generally accepted principles—and a key question is to what extent the principles at the international level correspond to those at the national level. Here, Rawls sees (again in contrast to Höffe) serious disparities[19]: he conceives of the principles of the law of peoples in three steps, which respond to three different constellations. To explicate this, Rawls fundamentally distinguishes (ibid. 4) between five types of societies:

1. *Liberal nations*[20] satisfy the two principles of justice. Here, essentially, western-type democracies are at issue.
2. *Decent non-liberal peoples* represent the key category of the Law of Peoples. Even though they have not fully implemented the two principles, liberal peoples should be able to live with them. Decent peoples must in any case conform to certain minimum standards. I'll return to this shortly.
3. *Outlaw states*[21] do not meet these minimum standards. Under certain, still-unnamed conditions, waging war against outlaw states may be justified.
4. Many societies are burdened by *unfavorable circumstances* (developing countries). According to Rawls, they need to be supported to some degree by liberal societies.
5. Some societies live under a *benevolent absolutism*. About these, Rawls has little to say.

Based on this classification, Rawls sketches the basics of the law of peoples in two parts, an ideal and a non-ideal theory, whereby the ideal theory is further divided into two sections.

Ideal theory part I extends the general contract theory from Rawls's earlier writings to a society of liberal and democratic peoples. *Prima facie*, this does not appear to be especially problematic. On closer inspection, however, Rawls carries out here a slight shift of emphasis within his theory. He first examines whether the following six conditions that must be present at the national level for a liberal conception of justice can realistically also have validity for such a conception on a global scale. This question receives an affirmative answer throughout, although with some attenuation at point 4:

1. A liberal conception of justice is possible on the nation state as well as the global level when it builds upon the laws of nature and aspires toward a certain kind of stability—namely stability for the right reasons.[22] In addition, it is possible to develop the appropriate principles of justice in a way that is practicable and applicable to institutions.[23] This would permit such a conception of justice to be *realistic*.
2. A conception can also be devised on both levels, which characterizes a reasonable and just society that is aided by political and moral ideals. The respective principles must also satisfy the criterion of reciprocity (see ibid. 14), that is, they would have to be acceptable to all the citizens who are subjected to them. Such a conception of justice would accordingly be—in a positive sense—*utopian*.
3. Political concepts, especially the "idea of a free citizen" (ibid. 15) cannot be determined by comprehensive[24] doctrines, but only by a liberal conception of justice. In other words, all the basic elements of this conception must be included in the category of the political.
4. Just as with the citizens of a nation state, the citizens of a society of peoples—and this is a very important point for Rawls (cf. Section "The sense of justice")—must acquire a sense of justice. This means that they need to be able to understand and apply the principles of justice, and that the citizens will normally "be moved to act from them as circumstances require" (ibid. 15). Thus the sense of justice is not only to be understood as a purely "theoretical" attitude, but, according to Rawls, also has an immediate practical effect in the actions of citizens. However, the phrase "as circumstances require," which does not appear in his earlier works[25] and is still directed at the nation state, suggests a slight restriction. There can thus apparently be circumstances that stand in the way of a direct application of the sense of justice. More important, however, is Rawls's formulation in the context of a society of peoples. Specifically, a greater degree of (reasonable) pluralism must be expected at the global level. The institutional conditions required for developing a sense of justice can "(may) differ from one society to another" (ibid. 18). Rawls assumes, therefore, that the strength of the peoples' *internal* commitments to the law of peo-

ples will differ. The respective internal commitment only needs to be "ideally speaking, sufficient" (ibid.). These remarks are not insignificant, and I will return to them momentarily.
5. In Rawls's view, social stability must be based on a reasonable political conception; it cannot simply rely on a balance of interests ("modus vivendi") or a balance of power. This is also true for a society of peoples.
6. It is possible—and here Rawls is uncertain (ibid. 16)—that a reasonable conception of tolerance must also finally be a part of the political conception of the society of peoples. This political conception may not, as already indicated, rely on religious or ideological teachings.

Since the six conditions have thus been sufficiently met at the international level, according to Rawls, the original position construction for this level can also be outlined. Here, Rawls constructs a second original state,[26] which, just as with the first one, is intended to serve only as an illustrative example. In the second *original position*, the representatives of the peoples—who reciprocally view each other as reasonable, free, and equal—come to an agreement. Here, the representatives and the peoples themselves (ibid. 30f.) are portrayed as rational actors, who—like the actors in the case of the nation states—find themselves subject to a "veil of ignorance" (ibid. 30), which denies them insight into their future situation after the contract has been settled.

The two original states differ in three points:

1. One people, at least if it lives in a constitutional democracy, does not have access to a comprehensive (shared) doctrine of the good.
2. The fundamental interests of a people here are also not defined by a doctrine of the good, but by the political conception of justice of contract theory. The people themselves are aware of these basic interests, and they are interested in their own independence, security, self-esteem, and also in recognizing the self-esteem of other peoples.[27]
3. The representatives of the peoples do not negotiate using various formulations of the two principles of justice—as with the actors in the first original state—but rather using different formulations of the Law of Peoples (ibid. 40). This law of peoples consists of eight principles in need of further interpretation and whose precise formulations are decided by the peoples on the basis of their fundamental interests. Rawls characterizes these principles as familiar (see ibid. 37); they are not newly constructed, but reflect "traditional principles of justice among free and democratic peoples" (ibid. 37):

a. "Peoples are free and independent, and their freedom and independence are to be respected by other peoples.
b. Peoples are to observe treaties and undertakings.
c. Peoples are equal and are parties to the agreements that bind them.
d. Peoples are to observe a duty of non-intervention.
e. Peoples have the right of self-defense but no right to instigate war for reasons other than self-defense.
f. Peoples are to honor human rights.
g. Peoples are to observe certain specified restrictions in the conduct of war.
h. Peoples have a duty to assist other peoples living under unfavorable conditions that prevent their having a just or decent political and social regime."

According to Rawls, these principles are superior to all other recommendations. Alternatives to them would not be possible. On the other hand, they must be interpreted and qualified to be actually applicable. This application will essentially lead to the establishment of three types of organizations, namely a) those that provide for fairness in global trade, b) lending organizations, and c) "a Confederation of Peoples" (ibid. 42) like the United Nations. The peoples should recognize that these organizations are beneficial to each of them over the long term and that the resulting inequalities in Rawls's understanding (see also the section "Rawls's theory of justice and its connection to order ethics") are functional, that is, they lead to the eventual betterment of the poorer peoples (see ibid. 42f.).

As with Höffe, Rawls, too, has a response ready for criticisms made from "realistic" or "pragmatic-political" viewpoints after he develops his position. His assumption here—at first only in the context of the *Ideal theory part I*—is that trade and the spread of democracy will lead to a peace among liberal peoples.[28] Wars would thus only be waged against so-called outlaw states.

This then, so far, is the unproblematic and more or less uncontroversial part of Rawls's *Law of Peoples*. His ideal theory, however, has a second part (see ibid. 59ff.). Here, Rawls no longer assumes the existence of a society based on exclusively liberal democratic peoples. Instead, he considers whether a) other peoples, who cannot be described as liberal, can agree to the law of peoples, and whether b) the liberal peoples can tolerate such decent non-liberal peoples, which is also to say, accept them as equals.

Rawls obtains the fundamental justification for such a question (ibid. 60) from earlier observations about the nation state. The same is true for various comprehensive doctrines (e.g., religious or philosophical). If they meet certain conditions—that is, if they can be viewed in a certain sense as reasonable and would thus have to be accepted within a society—then non-liberal societies would also have to be accepted by liberals, assuming they also meet certain conditions.[29]

These conditions are institutional in nature. To be more precise, Rawls formulates two criteria. Only decent non-liberal peoples able to meet both criteria could be "a member in good standing in a reasonable Society of Peoples" (ibid. 64, emphasis in original):

1. First of all, decent non-liberal societies are not allowed to pursue aggressive goals. They have to respect the organization of other societies and may only try to influence other societies by means of diplomacy, not violence.
2. The second condition consists jointly of three sub-conditions. In a decent non-liberal society

   a. human rights, that is, in particular the rights to life, liberty, property, and formal equality, must be ensured[30];
   b. members of society must, because of the legal system, have duties that are consistent with their notions of justice, that is, duties should not simply be enforced by coercion (as in the case of authoritarian regimes);
   c. judges and other officials must have sincere and well-founded reasons to believe that the law of their society is guided by a "common good idea of justice" (ibid. 71). According to Rawls, this common good concept of justice—according to which the legal system of a decent society should orient itself—is *not* to be understood as the shared *goal* of a people. At most, the pursuit of such a goal by individuals should be encouraged (see ibid.). This idea also requires a "decent consultation hierarchy" (ibid. 61, emphasis omitted): the members of decent non-liberal peoples must, at least in corporatist fashion, be represented in the hierarchy as members of different social groups. The representatives of these groups should at least be included in the political decision-making processes in an advisory capacity.

Rawls elucidates these criteria using a fictional example (see ibid., 75ff.): Kazanistan is an idealized Islamic state that is especially distinguished from liberal democratic states by the fact that it does not have an institutional separation of church and state. Public offices, for instance, have not been assigned independently of religious affiliation. Nevertheless, Kazanistan tolerates other religions domestically and does not pursue aggressive foreign policy objectives (e.g., the "Holy War" is interpreted only in a spiritual sense). In addition, this state utilizes policies that established a consultation hierarchy. As a consequence, all social groups must be consulted, compromises must be reached, and dissenting opinions must be heard. This has already led to reforms that have improved the status of women. While such a state, in Rawls's view, certainly cannot be viewed as perfectly just, it must, nonetheless, be regarded as decent. Under the given circumstances, and given the many prototypes in the real world, it would be the best that we could "realistically—and coherently—hope for" (ibid. 78).

In an "appropriate original position" (ibid. 69), decent peoples like the inhabitants of Kazanistan would, according to Rawls, choose the same eight principles of the law of peoples that liberal peoples would choose. They would advocate the law of peoples, because they would be especially interested in their own protection as well as the benefits of trade. To be sure—as Rawls explicitly points out (ibid. 70)—the *basic structure* of a state like Kazanistan could not be derived again from an original position, for it would otherwise be a liberal society. Nevertheless, at the international level, Kazanistan could be considered to be on equal footing with liberal societies. One can understand this to mean that Rawls distinguishes here between different problem areas[31]: at least for issues of international cooperation, the internal arrangements of a decent nation should be ignored. At the same time, one could certainly keep an eye on other problems in the "internal development" of a people toward a liberal and fair basic structure. Still, in doing so, one would need to focus on long-term policy changes without coercion. Force would only interfere with these changes and discourage their advocates. An attitude of mutual respect would be more productive (see ibid. 62). Even with regard to the question of whether non-liberal, decent societies should be offered incentives to develop into liberal societies, Rawls (ibid. 84f.) is more cautious. He rather endorses waiting for voluntary petitions for assistance to institutions such as the International Monetary Fund.

This concludes the ideal theory of the law of peoples. Rawls then proceeds to outline a non-ideal theory that is also urgently needed under the conditions of globalization. The central concern of this theory is how one should deal with others as liberal and decent peoples.

The non-ideal theory of the law of peoples aims to provide guidelines for how a) outlaw states and b) peoples burdened by unfavorable circumstances should be treated. This results in a) the just-war theory (ibid. §14), and b) a theory of distributive justice among the peoples. I will focus on each in turn.

Ad a): The just-war theory[32] concerns under what circumstances and in accordance with what principles liberal and decent (in short: well-ordered; see ibid. 89f.) peoples are entitled to carry out violence against outlaw states. Such a right to wage war, according to Rawls, only arises in cases in which fundamental freedoms and democratic institutions must be protected. In such cases, genuinely political citizens in liberal states as well as inhabitants of decent and absolutist states may defend themselves. The right to wage war, however, does not exist in those cases where economic prosperity, power, or the "acquiring [of] natural resources" (ibid. 91) are at issue. A state that would wage war in the latter cases would itself become an outlaw state.

A just war must otherwise be waged according to certain rules. Rawls (ibid. 94ff.) presents six principles for conducting a just war:

1. A lasting peace must be sought as the goal of a just war.
2. A just war is not to be waged between well-ordered peoples, but only by one or more well-ordered people(s) against not-well-ordered peoples.
3. A distinction must be made in a just war between responsible leaders, officials, and senior officers, on the one hand, and all other inhabitants of outlaw states, on the other.
4. In a just war, the human rights of inhabitants of outlaw states must be taken account of to the greatest extent possible.
5. Well-ordered peoples must make their objectives known already *during* a just war.
6. In a just war, the implementation of instrumental means-end thinking must be strictly limited, which means, for Rawls, in terms of the first five principles. The only exception is a situation of "supreme emergency."[33] Here, civilians may also be attacked, but only if the subsequent advantages are clear.[34]

Ad b): According to Rawls, liberal societies are generally obliged to assist at least some of the societies that are burdened by unfavorable circumstances. Burdened societies worthy of assistance are those that have not behaved aggressively, but—whether because of a lack of tradition, lack of technology, or lack of human capital—are not in a position to adequately supply their members with basic necessities.

In Rawls's view, the assistance is intended to follow three guiding principles. First, the aim of the support should not be to produce *great* wealth in such societies. Second, consideration must be paid to the assisted societies' political cultures. The elevation of the status of women, for instance, could greatly accelerate the progress of a burdened society.[35] Third, the assistance should not carry with it any paternalistic traits, but must rather be aimed at a situation in which the assisted societies are capable of managing their own affairs.

The remaining question is how far the assistance should go. Here, the theory of distributive justice comes to bear between the peoples. On this point, Rawls favors a much weaker approach than his student Thomas Pogge. While Pogge (1994) endorses an egalitarian principle at the global level and thus an—at least—more even distribution of basic goods,[36] Rawls opposes this "maximalist" view with his own "minimalist" one. He finds that the difference principle cannot be applied at the global level because it would lead to unacceptable outcomes. For example, according to this principle, countries with different savings rates would have to be assisted in equal measure (see ibid. 117). In another case, a society whose population growth has been reduced because of improvements to the career prospects of women is assisted significantly less than a country that has not made such improvements and thus continues to have high population growth and subsist at a lower level of prosperity. In both cases, the basic concern is that a global difference principle would create perverse incentives, which Rawls wants to avoid. Indeed, he does not operate himself with the incentive concept (see also the section "The sense of justice"), but rather only remarks that the law of the peoples is not interested in the individual welfare of cosmopolitans and citizens of a world state, but (only) in the stability of societies (which, indeed, also corresponds to the principal question pursued in this book).

Nevertheless, Rawls emphasizes that, while inequality does not necessarily always need to be regarded as unjust, it still might be desirable to reduce inequalities, since this would alleviate suffering, eliminate stigmatizations, and strengthen the degree of fairness in the political process within the society of peoples.

As in the case of Höffe earlier, a comment should be made here on methodology. Whereas Höffe prefers a "legal-moral methodology," which he explicitly opposes to preference-based, economic methods that only "deal with" property and are obviously primarily based on moral postulates, Rawls goes in another direction. In his view, it is precisely *not* the "task of philosophy to uncover a form of argument that will always prove convincing against all other arguments" (ibid. 123). Such arguments do not exist.[37] Peace is not achieved insofar as war is declared irrational, but only when a path is provided to peoples for developing a certain basic structure. This basic structure includes vital institutions whose formation—this is my addition—can only take place with the help of the individual disciplines and economics. Rawls thus fundamentally minimizes the role of philosophy.[38]

This perspective is also expressed elsewhere: according to Rawls, the principles of the law of peoples *cannot* be derived from practical reason; they cannot be justified by more and more refined and sophisticated lines of argumentation (ibid. 86f.). Rawls distinguishes his position here[39] in particular from a transcendental idealism, which has a completely different object than political liberalism. The idealist finally attempts (in my own terminology) to establish something that is culturally dependent and critical to the political process in a way that is culturally and politically invariable (metaphysical). Political liberals, on the other hand, see practical reason solely as a set of normative ideas (reasonableness, respectability, and rationality). A list of necessary and sufficient conditions for these ideas does not exist, however, so that "differences of opinion are to be expected" (ibid. 87). Although one suspects, according to Rawls, that the ideas of practical reason and the principles of the law of peoples will eventually develop into a coherent system, "there can be no guarantee" (ibid.). With this statement, Rawls once again downplays the role of ("reasonable") arguments in his conception.

The main theoretical attenuations and concessions that Rawls performs under the conditions of globalization may be summarized as follows:

1. He does not transfer the thinking in state contexts directly to the global level, but at most has in mind the idea of a confederation.
2. The differential system, which is so important domestically, is supposedly not valid on a global scale.
3. The third consideration relates to the sense of justice, which is crucial to Rawls.[40] While Rawls emphasizes in earlier writings (such as Rawls 1993) that a state can remain stable only if its citizens develop a functioning sense of justice, he weakens this condition in the "Law of Peoples." At first, Rawls remarks—albeit still with a view to the national, rather than the global level—that citizens of a society who have a sense of justice will be able to "understand the principles and ideals of the political conception, to understand and interpret apply them to cases at hand, and they will normally be moved to act from them as circumstances require" (Rawls 1999, 15). Even this formulation—with the double attenuation "normally" and "as the circumstances require"—is somewhat weaker than in earlier works (see Rawls 1993, 301f. and the section "The sense of justice"). More important, however, is the transmission of the sense of justice to the global level, which Rawls talks about next.

He offers the following concise summation:

> The degree to which a reasonably just, effective institutional process enables members of different well-ordered societies to develop a sense of justice and support their government in honoring the Law of Peoples from one society to another in the wider Society of Peoples. The fact of reasonable pluralism is more evident within a society of well-ordered peoples than it is within one society alone. An allegiance to the Law of Peoples need not be equally strong in all peoples, but it must be, ideally speaking, sufficient. (ibid. 18)

Here, Rawls clearly does not have in mind a one-to-one transfer of nation-state principles to the law of peoples, but rather takes account of the conditions of globalization. He acknowledges that on the global level the number of different (reasonable)[41] views increases and that one can thus only have limited expectation for the development of such a sense of justice.[42] This can be interpreted to mean that he takes into consideration the problem of the implementation of norms to an even greater extent than in his earlier writings.[43]

Despite the distinctions, I would like to summarize by highlighting the similarities that emerge out of what are certainly two of the more prominent philosophical approaches to the issue of globalization.

While Rawls rejects the world state, and also undertakes the indicated attenuations, he makes certain demands of the citizens of a society, even under conditions of globalization. Although Höffe explicitly notes that global civic virtues must be present, Rawls does not go so far. Just the same, it is necessary to bear two things in mind: on the one hand, the pluralism of opinions, lifestyles, and ways of life should constitute a *reasonable* pluralism, which presupposes a certain definition of reasonableness (more on this in the section "Reason vs. rationality") and excludes differing opinions, lifestyles, and ways of life. On the other hand, Rawls presumes that actors even in the age of globalization have a sense of justice, although one that possibly only functions in a limited way. The details of this capacity will be discussed in the section "The sense of justice." For the moment, it should only be understood that global civic virtues as well as a sense of justice represent two *anthropological requirements* for social stability under conditions of globalization. There are two capabilities or qualities at issue, in the sense mentioned at the outset, which are finally called upon normatively. On the one hand, it remains to be seen to what extent global civic virtues and a sense of justice can remain stable over the long term under conditions of globalization. On the other hand, it is debatable whether both skills and qualities are even necessary for social stability.

Further responses will be examined in this book in regard to the following two aspects. First, can the existence of the capability or quality in question be systematically relied upon over the long term? Second, is the capability or quality in question necessary for the stability of societies under the conditions of globalization? These issues are discussed in chapters 3 to 5 in reference to the approaches of Vittorio Hösle, Philippa Foot, Jürgen Habermas, John Rawls (except for the "Law of Peoples"), David Gauthier, Richard Rorty, James M. Buchanan, and Ken Binmore. Chapter 6 then presents a summary and seeks to put forward its own approach.

To start with, however, some of the basics of the conception of normativity to be used here require explanation. In the following, chapter 2 will present the outline of the book's main focus from a systematic and historical perspective, which it will then crystallize into a reference model.

NOTES

1. Certainly, the corresponding approaches typically suggest that the existence of the respective required normative foundations are also empirically plausible. The plausibility and methodological tenability of such clues will be examined (critically) below.

2. A problem already emerges here that H. L. A. Hart clearly recognized in his essay on the enforcement problem of morality (Hart 1967/1971): if one demands that a state should enforce moral standards by law, *because* it is likely to decay without such enforcement, this does not mean that the condition of decay may itself, in turn, be defined by the fact that there are no shared norms. This would reflect circular logic. (At any rate, Hart generally finds that it is neither sufficiently empirically nor theoretically grounded that a state must decay without the legal enforcement of moral standards.)

3. See basically Luhmann 1997.

4. See, for example, Stiglitz 2002, Bhagwati 2004, Razin and Sadka 2008, Baines and Ursah 2009, and Rodrik 2011.

5. See ibid. 54.

6. For a complete list, see ibid. 140f.

7. One in particular, namely the third principle, "resists simple formulation" (ibid. 79).

8. And this statement not only seems to be obviously intended for the nation state, but also for the global level.

9. In the section "The sense of justice" of this book, the similarly named sense described in the conception of Rawls should be distinguished from Höffe's term.

10. Rawls's "Law of Peoples" (1999), however, even in the later edition from 2002, is not cited. Höffe only quotes Rawls's eponymous Oxford Amnesty Lectures from 1993 (Rawls 1993/1996), although Rawls remarked that he was "not satisfied" with the lectures, finding them "not fully developed" and "open to misinterpretation" (Rawls 1999, preface).

11. I will pass over a few different versions of this thesis, see Höffe 1999/2002, 268.

12. See Rawls's argument (section "Modus vivendi, constitutional consensus and overlapping consensus"), according to which a *modus vivendi* is not stable.

13. Kant (1976, vol. 11, 204ff.), 1st Definitive Article.

14. See, for example, classically Doyle 1983; for an overview, Russett and Oneal 2001 and Brown et al. 1996.

15. The counterexamples are not unproblematic: the only somewhat convincing example of a war between democracies is, in my opinion, the war between the United States and Great Britain in 1812. This conflict, however, has a special status in that it was between a former colony and its former colonial ruler. With regard to the examples of India vs. Pakistan, as well as Britain vs. France after 1791, it would be necessary to determine whether the requirements of democratic states were actually fulfilled (at least on each respective side). The same applies to the First World War. Beyond this, ancient democracies are not directly comparable to ours, as Höffe (ibid. 285f.) admits himself.

16. Quite obviously such uncoerced recognition of rules should resolve prisoners' dilemma situations. See also the section "Society requires 1) rational motivation." As an example, Höffe cites missions of the UN, in which many have realized the benefits and only relatively few have had to contend with the associated costs.

17. Both processes of justification, however, can be used in parallel. Public authorities can thus be justified along both lines (see Höffe 1999/2002, 99).

18. For a general appraisal of the "Law of Peoples," see for example Beitz 2000.

19. Beitz also refers to "dramatic differences" between the "Theory of Justice" and the "Law of Peoples" (Beitz 2000, 688).

20. More specifically, Rawls emphasizes that his distinction concerns *peoples* and not states, especially for the purpose of detaching himself from thinking in terms of categories of the nation state. Peoples are conceived as those who are able to accept the law of peoples, while states are deprived of the right to deal with their people at their own discretion. In addition, Rawls believes that people rather than states act on the basis of reasonableness rather than rationality and thus are more likely to achieve stability than states *for the right reasons* (see Rawls 1999, 25ff. and in the following section "Reason vs. rationality").

21. Here, Rawls speaks of outlaw *states*, not of outlaw *peoples*, apparently to make clear that—especially in the case of a war—it is necessary to clearly distinguish between the population of an outlaw state and its representatives.

22. For further explanation, see the section "Modus vivendi, constitutional consensus, and overlapping consensus."

23. Rawls (ibid. 13) gives an explicit counterexample: Sen's so-called capabilities are "unworkable ideas."

24. For more on this concept, see the section "Rawls's theory of justice and its connection to order ethics."

25. For example, it is neither included in the "Theory of Justice" (Rawls 1971) nor in "Political Liberalism" (Rawls 1993). See the section "The sense of justice."

26. Rawls thus begins like Höffe: here, there are *two* original states; there, there is a *dual* world social contract. The differences, however, will become obvious in the following.

27. Unlike states, peoples are prepared to fully accept other peoples as equals. This necessitates that peoples even adhere—without additional incentives—to agreements where non-compliance would be more advantageous to them (see ibid. 44). One can interpret this as the solution to prisoner's dilemma situations, without (the threat of) sanctions. See also the section "Gauthier's conception of economics."

28. Rawls cites a number of historical examples, some of which directly contradict those cited by Höffe. A detailed discussion here, however, would lead us too far astray.

29. However, Rawls does not argue here—at least not explicitly—from the standpoint of the implementation problem: he does *not* say that decent peoples would have to be tolerated, *because* the law of peoples would otherwise not prevail on a global level. This kind of reasoning probably seemed to be dependent on too many contingent factors. See also the section "Modus vivendi, constitutional consensus, and overlapping consensus."

30. Rawls believes that these rights are not specifically Western or liberal.

31. In terms of methodology, it should be noted that, to Rawls, the principles of decency (1999, §15) are not derived from practical reason in the sense of a metaphysical instance. As Rawls (1985) has already pointed out with regard to principles of justice, a political basis rather than a metaphysical one is to be preferred for the idea of decency.

32. Rawls in all likelihood knew that this *term* alone would be a provocation to many of his readers.

33. Ibid. 99, no italics in original. According to Rawls, a fixed definition of a supreme emergency cannot be arrived at on a drawing board, as it were.

34. Rawls here cites examples from the Second World War. He considers, for instance, the bombing of Dresden to have been "clearly too late" (ibid. 99).

35. Rawls here refers to the work of Sen; see Sen 1999.

36. He thus calls for a resource tax; see Pogge (1994). See also the convincing critique by Crisp and Jamieson (2000) and the less convincing one by Allen Buchanan (2000b).

37. See also the section "Moral communication: towards a semantics of benefits" (on Brandom).

38. Buchanan (2000a) implicitly criticizes this point: he believes that Rawls would also have had to introduce strong principles of justice for the international level. Such principles, in Buchanan's view, would provide for more opportunities at the global level, more democratic participation in global institutions, and limit economic inequalities (see ibid. 711). In my view, Buchanan makes the mistake of not proceeding from the issue of *implementation*.

39. As already discussed in Rawls 1985.

40. The following remarks will be even more transparent in the light of the section "The sense of justice."

41. On the problem of rationality in Rawls, see the section "Reason vs. rationality."

42. Later, this attenuation seems less pronounced (ibid. 45); it is difficult to arrive here at a fully coherent picture of the Rawlsian view.

43. For more on the implementation problem, see the section "Order ethics as an ethics of benefits and incentives."

Chapter Two

Normativity under Conditions of Globalization

The Conception of Order Ethics

THE PROBLEM'S OUTLINE

Under normativity, I understand with Jonathan Dancy (2000b, vii) the general characteristic of everything that emerges on the side of "ought," or when one distinguishes between what is and what should be.[1] The previous chapter served to illustrate the development of the general framework under which a conception of normativity should be formulated today. It has become clear that modernity's pluralism[2] will assume new dimensions in the era of globalization, and to some extent already has. With that said, the question arises as to what conditions the members of a society—indeed, perhaps even members of the future world society—will need to meet in order for their society to remain stable. In other words: What requirements can be made of the individual members with the prospect of also actually influencing their behavior? The null hypothesis, which I will adopt in the following, states that the self-interest of individuals is sufficient for convincing the individual to systematically observe the organizationally embedded, sanction-based rules of a society.[3] But is self-interest actually enough, or are additional requirements necessary for a systematic compliance with the rules?

Most theorists are not satisfied with this null hypothesis, finding that compliance with the rules is not sufficient. The classical problem they pose is the following: Is it not also possible for rules to be unjust or to lead to unfair results and thus to unstable conditions? Is one, then, to be expected to comply with these rules anyway?

These queries are answered by the order ethics presented within the framework of this book. In building on elements of social-contract theory, it proposes a multi-level hierarchy of rules. This strategy will be discussed in more detail in the section "Order ethics as an ethics of benefits and incentives."

Most theorists, however, pursue different strategies. They represent the view that the members of society should not only comply with the rules, but also have to "bring with them" other qualities, namely, a moral surplus value, which I will define shortly. In the next chapters, the respective responses from Habermas, Rawls, Gauthier, Buchanan, and others will be discussed. I will challenge these answers and question whether this surplus value is a reasonable assumption that appears to be theoretically acceptable under modern conditions.[4] In particular, the question arises as to whether it is still sensible in the modern world to link the stability and functioning of a society to personal qualities, which the members of this society need to possess. Requirements like these not only seem to be problematic under conditions of globalization. Along with this, it becomes increasingly difficult to determine what distinguishes humans as humans, and to delineate potential competitors—such as intelligent computers, but also the intelligence of animals.[5] Höffe (1999/2002, 64) has isolated the following classical determinations of philosophical anthropology:

1. *zoon*: unlike angels or gods, a human being is not a creature of pure reason, but a bodily and living organism.
2. *zoon logon echon*: unlike animals, human beings have the capacity for thought and speech.
3. *zoon politikon*: the human being is dependent on fellowship with others.

Even these determinations, as relatively weak as they are, have not gone unchallenged. In particular, the second one has long been questioned within the context of socio-biological approaches (see, for example, works like Segerstrale 2000 and Alcock 2001)—however problematic the conclusions drawn from these findings may be.[6] This, however, will not be the focus here. The moral surplus values discussed in chapters 3 to 5 go beyond these classic determinations, or interpret them in a certain "strong" way, which particularly emphasizes the anthropological basis for the stability of modern societies.

In contrast to this view, an approach will be presented here along with order ethics, which holds that moral surplus values are superfluous. It assumes that actors who violate the rules, especially moral codes, do not demonstrate any personal defects.[7] A theoretical reconstruction of the behavior of these actors must rather assume that they cannot systematically violate *incen-*

tives. Actors behave one way, and not another, because of the constraints of a given situation, and especially due to the available interaction structures. To achieve improvements, these constraints must be reckoned with.

The problematic examined in this book touches on fundamental questions of philosophy—not only of ethics, however, but of all philosophic disciplines. Even in epistemology, the theory of science, philosophy of mind, aesthetics, and (if one prefers to use these terms) metaphysics and ontology, there are two opposed research programs. Roughly speaking, they can be simplified to the concepts of "naturalism" and "normativity." Many attempts have already been made to define the term "naturalism," as in the case of Quine (1995), Shimony (1993), Armstrong (1983, 82), Rosenberg (1996), and Vollmer (1995). While a detailed discussion of these attempts should not and cannot be undertaken here, the following key elements of the naturalistic program may be identified:

1) Rejection of a prima philosophia

Naturalism does not accord a special position to philosophy within the sciences. In particular, there can thus be no phenomena that are *fundamentally* inaccessible to scientific methods. This does not exclude the fact, however, that some basic presumptions are indispensable for scientific research for heuristic reasons. Naturalists, for instance, make the assumption that nature is primarily matter and energy and that all real systems are subject to evolution.

2) Empirical sciences as a model for philosophy

For the naturalists, both the method and the findings of the empirical sciences (not only the natural sciences, but also the social sciences) are the standard according to which philosophical theories must be measured. Nevertheless, this neither implies that the goal is a unified science, in which philosophy simply adopts empirical scientific methods whole cloth, nor that philosophy would have to recognize physics or biology as a leading discipline.

3) Evolutionary paradigm

The theory of evolution is a central theory of naturalism. Still, there are different perceptions among naturalists about *which* variant of the theory of evolution should be authoritative. Here, the theory of universal evolution is the basis according to which evolutionary processes are present at all levels.

In the present context, the first point is especially relevant, and, to a lesser extent, so is the second point: naturalists believe that all phenomena in the world can be dealt with scientifically. There is no one "domain" where philosophy has a systematically exclusive right.

Some schools of philosophy have a different opinion. For example, the views are represented that spirit, consciousness, culture, or the Big Bang cannot ultimately be understood scientifically. Normativity can also be counted among these schools. I recognize *normativists* as those theorists who postulate a "domain" of normativity precisely where philosophy has this exclusive right. The existence of norms, then, provides evidence of a fundamental limit to scientific analysis.

The order ethics approach advocated in this book is an *approach that has a naturalistic basis*. (I have chosen this wording because the concept of ethical naturalism has already been given a specific direction and is burdened by the constant suspicion of a naturalistic fallacy.)[8] Order ethics in the form presented here relies primarily on the observations of Karl Homann, which are formulated in Homann (2002 and 2003), Luetge (2005, 2012, and 2013), and Homann and Luetge (2004/2013). This conception, however, will be presented here from a new perspective, namely, that of naturalism. Below, I will discuss the essential features of the conception I refer to as *OE* (order ethics). At the same time, I interpret OE as a naturalistic research program that posits the null hypothesis (mentioned at the beginning of this chapter), according to which self-interest is sufficient for a systematic adherence to the rules. I will proceed in the following manner: first, in the section "Historical perspectives: precursors of order ethics," I will briefly outline the historical precursors. In the section "Order ethics as an ethics of benefits and incentives," OE itself will be presented by means of a thought experiment. The section "On the relationship of order ethics and individual-oriented approaches," finally, discusses individual-oriented approaches, which OE critically challenges, in order to present a stronger contrast.

HISTORICAL PERSPECTIVES: PRECURSORS OF ORDER ETHICS

It may initially appear that OE is primarily based on economic and other social-scientific work. It has its precursors, however, in the philosophical tradition. Some of these precursors are at the same time also (largely) naturalists.

The most important precursor of order ethics from the philosophical tradition is probably *Thomas Hobbes*. For centuries, Hobbes was one of the most important focal points of controversy for many writers in ethics, law, and political philosophy. It often seemed almost obligatory to refute him or to distance oneself from him.[9] Apart from the certain negative *view of human beings*[10] attributed to Hobbes, this is likely due above all to the fact that Hobbes's conception (similar to OE) does away with any (undoubtedly sympathetic) assumption that the members of a society might possess a socio-stabilizing capacity for reason. The Leviathan—constituted by and, in fact, identical[11] with all the members of society—only produces social stability by means of incentives and sanctions. (Further remarks on Hobbes follow in the section "Gauthier, Locke, and Nozick: The status of rights.")

David Hume, one of the main representatives of the European Enlightenment, employs his overall theoretical and practical philosophy to argue against metaphysical approaches. This probably finds its most extreme expression in the closing sentences of the *Enquiry Concerning Human Understanding*, which call for any book that is neither mathematical nor attributable to empirical science to be committed to "flames" (Hume 1748/1975, 165).

Hume's ethics is entirely conceived in this spirit. He consistently attempts to banish metaphysics from ethics (and also from socio-philosophy). Hume grounds morality *systematically* in its society-preserving and stabilizing function. According to Hume, morality neither serves divine commandments, nor those of reason, but rather the desires of people. But these desires are not determined by individual interests alone, but moreover by feelings of sympathy. Large parts of the *Enquiry Concerning the Principles of Morals* (Hume 1751/1975) consist in a descriptive study of the way morality, above all in the form of such feelings of sympathy, guides our existence. Hume analyzes the different types of passions (in particular, "good will" and "justice"), and sees a functioning society that is based upon them. The society should serve the good of all, including those who, as a result of these passions, subject their actions to restrictions. Hume tries to show that it is *generally* advantageous for everyone to behave morally.

The third volume of the *Treatise on Human Nature* supplies the theoretical foundations for this position. Like Hobbes, Hume recognizes the theoretical implications of the prisoner's dilemma: he sees that the cooperation of the actors in the prisoner's dilemma cannot occur because of the situational incentives. The actors are inherently self-interested

> or endow'd only with a confin'd generosity, they are not easily induc'd to perform any action for the interest of strangers, except with a view to some reciprocal advantage, which they had no hope of obtaining but by such a performance. Now as it frequently happens, that these mutual performances cannot be finish'd at the same instant. (Hume, 1739–1740/1978, book III, part 2, 519)

Because the one who offers a service in advance puts himself at risk of exploitation, the advance service is omitted (see Hume 1739–1740/1978, book III, part 2, 519):

> I will not, therefore, take any pains upon your account; and shou'd I labour with you upon my own account, in expectation of return, I know I shou'd be

> disappointed, and that I should in vain depend upon your gratitude. Here then I leave you to labour alone: You treat me in the same manner. (ibid. 520f.)

In view of this logic, Hume gives a rationale for shared rules: appeals will not help, for "correcting the selfishness and ingratitude of men" (ibid. 521) could only lead to "omnipotence, which is alone able to new-mould the human mind, and change its character in such fundamental articles" (ibid.). Self-interest cannot be abolished, so we must instead "give a new direction to those natural passions" (ibid. 521) and learn that "we can better satisfy our appetites in an oblique and artificial manner, than by their headlong and impetuous motion" (ibid.). Only the (selfish) tendency itself can keep the (selfish) tendency in check by giving it "an alteration of its direction" (ibid. 492).

In other words, a system of rules must be designed that is, on the whole, mutually advantageous (ibid. 579) and that—as an artificial, unnatural mechanism[12]—rests on an "agreement." Hume does not categorically reject contract theory, on the proviso that the idea of an original contract is explicitly viewed as a (useful) *fiction* (see ibid. 493). The mutual agreement would then provide a reliable foundation for rules.[13] On this basis, promises can be kept (ibid. 516) and a state entity can evolve.

In Hume's conception, however, two problems emerge, which I will discuss later in this book. On the one hand, the analytical access to the passions must be questioned. What status does the theoretical statement have that people can avail themselves to feelings of sympathy?[14] What problem is such a statement designed to address? These issues will be taken up again in chapters 3 to 5.

The second problem concerns whether Hume neglects *conflicts* of interest and relies too heavily on the assumption (understood differently by Adam Smith)[15] of a *harmony* of individual interests. Hume, indeed, recognizes this problem himself: when he sees the difficulty that some people might desire everyone else to follow the moral rules, but not do so themselves, *Enquiry Concerning the Principles of Morals* nearly ends in an aporia. This difficulty is the free-rider problem, which largely corresponds to the prisoner's dilemma. For Hume (1751/1975, section IX, part II), the only hope to solve the problem lies in the fact that these people would at some point see the futility of such a strategy. The free riders would have to recognize that in the long run any rule breakers would be caught and punished and that they would therefore be better off (in the long run) if they desisted from free riding. This attempt at a solution, however, has a distinct *ad hoc* quality that is ultimately not satisfying.

Despite these difficulties, Hume's approach represents an important attempt at a functional justification of morality. And he is to be regarded as the precursor of an order ethics insofar as he tries in his normative concept to manage with as "little" as possible. In the final analysis, this means primarily only with the desires (the *passions*) of human beings and then, only secondarily, with possible intellectual abilities (*understanding*, or even—what is not isolated in Hume—*reason*).[16]

Benedict de Spinoza's political conception in the "Tractatus theologico-politicus" (1670) and in the unfinished "Tractatus politicus" (1677) also tries to establish the groundwork for the stability of societies without assuming that human beings have additional socio-stabilizing rational abilities. Like Hobbes, Spinoza explicitly assumes that only the self-interested consent of everyone may be the basis of normativity.[17] This position is represented in particular in the "Tractatus politicus":

> man acts in accordance with the laws of his own nature and pursues his own advantage in both the natural and the political order. In both conditions, I say, man is led by hope or fear either to do or to refrain from doing one thing or another. (Spinoza 1677, chapter 3, §3, in: Spinoza 1670–1677/1951)

In the following, this position will be extended to (social) contracts as a basis of the state. According to Spinoza, parties who enter into a contract will actually only feel *bound* to this contract when they are able to connect with it the "hope of some greater good, or the fear of some greater evil" (Spinoza 1670–1677/1951, 203–204). Other binding effects, such as through reason or divine instructions, are not allowed by Spinoza.

In the writings of Immanuel Kant, there are (at least) two linkages for the conception defended here.[18] On the one hand, Kant contends that even exclusively self-interested beings can form a stable state:

> Das Problem der Staatserrichtung ist, so hart wie es auch klingt, selbst für ein Volk von Teufeln (wenn sie nur Verstand haben) auflösbar
>
> as hard as it may sound, the problem of setting up a state can be solved even by a nation of devils (so long as they possess understanding). (Kant 1976ff., vol. 11, 224)[19]

This remark implies that a state is not necessarily dependent on values, virtues, moralistic motivation, and so on.[20] The "private thoughts" (ibid.) of the individuals are sufficient; the state is not there for their moral improvement.

Second, reference can be made here to the Opus postumum's doctrine of self-positing ("Selbstsetzungslehre").[21] Eckart Förster (1992) reconstructs the following evolution in Kant, who continually pursues the problem of moral compliance[22]: in 1781 (Critique of Pure Reason), he still refers to God as the guarantor of morality; in 1785 (Grounding for the Metaphysics of Morals), he uses the concept of duty to substantiate compliance with norms *out of respect* for the law, but this appears only as an interim solution; and in 1788 (Critique of Practical Reason; in part, also in the Critique of Judgment from 1790), the reference to God is taken up again. None of these solutions seems to sit well with Kant, however. Only in the Opus postumum does he embrace the doctrine of self-positing, whereby God is an idea that one posits. *We invented* an idea in order to ensure the observance of morality. Further metaphysical requirements are not necessary.

At this point (in the historical chronology), it is appropriate to point to a philosopher who, to the casual observer, might be considered a precursor to order ethics. This classification, however, cannot in fact be supported. The philosopher in question here is Max Stirner, who, in his major work *The Ego and Its Own* (1845/1972), formulated the key philosophical statement: "Ich hab' mein Sach' auf Nichts gestellt" ("I have set my affair on nothing").[23] This dramatic rejection of more than just the views of German idealism demands that philosophical work be taken up with as few assumptions as possible (or indeed none at all). At first glance, this would seem to agree with one of the intentions of OE. On the other hand (and without exploring this in detail here), it must be pointed out that:

a. Stirner makes use of a Lockean concept of freedom, which does not recognize civil liberties in the sense of Hobbes as being socially constituted, but rather as extra-socially predetermined. This is a strong assumption that OE is not able to accept.
b. As an anarchist thinker, Stirner does not have an adequate theory of institutions.[24] He thus specifically does not call for *institutions* (including regulations) to be built on the weakest possible conditions (e.g., incentives), for he is more concerned with the world of ideas than with institutions (governmental or non-governmental). Even though the achievement of Enlightenment is acknowledged as having resulted in humanity's development toward a stage of self-organization, Stirner barely touches on its institutional outline.
c. Stirner claims to observe man "as he is," that is, in the sense of a phenomenalistic approach, rather than an exemplary reconstruction. On this point, see the section "On the relationship of order ethics and individual-oriented approaches."

With his conception presented in *Game Theory and the Social Contract* (Binmore 1994 and 1998), *Ken Binmore* foregoes stabilizing rational abilities in the most consistent manner. Binmore remarks pointedly: "Just saying yes" holds society together today and nothing else. This approach is discussed in detail in the section "Society requires (almost) nothing (Ken Binmore)." Here it should be noted, however, that even Binmore accepts a socio-stabilizing tendency, namely, *empathetic preferences*. Their status varies, though, in comparison to the capabilities postulated by other authors.[25]

These are just some of the precursors to order ethics.[26] Its underlying idea should be made apparent in the following on the basis of a thought experiment.

ORDER ETHICS AS AN ETHICS OF BENEFITS AND INCENTIVES

Order ethics (OE) has been described in different ways (see especially Homann 2002 and Homann and Luetge 2004/2013). Below, I will go about describing OE by utilizing a thought experiment. First, however, some preliminaries are required:

- OE is a conception of economic ethics. It relies partly on the findings of economics; if necessary—with due reflection to methodology—other disciplines can also be consulted.[27]
- The term *order ethics* refers to the conception's *objective*, that is, the order framework. The term *ethics of benefits and incentives*, or "benefit and incentive ethics," connotes the *means* of such a conception.
- The concept of order ethics touches on the problem areas of ethics and social philosophy. In particular, if not exclusively, the social conditions in the implementation of norms established by ethics are the subject of social philosophy, which, in turn, is based on economics and other social sciences. In this book as well, the two issues touch constantly. This points to an underlying assumption, namely, that the division between ethics and social philosophy is not only artificial, but also heuristically unproductive.
- The term *institution* is by no means intended as a plea for more juridification or regulation. Institutional arrangements can just as well *minimize* regulations and open free spaces for the effects of morality.[28] In addition, in the section "Derivation of order ethics," the effects of *informal* institutions—within the framework of open contracts—will also be discussed.

I will now first provide a brief overview of order ethics before discussing in more detail those aspects of the conception that are relevant to the topic of this book.

Order Ethics: A Brief Overview

Order ethics ("Ordnungsethik"), which can be considered the complement of the German conception of "Ordnungspolitik," highlights the importance of the order framework for ethical questions. This framework is needed not to tame markets, but to make them more profitable in the long run.

Unlike many other conceptions of ethics, order ethics does not start with an aim to achieve, but rather with an account of what the social world—in which ethical norms have to be implemented—is like: The modern social world differs strongly from the pre-modern one. Pre-modern societies played zero-sum games in which people could only gain significantly at the expense of others. This view of a "zero-sum society" is concisely expressed in the words of the successful fifteenth-century Florentine merchant Giovanni Rucellai (1772, written around 1450): "by being rich, I make others (which I might not even know) poor."

Modern societies, by contrast, are societies with continuous growth. This growth has only been made possible by the modern competitive market economy, which enables everyone to pursue their own interests *within a carefully devised institutional system*. In this system, positive sum games are played, which makes it in principle possible to improve the position of every individual at the same time. Most kinds of ethics, however, resulting from the conditions of pre-modern societies, ignore the possibility of win-win-situations and instead require people to be moderate, to share, to sacrifice. Indeed, this would have been functional in a zero-sum society: The types of ethics still predominant today have been developed within pre-modern zero-sum societies. And these conceptions distinguish—in more or less strict ways—between self-interest and altruistic motivation. Self-interest is seen as something evil.

Such an ethics is not functional in modern societies. Ethical concepts lag behind. Within zero-sum games, it was necessary to call for temperance, for *moderate* profits, or for a condemnation of lending money at interest. Within positive-sum games, however, the morally desired result of a social process cannot be brought about by changes in motivation, by switching from "egoistic" to "altruistic" motivation. Instead, in the modern world, the individual pursuit of self-interest promotes traditional moral ideals in a much more efficient way: These ideals are implemented in the order framework of a society. They govern the market, and via competition on the market, the position of each individual can be improved: the positive sum results. And this positive sum is visible in the form of innovative products at good value for money, of jobs, of income, of taxes and so on. So within the positive sum games of modern societies, the individual pursuit of advantages is in principle compatible with traditional ethical ideas like the solidarity of all.

Competition as a Social Condition

Competition is pivotal in this picture: Order ethics emphasizes the special role competition plays in a society which is characterized by market interactions throughout. Competition has many positive aspects (cf. Hayek 1978): It fosters innovation, the spreading of new ideas and it tends to erode positions of power (for example, those of former monopolists). Most important for ethics is that in competitive situations, morality is constantly in danger of getting crowded out. The prisoners' dilemma (see section 2.3.3) is the classic model for highly competitive situations which can work against morality, but which can also work in favor of morality if the rules of competition are set adequately. In particular, the incentives set by the rules should not thwart what is deemed ethical. As an example, if corruption is seen as unethical, then rules which allow for corruption (for example, allowing bribes to be deducted from tax) will promote unethical behavior—no matter what public calls for morality are being launched. Therefore, order ethics aims at changing the order framework of a society rather than at appealing to moral behavior. This does not imply that people cannot behave ethically, but rather that ethical behavior must not get punished by the incentives.

Actions and Rules

The second theoretical element introduced by order ethics is the distinction between actions and rules. Traditional ethics concerns actions: It calls directly for changes in behavior. This is again a consequence of pre-modern conditions: People in the pre-modern world were only able to control their actions, little however the *conditions* of their actions. In particular, rules like laws, constitutions, social structures, the market order, as well as ethical norms have remained stable for centuries.

In modern societies, this situation has changed entirely. The rules governing people's actions have increasingly come under control. In this situation, ethics should focus on rules, incorporating morality into incentive-compatible rules. Direct calls for changes in behavior without changes in the rules only lead to an erosion of compliance with moral norms: Individuals that continue to behave 'morally' will be singled out, because the incentives have not been changed. More precisely, there are three problems here: First, only changes in rules can change the situation for all participants involved *at the same time*. Second, only rules can be enforced by sanctions—which alone can change the *incentives* in a *lasting* way. Third, only by incorporating morality in the rules can competition be made productive, making the individuals' moves moral-free in principle. With the aid of rules, of adequate conditions of actions, competition can realize advantages for all people involved. In this way, Adam Smith's (1776/1976) classic idea of the market promoting the interests of all can be (re-)captured: If the rules are set adequately, self-interest as the dominant motive in actions can bring about the ethically desired results.

Thus, rules open up new opportunities in actions. But there is an even more important lesson to be learnt from this theoretical perspective: Rules and actions must be prevented from getting into opposition with one another.

Ethical behavior on the level of actions can only be expected if there are no counteracting incentives on the level of rules. In the classic model of the prisoners' dilemma (see section 2.3.3), the prisoners cannot be expected to cooperate, because the conditions of the situation (the "rules of the game") are such that cooperation is punished by defection on the part of the other player. In other words: In PD situations, actors are permanently faced with the possibility of being "exploited" by others if behaving cooperatively, and therefore they stop cooperating themselves pre-emptively. This leads to a situation where rational, self-interested actors end up with a result that leaves all worse and no one better off: Morality gets crowded out.

Actions are governed by rules, but what about rules themselves? In the order ethics picture, rules are governed by other rules of higher order. Higher order means that there is a greater degree of consent needed to put these rules in effect or to change them—as is the case with laws and constitutional rules, for example (Buchanan 1975 and Brennan/Buchanan 1985). Ultimately, the only normative criterion that is needed here is consent—the core criterion of the contractarian tradition (see sections 2.2 and 2.3.1).

Implementation and Advantages

Generally speaking, the relation between implementation and justification in order ethics is different from the one in many other ethical theories: Most ethical theories, whether consequentialist or deontological, proceed by first giving a justification for their norms and then looking for ways of putting these norms into effect. The problem here is that the social conditions for implementation, especially in modern societies, are taken into consideration only *after* a justification has already been established. In this way, there is no room for the idea that a norm may not be justifiable *because* there is no way to implement it: ought implies can. Consequently, order ethics changes the theoretical precedence: discuss problems of implementation already in the process of justification.

It should therefore be clear that moral norms which are to be justified cannot require people to *abstain* from pursuing their own advantage. People abstain from taking "immoral" advantages only if adherence to ethical norms yields greater benefits over the planned *sequence* of actions than defection in the single case. Thus "abstaining" is not abstaining in the long run, it is rather an investment in expectations of long-term benefits. By adhering to ethical norms, a person becomes a reliable partner for interactions. The norms do indeed constrain her actions, but they simultaneously expand her options in *inter*actions. And people consent to rules—in the sense outlined in the previous section—only if these rules hold greater advantages for them, at least in the long run.

In general, ethics cannot require people to abandon their individual calculation of advantages. However, it may suggest *improving* one's calculation, by calculating in the long run rather than in the short run, and by taking into account the interests of their fellows, as one depends on their acceptance for reaching an optimal level of well-being, especially in a globalized world full of interdependence.

The problem of implementation can now be placed at the beginning of a conception of order ethics, justified with reference to the conditions of modern societies sketched above. Under the conditions of pre-modern societies, an ethics of temperance had evolved that posed simultaneously the problems of implementation and justification. The implementation of well-justified norms or standards could then be regarded as unproblematic, because the social structures allowed for a direct face-to-face enforcement of norms. Pre-modern societies not only favored an ethics of temperance, they also had the instrument of face-to-face-sanctions within their smaller and non-anonymous communities. This instrument is no longer functional in modern anonymous societies, and so the problem of implementation has to be faced right at the start of a modern ethical conception. Simultaneously, an order ethics relies on the implementation of sanctions for enforcing *incentive-compatible rules*. In modern societies, rules and institutions, to a large extent, must fulfil the tasks that were, in pre-modern times, fulfilled by moral norms, which in turn were sanctioned by face-to-face sanctions. Norm implementation in modern societies thus works by setting adequate incentives in order to prevent the erosion of moral norms, which would happen if "moral" actors were systematically threatened with exploitation by other, less "moral" actors. This idea will be expanded on in section 2.3.1, with the help of a thought experiment.

Regarding the core normative criterion of order ethics, the above implies that neither is altruism equal to moral behavior nor egoism to immoral behavior. The demarcation line can be found rather between unilaterally and mutually beneficial action: In order to act morally, an actor should be pursuing her advantage in such a way that others benefit as well.

Thus, the conception of order ethics makes changes in ethical categories necessary. Instead of calling for temperance and sacrificing, ethics should promote investing. Instead of demanding redistribution, it should favor exchange. Self-interest should not be "domesticated," but unleashed. And abstaining (or refraining) from breaking rules is not really "abstaining," but an investment in the stability and further development of the social order.

A Thought Experiment

Bruce Ackerman begins his *Social Justice in the Liberal State* (Ackerman 1980) with a thought experiment that seems to have been taken from science fiction. In order to conceptualize the justification for the rules of a state, he does not exactly proceed in terms of classical and modern contract theory to postulate an *original position* here on Earth. Instead, he asks the question of how—that is, according to what principles—would we build a society, if we—or at least a sufficiently large group of people—were to land on a distant planet (see Ackerman 1980, 31ff.[29]). The planet is uninhabited and has a lot of food ("manna," ibid.) that is infinitely divisible, yet not available in unlimited quantities. Therefore, the problem of the resource allocation of manna cannot be avoided.

In Ackerman's fictional scenario, the landing on the planet is imminent and the spacecraft with the people aboard finds itself in orbit. Before landing, however, the occupants of the vessel must lay down the principles of the society in order to prevent anarchy. After such a determination has been made, the captain of the spacecraft will ensure that these principles are actually adhered to by all participants with the aid of the vessel's weapons technology (laser guns, etc.). No effective opposition is possible against this technology, which is to say that once the rules have been agreed to, all members of the society must submit to them without an option to defect. In this way, the theorist—by expressly setting aside the problem of the *implementation* of the rules—focuses on the issues of *explaining and justifying* them. Ackerman (1980, 34) explicitly emphasizes this aspect, believing that this is his approach's specific advantage.

Be that as it may, I recognize that this is exactly where the Ackermanian concept gets into trouble. It cannot be useful—especially in a thought experiment—to only deal with implementation problems retroactively and secondarily in effect with the help of a *deus ex machina* (laser cannons). In any case, this approach does not make sense if one assumes that the issue of implementing rule R must be systematically thought about along with the explanation of R. If one proceeds in the manner Ackerman has, one initially constructs an ideal model whose chances of implementation are then (presumably) taken into account after the fact, bit by bit. One thus must contend systematically with the "chasm" between model and implementation that cannot be subsequently eliminated, but at most—with daring bridge construction—provisionally traversed.

In reference to Ackerman's example, how is the idea to be arrived at in his conception that the conferral of (human) rights can be justified by means of (universal) self-interest? If these rights are *not* accorded to every individual, the disadvantaged and unsatisfied will tend to block all productive cooperation because of the structural dilemmas of modern societies (see the section "Categories of order ethics"). Human rights are thus productive. Such reasoning, however, can only be conceived of in terms of implementability. Ackerman resorts to this possibility.

Nonetheless, I find his thought experiment fundamentally warrants further development for two reasons:

1. The scenario avoids those original position models of contract theory that deliberately construct a purely fictional set of circumstances. Even if it is clear that a historical state is not at issue, the difficulty remains of convincing the various actors *why* it is necessary to reason with the aid of such a fiction. The rationale of the advanced theories is that the *self-interest* of the actors—in connection with the idea of possible cooperation gains—justifies, if not compels, the use of the *original-position* fiction. This idea will be upheld in the present thought experiment. However, if the fiction of the *original-position* is to be used in discourse as an aid to argumentation and have a practical purpose in mind, then I find the science-fiction associations today to be at least as appropriate, if not more so. Science fiction has been recognized as an important part of the public consciousness for decades, specifically for the purpose of refining intuitions or elucidating the consequences of philosophical ideas.[30] It builds on fundamental realities of modern society and exaggerates them for the sake of clarification.
2. The increasing pluralism in modern societies accompanying globalization is more clearly expressed in science fiction-based thought experiments than in the original position models. Even Rawls (1993) can only, as it were, integrate pluralism into his *original position* (explicitly understood as a construct) after the fact. As will become evident below, I see in Ackerman's model the possibility to put it systematically at the beginning.

The outline of the thought experiment now has the following contours.

It is assumed that a large number of people in the distant future are just about to land on a distant planet. These people come from Earth; they are aboard a spaceship that orbits the planet. As in Ackerman's approach, manna is available on the planet, which, however, still needs to be distributed. Before landing, the passengers intend[31] to agree to the rules for the future society. In regard to Ackerman's scenario, the following important changes should be noted:

1. The technology to ensure the enforcement of the determined arrangements is *not* available. There is no weapons technology; there are no laser cannons for guaranteeing that the rules arrived at through consensus will be respected. This means that the passengers of the spacecraft will already have to think about enforcement mechanisms at the time of agreement. These mechanisms must be available after the landing and be robust in the face of the actions of (self-interested) actors.

2. On board the spacecraft, rules are also already in place for communal living. The plan of the new social order does not reflect a "Stunde Null." The passengers of the spacecraft are already able to avail themselves of well-rehearsed conventions and institutions. So far, however, these have related to a confined world, namely that of the ship. They have not been adapted yet to a larger world. Either the old rules need to be adapted to the changed environment or completely new rules have to be devised. In any case, the old rules of the passengers, who have been on the ship for a long time, must be considered when the contract is finalized so that it will be accepted by one and all.
3. The spaceship occupants, moreover, have different *cultural backgrounds*. While they all come from Earth, they originate from every corner of the globe. They bring with them their diverse cultural histories, values, and norms. Thus a "Stunde Null" is neither in evidence in terms of the rules, nor in terms of the "mental models" (Denzau and North 1994) of the actors. Although the concern here is with the design of the order of a *new* society, remnants of an old order must be borne in mind. The availability of a shared moral conception cannot be assumed, nor expected over the long term. The passengers have different and very likely also conflicting moral codes.[32]

It seems appropriate to construct a thought experiment in this way given that the concept of an original position as a completely new beginning has experienced steady criticism. In opposition to Rawls, Buchanan (1972) thus already argued that a contract theory must always proceed from the status quo in order to have an impact. Only then will the contracting parties be *motivated* to act. This means that in the process of finalizing the contract the parties cannot expect unanimity with regard to goals or values or cultural norms.

This is the construction of the circumstances surrounding the contract settlement. A contract theory further requires a conception of the rationality of the contracting parties. Here, in accordance with Binmore (1994 and 1998), I would only assume an (economic) standard of rationality.[33] To justify this, and in view of the wholly unmanageable amount of literature, I would like to start by noting the following:

a. To date, a convincing alternative conception of rationality has yet to be put forward. The maximin conception, for instance, has proved to be extremely implausible and is defended by only a few authors (e.g., Chu and Liu 2001). "Bounded rationality" (Selten 1990, Simon 1983) can be attributed principally to standard rationality under certain conditions, in particular in light of informational constraints.

b. As economic standard rationality is the *simplest* conception, one should therefore begin with it. If success can be had in building a sustainable approach based on standard rationality, this would then be possible with other rationalities. If we are all intrinsically self-interested in the classical sense *and* our systems and institutions on the whole still remain stable, they will also remain stable on the whole if we behave more altruistically or (frequently) according to the principle of contingency.[34] While this, to be sure, would need to be shown in detail, I will simply presuppose it here. (Further arguments in defense of the use of standard rationality are cited in the section "Derivation of order ethics" and "Categories of order ethics.")

A contract theory, thirdly, must be able to the respond to the question concerning the parties' state of knowledge. How much do they know about the structure of the future society and their own position in it? A Rawlsian "veil of ignorance" (Rawls 1971, 19) that denies the actors absolutely any information about their future standing cannot be introduced in the situation described here. The actors know their individual skills and those of their fellow human beings from their previous life on Earth and on board the ship. They must proceed from this status quo. In this regard, I agree with Buchanan, who says: "'We start from here,' and not from some place else" (Buchanan 1975, 78, see also, Brennan and Buchanan 1985, chapter 5).

However, unlike in Buchanan's conception, the old situation does not transfer seamlessly into the new one. At issue is a new situation with new *natural* constraints, alongside which new *social* constraints must be placed. And plenty is known at the settlement of the contract of the functioning of the future society, here analogous to Rawls. With the help of a well-developed economy, the advantages of specific control systems over others can be theoretically verified.

The details of the social rules to which the actors of the described situation would agree could fill up its own volume. At this point, I am only interested in the *outlines* of a changed situation resulting from the contract settlement, which, in turn, will serve the theoretical introduction of OE.

Derivation of Order Ethics

The conception of order ethics may be indicated in four steps[35]:

First, the *problem* that OE is designed to solve must be clearly understood. The strict problem-centeredness and problem-dependence of all theory formation is, in my view, an area that has not yet been sufficiently addressed:

- In philosophy of science, Popper most notably remarks that "all life is problem solving" (Popper 1999), and points to the role of problems for

scientific progress and the development of theories. Even in his rudimentary ethics, Popper describes "practical moral" problems as the "basis of all ethics" (Popper 1945/1950, 630, italics omitted; see also Luetge 2001).
- In addition to Popper, Larry Laudan (1977) emphasizes the "fruitfulness in solving problems" as a central epistemological criterion for the quality of theories. However, he himself later removed this approach in large measure from his work.[36]
- The attempt to establish a formal theory of problems stems from Jagdish N. Hattiangadi (1978 and 1979). This attempt, though, seems to have been rather unsuccessful (see Giunti 1988).
- Gerhard Vollmer (1993) has also mentioned the role of *unsolved* and even insoluble problems in scientific knowledge. He sees this as part of the epistemological re-evaluation of the context of the discovery of theories (Reichenbach 1938/1983) and argues for a thorough reworking and systematization of unsolved problems in all disciplines.
- Homann (1988, 2002) and Andreas Suchanek (1994) have pointed to the problem-dependence of social-science research in particular. Model constructions such as the *homo economicus* can only be used effectively in reference to a specific *problem*.[37] Economic theory reports on the problem of social order (see Hayek 1973–1979), that is, on the question of how (modern) societies can be stabilized and made capable of development. Here stabilization is normally not possible without a capacity for development.[38]

It is at this point that order ethics enters the discussion.[39] Order ethics takes a soluble (practical) *problem* as its point of departure, namely, the problem of social order. In this regard, the tools of ethics are selected, especially social-scientific theories, methods, and findings (other tools, of course, are not excluded).[40]

In the thought experiment, it is precisely the following problem that is under consideration: the formation of a social order on a new planet, not on the basis of a "tabula rasa," but rather in light of a situation where the already existing rules and values from Earth of the spaceship occupants are taken into account. The new situation, however, requires that the rules be revised.

Second, since order ethics focuses on the problem of *social order*, it is clearly distinct from an *individual ethics*. Individual ethics[41] primarily directs its requirements at individuals. It can—of course only in an ideal-typical way—be characterized by a hypothesis and a requirement.

Hypothesis IE: immoral motives or preferences of the actors are to blame for morally questionable conditions.

Requirement IE: these conditions can be remedied insofar as moral demands are placed on the actors, prompting them to undergo a shift in consciousness. The moral control of society is thus the result of *appeals*, and also possibly of education.

Third, yet, when there are *social structures of the prisoner's dilemma type,* then an ethic that makes the individual the primary addressee of moral demands cannot have a lasting effect. An individual ethics must always be regarded as an attempt to put existing incentive structures out of operation, which for all intents and purposes remains unsuccessful.[42] Calls for a shift in consciousness and moral appeals requiring a correction of individual preferences have little impact. Order ethics responds to precisely this. Analogously to individual ethics, it can—and of course also only in an ideal-typical way—be characterized by a hypothesis and a requirement.

Hypothesis OE: it is not immoral preferences or goals that are to blame for morally questionable conditions, but instead specific social structures.

Requirement OE: for this reason, moral demands—at least if their practical implementation is to be an objective—must be oriented toward changing the conditions, which is to say the rules that are valid for all actors. (This does not mean, within the context of the logic of benefits and incentives, that there are no further opportunities for moral action because of systematically open contracts; see point e below.) The moral control of a society thus occurs by changing the *incentive structures*.

Order ethics is therefore adopted *tentatively*, so that dilemma structures prevail in the world. However, the fruitfulness of the assumption must be continuously checked on the basis of its practical utility in structuring social problem situations.

In the thought experiment, the spaceship passengers—who have social-scientific knowledge—also expect that dilemma structures will predominate in the newly founded society.[43] Given the interactions that will occur in a contentious world with shortage problems, such structures are inevitable. Faced with the problem of social order in a world made up of dilemma structures, the passengers must therefore come up with appropriate incentives and sanctions. They are not able to hope for a permanent and systematic change in attitudes or consciousness. There must be a consensus of the contracting parties, however. Yet, if the individuals agree on wanting to improve their situation, they will not fail to eventually adopt the OE perspective. Because of the already existing pluralism of values and the fact that the assumed size of the spaceship crew does not allow for a face-to-face society, the sanctioning can then only occur by way of the institutions. These may be developed by theorists and proposed to the contracting parties.

Fourth, in order to rebut some standard objections to OE up front, attention should be called to the following (mainly methodological) clarifications for the order-ethical program:

a) OE focuses on improvements for everyone, that is, (strict or strong) Pareto improvements that make *all* interested and affected individuals better off. It is important that Pareto superiority only be demanded as a criterion for *rules*, not for individual measures or actions. Individual measures that come into being through rules can always make individuals or groups worse off. However, Pareto superiority of rules means that these short-term "losers" are not only compensated within a reasonable time frame, but are also clearly able to *improve* their condition in comparison to their starting position.

b) Individuals can—both in an entrepreneurial and ethical sense—*invest* in the future. The objection that many people behave morally without being aware of their own advantage can be refuted in many cases by pointing out that these actions may be looked at as advanced payments in anticipation of future cooperation, as investments, in other words, with the hope of future compensation. Since people and businesses are able to invest in every way, why then not also in terms of morals? It is precisely those sophisticated actors who, in thinking of their (possibly *very*) long-term advantage, *must* make moral investments.

The fact that people act in this way, that they invest, must be distinguished methodologically from the skills that are viewed as *necessary* for a stable, modern society in the approaches examined in chapters 3 to 5. The necessary "surplus" postulated by these approaches lies in certain values, a certain notion of human beings, cooperative skills, and so on, that are determined by the respective conception *in advance*, and this "surplus" has precisely the ability to transcend the (long-term) pursuit of advantages. The authors discussed in chapters 3 to 5 stipulate what skills are equally necessary for all stakeholders. Nonetheless, *how* such investments are made cannot be determined in advance, either straightaway for all actors or for all time.

c) In determining Pareto-superior measures, adequate matching rules must be selected. A "nirvana fallacy"—in the sense of Harold Demsetz (1969)—cannot be employed, but instead the relevant alternatives must be called on. Relevant alternatives are above all future scenarios that could not have arisen or will not arise without rule changes. This is especially crucial if a proposed rule change for party A would, at least *prima facie*, result in a worsening of the initial condition T_0. A lands in condition $Z_1 < Z_0$ (the relation "<" means "is worse than") and would clearly not agree to such a change. If, however, it is to expected that A's situation would worsen *even further* without a change in comparison to T_1, that is, $T_2 < T_1$, then A's agreement *can* in fact be expected. A would therefore forestall a de facto worsening of his condition in an alternative, empirically plausible future scenario.

In this way, many of the empirically observable approvals resulting in *prima facie* worse conditions can be explained. Such apparently worse positions can still be Pareto-superior in the sense described. The consent of the white population in South Africa to the democratic reforms beginning in 1994 can serve as example, for without it this segment of the population would have had to contend with much worse conditions (violent revolution, etc.).[44] This point is of great importance for developmental policy as a whole: the corrupt elites of many countries must be convinced that by giving up power they still stand to be relatively better off compared with alternative scenarios.

> d) It is often argued against contractarian conceptions that the individuals would not even be able to recognize their own interests. Only on the basis of their "true" interests would they be ready to approve rules, which—at least in individual cases—would be contrary to their own interests. At this point, contract theories introduce arguments like the "veil of ignorance" (Rawls 1971, 19) or the "veil of uncertainty" (Brennan and Buchanan 1985, 28ff.). The individuals are placed in a situation in which they lack certain information to determine what is in their own interest in the future society and what is not.

Without going into the details here once again (see the section "A thought experiment"), I would only point out that the above-mentioned thought experiment contains this argument. As the occupants of the ship find themselves in orbit, they negotiate the rules for a situation to which, on the one hand, everyone brings their existing individual abilities, but which, on the other hand, also represents a new beginning for everyone. Despite their scientific knowledge, the space travelers cannot know how the rules *individually* will affect the future society. They cannot know how they themselves will react to the new constraints, to the new, changed composition and structure of society, and to the new rules. Accordingly, the information and uncertainty problems of modern society are at least captured, and the difference between "true" and supposed interests can be portrayed as the difference between long- and short-term interests (under uncertainty). The veil argument can also be understood with Binmore (Binmore 1994, 41) as a "device of the original position" that is possibly even evolutionarily rooted in us (see the section "Binmore's original position") and helps us to solve coordination problems. The theorist makes this "food for thought" explicit and presents it to the actors to solve their coordination problems. Whether the actors make use of it is another question.

Order Ethics in the International Context

Order ethics does not deal only with those rules which are incorporated in the law, but with rules on other levels as well. This includes, in particular, agreements at branch level and also self-constraining actions of individual corporations, and leads into the area of Corporate Citizenship and Corporate Social Responsibility (CSR). The underlying economic idea of mutual advantages, however, stays the same: To aim for a win-win situation.

According to M. Friedman's famous dictum, "the social responsibility of business is to increase its profits" (Friedman 1970), corporations would have—at most—responsibilities for the order framework of the market. However, corporations are in fact doing much more, like providing social welfare, engaging in environmental protection, or in cultural and scientific affairs.

There are several possible reactions to this: A stakeholder approach would explain these observations by insisting that a corporation has to take into consideration not only shareholders, but other groups as well. If one takes the order ethics perspective seriously, however, then it is difficult to justify why the claims of stakeholders, which are already incorporated in the formal *rules*—as taxes, salaries, interest rates, environmental and other restrictions—should be incorporated a second time in the *actions* of corporations. This is not to say that corporations should not account for stakeholder interests at all, but rather that the *justification* given is not strong enough.

A suitable justification for a greater political role of corporations can be developed along the lines outlined in the rest of this section. It is consistent with the order ethics conception, especially in view of two points: Ethical norms must (1) be implemented in an incentive-compatible way and (2) be built on (expected) advantages and benefits.

Order ethics proceeds by extending the concept of "order" to other, less formal orders. It therefore introduces another theoretical element, again from economics: the theory of incomplete (or open) contracts.

So far I have shown above all how OE applies to institutions as a solution to interaction problems. It must always be borne in mind here that OE does not fundamentally concern rules or institutions, but benefits and incentives. And as control mechanisms of modern societies, benefits and incentives can be understood apart from (formal) rules. The systematic starting point for this is the theory of open and incomplete contracts.[45]

This theory assumes that human interactions are generally governed by contracts, through both *formal*, codified laws and *informal* mechanisms (such as promises). Crucially, however, many of these contracts are *open* (or incomplete) in the sense that

- performances and rewards are not precisely determined,
- the fulfillment of these contracts is not objective or ascertainable by external authorities and therefore not justiciable, and
- generally, the enforcement (e.g., in court) is too expensive.

Open contracts lead to more uncertainty, and to the risk of stronger dependencies with corresponding opportunities to engage in opportunistic behavior *after* the contract's settlement (ex-post opportunism). Some typical open contracts are employment contracts, service contracts, long-term cooperation agreements, insurance contracts, marriage contracts, and also the classical corporate contract. The number of such contracts increases considerably under conditions of globalization, since uniform regulatory frameworks are less and less available.

On the one hand, the openness of the contract is a serious disadvantage: such contracts will initially lead to planning uncertainties, and especially to dependencies that cause rational actors to not even pursue interactions that could be Pareto superior. Open contracts also constantly require new or revised interpretations of the contract. On the other hand, the openness is also an advantage: it allows for dealing with insufficient information at the time of the contract settlement in a rational manner. The obligations arising from the contract are then only specified once the corresponding information becomes available, and this, in turn, leads to *higher productivity*.

This is precisely where a behavioral ethics can be applied systematically. Where the systematic openness of contracts must be compensated for, the actors are called on to clarify what is to be understood as "fair" in the case at hand. Ethics—understood as fairness,[46] integrity, trust, and so on—has the task of counterbalancing the uncertainty caused by open contracts and reducing the costs of the interactions associated with them.[47] This means it makes sense from the standpoint of self-interest to build up trust and reduce the risk of opportunism. The willingness to act fairly, however, must be signaled in a credible way, for instance with the help of supporting documents concerning the previous actions of the involved individuals.

It is important in this context that a behavioral ethics derived from the concept of open contracts is itself based *on benefits and incentives*. Benefits and incentives here not only make themselves felt by way of (formal) institutions, but also through informal factors.

A final, somewhat more detailed, methodological note: alongside the *original position,* the *homo economicus* is the main tool for thinking through order ethics. At issue here is the construction of a useful fiction.[48] In the section "A thought experiment," two tentative arguments were made for the use of this construction, specifically with regard to its advantages over alternatives and its simplicity. I would now like to demonstrate that the use of the *homo economicus* characterizes a specific scientific discourse that only deals with a specific *aspect* of reality. This has two facets.

First, it involves taking up a certain position within the *realistic* research program that integrates *constructivist* elements. Although much more might be said on this, I will only say at this point that I share an understanding of realism that approximates the one represented in Philip Kitcher's writings, especially in his *Science, Truth, and Democracy* (Kitcher 2001). Various perspectives, accordingly, are explicitly authorized with regard to the same phenomena. The knowing subject *constructs* knowledge, and she does this on the basis of her *interrogations* with the help of the prerequisites of her own knowledge *and* the empirical material.[49] The different perspectives on the same empirical material, however, are quite compatible with realism, which Kitcher (2001, 44ff.) explains on the example of the sculptor:

All of the various forms that a sculptor can chisel from a block of marble (e.g., Bernini's or Michelangelo's *David*) are always already contained in this block. The sculpture separates the various parts of the marble from each other, but he does not *create* them. Instead, he can separate out the (uncountable) infinite number of forms in the marble, which may already be seen in the block, but only—to speak with Shakespeare (*Hamlet*, I, 2)—before the "mind's eye" of the artist. Kitcher asks why this manner of articulating the problem should not be allowed. Only a relatively dull positivism could deny a priori that the different forms or perspectives are always already present in the empirical material and also—at least with an adequate gaze—identifiable. Aside from the details of the epistemological issues, which cannot be entered into here, this manner of articulating the problem seems fruitful: it would relativize some of the complications that arise when talking about those entities that are problematic for a *traditional*-realistic conception.

In my view, this allows the *homo economicus* to be conceived of as *a possible model of human beings* in a quite realistic sense. In the mind's eye of the economist—or that of the order ethicist—*the homo economicus* is already visible in the empirical human being, the *homo sapiens* (see Binmore's [1994 and 1998] terminology). Other models of the *homo sapiens* are visible in the mind's eye of the psychologist, the sociologist, and the biologist. Nonetheless, each one can be in complete agreement with reality. The constructivistic consequence—or what is somewhat unfairly alleged of constructivism, namely that the models can ultimately be selected *arbitrarily*—is avoided. To offer yet another example, some organisms are classified differently by different branches of biology. While general biology counts the round worm among the class of nematodes, parasitology includes it in among the parasites. And here, in the natural scientific context, the view seems even more plausible that nematodes and parasites are equally "real."

On the other hand, no discourse—whether naturalistic or non-naturalistic—can be applied to "the whole" of reality. This may sound trivial, but it is quite relevant: naturalistic approaches—and to these I include order ethics (see Luetge 2004a)—are regularly accused by non-naturalists of never attaining a certain level of reality with their explanations. This criticism is put forward in similar form in epistemology and the philosophy of science as well as the philosophy of mind and ethics. The argument generally proceeds as follows:

1. The naturalist explains only aspects A to E of the phenomenon at issue, but is unable to explain F.
2. For non-naturalists, however, aspect F is precisely the phenomenon's essential aspect. In the philosophy of mind, for example, F can stand for "the unity of consciousness" or "the inner aspect of consciousness"; in epistemology, "normative epistemology"; and in practical philosophy, "*commitments*" (see Brandom 1994 and also Luetge 2008).
3. The non-naturalist claims either to be able to explain F or that F is fundamentally inexplicable.

In the third step, different paths are taken by the respective authors. In the philosophy of mind, inexplicability is frequently chosen; practical philosophy, on the other hand, tends toward explicability by means of another, namely, non-naturalistic theory. In my view, the following is most relevant: if no discourse can grasp reality in its totality, then it is neither possible for the transcendental philosopher nor the philologist. This is clear to some of the respective proponents, but not to all of them. Robert Brandom (1994), for example, claims that naturalistic attempts to explain—or even to "create"—normativity must inevitably fail, since normativity is not naturalistically reconstructable. Rather, this sense of normativity is, on the one hand, specifically what distinguishes human beings from the rest of the animal kingdom,[50] and, on the other hand, this is where the task of philosophy comes to bear, according to Brandom.[51] It is supposed to examine just this area of the normative—the force of norms and the binding effects of *commitments*.[52] No naturalistic theory could take on this task, and nor could a naturalistic philosophy, Brandom claims.[53]

I will discuss these hypotheses in greater detail in the section "Moral communication: Toward a semantics of benefits" (and later in "Society requires (almost) nothing (Ken Binmore)"). But even here, I would point out that I find such a position to be highly problematic, as attempts at this kind of delimitation have often been found invalid. During its history, philosophy has unsuccessfully tried to demarcate its sub-disciplines like natural philosophy, epistemology, or philosophy of mind from evolutionary theory, neuroscience, linguistics, or theoretical physics. And from my perspective, Brandom has not managed to prove that such a normativity exists that is totally inaccessible to naturalistic explanations. Some of the examples he cites as not being explicable according to naturalistic binding effects, I view, on the contrary, as being *precisely* explicable in a naturalistic way, that is, in this case with regard to benefits and incentives as called upon by OE (see the section "Moral communication: Toward a semantics of benefits").

Morality does not just represent a language system that we neither can nor may reconstruct naturalistically. Brandom's view represents either inconsequential wordplay or—to put it rather bluntly—a prohibition on research.

Only from these points altogether, then, does a satisfactory understanding emerge of both the explanatory and the normative perspective of the order ethics approach. The efficacy of the *homo economicus* can only be first developed after taking these points into consideration. In fact, many of its customary representations yield little more than caricatures (in such cases one may speak more appropriately of "*homo stultus*" or "*homo stupidus*"[54]). I do not claim here that this perspective should not be abandoned under any circumstances, but rather that as long as it is fruitful, we should stick to it for now.

Categories of Order Ethics

Since order ethics makes the claim of presenting in some respects a fundamentally different conception than traditional individual ethics (see the section "Moral communication: Toward a semantics of benefits"), certain *categories* not only need to be reconstructed, but in some cases *newly constructed*. This should begin with the term *order ethics*.

Order ethics sees its goal in changing the basic *conditions* for individual behavior and *only indirectly*, not directly, in changing the behavior of the actors themselves. It might therefore be called an "ethics of conditions," which—paradigmatically—does not place its demands on the individual, requiring a change in her actions, motives, and reasons. Instead, it attempts to achieve changes in the rules and in the order framework.[55] Hence, the term *order ethics* is used in contradistinction to an individual ethics (as described).[56] Such an ethics can also be understood as "ethics on a naturalistic basis" (see the section "The problem's outline"). In this sense, the concern is with a research program that essentially uses individual scientific methods and findings in the natural sciences and also in the social sciences. They are not only used in general for providing additional support or subsequent enforcement of the established norms, but also systematically as part of the process of founding norms, that is, as concerns to the "heart" of ethics.[57]

The conception advocated here, of course, does not claim that rules could or should be established once and for all time. They are, in fact, further developed, and they *must* be because the societal consensus and conditions change. Rules that once corresponded to the given social consensus can, in the case of social upheavals and changes in the social structure, come into conflict with this consensus. Even a calculated *violation* of a rule can be beneficial to economic and social progress under certain conditions.[58]

The question is *how* such—even morally motivated[59]—upheavals and changes in the rules find expression. Indeed, an order ethics specifically does *not* want to represent the position that, beyond the rules, certain moral capacities, and so on, are *absolutely mandatory* for the stable functioning of a modern society. Categories, however, must be developed in order to adequately describe the role of moral ideals and visions *in the development and adaptation of the rules*. The concept of *heuristics* seems especially well-suited to this purpose.

Under the term *heuristics*, one understands instructions for solving problems, which (see Gadenne 1996, 61)

- are not precise and do not provide any guarantee of success; and
- offer points of orientation, but no problem-solving *algorithm*.[60]

Heuristics can thus be viewed as a technological tool or a mental instrument that fulfills certain tasks, namely, the production of new knowledge or, more generally, serves new solutions and problem-solving strategies. In this sense, the term is also useful for modern societies in the function of morality: it does not imply either that such a morality is strictly necessary or that it must lead to a solution, or that there might not be other, more suitable non-moral strategies. In the division of labor of the disciplines, it can turn out that other individual disciplines treat the concept referred to here as heuristics in other ways and with other terms. Heuristics can also be obtained from non-philosophical, non-moral, and non-religious traditions, such as art, literature, other cultures, or the social and natural sciences. Which heuristics is more *fruitful* than others must first be demonstrated, for it is not clear from the outset.[61]

The idea of leaving the economics concept of benefits open has certainly been part of the business ethics discussion for some time. It will be taken up here again, however, for the sake of clarification. Under *benefits*, one understands what the actors themselves view as benefits, whether it's monetary benefits, time, effort, energy, a feeling of satisfaction, a clear conscience, or the Aristotelian "good life." It is only when benefits are understood in this way that an order ethics can be developed systematically on the basis of benefits (and incentives). While it is not possible to go through this program in detail, it can be pointed out that (at least prima facie) many of the findings of the ethical discussion may remain in place. They should, nonetheless, be seen from another perspective and interpreted differently. In *descriptive* terms, many of the findings that point to the moral behavior of the individual can be reinterpreted *as if* these individuals pursue the benefits that are open to them. In *normative* terms, an order ethics calls for those norms deemed ethically positive to be *implemented* in such a way—or at least for the *proposals* regarding their implementation to be designed in such a way—that all the parties attain the *benefits*. A lasting and stable implementation, which is the foundation of order ethics, would not be possible otherwise. In the context of modern societies, individuals and small groups are able to acquire substantial power, systematically undermine productive partnerships, and, to a certain extent, throw sand in the works.[62] To move these individuals to cooperate, they must recognize the benefits for themselves. Moral reasoning could only develop systematically in pre-modern societies, and even then only because of the continuous, intensive face-to-face surveillance with its attendant informal sanctions.

The structures of modern societies that give individuals substantial power and make cooperation difficult have long been known in the philosophical-historical tradition (at least since Hobbes). In game theory, which order ethics draws from, these structures are represented as dilemma structures. This concept is frequently circumscribed even further such that modern society is characterized by *prisoner's* dilemma structures (see, for example, Buchanan 1975, Binmore 1994 and 1998, Homann 2002, and Luetge 2012). This idea, in turn, is sometimes criticized: dilemma structures—understood empirically—are either argued to be not as prevalent in a modern society as has been suggested or at least not *predominant*. Since a crucial theoretical element relating to the present approach is at issue here, a more thorough discussion is called for.

The first part of the above-mentioned criticism takes the view that the dilemma structures are fundamentally inadequate for characterizing modern societies (this criticism is sufficiently dealt with by Homann 2002, chapter 5). The second part maintains that dilemma structures are indeed a perfectly reasonable concept, but also that further, different embedded dilemmas may be found alongside the prisoner's dilemma. As useful as it is to speak more generally of dilemma structures, there are also good reasons—at least pragmatic ones—for *concentrating* on *prisoner's* dilemma structures, which are shown in figure 2.1.

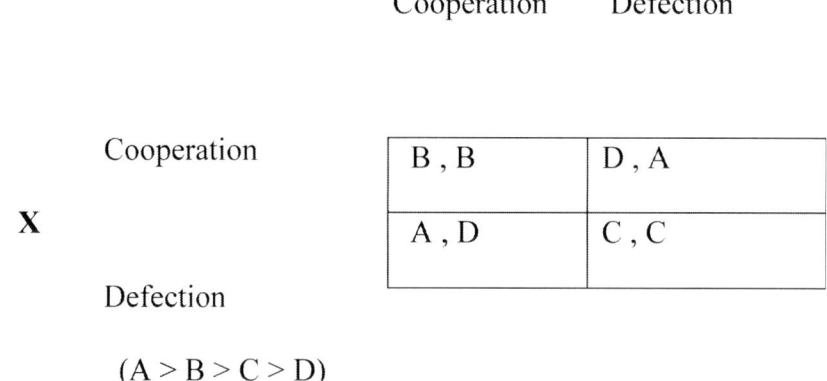

Figure 2.1. The prisoner's dilemma

The following alternatives to the prisoner's dilemma are suggested.

a) The Game of Chicken, a game related to the prisoner's dilemma

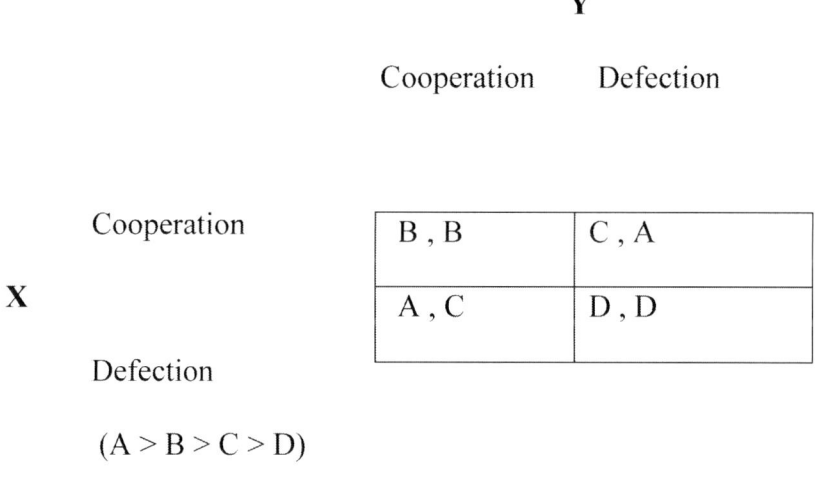

Figure 2.2. The Game of Chicken

For the purposes of the order-ethical conception, however, it is too obvious in the Game of Chicken that mutual non-cooperation (D, D) is bad for both actors. The threat of non-cooperation is less credible in this game than in the prisoner's dilemma. The actors are to some extent *condemned* to cooperate and can escape only at the cost of a "scorched earth" policy. In the Game of Chicken, defection is simply *too* risky.

b) The Battle of the Sexes. This model adequately represents certain aspects of social structures

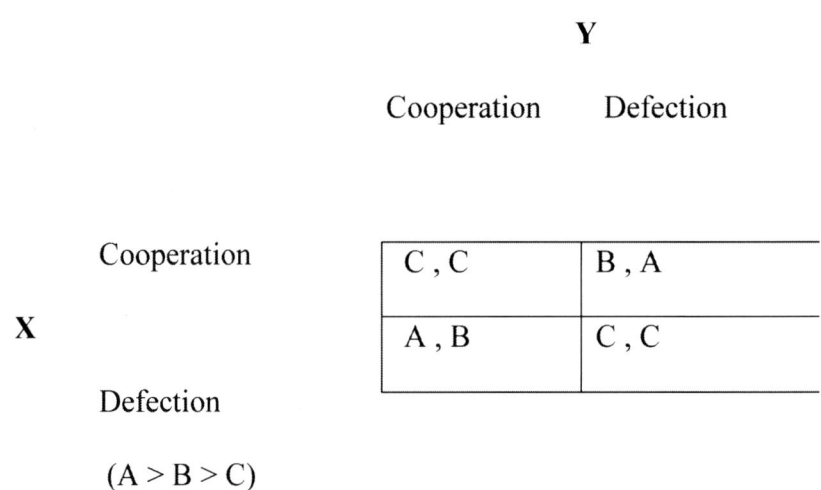

(A > B > C)

Figure 2.3.   The Battle of the Sexes

For the present purpose, this model is only somewhat suitable. Although Pareto improvements are possible in the (C, C) situations, in each case one wins more than the other. Therefore, it is generally difficult for the actors to agree on one of the two quadrants (B, A) or (A, B). To prevent an impasse, the one who—economically speaking—wins more could compensate the other. This is not provided for in the Battle of the Sexes, however. If there is compensation, a different game is being played. On the basis of this game, consequently, the mutual co-operational gains resulting from rule changes might be less plausible than in the prisoner's dilemma. Cooperation in the Battle of the Sexes is not entirely convincing.

c) The unproblematic Altruism Game (Other-Regarding Game)[63]

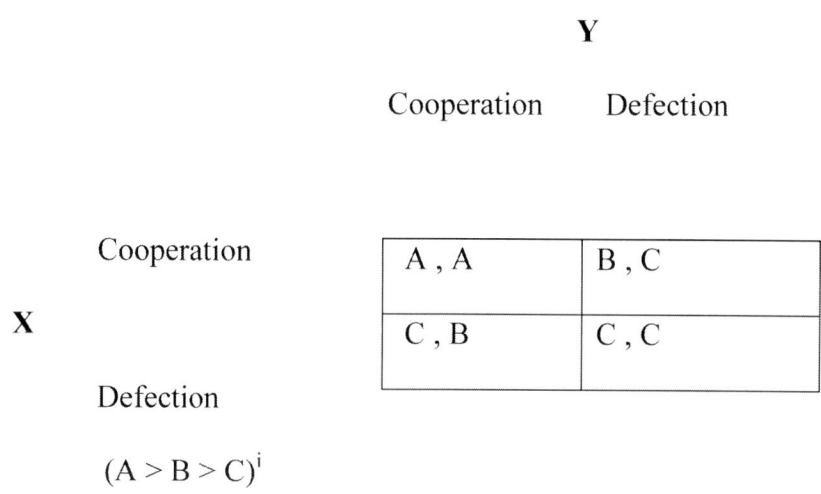

$(A > B > C)^i$

Figure 2.4. The Altruism Game. [i] This game is described here in somewhat simplified form. Sen originally had a situation in mind in which the asymmetric quadrants are "swapped" in the sense that the more favorable situation is chosen. This complication, however, is less relevant here.

In the Altruism Game, the actors select the best cooperative alternative for *everyone*, regardless of the actions of the others. This may be a useful model for special situations.[64] In general, however, one cannot assume such "fixed" modes of behavior in modern societies. The relevance of the Altruism Game is therefore rather limited.

d) Coordination games

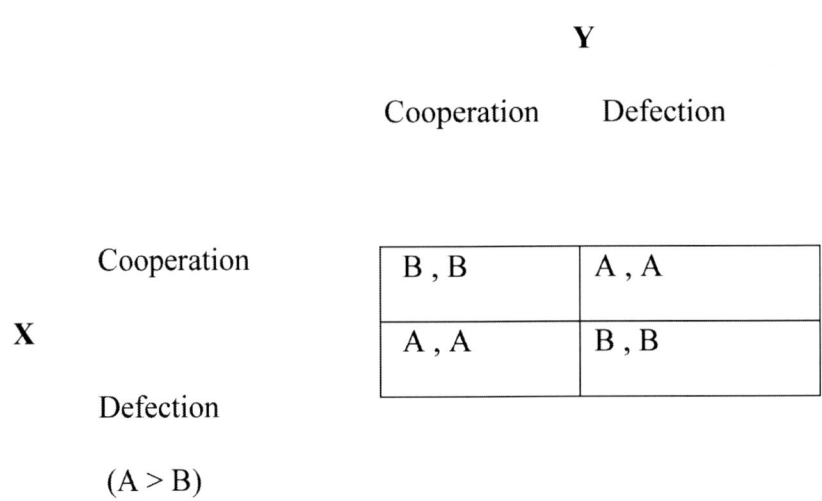

Figure 2.5. Coordination Games

Coordination games present no theoretical problems and are therefore not suitable as a model for the present purpose. The concern is merely with *which* one of the two situations (A, A) is to be realized. The order ethical conception itself, however, would suggest looking for a hidden (because overcome) dilemma structure, even in situations that *seem* to be pure coordination games. Coordination-game modeling is therefore only of limited use.

e) The Assurance Game has been utilized by Amartya Sen, among others, for ethical questions.⁶⁵ This model is characterized in figure 2.6.

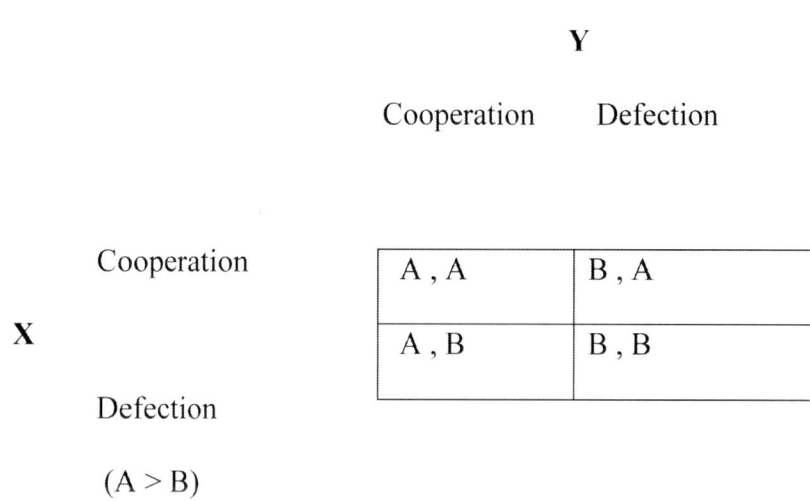

Figure 2.6. The Assurance Game

To be sure, as in prisoner's dilemma, the circumstances in this situation are such that X cooperates only in the case that Y also cooperates. If Y does not cooperate, both actors end up in the Pareto-inferior situation (B, B), which, indeed, reflects a second equilibrium that does not exist in the prisoner's dilemma. Most notably, however, the coordination with respect to the Pareto-superior outcome (A, A) can be achieved without sanctions and enforcement measures. The players agree on (A, A) without coercion, since *there is no threat of other, more individually favorable* cases. It is thus highly questionable whether the Assurance Game is suitable for modeling the conflict-laden situations that predominate in modern societies, which are either manifest or (temporarily) overcome with the possibility that conflicts can break out again at any time. An agreement without even *self*-imposed pressure is wishful thinking in too many societal cases.⁶⁶

54   Chapter 2

f) The Stag-Hunt Game

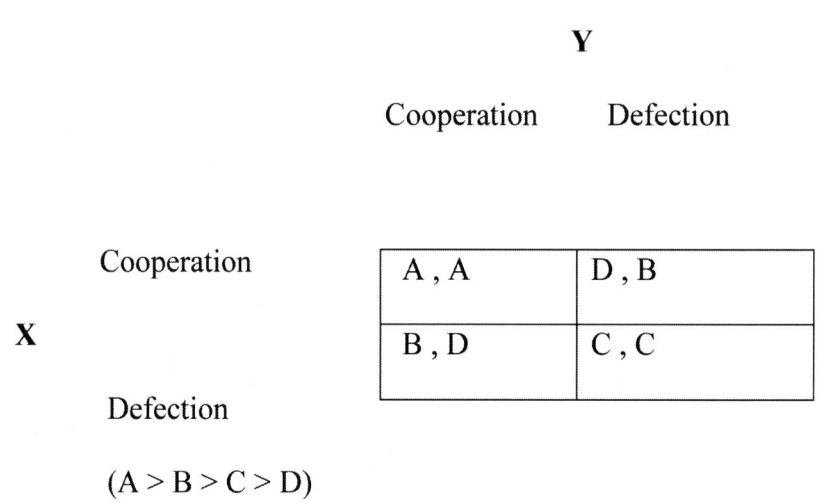

(A > B > C > D)

Figure 2.7. The Stag-Hunt Game

The Stag Hunt Game[67] is suitable for the purposes of Binmore, who often draws on it (see Binmore 1994, section "Derivation of order ethics"). He is concerned above all with the representation of a situation that—despite possible benefits for everyone—does not necessarily have to lead to cooperation. The reason for this is that an agreement on cooperation is difficult to implement, as the degree of (self-) commitment must be believable to the opposite party. In this respect, the Stag Hunt Game raises an issue that is also particularly relevant to OE, namely, the question of implementation. Just the same, it still appears less suitable for the present purpose than the prisoner's dilemma, the problem being that the rationality trap is missing: the situation, that is, in which one can do better for oneself at the expense of another than through cooperation. Thus the resulting betterment from cooperation is too obvious and the possibility of exploitation is absent. The prisoner's dilemma, hence, appears to be more suitable for the present purpose.

The observations above clearly show that when drafting proposals for institutional reform it is useful to view the society *as if* it were specifically characterized by prisoner's dilemmas, and not only dilemma situations in general. This is the only way to demonstrate Pareto improvements for all parties involved, to avoid rationality traps, and to identify opportunities for eliminating impasses. The prisoner's dilemma should thus not only be an essential category for business ethics, but for ethics in general.

Moral Communication: Toward a Semantics of Benefits

Above and beyond the preceding remarks, order ethics stresses a further, perhaps decisive point. OE does not reflect a purely economic approach, which by and large falls back on questions concerning institutional design, works with purely self-interested actors toward this end, and—setting aside questions of norm *justification*—focuses on the problem of norm *implementation*. This is by no means the case. OE is rather *precisely* geared toward the *justification* of norms. The order-ethical justification of norms, however, differs from traditional justifications: *only a (systematically) enforceable norm—and this means above all one that is organizationally framed and incentive-compatible—is also well-founded.*

This position has two aspects: first, it draws attention to the importance of institutions and their rational configuration for ethics.[68] On the other hand, not only must institutional reform proposals be based on benefits, but so must *norm justifications* when they are *communicated* to others. In other words, the justification of norm N must communicate the *benefits* of N's implementation to those on the receiving end of the explanation. I will call the semantics used in this case the *semantics of benefits*.[69]

A formulated conception of such a semantics of benefits as philosophical program does not yet exist. For the time being, it also cannot be presented here. Still, I would like to discuss some prolegomena to such a semantics of benefits, at least in rudimentary form.

Language philosophy could help to investigate the question of how benefits are communicated in justificatory discourses. If the theory of order ethics is correct that norm justifications concern benefits, then it must make sense to analyze such justifications in view of the respective—explicit or implicit—signaling of benefits, promise of benefits, and willingness to negotiate over benefits (bargaining). The famous quote from Adam Smith's *Wealth of Nations* is as follows:

> It is not from the benevolence of the butcher, the brewer, or the baker that we expect our dinner, but from their regard to their own interest. We address ourselves, not to their humanity but to their self-love, and *never talk to them of our own necessities but of their advantages.* (Smith 1776/1977, 13; my emphasis)

In my view, behind Smith's use of the word "talk" lies a philosophical understanding of language that until now—at least to my knowledge—has been neglected. How do we "talk" about the benefits to others? How does we justify norms—naturalistically, that is, regarding benefits—to others without appealing to metaphysical constructs or making the assumption, for example, that there is a rational motivation in the Habermasian sense (see the section "Society requires rational motivation for life forms capable of ideal")? As I see it, there are opportunities here for taking a new direction in the linguistic-analytical study of normative statements. Some preliminary considerations—more than this is not possible here—would be the following.

Brandom (2000 and 1994),[70] John McDowell (1994), and game theory-oriented philosophers such as John Broome (2000)[71] represent a motivation theory, which says that people with reasons, also especially moral reasons, can be directly motivated to act.[72] This view is also expressed in the following way, particularly by Brandom.[73]

People are normatively required to justify their actions to others with good reasons. A failure to present a justification is sanctioned, although with a type of *normative sanctions* that—and this is key—is not reducible (with the help of incentives and cost-benefit estimates) to sanctions in an "external" sense.

With this in mind, good reasons should oblige an actor to act in a certain way, and, indeed, in a way that, at least according to Brandom (2000, 91), is *unconditional*.[74] Actors who do not act in this way suffer from a character flaw: they are *weak-willed*. This theory thus attributes suboptimal results in interaction contexts to (typically referred to as irrational) weakness of the will on the part of the actors concerned.

Put differently: in order to convince a player A of the necessity of an action H, a proponent of OE recommends that A try to bear in mind the (long-term) benefits of H *for A personally*. A consistent advocate of Brandom's theory of motivation, on the other hand, must argue that A would have to be convinced with good reasons—whatever they may be—which *cannot* be ascribed to benefits.

In the following two examples, I would like to illustrate this difference in the interpretation of action situations and their relevant motivations and also make plain the possibility of a semantics of benefits, which helps benefits to be communicated in justification discourses.

a) As part of his criticism of so-called reductionist theories of practical rationality, to which he counts particularly consequentialist theories, Julian Nida-Rümelin (2002, 121f.) presents the following example. It is intended to show, first, how inadequate such consequentialist theories of rationality are, and second, to illustrate the concept of the "good reason":

> A woman sitting at a table next to me in a restaurant asks me to pass her the salt. This request is alone a good reason to meet it, at least under normal conditions. A further justification is not necessary. And in particular, "the consequences (and my subjective evaluation of them) seem to be irrelevant. . . . If I answer the question of why I passed the salt with consideration regarding the consequences of this action . . . then this would under normal conditions be considered discourteous to the person having made this request, as I apparently did not accept her request as a genuine reason for action." (ibid. 121; translated by C. R.)

This example may, indeed, prima facie have a certain plausibility. However, it seems important to add that Nida-Rümelin's reconstruction cannot be any sort of pre-theoretical description (which is not available), but is rather a *reconstruction* from the point of view of a theorist. As such, it is itself exposed to the possibility of alternative reconstructions. In my view, even more alternatives are conceivable from the perspective of OE, which operates with benefits and incentives.

First, one could argue that following the rule "pass the salt each time someone asks" is already advantageous because of its simplicity: it is simpler because it requires fewer (mental) resources to *always* pass the salt than to think about it each time in advance—at least as long as the act of passing the salt does not involve any greater costs.[75]

Second, one could call on the discussion of "social capital"[76] in economics: a person who regularly passes the salt to others at neighboring tables, especially if they are in an environment where she typically resides (community, village, pub), could be seen as investing in her social capital. The development of social capital, in turn, can result in the expectation of a direct increase (at least longer-term) of utility, principally in the form of new opportunities for cooperation. The investments must not exceed the long-term expected benefits; otherwise they are scaled back.

Third, it would be possible to introduce the category of "psychic costs." One could then argue that it inflicts psychic costs on an actor who deviates from learned "moralistic" behaviors. "Immorality" causes remorse. Again, this will only apply as long as the opposing incentives are not too great.

It is clear, however, that the reconstruction of the salt example with the help of "good reasons" is at least not the only possible example.

b) According to Brandom (1994), whose approach has already been referred to extensively, human beings, in contrast to animals, can be characterized by their "norm sensitivity" (ibid. section 1.4.2). This ability makes them receptive to good reasons, which has an impact on their social life. Brandom draws a sharp distinction between two types of rules or social practices: those in which non-compliance involves external sanctions (in extreme cases, corporal punishment), and those in which a failure to comply results in so-called normative sanctions (ibid. section 1.4.5). To distinguish normative from external sanctions, Brandom (ibid. 90) offers the following (fictional) example:

When entering a particular hut, the members of a tribe are supposed to present a leaf from a certain tree. Anyone who does not comply to this expectation is punished by being excluded from participating in the weekly festival.

For Brandom, this situation involves a normative sanction, which refers to the normative status of individuals and consequently differs from external punishments such as caning. Normative sanctions range within "normative network(s)" (ibid. 91), which *cannot* be attributed to non-normative elements.[77] Here, a gap emerges between non-normative and normativity that, at least for Brandom, appears to be so large that one can speak of an independent normative space.

An order ethics that relies on economics cannot comprehend this strict separation. Both caning and the denial of participation in a festival must be considered utility losses. In the latter case, the loss of benefits may well be felt less immediately. Nevertheless, both losses may be directly *compared* and weighed against each other. An individual who does not participate in the festival loses social capital; he misses out on opportunities for cooperation that will likely be negotiated there. There are thus accumulated opportunity costs, that is, costs of unused opportunities, which can easily be juxtaposed to a direct punishment—which seriously puts into question the foundation of Brandom's strict dichotomy.

Second, I return again to the concept of heuristics from the perspective of a semantics of benefits. The following *tu quoque* argument is made against the order-ethical conception: order ethics brings into play at another level abilities already found unnecessary for the operation of modern global societies. The concept of heuristics (see the section "Categories of order ethics") is not based on benefits and incentives, but rather on a kind of rational motivation. A modern society does not in fact need a rational motivation on the level of immediate action. The actions could (in principle) take place free of morality. However, to *change* the rules, or at least to arrive at concepts for the rules' further development, the members of society (or at least a portion of them) would have to be morally motivated or have a rational motivation. Is this criticism justified? Is heuristics to be equated with a moral surplus value (within the meaning of chapters 3 to 5)?

In response to this question, two different, but mutually supporting answers might be given.

First of all, I see a distinct difference between a heuristic, as outlined in the section "Categories of order ethics," and the moral surplus value of the approaches discussed later in chapters 3 to 5. To be sure, the heuristics postulated by order ethics does not concern the immediate benefits for those who behave according to this heuristic. It does, however, relate at a minimum to the *communication,* mediation, or promise of possible future benefits. This diametrically contradicts the statements of representatives of moral surplus values. Their—usually *explicit*—concern is that a motivation, informed, for instance, by a sense of justice (Rawls, see chapter 4) or a rational motivation (Jürgen Habermas, see the section "Society requires rational motivation for life forms capable of ideal role taking and constitutional patriotism (Jürgen Habermas)") precisely offsets the motivation informed by benefits. This, then, is in most cases connected with the demand that we *should* act in this manner, that is, follow a sense of justice or a rational motivation.

Second of all, even if the difference indicated between the concept of heuristics and the moral surplus value is not accepted, another difference remains: order ethics introduces a *two-tier* set of rules and actions, wherein the motivation of "another type" would come into play only at the second level—that of the rules. Yet this changed conceptualization would bring a theoretical advance, because the distinction between the levels of action and rules is not present in much of the philosophical—also partly economic—literature (for more on this, see the section "Society requires internalized dispositions for cooperation (David Gauthier)").

ON THE RELATIONSHIP OF ORDER ETHICS AND INDIVIDUAL-ORIENTED APPROACHES

Since order ethics is contrasted in this book with alternative approaches, I also want to give its counterpart more conceptual precision as an ideal type. This counterpart has already been denoted as individual ethics (IE, the section "Derivation of order ethics") by a hypothesis IE and a requirement IE. In the following chapters, different expressions of this ideal type in ethics and social philosophy are discussed and examined as to their effectiveness in the modern era. It turns out that all approaches—including Binmore's (see the section "Society requires (almost) nothing (Ken Binmore)")—contain individual-oriented[78] elements. Insofar as these elements go beyond the individual pursuit of benefits, I refer to them with the concept of *moral surplus value*. Their exact form can vary from one approach to another. A moral surplus value is *a moral capacity or quality* that citizens of a modern global society must possess[79] in order for their society to remain stable.[80] The moral surplus value is necessary to govern a society and to stabilize a democratic society, if not on its own then *in addition to rules and incentive structures*. The degree to which the moral surplus value is required also varies from one approach to another. OE, however, dispenses with this surplus value.

To begin with, it is important that in the discussed approaches the respective moral surplus value has a role in the governance of modern societies, which—in contrast to the concept of OE—is

- *permanent*, that is, the moral surplus value is not meant to serve the temporary closure of existing gaps in the regulatory system. In the concept of order ethics, however, moral resources are only used systematically in cases of open contracts (see Homann and Luetge 2004/2013, part 2).
- *systematic* in nature, that is, moral resources, as governing instruments, obtain a systematic location in the *theoretical structure*, and not only in a pragmatic or application-oriented discussion. OE, by contrast, assumes that the moral resources have been *systematically* (or paradigmatically)

exhausted in the governance of modern societies. In the model, that is theoretically, there is no place for them *in principle* as a null hypothesis. In any case, it can still be said in a pragmatic discussion, for instance on case studies, that moral resources can continue to be used (in a limited way) in controlling, for example, management processes[81]—although not permanently against incentives.

- *substitutive*, not supplementary to the rules. The discussed approaches want to *replace* the rules (at least in some areas) with moral surplus values in order to restore morality or—where possible—to not introduce rules at all because this brings about, or at least contributes to, the initial decay of a (supposedly functioning) morality.[82] In both cases, moral resources are seen as the primary governing instrument, not—as in order ethics—as something secondary that must be supported by rules or whose stability essentially depends on functioning background rules. OE does *not* assert that moral resources cannot be effective, which certainly is possible within the concept of open contracts. Moral resources simply cannot be actively *against* the logic of benefits and incentives or against existing incentives. Their compatibility with incentives must also first be (re-)established by means of appropriate rule reforms.

This permanent, systematic, and substitutive role of moral surplus values constitutes the core of the descriptive arguments of an individual ethics and a large part of the approaches discussed in chapters 3 to 5. In my view, they have two essential conditions:

- It is possible for the members of a society to systematically *infringe on* incentives. To this, accordingly, is also tied the *requirement* to ignore incentives and to act in a (supposedly) moral way (see the section "Derivation of order ethics").
- Morality avails itself in a meaningful way (only) to a phenomenalistic access. As *phenomenalistic*,[83] I refer in the following to those approaches that—even if usually only implicitly—assume that we have a non-theoretical access to individual, or a group of, phenomena. It should be possible to process this access with the use of everyday language; some of the respective approaches link to this the demand (or hope) that philosophy should embrace this access. Phenomenalist approaches, however, can be also found in other disciplines outside of philosophy (for example, in psychology and the social sciences).[84] In ethics, this is represented in the following way: moral intuitions do not have to be reconstructed, but are open to direct, non-theory-based access.[85] To some extent, this is even tied to the *requirement* that morality *may not* be reconstructed otherwise, as this would also encourage its decay.

- OE explicitly distinguishes itself from phenomenalism. According to current scientific theory, it does not make sense to assume non-theoretical access to phenomena. The phenomena of this world can only be addressed scientifically with a scientific language system *and* reference to a specific problem. This book aims to make a contribution in this regard.

For the sake of drawing a contrast, the statements from the section "Derivation of order ethics" are compared here once again in summary. The *role of moral resources* in OE is

- *heuristic,*
- to be considered above all in *pragmatic* terms, when applied to the particular case, and
- merely conceived to be *supplementary* to existing rules, that is, without the corresponding rules that generate incentive compatibility, moral resources cannot reach their full effect systematically.

Also, in contrast to the conditions of the discussed approaches, OE requires

- that individuals cannot systematically infringe on incentives, and
- that the theoretical access to moral resources is by no means phenomenalistic, but makes sense only under *systematic* inclusion of the individual disciplines, particularly the social sciences.[86] This also implies that the sanctions and institutions *behind* the moral phenomena must be taken account of.

Accordingly, the following candidates emerge for OE's possible demands on the actors.

Requirement 1: Adhere (out of your own self-interest) to the (political-legal) rules!

The view is sometimes expressed that this requirement is not necessary because compliance with the rules out of self-interest already results from the outline of order ethics. While this is true, this interpretation in my view ultimately results in the determination that compliance with the rules out of self-interest no longer has *any* ethical relevance. It appears as though ethics—at least semantically—is completely replaced by economics and other social sciences. This would not do justice, however, to order ethics, which precisely represents the view that compliance with the rules (motivated in particular by self-interest) is, to a great extent, *ethically* relevant. The *ethical* preferability of such acts is thereby secured by the rules, which everyone can agree on. If one were to leave out the predicate "ethical," one would run the danger of falling into a discussion in which a second, ethical level is put into place, alongside the economic-social scientific level. This would open the door to the argument that something can be economically right, but ethically wrong. In other words, that ethics and economics are two strictly separated discourses. Ethics and economics could then no longer be traced to a common root, as in Smith (1776/1976), and, in ethics, the issue of the implementation of ethical demands would again be placed in the background. It therefore seems appropriate to continue to view the self-interested adherence to the rules as an *ethical* demand.

Requirement 2: Commit yourself (out of your own self-interest) to changing the (political-legal) rules!

As a demand, adherence to the rules may not suffice. Indeed, rules in practice do not remain static, but must also be—normatively—adapted to the societal circumstances and the members' changing consensus, resulting from shifts in power.[87] It consequently seems intuitively obvious that, along with adherence to the rules, the further development of the rules must also be ethically mandated.

But is this requirement really necessary? If all members of a society are satisfied with the current rules, then must a further development of them take place anyway? Above all, what objective or direction should the development be based on? In the modern era, such an objective cannot come from external sources, but only be generated somehow by the society's members themselves.

In my view, it should first be noted here that the continued development of rules can only occur a) in practice if the affected individuals desire it, and only be demanded b) normatively under the condition that the individuals find this development desirable, since they would not implement it otherwise. Further rule development is ultimately not feasible when it is *against* the desires of those who are affected, even if it appears as a "moral" necessity.

But this is not the final word on the matter. The role of heuristics has already been addressed in the section "Categories of order ethics." Heuristics can reveal to the individuals new opportunities for mutual gains. They must be strictly distinguished, however, from the many varieties of a moral surplus value. The basic idea here, which has already been discussed, is that heuristics communicates the *benefits* for all parties, which the proponents of moral surplus values either explicitly reject or at least do not highlight. As we will see, Rawls (see chapter 4) and Habermas (see the section "Society requires rational motivation for life forms capable of ideal role taking and constitutional patriotism (Jürgen Habermas)") explicitly do *not* focus on benefits,[88] but rather position their own conceptions *against* a justification of the benefits of ethical norms. The benefits of virtuous and value-ethical approaches are also downplayed, including even in many parts[89] of the theory of deliberative democracy. A consistent focus on benefits is finally only to be found in Buchanan (with a few limitations, see the section "Society requires an ethic of work and an ethic of saving (James M. Buchanan)") and Binmore (see the section "Society requires (almost) nothing (Ken Binmore)").

The outline of the problem also shows that the happiness of the members of a society cannot be coerced. That is, they also cannot be compelled to make a *rule* change. If all members are actually satisfied with the existing rules, or at least a corresponding degree of satisfaction can be deduced systematically from their behavior, then there is not much that is left for the order ethicist to do. He can still of course make informational and educational proposals, but these ultimately remain non-binding.

Such a society can continue to be stable and serve the well-being of everyone. If, despite being informed, the people miss out on improvements to their situation, then the theorist has nothing more to say. The citizens of a democracy—in the words of Richard Rorty—can be "as privatistic, 'irrationalist' and aestheticist'" (Rorty 1989, xiv) as they choose, as long as they adhere to the rules.[90]

The question remains open whether order ethics, as outlined here, can still be assigned to ethics. Some authors maintain that such a program, which uses the tools of the social sciences and works with the concept of benefits, is too far removed from the tradition of ethics and is better located in the sciences. As I have indicated, however, order ethics certainly has a tradition in ethics, and is able to draw on theorists like Hobbes, Hume, Spinoza, and possibly even Kant. As ethicists, these philosophers were also interested in social stability as a major ethical goal, and they also highlighted the mutual benefits for the actors.

Could it be, then, that an order-ethical program has been represented in the *entire* tradition of ethics? Might not the *entire* tradition be reconstructed to show that its representatives have always had in mind a fundamental normative criterion of universal consent? Such a thesis seems problematic, for it does not indicate whether or not the *consent* in the theoretical reconstruction takes place—at least systematically—out of self-interest. Order ethics sees it this way, but the tradition presents fundamentally divergent opinions on this point.[91] Some of these opinions are called on by the approaches discussed in the following chapters.

Can such a program, therefore, be described as belonging at all to ethics? I think so, and I have aimed in this chapter to show the extent to which OE with regard to this particular question is an ethical conception. But even if one were to ignore the term *ethics*, OE can just as easily be understood in its broader outlines as a research program of *practical philosophy* that combines the different branches of philosophy and, in doing so, is able to invoke at least two prominent philosophers: Aristotle and Adam Smith.

NOTES

1. The contributions to the largely relevant volume *Normativity* (Dancy 2000a) seem to me to suffer from a series of problems: they do not, or at least barely, draw on the results or methods of other disciplines; they are not aware—as explained below—of the two-tier system of rules and actions; and they use the concept of volitional freedom in a phenomenalist way (see the section "Moral communication: towards a semantics of benefits"). They also only treat the *implementation problem* of moral standards in a single respect: while Raz (2000, 58) explicitly dismisses the problem, Railton (2000, 3ff.) and Dancy (2000b) stress that norms do not have coercive power and that the normative "domain" is the "domain" of freedom (see ibid. xv). Thus, while the implementation problem is in fact acknowledged in the approach, the dualistic opposition between freedom and coercion also leads to an aporia.

2. I use the term *modernity* not as a historical concept, but as a structural term—in the sense, for example, of Niklas Luhmann and Daniel Lerner (1958/1964)—in order to distinguish between modern and traditional societies. This makes irrelevant those criticisms that aim to show on the basis of historical events that modernity did not begin at all or did not begin suddenly or began later than alleged.

3. "Systematic" is not intended to mean in every single case; of course, there are always violators of the rules that occupy the judiciary. Such typical infringements of the system, however, do not represent a danger to the stability of society as a whole. See also, similarly, Hirschman 1994.

4. I deliberately avoid the term *realistic* and the formulation "are these views realistic?" In my opinion, the discussion surrounding realism and constructivism are not central to the controversy about the moral value surplus. One can postulate or demand such a surplus either as a realist or as a constructivist. See also the section "Derivation of order ethics."

5. This diagnosis is also the focus of Robert Brandom in his seminal book, *Making It Explicit* (1994). He draws from it different conclusions than I do, however. Similar to the indicated theorists, he focuses on strengthening the normative anthropological conditions. See also the section "No commitments!"

6. For a discussion on this topic, see, for example, the contributions in Bayertz 1993.

7. See, by contrast, the views of Foot, in the section "Society requires a shared conception of humanity as a basis for virtues (Philippa Foot)."

8. Whether this is actually a fallacy in a strictly logical sense as a number of authors have suggested will not be examined here (see, for example, Sober 1991; Frankena 1939 also already makes necessary corrections to the classical view of the naturalistic fallacy).

9. On this point, see the contemporary responses in Rogers 1995, and the works of Hampton 1986, Kavka 1986, and Gauthier 1969/2000.

10. It would lead too far astray to pursue the question here of whether Hobbes's characterization of "man as a wolf to man" (which is not in the Leviathan, but in the dedication of "De Cive" and is known to go back to Plautus) can be understood not only as an image of humanity, but also possibly as a theoretical *construct* for certain ends.

11. It is not clear that the Leviathan is to be equated with *one* ruler. Hobbes himself wrote in a crucial passage that members must "conferre all their power and strength upon one Man, or upon one *Assembly of men*" (Hobbes 1651/1991, 120, italics mine).

12. On this contradiction, see Hume 1739-40/1978, book III, part 2, 497f. and 533f.

13. Hume developed his concept of consent in Hume 1739-40/1978, book III, part 2, 489ff.

14. Binmore (1994, 285ff.), for example, believes that Hume's concept of "sympathy" is (largely) satisfied by his own concept of "empathy." See also the section "Empathetic preferences."

15. Smith (1776/1976, book I, 69f., 133ff.; book IV, 107ff.; book V, 213ff., 282ff.) indeed specifically discussed possibilities for bringing about this harmony by means of rules. His *Wealth of Nations*, however, did not appear until 1776, twenty-five years after the publication of the *Enquiry Concerning the Principles of Morals*.

16. Prima facie, Hume appears elsewhere (Hume 1748/1987) to reject a contractual moral justification. But, along with Mackie (1980) and Gauthier (1979), I also read Hume as a

contractarian, at least in an explanatory, if not legitimatory, respect (on this point, see also Binmore 1994, 29f.).

17. A close relationship exists with Rousseau, who writes at the beginning of *The Social Contract*: "In this inquiry I shall try always to bring together what right permits with what interest prescribes so that *justice and utility are in no way divided*" (Rousseau 1762/1977, 49; in the original: "Je tâcherai d'allier toujours dans cette recherche ce que le droit permet avec ce que l'intérêt prescrit, afin que la justice et l'utilité ne se trouvent point divisées").

18. My remarks here can of course only present very rudimentary details.

19. Interestingly, Höffe (1988, 56ff.) uses this quote in a slightly different sense: for him, this passage is rather proof that the state whose gradual demise has been predicted by some authors will in fact also remain relevant in the future.

20. See also the following section.

21. For more details, see Förster 1992 and 2000.

22. I have limited Förster's question to the issues relevant here.

23. Stirner 1845/1972, 3. As it is well-known, this is a quotation from Goethe's poem "Vanitas! Vanitatum vanitas" (Gesellige Lieder, Goethe 1991, vol. 6.1, 93).

24. Although after writing *The Ego and Its Own*, he translated Smith's *Wealth of Nations* and J. B. Say.

25. For a more thorough discussion, see the section "Discussion: Can't society also dispose with empathetic preferences?"

26. This list is, of course, not exhaustive. Another candidate is also worth briefly mentioning here: the sociologist Jean-Marie Guéhenno. In his book *The End of Democracy* (1993), Guéhenno developed the thesis that the state of the future will only be a state of civil law (I refrain here from discussing Guéhenno's other theories). For future society, civil law is the only relevant law, because only individual interests would come together. An approach such as this coincides with OE insofar as the conditions for a functioning society are considered to be very weak.

27. See Luetge 2012 and 2013 and Pies et al. 2009.

28. On this point, see Pies et al. 2009.

29. Here, I greatly simplify the thought experiment. Ackerman uses it in many more contexts and clearly derives many more conclusions from it.

30. I am thinking here of films like *A.I.* (2001), *Contact* (1997), *Blade Runner* (1982), or *Terminator 2* (1991) that address philosophical questions quite seriously.

31. However, no one can be forced to agree. The question of a possible time limit for the agreement process will be passed over however in order to avoid overcomplicating the issue.

32. This changed—and certainly due to globalization at least partly forced—manner in dealing with other cultures is also apparent in science-fiction literature, as in the example of the development of the series *Star Trek*, which reflected the various societal concepts of the 1960s, 1980s, and 1990s. See Gregory 2000, and on the philosophical dimension of *Star Trek* Barad and Robertson 2000.

33. Binmore himself also discusses his respective analyses in reference to the alternative Rawlsian maximin-rationality. I will have to pass over this (see the section "Society requires (almost) nothing (Ken Binmore)").

34. This requires two additional points be made: 1) sometimes in the context of standard-rationality it makes sense to act in terms of the principle of contingency such as in cases of uncertainty or to disrupt a balanced incentive structure (e.g., in the example of Buridan's Ass); 2) however, if we were ever to systematically and permanently adjust our actions in terms of a perhaps even "absolute" (quantum-) system of contingency no society at all would be possible. Then, indeed, no knowledge of nature, social theory, or ethics would be possible.

35. The fourth step is different from the others in that it concerns the rejection of some standard criticisms, in order to avoid some possible misunderstandings about OE.

36. See Laudan 1987 and 1990.

37. See also the section "Gauthier, Locke, and Nozick: the status of rights" and "Binmores conception of rationality."

38. One could also speak more precisely of a coordination or alignment problem, which would better reflect the fact that order does not come from "above." Instead, individuals make

it themselves and coordinate reciprocally. However, as the above manner of speaking has fallen into common usage, I will adhere to it.

39. Here, I partially draw on Homann and Kirchner 1995.

40. One could also say: "problem" is in this approach a more primitive, that is to say, irreducible basic concept (on this concept, see Binmore 1994, 138).

41. To be clear: an *individual ethics* is not necessarily associated with a *methodological individualism* and, conversely, a methodological individualism does not necessarily lead to an individual ethical position. A methodological individualist (as opposed to a methodological collectivist) merely claims that social conditions can be explained by the interaction of the various individuals. On the *descriptive* side, both individual and order ethicists can hold such a position.

42. It should be noted that it is perfectly legitimate to focus on the question of the *justifications* of abstract ethics; one needs to be aware, however, that it is not possible in this way to conceive of an ethics under modern conditions.

43. Rawls (1971) is at least not explicit on this point, although he assumes that the contracting parties in the *original position* are aware of the general functional principles of the future society.

44. Gauthier (1986, 195f and 1988, 181) cites this example as evidence that coercion can also play a role in the settlement of a contract. This represents a problem for him, because the consent of the parties in his conception cannot be forced. The idea of a Pareto-superior worsening in relation to the status quo is easily conceivable in OE, for this conception does not recognize the categorical opposition between freedom and coercion (see Homann 2003, chapter 8).

45. On the theory of *incomplete contracts*, see for example Oliver D. Hart 1987 and Grossman and Hart 1986. Along with Homann, I prefer the term *open contracts*, as it is oriented more toward the positive aspects of this concept (see Luetge 2012 and 2013).

46. On the concept of *fairness*, see also Rescher 2002.

47. The prerequisite for the realization of the positive effects of incomplete contracts is that corporate actors and companies in particular understand how to compensate for the problems of incompleteness with the management of so-called "soft" factors such as morality and culture.

48. See also the section "Binmores conception of rationality." Hume already does not consider the self-interestedness of human beings to be a factum brutum, but derives it from the constraints of reality: "The selfishness of men is animated by the few possessions we have, in proportion to our wants" (Hume 1739-40/1978, book III, part 2, 495).

49. I am translating here into my own terminology.

50. Brandom (2000, 35) writes:

> My hope is that by slighting the similarities to animals which preoccupied Locke and Hume and highlighting the possibilities opened up by engaging in social practices of giving and asking for reasons, we will get closer to an account of being human that does justice to the kinds of consciousness and self-consciousness distinctive of us as *cultural*, and not merely *natural* creatures.

In my view, this can be understood as Brandom's credo, or at least his most central research objective.

51. See also Brandom (2002). In Brandom (2001), it is similarly argued that the preference concept requires the concept of identifying reasons. According to Brandom, reasons, as "minimal Kantianism" (ibid. 13), are fundamental.

52. In this respect, Alan Gewirth (1978) represents a similar position. To be sure, it is Gewirth's goal to establish morality through rationality while—in contrast to Brandom—explicitly setting aside the self-interest of the actors. At the same time, however, Gewirth postulates a normative binding effect of *logical arguments*, according to which the members of a linguistic community understand the legal claims, stringently accepting them on logical grounds and also taking account of them when completing actions. The question of the actual implementation and enforcement of legal claims—for example through institutions—is not the focus of this approach.

53. Which according to Brandom probably by definition cannot exist.

54. Hence, for instance, the "rational fool" in Sen (1977; also in Sen 1999 the *homo economicus* is "sold below its value"). Why shouldn't rational actors rationally invest in the future? The devil himself can, and even over the very long term, like Mephistopheles in Goethe's *Faust* (Goethe, 1991, vol. 18.1). In this sense, Hobbes's "Foole" (Hobbes 1651/1991, chapter 15) is not at all "stupidus"; in fact, he says only that societal stability does not need a "more" of normativity beyond the sanctioned rules. There are few authors who might rightly be accused of drawing on these caricatures of the *homo economicus* (possibly: Stigler 1981). Nonetheless, poor strategies are used to defend this model—in particular the classical "proofs" that refer to human nature, such as those of John Stuart Mill (1863/1975).

55. Hermann Krings already emphasized the role of institutions for ethics, when he remarked: "The conscience of the individual cannot compensate for the failure of the institution" (Krings 1991, 230).

56. The opposite term of *individual ethics* is actually *social ethics*. The latter, however, is often too closely associated with the Catholic social doctrine and correspondingly institutionalized.

57. For more detail on a naturalistic ethics, see Luetge and Vollmer 2004.

58. This argument goes back to Friedrich August von Hayek.

59. In other words, it may come to a point where we believe that we are capable of actually implementing more moral ideals than previously. In Germany, the step-by-step introduction of social insurance since Bismarck's times is a classic example.

60. Similarly, see Kuhn's rejection of the notion of an algorithm of theory selection (Kuhn 1977, 326ff.).

61. It is important to delineate heuristics from other ethical and moral concepts. See also the section "Categories of order ethics."

62. The global impact of September 11, 2001, might serve as an example.

63. See Sen 1974.

64. Also possibly for situations in which the actors have fixed dispositions. See the section "Society requires internalized dispositions for cooperation (David Gauthier)."

65. See Sen 1974.

66. See also the above remarks on Brandom.

67. Binmore calls it the "Stag-Hunt Game." This game refers to a metaphor in J. J. Rousseau's "Discourse on Inequality." See also Rusch/Luetge 2013.

68. I will return to this repeatedly in the course of this book (see sections "Society requires 1) rational motivation," "Gauthier, Locke, and Nozick: the status of rights," and "Solidarity: the source of shared experiences of suffering").

69. Loosely drawing here upon the business-oriented way of speaking, "to communicate benefits."

70. As already mentioned, Brandom links this view to the theory that the special character of the *homo sapiens* is the receptivity of (good) reasons.

71. See, for example, Broome's concept of "normative requirements" (Broome 2000).

72. See, for example, Snare 1991, Broome 1997, and my discussion of Philippa Foot in the section "Society requires a shared conception of humanity as a basis for virtues (Philippa Foot)."

73. I paraphrase the relevant elements of this position for the questions currently under discussion.

74. A discussion of Brandomian "inferential semantics" would lead us too far astray.

75. This could be determined by examining whether people change their salt-passing behavior when the costs for them go up, such as when they themselves and several of their family members at the moment are eating eggs and cannot spare the only available salt shaker without causing violent protests from the children. Nida-Rümelin, though, seems to allow for this insofar as his example only applies to "normal conditions." However, if conditions do in fact play a role, why does Nida-Rümelin then reject an impact evaluation that would take such conditions into account?

76. The concept of social capital can be introduced economically in reference to the concept of trust—as a relationship between the trustee and the trustor—if we extend this relationship to

a third subject. If a trustee acts in the manner intended by the trustor, he acquires a moral claim in a "trust community" against third parties. If a group, a community, or a whole society constitutes such a "trust community," they have at their disposal social capital. A prime example of this, for instance, is alumni associations, where university graduates from the same institution can expect help from each other, even if they have never met in person. In this context, social capital can facilitate interactions considerably because it saves resources. If one can trust one's counterpart, complex controls are no longer necessary. However, social capital must be protected with sanctions on the abuse of trust and the misuse of social capital. These sanctions can be imposed by the trustor as well as by third parties. Because of the implicit nature of the contracts, this is mostly done through informal sanctions such as reputational damage, public contempt, or social exclusion. Cf. Homann/Luetge 2004/2013.

77. Once again, I am unquestionably abridging this discussion; a more comprehensive look at the Brandomian approach is beyond the scope of this book. I also pass over, for instance, Brandom's discussion of the "gerrymandering argument" (see ibid. section 1.3ff.), following Kripke (1982).

78. I extrapolate from OE to "individual-oriented approaches," as it is not only concerned with *ethical* questions (in the traditional sense).

79. According to the view of the respective approach.

80. In the German-speaking world, this kind of hypothesis became well-known in particular through Ernst-Wolfgang Böckenförde (1967/1991, 112), who claims that the modern state subsists due to requirements that it itself cannot even guarantee. (This proposition had already been made by Wilhelm Röpke, but is probably much older.) Although I will briefly discuss Böckenförde (in the section "Society needs shared values (material value-ethics)"), his position nonetheless seems to me to not be sufficiently developed to require an extended discussion.

81. This discussion is conducted, for instance, by Wieland (2001).

82. Bohnet, Frey, and Huck (2001) attempt to substantiate this view by means of game theory.

83. I have deliberately not chosen to use the term *phenomenology* to avoid confusion with the school that goes back to Husserl. A phenomenalistic approach does not necessarily have to derive from Husserl's phenomenology.

84. The approach of Sen (1977, 1999) has already been indicated (see the section "Derivation of order ethics," no. 4). For other examples, see the section "Morality in Buchanan's later work."

85. Homann (2002, chapter 7) suggests that morality in such an approach is employed as an explanans, not, as in order ethics, as an explanandum.

86. Incidentally, this is analogous to epistemology, which also can no longer manage without the individual disciplines. See the discussion on naturalism in epistemology (e.g., Kitcher 1993a and Rosenberg 1996 and also Luetge 2004b).

87. Binmore (1994, 1998) examines this in detail. See also the section "Society requires (almost) nothing (Ken Binmore)."

88. Some commentators welcome this (see, for example, Barry 1989); I do not.

89. Representatives, such as Charles F. Sabel, have already made considerably more headway here. See, for instance, Cohen and Sabel 2001.

90. I do not agree with Rorty, however, that the cohesion of modern societies is largely facilitated by emotional experiences, such as those involving compassion. Generally speaking, I view Rorty's approach very critically. Despite some interesting ideas, he remains by and large on the level of individual ethics. For more detail on this, see the section "Society requires shared feelings of sympathy and solidarity (Richard Rorty)."

91. For instance, in the tradition of discourse ethics; see the section "Society requires rational motivation for life forms capable of ideal role taking and constitutional patriotism (Jürgen Habermas)."

Chapter Three

Society Requires Capacities of the Individual

SOCIETY NEEDS SHARED VALUES (MATERIAL VALUE-ETHICS)

The first theoretical position examined in this book *claimed* that it is also possible under the conditions of modernity for everyone to objectively recognize universally valid, *substantively determined* values. It consequently follows that this position must at the same time *require* that all people also adhere to these common values. While, strictly speaking, it goes beyond the assumption of a moral surplus value, here it will be discussed as a reference position.

A *material* value-ethics stands in contrast to most varieties of *formal* ethics of, for instance, Kantian character, which do not specify the substance of common values, but only emphasize procedures. Material value-ethics in its classical form is represented by Max Scheler (1916/1980), Nicolai Hartmann (1935), and Hans Jonas (1979).

A newer version has been developed by Hösle in his book *Morals and Politics* (Hösle 1997) and is also supplemented in particular by applications to a variety of political issues. Drawing on this book, the stance of a material value-ethics will be illustrated in regard to the question of the required moral surplus value for a modern society.

Vittorio Hösle on Morals and Politics

Hösle's *Morality and Politics* (1997) offers commentary on a range of political issues. In an undertaking of encyclopedic dimensions, economic policy, property concerns, cultural policy, the question of a just war, and problems of international organizations are all submitted to an ethical evaluation.

Here, Hösle endorses using the following *theoretical model of the relationship between morality and politics*: while against separating the moral and political spheres (a position he attributes to Hobbes and Machiavelli, see Hösle 1997, 15), he adopts the Aristotelian view of a unity of ethics, politics, and economics and also ultimately Adam Smith's conception. However, Hösle does not have Smith's methodological unity of ethics and economics in mind, but rather wants to ascribe, on the one hand, a political function to ethical arguments and, on the other, maintain ethics as the basis of political philosophy (see Hösle 1997, 15). In doing so, he describes in detail the following model of the relationship between ethics and politics or political philosophy.

Ethics, first of all, has the task of determining valuation principles. In a second step, using social scientific knowledge if necessary,[1] these principles should be applied to activities and institutions. Hösle thus, on the one hand, subscribes to the traditional model of the relationship between ethics and morality, while attributing a role to the individual sciences, on the other. Indeed, it is inevitable that the social sciences should be utilized for application problems. At the same time, however, ethics—as the final authority in valuation matters[2]—should remain unaffected by individual scientific findings or theories in its standard justifications. According to Hösle, morality's autonomy must be categorically defended,[3] for otherwise the moral evaluation of a doctrine would merely be reducible to a successful outcome. Even Hitler, therefore, would have been morally right in the event of his victory (see Hösle 1997, 113).

Hösle wants to avoid this consequence at all costs and finds that the only way to do this is by appealing to substantively determined values.[4] These values are to be identified objectively and already in fact in pre-human nature (ibid. 355ff.). Here, intrinsic values are present, and even in inorganic nature there is "a lot . . . of value" (ibid. 355). Symmetries, for example, permit something intrinsically valuable to be identified, since they are already noteworthy for logical reasons (ibid. 355). The analysis of ordinary language also demonstrates: "Beautiful, on the other hand, is something in and of itself" (ibid.).

For organic nature, it is possible to present a model for the "appropriate existence" of a species (ibid. 357). Each species—especially humans—should live according to its kind in the way that has been objectively predetermined by nature.

In order to determine what is appropriate for humans, Hösle has developed (ibid. 288ff.) an anthropological theory, which refers to, among other works, Scheler's "Die Stellung des Menschen im Kosmos" (Man's position in the cosmos; Scheler 1928/1988). According to this theory, although a human being is not actually strictly biologically determined, a person may nevertheless oppose her biological conditions, perhaps separate herself from her drives and live in an ascetic manner or kill herself. Unlike what is suggested by "those Hobbes-influenced social sciences" (ibid. 292),[5] humans are in no way simply "nothing more than a very clever rat" (ibid.). With regard to political-ethical issues, this means that approaches imputing utility maximization to humans have fallen short. Every utility and every self-interest, namely, can be problematized: no one—not "even the most morally challenged" (ibid.) human—can dismiss the question of whether their interests are also *legitimate*. The intrinsic qualities of human nature inevitably force this question upon everyone. Hösle does not seem to view this as a necessity, but rather to believe that everyone *effectively* poses this question on their own. Hösle explains: everyone asks themselves (permanently?) whether their interests actually "come from themselves alone—or whether they should be ashamed about them" (ibid.). This means that not only are a person's interests not fixed, but also that the self underlying those interests is not a definite variable. The self is rather much more "a task for the ego" (ibid.).

Along with this theoretical conception of an anthropologically grounded material value-ethics, a certain *time-period diagnosis* appears in Hösle, which assumes

- that the increased wealth in affluent parts of the world has not made people more content (see ibid. 13),
- that the ideal of brotherhood has degenerated into an attitude of general indifference (ibid.),
- that scientific-technical progress and the rationalization of broad areas of society have led to a "collective mania" (ibid. 14) lacking any normative orientation.

Hösle is therefore of the opinion that most of the Western world finds itself in a crisis that has essentially been caused by its own progress. His proposed therapy, as already indicated, is to strengthen the values, that is, to demand more normativity.

To implement this therapy, Hösle postulates "criteria for morally correct decisions" (ibid. 199ff.). There are three criteria. Morally correct decisions should accordingly

   a. be made on the basis of a universalistic ethics. The Kantian requirement of universalizability is understood in Hösle as the apex and the terminus of a culture's development. By contrast, the actions of members of a *pre*-universalistic culture, who promote a kind of group egoism, are only then to be viewed as morally positive if they apply their own ideas to themselves, *even when it infringes on their own interests*. Hösle thus does *not* assume that self-interested actions can-

not be condemned in societies that do not have effectively anchored universalistic ethics, but demands specifically also in these cases that self-interest be intruded upon.
b. follow the *correct* values. This means that the correct values must first be specified, which is precisely where material value-ethics achieves its breakthrough.[6] To be sure, Hösle believes that it is only possible to *approximate* an objective hierarchy of values (ibid. 163f.), and he admits that—"at least given the current state of ethics"[7] (ibid. 163)— no valid hierarchy can be provided for *every* practical problem. For specific issues, however, solutions may found by calling on values, whereby it may be the case that different values can be put into use with regard to different individual matters (ibid. 164).
c. only after the appropriate means of implementation have been determined and the side effects of the decision have been researched. Here, the empirical framework must be taken into account. This gives Hösle's concept a certain flexibility, which has definite advantages, because although the foundation of moral valuations should be values, it remains difficult to apply these values. They cannot be directly translated into the social world. At the same time, the decision-makers need to be guided by additional criteria such as appropriate choice and an assessment of the side effects.

From Hösle's value-ethical point of view, a good government is one that puts the *natural law* into effect (see ibid. 776). This means that Hösle takes a position that ascribes rights to humans that precede a possible social contract and therefore may not be questioned under any circumstances. He stresses that he does not see these rights as being anchored in (biological) nature (there one only finds the right of strongest), but that it rather concerns rational rights, which are to be understood as reasons stemming from a reason-based morality (see ibid.). While this natural and rational law[8] cannot determine individual laws, it can nonetheless make certain minimum requirements. The core of the material natural law consists in the demand that citizens be treated equally before the law (ibid. 785). Another decisive natural-legal norm says "that the (subjective natural-legal) rights of legal entities must be protected by force" (ibid. 793). At this point, it becomes clear that in Hösle's conception the enforcement problem has a high priority. In addition, he uses—with recourse to Hegel—the argumentation that expansions of freedom are only initially possible through coercion and that "freedom is first realized within limitations" (ibid. 796). This corresponds to the view of OE, according to which freedom is not something protected *from* the state, but rather should be expanded *through* state institutions (see chapter 2). Just the same, Hösle does not limit himself to a functional justification, but adds a value-ethical viewpoint, which allows the government measures along with the (absolute) value of legal assets to be justified (see Hösle 1997, 797).[9]

In the event that natural rights can no longer be guaranteed, a civil war would possibly be preferable to the government itself. Hösle emphasizes that the right of resistance against state power also stems from nature (actually: the law of reason) and should not be overly downplayed.

In the area of the economy, natural law sets the following conditions: first, a morally good economic system must satisfy everyone's basic needs; second, it must ensure a wide degree of freedom; and, third, it must recognize the merit principle (ibid. 864). To fulfill these requirements, it is, for example, necessary—and this is just one of the many individual requirements enumerated by Hösle—that "inhumane forms of competition" (ibid. 865) are excluded from the market, specifically those which "are based on deception and lies" (ibid.).

Generally, parameters are necessary to exploit the market's benefits (see ibid. 866ff.). The state regulatory framework, which Hösle actually justifies with different reasons than OE, also still provides in its conception the basis for social progress through the market.

According to Hösle, it is important for a state and its economy to be orientated (in terms of its material value-ethics) toward the right goals.[10] Hösle understands these objectives as still being substantively determined, beyond the natural rights or rights of reason already indicated. He thus sees it as a necessary goal of a society (and an economy) to reach a state of equilibrium and to enable growth to come to a conclusion. This is possible once all of society's affected members reach the level "of a dignified life" (ibid. 874). Such a materially saturated society should be welcomed because then the people—according to Hösle—would able to devote themselves again to "higher" non-material values.[11] In this way, they would also avoid the constant "inner restlessness" (ibid.) he finds in the present society and which he considers lamentable. An economy that always strives for more growth does not necessarily lead to more happiness.[12] The expectations become sky high without the prospect of a satisfactory state of equilibrium. To achieve this state, Hösle assigns a central role to religions, on the one hand, and to the elites of a society, on the other.

Religions belong to the institutions that impart to the state "those moral forces without which the society would fall apart" (ibid. 883). A state could not function without such ancillary institutions (or, hence, also without one of the moral surplus values demanded by the other approaches examined in this book[13]). Further, and more or less alongside the various religions, art would be necessary, and perhaps even philosophy (though its potential role should not be overestimated; see ibid. 884). Religions, however, would take an especially prominent position among these institutions. They would foster the basic level of trust, which in turn would lead to a feeling of brotherhood and "overcome prisoner's dilemma situations" (ibid. 883). Hösle, at any rate, does not develop this thought to its logical conclusion. On the one hand, he is interested (as shown) in the implementation problem and, on the other, he writes that the religious "attitude may not be forced" (ibid.). While any religious affirmation is to remain voluntary, it is nonetheless apparently to be encouraged by the state, even though religions, for instance, would be able to decide on their own internal organization. The resulting—perhaps somewhat less democratic—organization would still have a positive function though, since it would put into place organizational elements that are always vulnerable under a democracy to the tyranny of a majority (see ibid. 883f.).

Along with the religions, the elites, especially the economic leaders, are expected to serve as role models for a society (see ibid. 1074). As such, they would help promote an orientation toward the right objectives. Above all, the elites are expected to encourage a general shift in values away from those based on the ideal of continuous growth, toward those that adhere to the ideal of *sufficiency*. Companies should limit their advertising to avoid arousing even more wants. The elites should *communicate universalizable preferences* so that more people refrain from defining their success according to the extent of their wants, but rather with regard to "the feeling of dignity that comes from restricting one's wants" (ibid.).

The practical *suggestions* Hösle derives from these theoretical deliberations can also be gained, at least in some measure, from other theoretical approaches and are thus rather uncontroversial (ibid. 1112ff.). Here, calls are made to reduce public debt, to *accept* (and not deny) the challenge of globalization, to have less protectionism, to minimize the welfare state, and even, under certain conditions, to legalize drugs.

Hösle, however, endorses a model that gives ethics a superior position to "the economy." Ethics must provide the categorical imperative, which then instills the economy with legitimate aims. Only an economy with such specified aims can be morally acceptable (see ibid. 114).

In Hösle, the moral reservations against "economic activity" seem to some extent to come from the fact that he, first, recognizes an "economic sector" and, second, ascribes to it the function of meeting demand (see ibid. 568f.). The difficulty of thinking in terms of sectors was already discussed in chapter 2. The statement, however, that "the economy" serves to meet demand can only be viewed as stemming from a pre-modern conception. Under modern conditions[14] one must always proceed from the assumption of means and ends being interdependent, not from the existence of predetermined goals. Individuals have goals. Modern society, by contrast, is in the middle of an evolutionary process, which human beings can certainly influence, but by no means control. Alongside changing limiting conditions, this especially impedes the simultaneous presence of shared *and* conflicting interests, which forces interacting groups to deal with each other in a completely different manner conceptually than individuals.

Problems of Value-Ethics

A value-ethical conception of the type Hösle proposes can be criticized in numerous respects. One strand of criticism, for example, takes aim at the fact that material value-ethics must ultimately require an objective hierarchy of values. Under modern conditions—that is, taking into account both the findings from the modern natural sciences and the modern social sciences since Max Weber—such a requirement is highly problematic and neither ontologically nor methodologically tenable.

With regard to the focus of this book, however, I am especially interested in pursuing two points. First, I would like to take issue with the anthropological foundation of Hösle's ethics.[15] On the other hand, I would also like to highlight in terms of OE the *constructive* contribution of a value-ethics in comparison to stronger formal-ethical conceptions. Hösle leaves more space for a pragmatic weighing (of values) and thus for the consideration of empirical (above all social) limiting conditions in ethics.

First, some observations on Hösle's anthropological foundations. As already noted, he shares the view with many philosophers[16] that human beings can be motivated by reasons and that this trait distinguishes them from animals. This characterization is linked to the rejection of a motivation that is based only on self-interest. As evidence of this, Hösle makes the claim that a purely self-interested individual in a desperate situation with nothing to lose would tend to undertake actions that could have disastrous consequences for numerous others. The terminally ill might become mass murderers. The elderly might consume their entire wealth. Since this is not the case (at least not to a wide extent), one can conclude that human beings are not simply motivated by self-interest, but also by (rational) reasons.

Two strategies present themselves for responding to this argument. First, one could still try to interpret the decision to forgo mass murder or wasteful consumption prior to death as a self-interested action. Second, the question may be asked as to whether Hösle's allegation is empirically valid or whether phenomena such as those he has rejected can in fact be observed to a significant degree.

As to the first point: in the economic discussion, there are a number of considerations relating to Hösle's cited courses of action that could be interpreted as self-interested. First, uncertainty plays a role. How certain is the death of the terminally ill patient? What if she perhaps still holds out hope for a (however small) chance of being cured? To view the problem from this economic perspective, it is however necessary to reject simple alternatives (terminally ill: yes or no) and to recognize the economic character of all kinds of considerations.

As to the second point: Is it true that human beings who have little or nothing to lose or intelligent suicidal individuals shy away from actions like those enumerated above? In reality, such behavior seems to be more common than Hösle is willing to admit. It is not necessary to recall the events on September 11, 2001, to point out the actual willingness of individuals to destroy the lives of thousands of people in suicidal attacks, including their own. The less people have to lose (e.g., those at the bottom of the social scale or the globalization losers),[17] the more likely they are to commit acts without regard to others. I do not see how Hösle could position morality in a way to solve political problems. The concern is rather to bring about improvements for the globalization losers (or at least hope for improvements) through institutional reforms (or at least through the prospects of such reforms). It is the task of economics to concretely develop such proposals.

Within certain limits, Hösle—in contrast to many of the other positions discussed in this book—explicitly allows for normative considerations to be made in regard to empirical limiting conditions. There is a certain comparative advantage to his position, which he shares with other approaches from the context of Neo-Aristotelianism. Proceeding from Aristotle's theory of the golden mean, these approaches emphasize that moralistic actions cannot be completely subsumed under a theory of morality, for residual problems remain that can only be solved through practical implementation.[18] Such approaches thus offer room for pragmatic considerations in the context of moral issues, although there is still no systematic theory here on the relationship between self-interest and morality. It is thus more or less accidental. In addition to this, most institutions in Neo-Aristotelianism do not assume a systemic role.[19]

What role can values still be assigned in modern societies? Albert Hirschman (1994) poses this question in discussing the value of "community spirit" (Gemeinsinn)[20] and concludes that, at most, *constitutional patriotism* would be a prerequisite for liberal societies (on this discussion, see the section "Society requires 3) constitutional patriotism"). All the other values represented in such a society would result spontaneously from conflicts. This position, therefore, only sees *one* value as being an indispensable condition. The existence of the others is established only descriptively. Homann (2002, chapter 4) even goes a step further. He recognizes values as generally having only a heuristic role: they should help in the search for rules, which, in turn, should be formulated and implemented in an incentive-compatible way. The problems of modern societies, however, are no longer solvable by a direct appeal to values.

All of the approaches discussed in the sections "Society requires rational motivation for life forms capable of ideal role taking and constitutional patriotism (Jürgen Habermas)" to "Society requires (almost) nothing (Ken Binmore)" take a pluralistic society as a given—at least on the basis of their own statements—and do not consider a return to pre-modern conditions to be a serious alternative. I will, nonetheless, ask how *consistently* the solutions of these authors (including Ken Binmore's, see the section "Society requires (almost) nothing (Ken Binmore)") are adapted to the structures of modernity. In practical terms, there is only a slight difference between the assumption of a moral value surplus and that of a material value-ethics suggesting that a modern society requires objective values in order to function. Therefore, the question about their modernity not only needs to be asked in reference to value-ethics, but also in reference to the other approaches under discussion in this book. This will be the focus of the following.

SOCIETY REQUIRES A SHARED CONCEPTION OF HUMANITY AS A BASIS FOR VIRTUES (PHILIPPA FOOT)

Moral theories that view virtues as a central concept of ethics have been a fixture in the ethical debate since antiquity. The list of their representatives is long, extending over the history of philosophy from Aristotle[21] through Thomas Aquinas[22] to Martha Nussbaum. The renaissance of virtue ethics began in the 1960s and 1970s in language philosophy, with the approaches of Georg Henrik von Wright (*The Varieties of Goodness*, Wright 1963), Peter Geach (*The Virtues*, Geach 1977), and Philippa Foot (in her work from about 1958). It is possible to speak of a flood of successors who came afterward (for a recent overview, see for example Swanton 2003). I will focus here on Philippa Foot, whose reflections appear to be characteristic of virtue ethics. As Foot remarks: "We need a firm idea of human nature (a conception of humanity) as the basis for virtue."

The primary aim of Foot's ethical approach is directed against utilitarianism, which has long played a dominant role in Anglo-Saxon moral philosophy (and still does today).[23] Foot criticizes utilitarianism with reference to several classical arguments, which have been an enduring part of the debate. In the following, I will briefly describe this critique of utilitarianism (see the section "Basic principles") and then give an outline of Foot's own virtue-ethical approach. I will especially examine the importance Foot accords to the conception of humankind and ethical viewpoints on human nature (see the section "The conception of humanity that is required for ethics"). After this problem-centered account, I will examine how virtues from the perspective of OE take on a heuristic function and can address certain types of problems in ethical theory (see the section "Virtues as a heuristic").[24]

Basics Principles

Foot contends that ethical theories of the twentieth century made a fundamental mistake by largely dismissing absolute concepts. In particular, the author believes that ethics can—and must—determine *absolute* duties for all people (see Foot 1997, 24).[25] Foot rejects moral relativism, but not for the reasons that (until that point) had generally been given by the exponents of Anglo-Saxon moral philosophy (Foot 2002, 20ff.). The latter, following Wittgenstein (1953/1984), mostly countered moral relativism with language-philosophical arguments. Here, a theory of relativism is not satisfactory since moral terms may be used in language games.

In contrast, Foot takes the view that the problems of moral relativism cannot be solved by reference to "some points of linguistic usage" (Foot 2002, 25). The debate thus needs to be conducted on a much more fundamental level. Language-philosophical arguments try to forgo substantive moral concepts such as "value," "happiness," "love," "nature," and so on (ibid. 34ff.), yet they inevitably fail. Only when these terms are reintroduced into ethical theory as *absolute* concepts is it also possible to reject relativism. Among other things, the ethical theory of Thomas Aquinas should serve as a model, which is based on the idea of absolute values (Foot 1978, 1ff.).

Foot resorts to the following three (mostly classical) arguments,[26] some of which had already been used by other authors against utilitarianism.[27] First, utilitarianism cannot reliably secure human rights, which puts minorities at risk of being repressed by the majority (or, alternatively, the majority could be repressed by well-organized minorities). Second, the idea of achieving a possible optimal state has to be rejected. And third, under certain circumstances, *every* action may be justified in the context of utilitarianism.

As to the *first* argument: David Lyons (1965) already argued utilitarianism takes for granted that individuals may suffer as long as it is offset by a benefit of sufficient size for the vast majority of others. Indeed, the core of utilitarian theory maintains that a criterion for ethical improvement should be the larger *general* (not personal or individual) utility.[28] This overall utility is somehow distilled from the use values of individuals. Then, a norm (or measure) A can be distinguished that increases this overall benefit the most, making it preferable to norms B through Z. At the same time, the distribution of this overall benefit among individuals does not (at least in principle) play a role[29]—with the risk being run that individuals or groups may be systematically repressed. As Foot puts it, utilitarianism cannot guarantee fundamental rights (see Foot 1997, 16).

Foot's argument is expressly shared by OE. Despite occasional assertions to the contrary, OE does not by any means reflect a variation of utilitarianism. As shown, it is rather based on a contract-theoretical approach with a theory of consensus. This consensus theory implies that *each individual* among those affected must be able to agree to, if not each individual policy measure, then certainly the rules by which these measures are adopted. The affected individual who sees herself not only disadvantaged by the rules in one particular case, but systematically, will withdraw her consent from the respective rule-bearing arrangement. This, in turn, will have adverse consequences for everyone in interaction structures of the prisoner's-dilemma type, for even a single defector can bring down the whole system into a rationality trap. Indeed, to induce others to undertake a "preventative counter-defection" (Homann) (see the section "Order ethics as an ethics of benefits and incentives"), the *threat* alone to defect is already sufficient, as is the *possibility* of the existence of a defector. This case can be avoided only if every individual—in her own interest *and* in the interest of everyone else—is attributed fundamental rights that must not be violated. Only then will everyone let themselves become involved in social cooperation.

OE can thus make the claim of having a better theoretical basis than utilitarianism. Unlike Foot's approach, though, these rights are not absolute, since they are achieved through consensus. For Foot, this would not seem to be adequate.

Foot's *second* argument is directed against the idea that there is an optimal state that could be sensibly posited as a goal for normative questions.[30] This critique has been familiar for some time in economics as a critique of social-welfare theory. Authors such as Kenneth Arrow, Amartya Sen, and James M. Buchanan have long challenged the existence of collective welfare functions.[31]

Foot herself raises the question of whether her criticism is directed against utilitarianism *overall* or only certain forms of it such as act utilitarianism.[32] She would thus not object to having her own reflections confirm *rule* utilitarian insights (see Foot 1985, 36). She considers this unlikely, however, due to the very different starting points. In fact, from the perspective of OE, rule utilitarianism is indeed preferable to act utilitarianism. The former allows for the assessment of action *sequences*, and leaves room for the possibility of investments—short-term disadvantages in favor of longer-term net benefits. However, OE should not be equated with a rule-utilitarian viewpoint. This is because OE does not claim that a public good should be promoted or maximized, but rather that *from the perspective of each individual* an ethical solution must result in benefits.[33] Only then can the solution be implemented, and only then can it be justified. By contrast, rule utilitarianism adheres to external normative criteria.

As to the *third* argument: according to Foot, any action can be potentially justified in the context of utilitarianism. This leads to the danger of arbitrariness in moral philosophy:

> Could it then be the case that in a culture the ultimate criterion of the good or bad, of good or bad human behavior, has to do with such proscriptions as running around a tree in a clockwise direction or watching hedgehogs in the moonlight? (Foot in 1997, 17)

Foot contends that Richard Hare would answer yes to this question. She is herself of the opinion, however, that there is already included in the *concept* of morally good action criteria of good or bad. Her argumentation relies on the notion of a conception of humanity that necessarily requires ethics. I will now discuss this is greater detail.

The Conception of Humanity That Is Required for Ethics

In Foot's view (see Foot 1997, 41), the concept of human nature is the overarching concept of moral philosophy.[34] There are constants in human nature that are of vital importance for social life and for ethics. Foot (see ibid.) is explicit on the point that this idea cannot be considered obsolete even in the modern era. Even in modern society, Foot suggests, ethics must be built on concepts such as freedom, home, family, love, and respect (see 40ff. and Foot 2002, 35).[35]

She appears to assume that even in the modern era individuals are able to commit to shared norms. Unlike Hösle (see the section "Society needs shared values (material value-ethics)"), Foot does not derive these shared norms from objective values (at least not explicitly), but from an objective and largely unchanging idea of human nature, a conception of humanity. She maintains that human beings are dependent on a certain degree of freedom, love, a family environment, and general happiness (see ibid. 43).[36] The psychological theory of egoism is incorrect.[37] Ethics must not only seriously acknowledge this, but, according to Foot, it could also actually derive substantive statements from these constants.

This would then establish the basis for a "modern" virtue ethics. Human beings need moral virtues to live—just as plants require water or wolves the hunt (see Foot 2002, 199). When orienting their lives according to these virtues, they finally achieve a state in which they arrive at the necessary degree of happiness, freedom, love, and so on. Here, Foot draws entirely upon the classical Aristotelian idea, which she wants to adapt to the present. Today's four cardinal virtues, therefore, are still the classical virtues of courage, temperance, wisdom, and justice (Foot 1978, 2).

This position has numerous implications. On the one hand, Foot concludes that within a species whose members cooperate with each other, free riders in prisoner's-dilemma situations are "defective" (Foot 2002, 200, italics omitted) and in some measure disturbed personalities. I interpret this as follows: the free riders would not recognize that cooperation would be beneficial to them and their short-term exploitation of others would exclude them from the longer-term benefits to the species, since the others would no longer be willing to cooperate with them. That is, for moral reasons and for reasons of personal interest (in Foot they do *not* appear to be mutually exclusive), it inherently makes sense for me to cooperate when others act similarly.

This argument is justified within certain limits. It is also found in Gauthier (see the section "Society requires internalized dispositions for cooperation (David Gauthier)") as well as in game theory[38] and goes back to Hume's moral theory.[39] Just the same, this convergence is more problematic than these theorists seem to recognize. As a rule, they do not discuss—and here Foot makes no exceptions—what the *implementation* of this convergence should look like in modern society. While one could still expect in the face-to-face relationships of a pre-modern society the informal sanctioning of violations and free-riding, this is no longer possible in the anonymous contexts of modern society. Here, formal institutions are necessary. Their significance, however, is neither discussed by Foot, nor, quite analogously, by Gauthier (see the section "Society requires internalized dispositions for cooperation (David Gauthier)"). In my view, philosophy cannot solve this problem on its own, but only through interdisciplinary collaboration. This is where economics and its theory of institutions come into play (see the section "Order ethics as an ethics of benefits and incentives").

If one turns to social-scientific theory, it makes little theoretical or strategic sense to tie down the concept of human nature as Foot and others do. In such instances, the special characteristics of the situation and the social interaction are systematically ignored. It is assumed that actors can repudiate incentives. And, finally, human traits are taken—in a phenomenalist way—as a *facta bruta*, derived more or less by means of direct evidence or intuition. At the same time, realists also admit there is no way to access reality without theory (see Popper 1963/1969, 66f.) and that this access is always filtered through a certain perspective and selection of our cognitive apparatus, and also necessarily restricted by a theoretical framing of the problem.[40]

Virtues as a Heuristic

It would be too easy to dismiss Foot's conception of a renewed virtue ethics (Foot 1978, 1ff.) by simply point out the conditions of modern societies. Certainly, the question arises in the context of OE whether virtue-ethical conceptions reflect societal changes *at all*. In my opinion, Foot also tries in her recourse to Aristotle and Thomas Aquinas's *Summa Theologica* to apply their ethics too directly to modernity. (The *Summa Theologica*, she notes, is "one of our best sources of moral philosophy" [ibid. 2] and is *even more* applicable today for ethics.)[41]

Be that as it may, I would now like to work out what a conception like OE can learn from virtue ethics, or, at least, how they might be brought into agreement with each other. The crucial point here, in my view, is the concept of morality that underlies both conceptions. It turns out, namely, that Foot criticizes a specific direction of moral philosophy in much the same way as OE. She rejects approaches that rely on the theory of motivation, which states—in Foot's reconstruction (see Foot 2002, 204, and the section "Moral communication: Toward a semantics of benefits")—that moral judgments are already motivating reasons to act. This means, one could assume that morality is already per se useful—that a good moral reason or a good moral justification already motivates human beings to conduct themselves in an appropriate manner (ibid. 3). From this perspective, then, there is no particular problem of *implementation* with regard to a morally justified claim. Instead, a form of "rational motivation" is postulated. This approach has been adopted repeatedly, particularly in the Kantian tradition, by philosophers leading up to Habermas (see the section "Society requires rational motivation for life forms capable of ideal role taking and constitutional patriotism (Jürgen Habermas)"). This rational motivation (for a more detailed discussion, see the section "Society requires 1) rational motivation") is supposed to make implementation possible and thus circumvent the path of "benefits and incentives" (Homann 2002).

Foot, however, argues that one cannot assume descriptively *and* one should not assume normatively that the moral justifications in the minds of individuals generally always have priority. Under "'moral considerations,' one would rather have to understand comprehensive 'moral judgment'" (Foot 2002, 195). Once all the relevant circumstances have been taken into account and carefully weighed, such a judgment should be made by everyone. To Foot, the primacy of the moral simply means "keeping one's head" (ibid.) and not losing sight of the *overall* judgment.

By this perspective, Foot apparently understands that an overall judgment is made after a whole range of virtues have been contemplated. Here, no single consideration would tip the scales. In contrast to the moral theories she criticizes that usually put *one* principle or *one* maxim at the heart of ethical considerations, Foot here aims for greater flexibility.[42] For example, in contrast to Kant, she finds that morality can only claim to know *hypothetical* imperatives. She deems Kant's argument for a clear distinction between moral judgments and hypothetical imperatives to be unfounded (see Foot 1978, 157). Foot considers hypothetical imperatives to be both sufficient and to reflect the only possible form of moral judgments. While the virtues she privileges are evidently to be understood as being valid without exception, a pragmatic assessment is always to be made when it comes to the actual implementation. For this reason, an "immaculate conception" of morality is not possible.

In my view, this can be reformulated from the perspective of OE as follows. On the one hand, in accordance with OE, hypothetical imperatives are also completely sufficient for ethics. On the other hand—and this is the crucial point—Foot's position (once one looks past the general problematic of a virtue ethics under modern conditions) allows for a much greater consideration in ethics of empirical—that is also to say social-scientific—limiting conditions than other approaches. In rejecting any motivational theory that sees moral judgments as motivating reasons for action, she thus simultaneously emphasizes the importance of the implementation problem in ethics. If there is no rational motivation to ensure the compliance with moral norms, then the problem of the *implementation* of these norms must be already thought through concurrently with the process of their *justification*. Foot considers it an illusion that further branches of moral theory ascribe the "'ought' a more or less 'magic force'" (ibid. 167).[43] In an entirely similarly manner, the OE conception criticizes approaches that focus on a change in consciousness or appeals to reason or on the conscience of the individual.

Only from this perspective is it possible to also see the limits of Foot's conception: she assumes that lived virtues keep a society together. At the same time, cases of conflict fade into the background—or more precisely interaction structures, where even a similarly strict orientation toward virtues cannot help the individual. Foot particularly overlooks the problem of the prisoner's dilemma, and thus the need for implementation with the help of all relevant institutions rather than (ultimately non-binding) virtues.[44] As a freestanding conception, virtue ethics could only be successful in a (pre-modern, idealized) society with shared norms and virtues.[45]

As I see it, this does not have to mean that virtues and virtue ethics as a theory of the virtues would not have a certain role to play—if a limited one—under modern conditions. In particular, virtues could assume a heuristic function in interaction situations, which are not (or not fully) regulated by functional institutional arrangements. Individuals who are looking for solutions to moral problems *below* the level of formal rules[46] could find food for thought in a conception of virtues. At the same time, the specific virtues Foot references (courage, temperance, wisdom, justice) do not appear to me to be very helpful. Instead, her general—Aristotelian—approach requires a well-considered decision, in which many factors are contemplated and no single moral element is overemphasized. This conception thus allows for pragmatic adaptations of ethical theory that fit local contexts. Their fruitfulness, of course, is not immediately evident and would have to be investigated in an actual case.

SOCIETY REQUIRES RATIONAL MOTIVATION FOR LIFE FORMS CAPABLE OF IDEAL ROLE TAKING AND CONSTITUTIONAL PATRIOTISM (JÜRGEN HABERMAS)

Habermas's conception of discourse ethics has been greatly expanded upon over the years. Numerous authors have also elucidated many of its aspects and further refined it. Due to the conception's complexity, it will therefore not be possible to present a comprehensive discussion of it here. Even a summary, for example, of its primary philosophical-historical influences would go beyond the scope of this book. I will therefore have to limit my reflections on discourse ethics to addressing a very specific question, which—against the backdrop of OE—is aimed at all the conceptions under discussion in the present context. The question, namely, is: What skills or qualities—what moral surplus or surpluses—must a functioning modern society demand of its citizens beyond compliance with sanctions-bearing rules?

I will pursue this matter with reference to discourse ethics by first discussing the conception's main idea, specifically, discourse and its particular functions (see the section "Basic principles: the principle of universalization as a rule of argumentation"). I will then reconstruct in three steps the three theoretical concepts that Habermas tries to demonstrate are essential for a modern society. These are as follows: a rational motivation of the members (see the section "Society requires 1) rational motivation"), a particular life form (see the section "Society requires 2) viable forms of existence for ideal role taking"), and a certain attitude that is designated as constitutional patriotism (see the section "Society requires 3) constitutional patriotism"). Then, I will present a critique of both the necessity and the implementability of these three concepts (see the section "Criticism: And what if a performative contradiction does not disturb me?") in order to finally propose a potentially constructive reinterpretation of Habermas's conception in the context of OE (see the section "Discourse as a heuristic for rule reforms?").

I refer below to the discourse ethics discussed in *The Theory of Communicative Action* (Habermas 1981) and developed in works from the 1980s and 1990s (Habermas 1983/1999a, Habermas 1983/1999b, Habermas 1991) and then further supplemented in *Between Facts and Norms* (Habermas 1992) and other subsequent works (see, for instance, Habermas 1996, Habermas 1998).

Basic Principles: The Principle of Universalization as a Rule of Argumentation

Habermas considers normativity to be essentially social in nature. This general statement about discourse ethics can be approached in two ways.

On the one hand, discourse ethics maintains that normativity can only be derived from a *social* process. It makes no sense to say that Robinson either acts or should act morally. Only members of a *society* can determine ethical maxims for themselves. According to Habermas, however, these maxims are not chosen (monologically) through an examination of conscience, but rather selected in discourse (dialogically) with others (see e.g., Habermas 1991, 51f.). Habermas sees Kant as the paradigmatic representative of the monological model. Kant argues that the categorical imperative may be affirmed by any individual for rational reasons. A dialogue or discussion with others is thus unnecessary.[47]

Discourse ethics, by contrast, is based precisely on the notion of reasoned debate with others. To this extent, it parts ways with Kant—or rather a particular interpretation of Kant. Then again, discourse ethics also has Kantian roots, for it examines the conditions of the possibility of discourse (see Habermas 1981, xli ff. and Apel 1990/1996). It examines (somewhat transcendentally) the preconditions each participant implicitly demands, expects from others, and thus must accept as a given in such discourses.[48] To this end, Habermas relies on the findings of language philosophy, above all the work of Peter Strawson, who analyzed expressions of resentment and indignation. With Strawson, Habermas sees in our everyday practice—in the practice of the "lifeworld"[49]—a "web of moral feelings" (Habermas 1983/1999a, 50), which refers to transpersonally valid standards. That such standards exist corresponds to our intuitions about morality, which is where discourse ethics wants to orient itself. And we could only defy these standards at the risk of committing a performative contradiction.[50]

On the other hand, Habermas resorts to the argumentation theory of Stephen Toulmin to characterize the structure of argumentation in discourses, specifically using the concepts "expressions of emotion" and "argumentative structure."[51] From the viewpoint of discourse ethics, both expressions of emotion and argumentative structures refer to necessary preconditions of arguments that each participant would have to recognize.

These necessary preconditions are conceived by Habermas in a way that goes well beyond language philosophy and are even explicitly distinguished from the latter's constituent parts. Habermas at this point introduces a further theoretical building block that goes back to George H. Mead's work on social psychology. Mead's primary concern was with interactions (hence his "symbolic interactionism"; see Blumer 1969/1986) and not individual actors (see Habermas, 1981, vol. 1, and Mead, 1934). He analyzed the structures of different types of symbolically mediated interaction. Habermas draws on these studies, and adds the concept of consensual coordination of action. These building blocks permit him to construct a model of a social process. This model is to be understood as an ideal reconstruction of the actual process of norm creation. It assumes that the actors involved can only establish shared norms by means of mutual agreement, that is, by consensus:

> Only those norms can claim to be valid that meet (or could meet) with the approval of all affected in their capacity as participants in a practical discourse. (Habermas, 1983/1999a, 66)

This is the pivotal *principle D*. It introduces the concept of *discourse* and is supposed to ensure that no one subjected to a norm is ignored in the establishment of this norm. Now, however, the question arises as to how the consensus of the participants can be achieved. Habermas's key concern is to emphasize the fact that it is not about simply achieving an actual consent from all parties involved. Such a de facto agreement could in fact develop from the "wrong" motives. It is important, though, that the actors do not simply choose one of the available alternatives due to their own interests or preferences (see Habermas 1983/1999a, c. 72f.). This would "only" result in a balance of power, a coordination of interests, and the generalized arbitrariness of individuals would prevail.[52] According to Habermas's argument, this would contradict our moral intuitions (see Habermas 1983/1999a, 72, and also Habermas (1991), 31f.). These moral intuitions, which discourse ethics aims to reconstruct with the help of language philosophy, demands that decisions be reached impartially.

According to discourse ethics, however, only *justified* wishes may be taken into account. The parties would have to enter into an argument—a discourse. A real argument, however, comes about only if certain preconditions are met. Such preconditions for an argument can be divided into three tiers, of which the third is decisive for discourse ethics (see Habermas 1983/1999a, 87ff.).[53]

First, the discourse participants would need to uphold certain logical rules. For example, they are not permitted to contradict themselves.

Second, each discourse participant would need to come up with certain pragmatic preconditions. She would have to assume, for instance, that all other participants are of sound mind and sincere.

Third, the communication process itself would need to be structured in such a way so that a consensus could be arrived at not only as a compromise between interests, but as a "rationally motivated recognition" (Habermas 1992, 31). While Habermas originally identified these kinds of preconditions as features of an "ideal speech situation" (see Habermas 1973, 252ff., and 1981, vol. 1, 25ff.), in later works (see Habermas, 1983/1999a, 89) he assumes that logic of language requirements (discourse rules) are at issue that arise from the general structure of argumentation. This methodological adjustment seems to be based on an aim to provide a more *realistic* model of discourse rules. Habermas at this point evidently finds that the construction of the ideal speech situation was too ideal.[54] A more fruitful way for him seems to be to characterize rules of discourse as the "*form* in which we present the implicitly adopted and intuitively known pragmatic presuppositions of a special type of speech" (Habermas 1983/1999a, 91, emphasis in original). And indeed everyone who enters into this special speech practice inevitably *must* recognize the rules of discourse. Should this not be the case, a person would commit a performative contradiction. As an example, Habermas remarks that A would not be able to say that he had *convinced* his opponent B of something by means of a lie, because B would have formed a conviction under conditions in which a conviction could not have formed. It is one of the preconditions of an argument that A would have to accept upon entering a discussion that a person cannot use a lie to convince an opponent, but only to *persuade* him.[55] A can therefore only say that she has talked B into believing something to be true (see Habermas 1983/1999a, 90f.). This would mean, though, that A had not entered into an argument at all.

Discourse ethics sees the following rules of discourse as requiring acceptance above all (see Habermas 1983/1999a, 89)[56]:

1) Everyone may participate in a discourse who can speak and act.
2a) Everyone may problematize any assertion.
2b) Everyone may introduce any assertion into the discourse.
2c) Everyone is allowed to express his attitudes, wishes, and needs.
3) No one may be forcibly hindered from claiming her rights to 1) and 2a)-c). This means that no one may be prevented from participating in discourses, problematizing, or introducing assertions or expressing her attitudes.

The most crucial point is certainly number 3, since it is intended to ensure that entirely rational arguments will win the day in a discourse. Habermas famously emphasizes that the participants involved in an argument are necessarily subjected to the "peculiarly constraint-free force of the better argument" (Habermas 1981, vol. 1, 24, see also 28). Due to the power of performative contradiction and rational motivation (see the section "Society requires 1) rational motivation"), the force inherent to the preconditions of argument is also a necessary feature of our lifeworld and thus irreducible.[57] In this unforced forced, Habermas seems to recognize the only power that philosophy can genuinely claim for itself.

From these general conditions for every argument follows the validity of the *universalization principle U* (see Habermas1983/1999a, 86f.). On the basis of principle D, U must already be taken as a given. According to D, the fact that norms can be derived from discourse is only possible and consistent with our moral intuitions *because* the preconditions for argumentative debate in these discourses already imply the validity of principle U, which in turn, reflects our moral notions of impartiality.

U demands each participant in a discourse—presumably temporarily—to empathize with the other participants and to take on the role of everyone else (see Habermas 1991, 51f.). This concept of "ideal role taking" (Habermas 1991, 49) comes from Mead (see, for instance, Mead 1934). However, while Mead especially has in mind the private adoption of an individual's role by another, Habermas aims for a more public type of role taking (see Habermas, 1991, 59f.). The individual would be publicly compelled—and this means in her (public) arguments with others, in public discourse—to take on the roles of others. It is only through such an attempt toward identification and empathy that it is at all possible to seriously enter into an argumentative debate. Should the members of a society not be ready to engage in role taking or be no longer capable of empathy due to different (physical and/or mental) aptitudes or cultural backgrounds, a society (it seems reasonable to assume) would not be able to remain stable. According to Habermas and discourse ethics, this compulsory role taking that results from U is therefore a necessary "extra" to be demanded of the members of a society beyond an adherence to the rules.

From the perspective of the OE model, two provisional results emerge from the discussion so far:

1. Due to the rejection of a monological moral justification, the discourse-ethics approach offers the opportunity to establish ethical norms based on a theory of human interactions. Through an analysis of such interaction structures, it would be possible—similar to OE—to work out the conditions of modern societies and on this basis to establish an ethics. In the following sub-sections, however, it will be shown that discourse ethics, on the one hand, reconstructs these interaction structures differently from OE, particularly with different theoretical methods. On the other hand, it also ascribes to these structures a different theoretical status. Over all, then, discourse ethics arrives at a different justification of normativity and other tasks for ethics.
2. Discourse ethics aims to achieve a consensus of all parties. Once all participants of a discourse have agreed to a norm, this norm is then in force. At the same time, however, certain underlying conditions are required for this consensus that make relatively strong demands such as the possibility of ideal public role taking and the existence and effectiveness of rational motivation (see also the section "Society requires 1) rational motivation"). To more sharply delineate the theoretical difference between OE and discourse ethics in the question of the status of consensus, one might therefore say that discourse ethics—unlike OE—does not *derive* normativity from the consensus, but merely assigns it to the *preconditions* of consensus. Although arrived at by different means than those determined through consensus, these

preconditions already contain a certain normativity. Discourse ethics must prove that rational motivation and ideal public ideal role taking are possible and actually effective. In the following, I will examine the supporting evidence for the concept of rational motivation (see the section "Society requires 1) rational motivation"), the concept of ideal role taking (see the section "Society requires 2) viable forms of existence for ideal role taking"), and the supplementary concept of constitutional patriotism from Habermas's later writings (see the section "Society requires 3) constitutional patriotism").

Society Requires 1) Rational Motivation

Habermas's argument for the importance of discourse is based on a key presupposition: the actors involved in discourse must be able to let themselves be moved in their actions (at least partially) by a "rational motivation" (see Habermas 1981, vol. 1, 26 and 29; Habermas 1983/1999a, 58 and 109; Habermas 1992, 5). With the help of this concept, the distinction between strategic and communicative rationality—Habermas's central antagonism—becomes explicit. Whereas strategic action is influenced by incentives and sanctions, communicative action is based on a rational motivation (see Habermas 1983/1999a, 58).[58] The communicative agent must not be guided by the social *worth* of certain norms, but rather exclusively by their (moral-philosophical) *validity*. The additional conceptual contrast denoted here is crucial to Habermas.[59]

The concept of rational motivation thus assumes a decisive role in discourse ethics. But how is this rational motivation defined and how is it different from other types of motivation?

It is difficult to find an answer to these questions in Habermas's writings. In the "Theory," he writes: "If arguments are valid, then insight into the internal conditions of their validity can have a rationally motivating force" (Habermas 1981, vol. 1, 29).

A few pages earlier, however, a footnote appears in which he admits himself that the concept of rational motivation has not yet been satisfactorily analyzed (see Habermas 1981, vol. 1, 26/411, fn. 28). Thus the "Theory," as I see it, mainly stays with postulates. Rational motivation simply *exists* (see also Habermas 1981, vol. 1, 42). Later works unfortunately do not offer much more help. In Habermas (1983/1999a), he repeatedly emphasizes the need for rational motivation (see pp. 58, 72f., 119), but its existence is simply postulated or assumed as a general rule.[60] In this particular work, he offers a justification in only one place:

> in communicative action one actor seeks *rationally* to *motivate* another by relying on the illocutionary binding/bonding effect (Bindungseffekt) of the

offer contained in his speech act. (Habermas, 1983/1999a, 58, emphasis in original)

Here, Habermas justifies the rational motivation with recourse to speech-act theory. He appears to assume that speech acts may compel actors to perform or refrain from certain actions. The core of this assumption is the idea of performative contradiction, to which Habermas assigns an essential role (see Habermas, 1981, vol. 1, chapter III). Rational motivation can be explained with the help of the concept of performative contradiction: in order to avoid a performative contradiction, the rationally motivated agent allows himself to be persuaded.

The question is whether it makes sense to attribute such a binding effect to a speech act. Habermas himself appears to recognize this as a central problem, and, in Habermas (1983/1999a), he debates at length a fictional "skeptic," who, among other things, specifically raises doubts about the binding force of speech acts and thus the effectiveness of rational motivation.

Formally speaking, the discussion involves an ethical cognitivist and an ethical non-cognitivist, who is designated a skeptic. In a first step, this skeptic doubts whether there is such a thing as moral phenomena (part 1). Habermas believes that he has already successfully dismissed this uncertainty with the indicated language-philosophical considerations, and especially Strawson's, which point to the existence of moral standards. In a second step, the skeptic doubts whether moral statements are capable of being truth-apt (parts 2 and 3). Habermas tries to get around this suspicion by only conferring moral statements a status "*analogous to truth*" (Habermas, 1983/1999a, 56; italics in original). The skeptic, however, disputes the justifiability of this truth-analogous status. Habermas dismisses this objection with reference to principle U, which functions as a *rule of argumentation* (parts 4 and 5). In a fourth step (parts 6 and 7), the skeptic then doubts that U can be a universally valid moral principle. In his view, it is much more an expression of the moral intuitions of a particular culture and therefore cannot be sufficiently justified given the global plurality of cultures. Habermas next clarifies the status of U: it is not (unlike in the view of Apel [1984]) secured by a final justification, but rather concerns more an inevitable precondition that is due to language-philosophical reasons. These reasons are also described in the section "Basic principles: the principle of universalization as a rule of argumentation": a sharper distinction is supposedly to be made between conviction and persuasion in language philosophy. A performative contradiction is committed when a person believes she has *convinced* someone under conditions in which the ability to convince another is not possible (see Habermas 1983/1999a, 90f.). Thus "if one is to argue at all" (Habermas, 1983/1999a, 95), U is always to be recognized as an inevitable precondition. U is therefore culturally invariant and must already be present in *every* cultural group, regardless of specific local moral standards.[61]

The existence of performative contradictions is thus used as an argument against cultural relativism. A justification for the binding effect of the underlying speech acts is not given, however. The following fifth step (part 8), in which the skeptic raises yet another criticism, is accordingly the most important in the present context. His objection this time is that one could in fact simply reject the discourse. What if a person did not want to argue at all? In that case, what effect could a performative contradiction have?

Habermas's response resembles Bertrand Russell's answer to the epistemological skeptic (see Russell 1946/2004, 611ff.). Russell emphasizes that the epistemological skeptic (such as Hume) can make logically consistent arguments, but cannot accomplish anything with his position. He must remain unable to act. Habermas responds similarly to the ethical skeptic: by consistently refusing to engage in discourse, this person could do nothing more than "assert his position mutely and impressively" (Habermas, 1983/1999a, 100).[62] Yet he still could not withdraw from daily communicative practice. Because this daily practice only *functions* due to the established preconditions of discourse, they would also have to be recognized by the skeptic. Otherwise he would wind up "regressing to . . . schizophrenia and suicide" (Habermas, 1983/1999a, 102). He could not decide between strategic, incentive-motivated action, on the one hand, and communicative, rationally motivated action, on the other (ibid. 111f.). Habermas points out—and sees this as "a factual observation" (ibid.)—that our world has inevitably always been influenced by cultural traditions and socialization and that the processes of tradition and socialization can be carried out on their own through communicative action and hence rational motivation. At the same time, we would not have a choice. Habermas now finds the refutation of the skeptic to be certain.

Many questions remain unanswered, though. Above all, it is unclear whether Habermas's analytical access to the communicative processes of everyday practice is the *only possible* access. Is it reasonable to assume that such processes are *not* only controlled by strategic action? This is Habermas's claim, which obviously also implies that we can repudiate incentives in daily communication due to rational motivation. But if—as with OE—one takes prisoner's-dilemma situations seriously, one would have to reject the position of discourse ethics. *If* prisoner's dilemmas can also be reconstructed in everyday contexts, then it must be logically concluded that these contexts cannot permit communicative action that *repudiates incentives*. I will again take up the problem of the prisoner's dilemma and its implications for discourse ethics in the section "Criticism: And what if a performative contradiction does not disturb me?" However, I would already note here that according to OE, everyday practical contexts are also reconstructed as being riddled with such dilemma situations. Just the same, these situations do not usually involve manifest dilemmas, but those that have been *overcome*, and yet are latent and persistent. The individuals concerned could successfully form interactions, overcome social traps (through formal or informal institutional solutions), and "reap" the advantages of cooperation. These dilemmas that have been overcome, however, are not visible from an approach that dwells on phenomena, that believes it can relate a quasi pretheoretical (life-world) perspective to these phenomena, and that, from this perspective, can identify the phenomenon "rational motivation." It may be useful for some objectives to adopt such a phenomenalistic perspective. The problems of modern society, however, can only be addressed in this way in a limited manner. I will discuss this, as well as a possible constructive role of discourses, in sections "Criticism: And what if a performative contradiction does not disturb me?" and "Discourse as a heuristic for rule reforms?"

Habermas's thinking evolves in the works that come after Habermas (1983/1999a). The essay "Discourse Ethics: Notes on a Program of Philosophical Justification" (Habermas 1983/1999a) is key, especially with regard to the clashes with Wellmer (1986) and Apel (1988), where the problem of the skeptic is raised again. First, Habermas responds to Wellmer's sharp contrast between rational and moral action by remarking that a cognitivist ethics, like discourse ethics, by no means needs to claim that "moral insight is already a sufficient motive for moral action" (Habermas 1991, 33). Moral commands and insights could claim for themselves only "the weak motivating force of good reasons" (ibid.) Commands and insights indeed imply a moral obligation. However, it is possible that they are not followed due to a "weakness of will" (ibid.). And shortly afterward he remarks:

> Since Schiller, the rigidity of the Kantian ethics of duty has been repeatedly and rightly criticized. But autonomy can be reasonably expected (*zumutbar*) only in social contexts that are already themselves rational in the sense that they ensure that action motivated by good reasons will not of necessity conflict with one's own interests. The validity of moral commands is subject to the condition that they are *universally* adhered to as the basis for a general practice. (Habermas 1991, 34, italics in original)

The last sentence of this quote is especially revealing. As in OE, the idea is incorporated here that the degree of compliance with norms (according to the principle "'ought implies can,' which though not mentioned explicitly by Habermas is certainly in the background") affects the *validity* of these norms. This would also imply that in a prisoner's-dilemma situation, the norm "You shall cooperate!" can have no validity for the individual because she would have to assume the defection of everyone else. This thought would go beyond Habermas's original idea that while an adherence to norms might not be sufficiently secured because of a weakness of will, the (moral-philosophical) *validity* of these norms is simultaneously not impinged upon. Consequently, it also would no longer be possible to speak of a practical effect of rational motivation. This is because rational motivation apparently could not exist in opposition to the incentives posed by the situation.

Immediately following the sentence quoted above, however, Habermas still only speaks of a condition of the "reasonableness of imposing moral demands (*Zumutbarkeit*)" (ibid. 34, 65, italics in original). He accordingly weakens the preceding sentence, for the reasonableness or unreasonableness of a norm (vis-à-vis its observance) presumes its validity. Merely complying with this norm is not reasonable, for instance, because its *general* observance is not assured.

The condition of reasonableness is clarified at a later point in the same essay. Habermas writes that a judgment could follow from a norm, which had been identified as the only one that is appropriate for a particular situation, but which also requires the actors to undertake an action that "cannot be reasonably expected from an existential point of view" (ibid. 87). This question, however, first arises in legal-theoretical discourses, not yet in ethics. In the law,[63] the argument is made that a norm can only be regarded as valid if general compliance with the norm can be expected. If this is not the case, then norms "cannot be reasonably imposed, regardless of whether they are valid" (ibid.).

It is unclear how these two sentences that immediately follow each other can be brought into agreement. If it is likely that a large proportion of those affected will not follow norm A (for instance, as a result of a prisoner's dilemma structure), is A then valid but not reasonable, or neither valid nor reasonable? Read in conjunction with the earlier quote, what is ultimately at issue seems to be a question of reasonableness that, nonetheless, does not come up in the field of ethics, but rather only in the field of legal theory. For Habermas, this transition permits him to introduce institutions into his conception: "Legal institutionalization alone can ensure general adherence to morally valid norms" (ibid. 88).

The following development in Habermas's thinking is thus disclosed: while in the works before the "Notes" institutions only played a minor role,[64] Habermas now recognizes that the question of implementability and of the actual effectiveness of discursively justified norms needs to be given more prominence. He acknowledges that it is neither sufficient to simply postulate the existence of rational motivation, nor to exclusively appeal to Kohlberg's developmental psychology (1981, 1984) for empirical support (for more on this, see the section "Society requires 2) viable forms of existence for ideal role taking"). Habermas seeks to secure the assistance of another discipline: legal theory.[65] There he apparently sees the theoretical possibilities for justifying the need for institutions within discourse ethics, without at the same time completely giving up on rational motivation as a concept.

This is made especially clear in *Between Facts and Norms* (Habermas, 1992). Habermas's legal-philosophical outline indeed centers on the significance of legally codified and sanctions-oriented norms. At the same time, however, the assumption is made that the citizens subjected to these norms have a moral surplus value at their command. They should continue to recognize normative validity claims, which follow from certain idealized preconditions of linguistic argumentation (see, for instance, Habermas 1992, 34 and 18 and 151ff.). And Habermas further sees this recognition as facilitating action: he still assumes that "language can be mobilized to coordinate action plans" (Habermas 1992, 18), which—according to what has been said so far—must presuppose the existence of rational motivation. He, moreover, distinguishes strongly between a form of control based on the law and on economic incentives:

> The socially integrative force of solidarity, which can no longer be drawn solely from sources of communicative action, must develop through widely diversified and more or less autonomous public spheres, as well as through procedures of democratic opinion- and will-formation institutionalized within a constitutional framework. In addition, it should be able to hold its own against the two other mechanisms of social integration, money and administrative power. (Habermas 1992, 299)

This quote shows both the coexistence of communicative action and legal control as well as the way in which Habermas positions the law (as he does with communicative rationality in earlier works) against economic incentives.[66] Thus, despite some development, there is also a high degree of continuity in Habermas's writings since "Theory."

In summary, the following picture of the interplay between rational motivation and motivation through sanctions-based institutions becomes apparent in discourse ethics. The importance of institutions is certainly recognized by Habermas. On the one hand, they secure the preconditions of rational argument. They can neutralize external influences on the discourse participants and thus ensure at least somewhat that the idealized preconditions of D are satisfied (see Habermas 1983/1999a, 92). On the other hand, the validity determined by legal theory in the legal sense provides the necessary enforcement that is required for implementing norms in a state, while also guaranteeing that the justifications for the norms are issued (see Habermas 1992, 32f. and 104ff.). In this way, the legality *and* legitimacy of the codified norms of a state are guaranteed by the law.

Here, Habermas combines several theoretical elements: he both focuses on motivation by means of institutions and he continues to require motivation by means of justifications and arguments, that is, rational motivation. Two major differences between discourse ethics and OE can therefore be clearly identified. One concerns strategic theory; the other is more facilitative of action.

Whereas OE reconstructs the stability of modern societies on the basis of its institutions and the incentives that come from them in a theoretically stringent manner, Habermas starts out by bringing several theoretical elements together, specifically, the rational, language-philosophically grounded motivation of discourse theory and the state enforcement of legal theory, whose necessity he recognizes in *Between Facts and Norms*. He then attempts to substantiate legal theory on the basis of discourse theory and, in doing so, to restore the theoretical coherence.

The first question that emerges, however, is how the discourse-theoretical reconstruction can be reconciled with an economic reconstruction of the law (see for instance Posner 1973/2007). Is the former just as effective as the latter?

Second, it is debatable whether the discourse theory of law does not neutralize the independent force of law, in other words, the state coercion that Habermas would in fact harness for his purposes. In my view, what ultimately remains for the discourse theorist, on both the discourse-theory and the legal-theory side, is only rational motivation.[67] Legal theory for Habermas would then certainly be theoretical consistent, but provide no independent support.

While OE consistently tries to conceptually avoid relying on moral surplus values, discourse ethics must assume here at least *one* such surplus value: the existence of rational motivation.[68] Discourse ethics recognizes the role of institutions and sanctions, but only concedes to them *one* role among many in the "concert" of social influences. Rational motivation could (and even according to *Between Facts and Norms* does) neutralize the incentives originating from institutions and social structures such as dilemma structures. I will critique these hypotheses in the section "Criticism: And what if a performative contradiction does not disturb me?" from the perspective of OE. Then, in the section "Discourse as a heuristic for rule reforms?" I will attempt within OE to confer a possible constructive role to a functional analogue to rational motivation, whose existence and effect are nonetheless reconstructed differently theoretically than in discourse ethics. First, however, two additional—and according to Habermas necessary—preconditions for the stability of a modern society will be described.

Society Requires 2) Viable Forms of Existence for Ideal Role Taking

As we have seen, Habermas assumes that the members of a modern society must be guided by rational motivation. This alone, however, is not sufficient to keep such a society stable. Rather, as already mentioned, the members must be capable of *ideal role taking* in the argumentative public debate. They must be able to put themselves into the shoes of their fellow citizens *to motivate them argumentatively*. Forms of existence that make this possible would accommodate a universalistic morality and be necessary to allow this morality to be effective. Habermas already stresses this in the "Notes," which is to say, before he ascribes greater importance to institutions in his later works:

> Universalist moralities are dependent on forms of life that are rationalized in that they make possible the prudent application of universal moral insights and support motivations for translating insights into moral action. (Habermas, 1983/1999a, 109)

This means the implementation of moral insights requires that the forms of life interested in this implementation must correspondingly motivate their fellow forms of life. Habermas does not say at this point, though, whether this would occur through social control, arguments, or sanctions. Still, argumentative motivation cannot be all that is intended here, since—according to Habermas (see ibid.)—this does not in fact lead yet to implementation.

To determine whether such forms of life actually exist, Habermas relies on the development psychology of Lawrence Kohlberg. Kohlberg's work shows that the "abstractive achievements required by the moral point of view" (Habermas, 1983/1999a, 109) can also actually be undertaken by human beings.[69]

Kolberg's stage theory of the development of moral consciousness reconstructs a total of six stages, wherein morality develops as a cognitive phenomenon (see especially Kohlberg 1981 and 1984). It distinguishes between two pre-conventional, two conventional, and two post-conventional stages. What is decisive for Habermas is, on the one hand, the rise from conventional to the post-conventional moral consciousness (i.e., from stage four to five, which I will ignore here) and, on the other, the transition (within the post-conventional type) from the fifth to the sixth and highest stage (see Habermas 1983/1999b and Habermas 1988/1991). Individuals at the fifth stage accept norms, rights, or principles, because they see these to be the result of a social contract that provides all parties involved with the maximum benefit. This does not yet exhaust the opportunities for development, however. Post-conventional stage six designates a moral consciousness that adheres to universal ethical principles—and not as a result of benefit calculations, but rather an "intrinsic" motivation, namely, the recognition of the necessity of acting according to principles.[70]

It is important that Kohlberg thinks it is possible to learn moral behavior. In his conception, to move from one stage to another higher stage means to go through a learning process. This learning process is not controlled by external influences (apparently meaning incentives or sanctions), but rather the result of "a creative reorganization of an existing cognitive inventory that is inadequate to the task of handling certain persistent problems" (Habermas 1983/1999b, 125). With such recurring problems, Kohlberg argues that phenomena heretofore recognized as factual do not by any means turn into fixed facts. The individual comes to realize that these facts may be the case or not. Adolescents find that social arrangements that previously appeared sacrosanct are not really so self-evident and that their legitimacy is not as secure as it once seemed. A person does not simply return to a recognition of previously accepted standards, but instead constructs a new view of morality, which helps her to provide her own norms and especially to differentiate morally valid norms from prevailing norms (see Habermas 1983/199b, 137). In the end, from this viewpoint, "all that remains is a procedure for a rationally motivated choice among principles that have been recognized in turn as in need of justification" (ibid.). Rational motivation and not recognition due to sanctions would thus stand at the end of the moral-psychological development process.

Without going into all the particulars of Kohlberg's concept, I would merely like to summarize the importance of his approach to discourse ethics. His developmental psychological work allows Habermas to suppose that the communicative action necessary for role taking is cognitively possible and, moreover, empirically grounded. The moral development that takes place in adolescents indicates the basic outlines of the process according to which adult citizens (and apparently even whole societies) could also improve their moral perspective in a Habermasian sense. Only then can discourse ethics recognize a controlling influence in discourse. It is thus only when the existence and effectiveness of rational motivation finds its basis in the cognitive processes, when forms of life exist that comply with the universalistic morality of discourse ethics (see Habermas, 1983/1999a, 109), that Habermas can assert that arguments can even prevail over incentives.

In the present context, two points in Kohlberg's theory seem especially notable.

First, the methodological question is unclear as to what form psychology would take as an empirical science in supporting ethics. In particular, it is not apparent how the psychological reconstruction of moral learning would be reconciled with other—for example, economic—reconstructions. The problem of interdisciplinarity with respect to economics and the law already discussed in the section "Society requires 1) rational motivation" emerges here once again: Are psychological and economic reconstructions equally effective? Do they respond to different problems? The psychological theory seems a) better suited to addressing individual developments and b) the results of these developments are sometimes more compatible with the intuitions of the members of a society.[71] Economics, by contrast, seems a) better suited to addressing systematic problems of social consequence, that is, problems that not only affect individuals but groups and entail changes in statistical variables, such as the unemployment rate or the savings rate. And some of its results are b) to a large extent counterintuitive and provide recommendations for institutional reforms that, at least *prima facie*, go against everyday experience and moral intuitions. I will return to the various tasks of psychology and economics in the section "Discourse as a heuristic for rule reforms?"

Second, even after the reconstruction of different problems in economics and psychology, the question remains as to which manner of framing of problems is more relevant for ethical theory. Is it more important that ethics conforms to our intuitions or that it can be adapted to the realities of modern societies?

In ethics, the view is usually taken that the moral intuitions of people—that is, not their preferences or desires—reflect the touchstone for ethical theories.[72] An ethics that runs counter to these intuitions is therefore to be rejected. This position, however, overlooks one consideration, namely, that moral intuitions are formed in a "moral mesocosmos" (see the section "Binmore's original position" and "Gauthier's point of departure for a functional justification of morality"). They did not develop under the conditions of modern societies. It has long been understood in epistemology and the philosophy of science that our intuitive beliefs about the world, which have been adapted to the dimensions of everyday life—that is, the mesocosmos (see Vollmer 1983)—do not always adequately assess modern scientific theories. Why should one not therefore also suppose that moral intuitions can fail in ethics? I do not intend to suggest here that the consent of all members of society is unsuitable as a criterion for the validity of rules or the solutions typically put forward for the problems of modern societies. The claim I want to make does not concern the wishes or preferences of individuals, but rather their moral intuitions. I argue that it is not moral intuitions that are decisive for assessing the consequences of an ethical theory, but instead the approval or non-approval—which is *not* necessarily based on moral intuitions but cost considerations—of these consequences by all those affected.

The relevance of moral intuitions, however, is not to be denied. At this point, OE introduces the distinction between rule compliance and rule heuristics.

Rules are consequently followed on the basis of the actors' cost-benefit calculations. The actors estimate the advantages and disadvantages of the specified incentives, and act accordingly. Moral considerations *against* incentives *cannot* permanently have the upper hand. To endure in a world dominated by dilemma structures, morality must be systematically tied to advantages for the acting individual. Therefore, rules and institutions that are supposed to implement and enforce moral ideas should be made incentive compatible so that the consequences of these rules do not run counter to the original (moral) intentions of the rule creators. Here is where rule heuristics comes into play. Of course, ideas and recommendations regarding how the rules should be designed should be present and communicated in a society. These ideas and recommendations can certainly draw upon (traditional) moral "inventories." These inventories can be studied and "nurtured" by psychology so that there is always a sufficient amount of ideas and suggestions available for undertaking rule reforms. Under nurturing, I understand that the psychological adequateness and relevance of these moral intuitions can be examined under the current societal conditions. This task must be ignored by economics. The cognitive circumstances of the affected individuals are not its focus.

If one divides up the tasks between economics and psychology in the manner indicated—that is, by assigning economics the responsibility of shaping the rules in an incentive-compatible way and psychology that of reconstructing and nurturing of moral intuitions—then ethics will not be able to dispense entirely with either one of the two disciplines. Just as much emphasis needs to be placed on the effective institutional enforcement of its norms as on the nurturing of its reservoir of ideas. Nonetheless, an ethics that goes about systematically—like OE—in dealing with the problem of norm enforcement must inevitably give economics a weightier role. Norms that cannot be enforced under modern conditions also cannot be justified. In addition, the question of *where* the ideas come from for the enforcement of norms is also important (this is, of course, also conceded to psychology within OE). Still, the question does not necessarily need to be answered only by psychology.[73] The reservoir of proposals for future regulation reforms can also be examined, reconstructed, and nurtured by other disciplines such as philosophy, but also by completely different undertakings such as those in the field of literature and art (see also the section "Discussion: Can't society also dispose with empathetic preferences?"). The task of economics, in my view, can hardly be assumed by another discipline. For this reason, it seems problematic to rely solely on psychology as a basis for the existence of suitable forms of life.

Society Requires 3) Constitutional Patriotism

In his later writings, Habermas added for citizens in the modern era a third crucial trait to the two concepts of rational motivation and public ideal role taking: citizens should be capable of adopting an attitude that he calls *constitutional patriotism* ("Verfassungspatriotismus"). This term was coined by Dolf Sternberger, who first used the concept in 1970 (systematically in 1979).[74] Sternberger (1982/1990, 20ff.) refers to a disposition that is distinguished from national or nationalist patriotism insofar as it is not predicated on a nation *without regard to its state constitution*, but instead on a *specific state order*. This constitutional patriotism, as Sternberger demonstrates, is older than national patriotism. There is evidence, for example, of its existence in Germany as early as the eighteenth century.

Habermas made use of this term for the first time in 1986 during the *Historikerstreit* (see Habermas 1986/1987, 50) and in the subsequent debates about a possible return (feared by Habermas) to conservative-national positions in the political landscape. The representatives of such positions advocated, among other things, encouraging patriotic attitudes. In stark opposition, Habermas insisted that in his view the only acceptable patriotism could be a "constitutional patriotism" (ibid.).[75] For Habermas, what apparently matters here most is an attitude that neither exhibits an affective bond vis-à-vis the nation nor an ideology.

Constitutional patriotism is dealt with more fully in the lecture from 1990 "Citizenship and National Identity" (Habermas 1992, 491–515). Here, it is suggested that this attitude should involve a sense for the *variety* of different forms of life and for their integration into a state (see Habermas 1992, 496). These forms of life should learn to interpret the constitution from their own cultural perspective.[76] In this way, a constitutional patriotism could then develop that would provide social cohesion even where it might no longer seem possible. Habermas's constitutional patriotism—in its first approximation—thus seems to resemble Rawls's "overlapping consensus" (see chapter 4), which also consists of consensus-oriented solutions that can be justified on the basis of different cultural backgrounds. However, Rawls's overlapping consensus is a more far-reaching concept, for it not only needs to relate to the contents of a constitution. On the one hand, it can be targeted at noncodified rules. On the other, it was also especially developed by Rawls for trans*national* levels. On this point, Habermas is explicit: constitutional patriotism is *not* conceivable at the global level (see Habermas, 1998, 163f.). In his view, the notion of a society of world citizens remains utopian. At the global level, other social blueprints are better suited as reference models (see ibid. 166f.).

In general, constitutional patriotism does not have the same systematic significance in Habermas's approach as rational motivation and public role taking. It rather seems to be more of an *added* supporting element, which helps Habermas to bring together several ideas. It is nevertheless important for the present context, since it concerns a further moral surplus value that is demanded[77] of the members of a society, particularly in Habermas's later publications.[78]

Criticism: And What If a Performative Contradiction Does Not Disturb Me?

The previous subsections have already highlighted the basic outlines of my criticisms of Habermas. In order to refine this criticism, I will now focus on what are the two main difficulties of discourse ethics for the question being pursued here: the possibility of rejecting a discourse and the problem of rational motivation.

Habermas's expectation of resolute, discourse-resistant actors was already made clear in the discussion of his confrontation with the fictional skeptic (see the section "Society requires 1) rational motivation"). He obviously recognizes that not only is the essentially random refusal of a few individuals at issue, but moreover that this points to an inherent systematic problem. *For solving social problems*, is it possible to assume that individuals can be brought to change their behavior by means of argument, justification, and persuasion? Is the implementation of ethical norms possible through argument? Or can one also—generally speaking—withdraw from argument and discourse?

As shown earlier (see the section "Society requires 1) rational motivation"), Habermas comes to see this problem with increasing clarity. In the "Notes," he nearly concludes that the conditions of implementation have an influence on the validity of norms. He then resorts, however, to the distinction between the validity and reasonableness of norms. Be that as it may, this distinction also reflects an evolution, because it is now possible that a norm, which has been won by argument, is nonetheless unreasonable for the affected individuals. The discourse is thus not sufficient by itself as a foundation for norms. This line of argument is further pursued in *Between Facts and Norms*. Here, Habermas admits that not only is argument necessary for the implementation of norms, but so are institutions. He writes:

> Modern societies are integrated *not only* socially through values, norms, and mutual understanding, *but also* systemically through markets and the administrative use of power. (Habermas 1992, 39; my emphasis)

This means that, through deliberative politics, it takes "elements from both sides" (Habermas 1992, 296), that is, from both a liberal and a republican viewpoint. They are thus based on interest compromises as well as the time-honored cultural background consensus of the citizens. One can no longer accuse Habermas here of completely ignoring the implementation problem and the role of institutions. *However,* a new problem arises: namely, that of the linkage between systemic or institutional integration, on the one hand, and value integration, on the other. This linkage, though, occurs in Habermas—as already indicated in the section "Society requires 1) rational motivation"—in a merely accidental, cursory manner. He is forced to abandon the higher conceptual unity of his earlier work and now sets discursive understanding and institutional implementation alongside each other without any theoretical relation. At any time, the actor should be able to perform a "motivation switch"[79] from strategic to communicative action.

The critique of Habermas must consequently begin with his theoretical patchwork: for how can the changes in the behavior of citizens that are still *methodologically controlled* be attributed to discursive processes or to institutions? Habermas does not seem to have a systematic answer in mind.[80] It therefore remains to be answered whether the solution of social problems ultimately takes place through discursive processes, or whether, in view of the conditions of implementation, there would finally need to be an institutional solution which even someone who rejects discourse would have to recognize.

Discourse ethics' second serious problem is closely related to the first: What is meant by rational motivation? How can we justify using this concept?

The discussion of the status of rational motivation in Habermas's approach (see the section "Society requires 1) rational motivation") showed that Habermas himself still finds the concept to require clarification. He, nevertheless, proceeds based on an assumption of the actual effectiveness of rational motivation: it is supposedly capable of neutralizing incentives. If this is true, then even the skeptic from (2) might be satisfied. The dogmatic rejection of discourse would be excluded as a possibility, since the holdout could ultimately be rationally motivated despite existing incentives.

Habermas tries to prove that it is possible to neutralize incentives with (at least) two arguments. First, he relies on Kohlberg's psychological work, which he believes demonstrates the existence of rational motivation in child development. This was discussed earlier in the section "Society requires 2) viable forms of existence for ideal role taking." There I drew attention to issues of interdisciplinarity as well as to Kohlberg's theoretical framing of the problem, which may not be suitable for the issues of modern societies explored by Habermas.

On the other hand, arguments are used from the tradition of pragmatism and analytical language philosophy, a cornerstone that seems to be (at least for the time being) more relevant to Habermas and other discourse ethicists than psychology. It is not possible to respond to all or even most of these arguments within the scope of this book. Nonetheless, *one* essential philosophical-historical underpinning for discourse ethics deserves closer examination: Charles S. Peirce's concept of the unlimited community, which serves as a model for the conditions of discourse.[81]

Habermas also sees this concept as being decisive in later works. This is demonstrated by the fact that he refers extensively to Peirce in chapter 1 of

Between Facts and Norms, as well as in later works (see Habermas 1999). Habermas reconstructs Peirce's ideas in the following manner (see Habermas 1992, 13ff.): for Peirce, communication is the central concept; communities, especially communities of scientists, form their shared life-world through communication. In such a community, diverse *truth claims* are proposed at first. These, however, finally converge under ideal conditions into a "final opinion" (ibid. 14)—into a consensus that can only be reached by the unlimited communication community that bridges "all local and temporal distances" (ibid. 15). This communication community of scientists from all eras is to be understood as an ideal republic of letters (see ibid. 16) who have committed themselves to the "cooperative search for truth" (ibid.).

That said, Habermas first reconstructs the Peircean communication community by ascribing to it a cooperative character.[82] He then postulates that the members should be able to gain the "*rationally motivated* agreement of the interpretation community as a whole" (ibid. 29; my emphasis).[83] Finally, he emphasizes that "learning processes" (ibid. 31) take place in this unlimited community, which lead the community to move more closely toward the ideal consensus.

A very different picture of Peirce's approach is offered by Thomas Haskell (1984, 210ff.) and Nicholas Rescher (1978, 15).[84] Both emphasize a) that the members of the communication community are anything but cooperative. In Peirce's model, they also specifically see b) not rational motivation at work, but the self-interest of researchers. And, lastly, both Haskell and Rescher emphasize c) that the community moves toward consensus via a mechanism that is reminiscent of the economic market mechanism, not a learning process—at least insofar as the latter connotes the reflective insights of individuals. More specifically[85]:

a) Peirce stresses precisely that rivalry and competition in the community of researchers plays a much bigger role than feelings of goodwill. Haskell writes:

> Indeed, upon close examination it appears that Peirce's community reproduces within itself the perpetual conflict and struggle for supremacy of a competitive market society. . . . Peirce's community is finally more critical than loving. (Haskell 1984, 210)

The researchers criticize each other intensely. The "most antagonistic views"[86] come into conflict. Entirely in the spirit of Popper (1934/1994 and 1963/1969), it is possible to speak of a process of conjecture and refutation. Claims and counterclaims are made, and errors are criticized mercilessly. Gestures of goodwill are interpreted as cowardice. It is not possible to speak here of cooperation in the interest of science or truth.

b) It is much more the self-interest of the researchers that is the chief impetus. Peirce clearly rejects any interest in strictly *monetary* rewards and capitalism's "Gospel of Greed" (Peirce 1893/1998, 6.294). Researchers, he suggests, are not interested in money. They are in his opinion at any rate very interested in their *reputation*. As he indicates in the concluding remarks of *The Fixation of Belief* (Peirce 1877/1998):

> The genius of a man's logical method should be loved and reverenced as his bride, whom he has chosen from all the world. . . . [H]e will work and fight for her, and will not complain that there are blows to take, hoping that there may be as many and as hard to give, and will *strive to be the worthy knight and champion* of her from the blaze of whose splendors he draws his inspiration and his courage. (Peirce 1877/1998, 5.387; emphasis added)

In Peirce's model, there can thus be no talk of rational motivation, understood here as the opposite of motivation that is brought about through incentives and benefits. Researchers need to love their own ideas—to view them as their "creation," which requires "cherishing and tending" (Peirce 1893/1998, 6.289). Peirce refers to this as the demand for "synechism" (ibid., italics omitted). Its equivalent is found in OE in the use of a broad benefits concept, which includes *everything* that the actors may perceive as advantageous.

c) How can Peirce then assume that a meaningful consensus will still emerge from such social conduct? The answer lies in the nature of the social mechanism that motivates the self-interested members of the research community. On this point, both Rescher (1978, 1976) and Haskell (1984) contend that is *not* learning processes that are actually at work, but instead a market mechanism that, entirely in the spirit of Smith and Mandeville, brings about progress through competition. One is able to speak in this case of the presence of an invisible hand in science that, however, does not remain a metaphysical metaphor insofar as it is embodied by the price mechanism. Rescher (1978, chapter 1) underscores that the research process is self-correcting, an idea that has been taken up again in economic theory.[87] And Haskell (1984, 211) even draws direct parallels to Smith[88]:

> The convergence of opinion within the community therefore does not depend upon its members' benevolence any more than the provision of our dinner depends upon the benevolence of the butcher, the brewer, or the baker.

In other words, Habermas's key witness for the effect of rational motivation, Peirce, is in fact an advocate for the opposing side.[89] Both OE and the economic theory of democracy can easily interpret Peirce within the framework of their approaches.

To summarize: On the one hand, Habermas defends his approach against the possibility of a rejection of discourse, but only with recourse to a theoretical patchwork. On the other hand—at least in the exemplary case of Peirce—he *wrongly* draws upon the philosophy of language in order to lend support to the concept of rational motivation. Both criticisms are therefore ultimately not responded to satisfactorily.[90]

Discourse as a Heuristic for Rule Reforms?

In the following, I will discuss three starting points for *constructively* interpreting Habermasian discourse ethics. First, Habermas points out that the citizens of a democracy must view their institutions as changeable and cannot take them to be sacrosanct. Second, Habermas's approach has the advantage of being potentially more adaptable to the intuitions of citizens of a democracy than the other approaches discussed here.[91] This is particularly true for *specific* questions of utility. Third, some of the features of discourse ethics can potentially find new relevance if one looks at the development of the Internet and attempts to evaluate its significance for democracy. These issues will now be discussed in turn.

As already mentioned, *Between Facts and Norms* does not in fact present a fundamental evolutionary leap in Habermas's thinking. It is nonetheless possible to find some ideas—particularly regarding the role of institutions—that are at least emphasized more strongly than before. We have already seen (see the section "Criticism: And what if a performative contradiction does not disturb me?") that both institutions and values contribute to the integration of societies. We have also seen (see the section "Society requires 1) rational motivation") that ultimately discursive rationality can and must prevail against systemic rationality. This idea may—at least to some degree—be constructively interpreted within the framework of OE:

There is in fact an interesting observation to be found in a footnote (see Habermas 1992, 43, fn. 18): Habermas admits here that strategic interactions continue to play a part in the actors' lifeworld, despite the effects of communicative rationality. Yet this lifeworld would not determine the actors' behavior:

> Those who act strategically no doubt also have a lifeworld background always behind them; but this background is neutralized in its action-coordinating force. It no longer provides a shared consensus in advance, because strategic actors encounter normative contexts, as well as other participants, *only as social facts*. (Habermas 1992, 26, fn. 18, my emphasis)

Habermas obviously finds it important that the institutions are perceived by the actors as *changeable*. In other words, it should not be the case that the citizens would merely accept the institutional framework as if it had dropped from the sky and thus no longer scrutinize it. The framework must be constantly examined and tested for possible improvements (in terms of OE: for cooperative gains).

Habermas also clearly sees that this problem is a particular problem of *modern* societies: in pre-modern times, limiting conditions were *regarded* as sacrosanct. Sociological and economic theory construe this as rational under the social conditions of the pre-modern period, which still had yet to experience societal growth (see Luetge 2012). The demise of "sacralized belief complexes" (Habermas 1992, 25) and ever-increasing societal differentiation presented the problem of stabilizing the social order in an entirely new form, however. The institutional framework is crucial for this stabilization, but so is *heuristics* for *altering* these conditions. Habermas's statement hints at a possible heuristic function for communicative rationality: the actors should constantly be reminded—and OE stresses this as well—that they have to continue to develop the framework in a way that properly accounts for the social dynamics of modern societies and shows that (willing) participation in such societies can also be advantageous in the future for all members. Suggestions for modifications to the framework can thus be given, which are then subsequently developed in detail by the social sciences in such a way that they are incentive compatible. However, the suggestions themselves would have to be generated by the actors, with ideas such as discourse and communication—along with many other sources of suggestions—making a contribution to this process without coercion. Such a view is represented—at least to some extent—by Sabel and Cohen (2001), who, for example, advocate "directly deliberative polyarchies" as ruling structures for certain parts of modern societies.[92]

A second constructive starting point is the requirement that solution recommendations for social problems not only need to be incentive compatible, but also—to a certain extent—satisfy the moral intuitions of society's members. I have already discussed the difficulty of such claims in the section "Society requires 2) viable forms of existence for ideal role taking." Within the context of OE and evolutionary theory it was pointed out that intuitions of all kinds have been formed by our evolutionary past, which no longer adequately represents today's world, and that the compatibility, for example, of natural-scientific theories with *intuitions* cannot be expected.

On the other hand, our intuitions do not simply exist as *facta bruta*. Intuitions, and even moral intuitions, can hence only be meaningfully discussed from a *theoretical perspective*. From the perspective of OE, for instance, actor A ultimately forms a moral intuition in order to serve his (long-term) self-interest. The predominant structure in our evolutionary past of the small group could still be directly controlled with the help of such moral intuitions.[93] However, as evolutionary theory also indicates, this adjustment is no longer optimal today—not only due to modern natural-scientific theories, but also because of the conditions of modern societies. Intuitions cannot be used any longer in the *direct* control of societies. Nevertheless, it remains the case that intuitions were originally intended to improve a person's individual circumstances. Why shouldn't an intuition serve this purpose under modern conditions, if only *indirectly*?

From the perspective of OE, this means that discourses can certainly play an important role in modern societies, but also that the *benefits* for the individuals involved in them must be communicated. The justifications of norms or rules need to address the self-interest of the stakeholders and demonstrate that an existing or proposed regulation serves the interests (at least long-term) of those who are subjected to it. It is not possible to speak here of a rational motivation that is not influenced by individual benefits and thus to sharply distinguish between the two motivations. Instead, the clear separation between seemingly "economic" and seemingly "non-economic" or "rational" motivations and practices needs to be abandoned. Such artificial antagonisms undermine research and society. They hinder the realization that we are only able to control modern societies with the help of benefits and incentives. Habermas, in fact, even pursued this insight himself. As part of his speech in Beijing in 2001 before the Chinese public and the party leadership, he did not legitimize human rights with reference to the philosophically grounded universality of such rights. He rather legitimized them functionally, that is, in terms of their benefits for the country: the systematic observance of human rights would in fact promote the productivity improvements that the Chinese wanted to achieve (see Maass 2001).[94]

When Habermas speaks himself about benefits in discourse, then others must be permitted to do so as well. Thus rules can be designed in a way that makes them compatible with our intuitions, without creating a conflict with their *incentive* compatibility. This, consequently, makes it possible to do away with the clumsy theoretical patchwork: ethics, economics, and legal theory have the *same* theoretical root, and each discipline is able to work with the micro theory of the self-interested actor.

Quite in passing, a third possibility is disclosed for a constructive linkage to Habermas's discourse ethics. The Internet can in principle quite naturally be seen as an opportunity to implement the ideals of discourse ethics in a new way. In particular, discourses in the Internet have a structure that comes at least very close to domination-free communication. The Internet offers—in the form of social networks, forums, newsgroups, mailing lists, and so on—the possibility of engaging in debate, where the users themselves determine the topics, can participate on equal footing and without coercion, and where there is no predetermined end. Here, the informality of such discussions is emphasized as much as anything. Each user can take part in a discussion at any time, anonymously and without fear that her statements will have any negative consequences.[95] Moreover, she can always withdraw from current debates and start new ones.

The Internet is rarely mentioned in Habermas's own work, and the few indications suggest a rather skeptical point of view. He thus writes in *The Inclusion of the Other*: "The publics created by the Internet remain closed off from one another like global villages" (Habermas 1996, 121). This statement suggests that Habermas finds public spaces in the Internet to be lacking and that he fears particularization.

The Internet, however, may still be employed to Habermas's own purposes. In "Notes," he looks for a way to illustrate the concept of the ideal communication community in order to explicate the idea of validity as kind of rational acceptability. In conclusion, he states: "The model of a public sphere accessible to all participants, issues, and contributions comes closest to the notion envisaged" (Habermas 1991, 54).

The Internet in many ways comes quite close to the kind of model described here. Anyone can participate in discussions, any topic can be addressed, and no contribution can be permanently censored. Elsewhere, though, Habermas (1992, 316f.) criticizes Robert A. Dahl (1989), who advocates technological means for improving democratic processes, especially new communication technologies like televoting. (Obviously the future role of the Internet was not yet appreciated in 1989.)[96] Habermas considers Dahl's recommendations abstract and utopian (see Habermas 1992, 317). Yet if one looks past Dahl's specific (and also dated) proposals, opportunities for further democratization through telecommunications can be recognized that Habermas not only did not see in 1992, but which he has also yet to systematically deal with up to this point. Should it be disposed to investigate the conditions of the Internet, discourse ethics will be able to take advantage of untapped possibilities.

SOCIETY REQUIRES INTERNALIZED DISPOSITIONS FOR COOPERATION (DAVID GAUTHIER)

In his book *Morals by Agreement*, published in 1986, David Gauthier presented a widely discussed approach for justifying moral norms. Gauthier has himself modified this approach in certain aspects in his writings since about 1990 and now focuses to some extent on other concerns than those that were emphasized in his original work. Both the original approach and the modifications have arguments that are valuable from the point of view represented here and those that seem rather problematic. It is therefore worth taking a close look at Gauthier's position. I will begin by introducing his starting points for a functional moral justification ("Gauthier's point of departure for a functional justification of morality"). I then address his underlying conception of economics ("Gauthier's conception of economics") and his understanding of justice and the role of dispositions ("Gauthier on justice and dispositions") as well as his position with regard to the establishment of rights ("Gauthier, Locke, and Nozick: The status of rights"). This will outline all of the essential theoretical elements for assessing Gauthier's position. My critique will concern, on the one hand, the complications of dispositions given the issue of implementation ("Gauthier, Locke, and Nozick: The status of rights"), and, on the other hand, the sharp juxtaposition of duty and longer-term interests ("Criticism: Can't duty be understood as 'nothing more than' (longer-term) interest?").

Gauthier's Point of Departure for a Functional Justification of Morality

From an examination of the basic elements of Gauthier's position in *Morals by Agreement*, it is possible to identify, in a first step, four points that appear to be compatible with OE.

Gauthier's starting premise is largely consistent with that of OE: namely, that morality results from a society's functional requirements. Reasonable deliberations cause its members to want moral norms so that morality can be used to solve certain interaction problems. Gauthier makes clear that conflicts inevitably result in a society when everyone pursues their own interests. In particular, these conflicts include the prisoner's dilemma, which was thoroughly discussed in chapter 2. To Gauthier's way of thinking, morality was "invented" precisely for the resolution of prisoner's-dilemma situations. The *way*, however, in which morality comes into play at this point differs fundamentally from the conception of OE. I'll return to this point in the section "The problem of implementation in Gauthier: dispositions with respect to dilemma structures."

Second, Gauthier emphasizes that moral theory can be developed only on the basis of a theory of interactions and that a theory that instead analyzes the decision-making situation of a single actor as the basis for an ethical theory is not sufficient. Gauthier identifies an opposition between two types of rationality: *parametric rationality* (see Gauthier 1986, chapter II) and *strategic rationality* (see ibid. chapter III). While *parametric rationality* is only apparent in contexts lacking interaction, that is, in Robinson situations, *strategic rationality* designates a rationality type that is disclosed in interactions. Gauthier criticizes economic theory because it stops at *parametric rationality* (I will discuss this in the section "Gauthier's conception of economics"). His own morality, conversely, is developed on the basis of *strategic rationality* (this will be the subject of the section "Gauthier on justice and dispositions"). OE also emphasizes the importance of interactions and assumes a theoretical perspective that already presupposes at its core that interaction conflicts are a determining factor of human existence. Nonetheless, in contrast to Gauthier, the OE model does not construct different *types* of rationality. I will come back to this in the sections that follow.

Gauthier's third basic premise is that moral behavior and rational choice are by no means mutually exclusive. Gauthier (1986, 4) correctly points out that Rawls, who also centers on the relationship between morality and rational choice theory, considers both approaches with categorically distinct objects that in no way stand in a derivation relationship with each other.[97] The concept of *Morals by Agreement*, by contrast, is based on the idea of creating a truly functioning, rational market *through morality*. This means that morality can immediately enter into the calculations of rational actors and directly influence their rational behavior. OE also sees no fundamental conflict between morality and rational choice. However, Gauthier conceives of their relationship—for instance, in the case of the prisoner's dilemma—completely differently than OE. This is the subject of the section "Gauthier's conception of economics."

The fourth point concerns the relationship between the theory of "Morals by Agreement" and the existing moral intuitions in a society. Here, Gauthier notes—in contrast to most of the other authors discussed in this and in the next chapter—that a functioning morality must go beyond the scope of available intuitions. Unlike Rawls or Habermas, for instance, he does *not* see his primary task in providing a theory that is compatible with intuitions and could also be considered appropriate from the viewpoint of the actors in a modern society. Instead, the task of morality should be to also provide counterintuitive recommendations. When in doubt, according to Gauthier, theory should be trusted over intuitions (see Gauthier 1986, 269).[98] This claim can only be underscored by OE. It is not enough to design an intuition-compatible moral theory for the problems of a modern society. Intuitions are shaped by our cultural and biological origins. In other words, we come from a moral and social "mesocosm" (Vollmer 1983). We should therefore assume that all of these theories coming from the mesocosmos will abandon us when we attempt to apply them to a modern society.[99] A moral theory under modern conditions will also arrive at recommendations that are at least not *directly* linked to our moral intuitions. This linkage may occur indirectly insofar as these recommendations may be reconstructed under current conditions with regard to the implementation of traditional ideals like solidarity and justice. However, this relates only to basic ideals, not the widely shared ideas about how these ideals should be *applied*.

Gauthier's theory and OE are consequently quite similar in terms of their starting points. Both approaches consider morality as a possible functional means for controlling societies; both emphasize the importance of interactions; neither one sees a fundamental conflict between morality and rational choice; and neither one is opposed to the possibility that an ethical theory goes beyond present moral intuitions. Their differences, on the other hand, are already evident in Gauthier's conception of economics, which I will now address.

Gauthier's Conception of Economics

Because Gauthier set about the task of demonstrating the compatibility of morality and rational choice, he must turn to economics as a discipline that deals with rational choice behavior. His view of economics is informed by some preliminary theoretical points:

First, under economics Gauthier simply understands an idealized version of neoclassical theory. He contends that economics makes use of highly radical idealizations. It hence only knows the rational choice of individual actors, the *parametric choice*, not the choice that is made in interaction contexts, the *strategic choice* (see Gauthier 1986, chapter III). Furthermore, economics perceives the market as a "morally free zone" (Gauthier 1986, 13 and chapter IV) and as "moral anarchy" (Gauthier 1986, 84; italics omitted). It deals with the market as an idealized phenomenon that is characterized by the free, wholly unrestricted activity of its participants (see Gauthier 1986, 92) and recognizes no morality. This is the case for both the actions of its participants and even apparently the possible underlying structures or general frameworks, since such frameworks are by definition absent. Gauthier, accordingly, constructs a sharp opposition between the market and morality (see also Gauthier 1986, 13), aiming to illuminate with the ideal of the moral-free zone the possibility and the necessity of morality in a non-ideal world. The argument is as follows.

In the ideal world of the market, morality would neither be necessary, nor possible as an instrument of control. Interest conflicts between the actors would sort themselves out, since the market—according to Gauthier's reconstruction—would tie each individual's pursuit of her own self-interest with reciprocated and universal benefits, without any need of coercion. The establishment of a market without any restrictions would thus be sufficient for settling a conflict. However, because the real world does not actually correspond to the ideal of economics, it is necessary to place moral restrictions on the actors (see Gauthier 1986, 84). In the real world, there exists the phenomenon of market failure, which is illustrated by the prisoner's dilemma (see ibid. 103 and 116ff.). This phenomenon, Gauthier finds, is the source of morality. He contends that the individuals in the prisoner's dilemma recognize the need to cooperate *out of their own self-interest*. That is, they see that they have to coordinate their actions beyond the extent that is required in an ideal market. They must set limits themselves on their actions.

For Gauthier, in a first reconstructive step, the prospect of a world full of market failures results in the justification of morality out of self-interest. Gauthier finds that economics neglects problems of the prisoner's-dilemma type. Economists do not focus on the coordination problems that develop out of interactions, so that for these kinds of cases, it would make more sense to consult game theorists. As mentioned above, economics is only acquainted with *parametric rationality. Strategic rationality*, on the other hand, belongs to the domain of game theory.[100] The latter is also less restricted methodologically because it is not limited to using the *homo oeconomicus* as a tool of analysis. Because we are *not* in fact all *homines economici* (see ibid. 317 and 322f.), this is in fact only an unrealistic caricature. As for whether this caricature might be constructed for a specific purpose, the conception of *Morals by Agreement* has nothing to say on this point. The conception also systematically neglects the importance of institutions, and its understanding of economics is limited to the extent that it ignores institutional economics and related approaches. I will return to these concerns in the section "Gauthier, Locke, and Nozick: The status of rights" in the context of discussing the design of institutions.

It is also interesting to note that Gauthier does not assume that the introduction of the market leads to an erosion of morality. His opposition between morality and markets does not connote a theory of decline. Instead, morality serves to bring about a fully functioning market in an imperfect world. The next section will further elaborate on the access to Gauthier's moral justification.

Gauthier on Justice and Dispositions

Once again, for Gauthier the problem of morality arises due to market failures.[101] Individuals find that the general pursuit of self-interest leads to results that are unacceptable not just for some, but for *all* parties.

As a starting point for morality, two different lines of argument now emerge: Gauthier could either require (a) that individuals immediately restrict their self-interest *out of a "moral" intent*—either on their own or through coercion—or he could (b) call on individuals to make a better calculation of their own interests. Interestingly, Gauthier does not adopt path (a), which is followed by many of the approaches presented here. Gauthier believes rather that path (b) is the more viable of the two. He contends that individuals should agree to bind themselves to a certain principle of justice out of their own interest and that they will in fact do so. The internalization of this principle by all actors, then, will help situations of the prisoner's-dilemma type to be resolved in everyone's interest.

The two-tier system in Gauthier's conception should also be noted, which is, nonetheless, different from OE's, since institutions do not play a role. The proposed principle of justice is at first chosen by utility-maximizing actors out of their *own self-interest* (see Gauthier 1986, 145). Yet in the later actions of the same actors, it is precisely the same principle that *should also limit the pursuit of self-interest*. Out of self-interest, the actors decide to not pursue their self-interest at every opportunity (or without using certain methods).[102]

The substance of this principle of justice is determined by Gauthier as follows: it involves the principle of "minimax relative concession" or, in brief, the MRC principle (Gauthier 1986, 157). Each individual is then to follow an arrangement in which her highest relative concessions to others are minimized as much as possible. That means—and this is also shown formally by Gauthier (141ff, 1986)—that all actors would be interested (and act accordingly) in minimizing the negative effects of a worst-case scenario.[103]

Gauthier suggests that this MRC principle is supposed to be internalized by the individuals. The members of the society are supposed to acquire a disposition out of self-interest, which limits their concrete actions. This disposition is also known as the "idea of mutual benefit" (Gauthier 1986, 157), which the individuals must accept for a society to be able to function. This means Gauthier attempts to do justice to his original aim of demonstrating the compatibility of morality and rational choice by assuming that rational use-maximizing actors would give themselves definite dispositions that maximize their advantages (see Gauthier 1986, 182ff.).[104] The extent to which this idea can actually be implemented and the difficulties it would likely encounter are considered in the section "Gauthier, Locke, and Nozick: The status of rights."

In light of what has already been discussed, it is clear that *Morals by Agreement*—as the title indicates—does not provide a contract theory in the classical sense, but a *moral* theory.[105] Gauthier speaks of an original consent of the individuals. These actors, though, do not agree to a constitution, but rather to moral norms and their internalization.[106] By contrast, "genuine" contract theories, including those from Hobbes, Rawls, or Buchanan, attempt to establish *rules and institutions*.[107] Some of these theories, indeed, presuppose specific lived forms of morality (see, for instance, Rawls, chapter 4; on Buchanan, see the section "Society requires an ethic of work and an ethic of saving (James M. Buchanan)"), but none attempt to solve institutional problems of social cooperation directly by means of internalized dispositions.[108]

Gauthier, Locke, and Nozick: The Status of Rights

In terms of contract theories, a second area of correspondence exists. With regard to the status of rights, Gauthier endorses a position that sees rights as being prior to a contractual agreement. I will explain this in what follows.

In his remarks on the "initial bargaining position" (Gauthier 1986, chapter VII), Gauthier makes it plain that he considers it essential to assume, already in the state of the original contract (as far as one can meaningfully speak of this; see the section "Gauthier on justice and dispositions"), that there are universally accepted rights. Gauthier hence takes up the quasi-natural law position of Locke and Nozick. He speaks of a necessary "Lockean proviso" (Gauthier 1986, 202). This *proviso* states that the individuals may only have access to an initial endowment that was appropriated by every individual from the beginning without exploiting anyone else (ibid. 201ff.).[109] No portion of the initial endowment of A can be due to the fact that A took this portion from person B, unless A would have otherwise made his own situation worse in doing so. This means that each actor in the "initial bargaining position" is awarded his own sphere, a "moral space" (ibid. 202) that no one else is allowed to interfere with or take away. This corresponds to the position of Robert Nozick (1974). Gauthier, however, attenuates Nozick's requirement with the addition that the individual actor cannot be expected to experience a deterioration of his own position. Nevertheless, it remains the case that the original negotiating situation is already given certain conditions in advance. Gauthier explains this with the intention that was laid out in the section "Gauthier's conception of economics": the individuals maximized their benefits precisely because they accepted such conditions.

It will be noticed that the actors in the *initial bargaining position* are—like the actors in Rawls's *original position*—straightforward maximizers, not limited maximizers (this will be further explained in the following section). The actors in the *initial bargaining position* immediately accepted the "Lockean proviso" out of their own self-interest because they were under pressure from others, who were similarly pursuing their own interests. According to Gauthier, these others would not tolerate barriers, but instead prosecute rule breakers. In a sense, the *Lockean proviso* is therefore *self-enforcing* by way of self-interest. It would be accepted without further ado by all stakeholders.

Paradoxically, Gauthier situates himself precisely in the tradition of Hobbes with this Lockean position (cf. Gauthier 1986, 259).[110] He explains this as follows: Hobbes requires in the state of nature "*that every man, ought to endeavor Peace, as farre as he has hope of obtaining it; and when he cannot obtain it, that he may seek, and use, all helps, and advantages of Warre.*"[111] Gauthier interprets this to mean that the concern is with a requirement that individuals already accept in the natural state prior to the settlement of the contract. This thus exhibits the same status as his own Lockean *proviso*:

> What Hobbes envisages is a rational bargain in which each accepts certain constraints on his freedom of action so that all may avoid the costs of the natural condition of war. (Gauthier 1986, 159f.)

In my reading of Hobbes, his peace requirement is intended differently, namely, as a heuristic in the sense of OE. It is an instruction that only binds individuals *in foro interno*, that is, not yet in their actions. It is not a guide to action of the type that demands "keep the peace!" Hobbes neither says that the individuals are always bound to this requirement of peace, nor how this stipulation should be interpreted. Hobbes, as I understand him, does not by any means want to say that the requirement of peace excludes certain behaviors from the outset (i.e., for instance, the encroachment on others' initial endowments). It further seems to me that the acceptance of this requirement by individuals—if it even makes sense to speak of *acceptance*—has a completely different status than the acceptance of the *social contract* (in Hobbes) or the acceptance of the *Lockean proviso* (in Gauthier). Certainly, in the first case, the concern is with—in Hobbes's terminology—a "Law of Nature" (Hobbes, 1651/1991, 92), which, however, only says something about the *goals* of the individuals: everyone seeks their own betterment. Consequently, the first condition is peace. But the goals of individuals are initially only *in foro interno*. Thus what occurs in their actions *in foro externo* is not prejudiced.

In the latter case, the Hobbesian social contract like the *Lockean proviso must* be accepted per force because of its benefits (for society's members), or else the result will be anarchy. Still, Gauthier says that social cooperation—in terms of his MRC principle of justice—must be fair *in order to* produce stability (Gauthier 1986, 230). That is, he defines stability as a condition that is attributable to fair conditions, whereas fairness was *previously* determined *independently* of such stability. This will be examined further in the following.

The Problem of Implementation in Gauthier: Dispositions with Respect to Dilemma Structures

Gauthier recognizes that not all problems are solved with a demonstration of the use-maximizing dispositions of rationality. He realizes that the crucial question remains as to whether the individuals—even if they have assumed the appropriate dispositions—will actually persistently and systematically adjust their actions in the proper manner. It is not enough to simply postulate the internalization of this disposition. Gauthier, though, does not make any attempt to factually substantiate this internalization with psychological findings.[112] Instead, he sees the compliance problem as an entirely separate concern.

Gauthier characterizes this compliance or enforcement issue as being similar to the problem of Hobbes's *Foole*. Hobbes introduces the *Foole* (Hobbes 1651/1991, chapter 15) to show that the actors are not sufficiently motivated after the contract settlement to observe the contract later on. The *Foole* allows Hobbes to reject the assumption that there is a more or less "automatic" adherence to a contract that has been consented to. To be sure, the *Foole* sees that it is in the interest of everyone to abide by the contract, but, at the same time, he recognizes the evolving prisoner's dilemma: it would be better for the *Foole* if everyone were to stick to the contract, except for himself. Hobbes solves the problem of non-compliance with the threat of sanctions.

This solution, however, does meet with Gauthier's approval. He deems the threat of sanctions to be merely a political, not a moral, solution (Gauthier 1986, 163). Thus, a basic distinction between morality and interest that Gauthier repeatedly emphasizes is blurred: "Were duty no more than interest, morals would be superfluous."[113] At first, this sounds little more than a definitional problem. But there are profounder difficulties at issue. Gauthier stresses that, in order to have a guiding effect, morality cannot directly address the interests of the actors. Morality may *not* count on sanctions for its enforcement, but must be self-enforceable. This is because political solutions can be very expensive. Costs would accrue with regard to the monitoring and enforcement of the applicable arrangements (see Gauthier 1986, 164f.). The individual's voluntary moral compliance would be significantly cheaper. It would at least spare the need for *some* institutions.

This means that Gauthier is not against political or institutional solutions to interaction problems *in principle*. He assumes, however, (or at least hopes) that they will not always be necessary. Moral solutions should save costs for everyone. Therefore, Gauthier argues, everyone should recognize that morality is personally valuable and be guided by it. The observance of moral norms should be the best way for every individual to maximize her own benefits. The core idea is that the person who does not comply with the norms is exempted from cooperating with others and thus from the related gains. She risks being denied by the others of the opportunity to cooperate.

Gauthier remarks that to the extent that the individuals eventually learn that they would be cut out of any proceeds because of non-compliance, morality starts to emerge. The individuals internalize moral dispositions that limit their behavior. In this way, groups form of "*constrained maximizers*," who are confronted by the "*straightforward maximizers*" (see Gauthier 1986, 167). Gauthier's construction of the *constrained maximizers* is one of his key theoretical building blocks.[114]

Both types of actors—the *straightforward maximizer* (SM) as well as the *constrained maximizer* (CM)—maximize their benefits. But a CM maximizes her benefits under the condition that others will benefit as well. A CM adheres to previously agreed-upon moral norms when she assumes that her expected benefits resulting from a general compliance with these norms would be *greater* than if she were to act in as personally selective a manner as an SM. She thus puts up with the fact that individual actors defect, as long as this defection is not widespread. A CM will continue to cooperate, and defection is in fact *not* punished with counter-defection, as in a tit-for-tat strategy. An SM, however, always tries to *directly* maximize her benefits. She does not have internalized behavioral constraints that might cause her to yield to urges beyond those of her own self-interest. The difference between a CM and an SM can also be conceived slightly differently. I will return to this momentarily.

As Gauthier shows, CMs have an evolutionary advantage over SMs if in a society they are able to frequently meet with other CMs. The partners realize cooperation gains from such an interaction, which consequently makes them better off than non-cooperative SMs. In this way, Gauthier suggests, the CM disposition can spread in a society.[115]

However, when all other members of society are SMs, then individual CMs are unable to accomplish anything. Gauthier concedes that CMs must then in this case also behave like SMs. If everyone else behaves like Hobbes's *Foole*, then moral actions are not possible in Gauthier's view (see Gauthier 1986, 181f.). But, he emphasizes, this should not be understood to mean that a CM is basically nothing more than a shrewd SM, always keeping an eye on her own benefits, while ignoring the other stakeholders. A CM does not presume that she can count on the reciprocal cooperation of others for her cooperation. Instead, she cooperates even if she does *not* expect any positive "repayment" (ibid. 169f. and especially fn. 19), and she further does so because of her disposition, which makes her a moral actor. Moral action must therefore arise from such an independent disposition and be disconnected from any thoughts of the pros and cons, as it were.

It is precisely this *difference in motivation* that fundamentally distinguishes CMs and SMs. They each have different *natures*. The nature of a CM differs from the nature of an SM at its core. These natures are not completely fixed, because a CM indeed behaves in certain situations like an SM. It is a matter of the "relatively absolute" *personal* traits of individuals. Gauthier insists that the members of a society—at least the vast majority—must have certain *personal* traits (as a moral surplus value) so that a productive cooperation and a stable society can develop.

For Gauthier, the difference to contract-theoretical approaches in the classical sense also arises from his conception of *constrained maximizers*. As described in the section "Gauthier on justice and dispositions," Gauthier's approach cannot be described as a contract theory in the classical sense, but rather as a moral theory with contract-theoretical elements. Gauthier verifies this himself, for he clarifies his critique of the *homo economicus* by remarking that the *homo economicus* has a "*radically contractarian* view of human relationships" (Gauthier 1986, 319, emphasis in original). It treats all inanimate objects only as instruments for exploitation. Certainly, Gauthier notes, the *homo economicus* cannot instrumentalize people in the same way as it does objects. However, it does in fact do this when it lets itself be instrumentalized as a form of compensation. The *homo economicus*, consequently, only views other people as contracting partners with whom it interacts for the sake of mutually beneficial collaborations.[116] It considers all possible forms of human relationships only from this contractual perspective and constantly analyzes them to see if they may no longer serve his interests. Gauthier acknowledges the liberating effect of the idea that human beings no longer need to depend on the goodwill and collective emotions of others (see ibid.) The "economic man," though, represents an extreme version of this idea, since it can no longer voluntarily become involved in affective commitments. He possesses only "asocial motivation," that is, he is not motivated by the intrinsic value of human relationships. He is thus also "asocial" and even irrational, because—as Gauthier's sees it—it is rational for a person to comply with intrinsic values in order to serve her own self-interest.

Gauthier's moral surplus value—in the guise of moral dispositions—therefore ultimately helps to solve a stability problem.[117] This stability problem consists in the following set of facts.

According Gauthier, the rules of a society must be accepted and followed by everyone or at least a sufficient number of members of the society. If all members of a society were SMs, their acceptance of the rules would then be completely dependent upon whether these rules serve their short-term self-interest. However, since these personal interests can change—for example, today I am childless and single, whereas tomorrow I am a married father with very different interests—the level of acceptance of the rules must also constantly fluctuate. Gauthier contends that no modern society can be permanently stabilized on such an insecure basis.[118] In particular, for the sake of stability, the MRC principle of justice would have to be internalized by all actors (see Gauthier 1986, 179).

As part of the stability problem, Gauthier also includes the issue of how to bring about the internalization of such personal traits. Like Habermas, albeit for different reasons, he stresses that the acceptance of social norms and informal rules must occur without force. If coercion in the form of sanctions were needed to secure this acceptance, this would result in unproductive transfers in a society. Sanctions are unproductive per se because the resources they utilize would not be required if everyone adhered to the sanctioned rules. Such unproductive transfers would find little acceptance overall, since the individuals would not appreciate having to permanently spend resources to force others (and ultimately themselves) to comply with the rules. The others, it is argued, would have to realize that a failure to comply over the long run would mean a self-inflicted increase in the shared expenses. The resources being "squandered" here could be used more productively elsewhere.

The result of these kinds of considerations is supposedly that no reliable agreement on sanctions can be made. Consequently, when sanctions are relied on as the only guarantee of rule compliance, there is a risk of instability (see Gauthier 1986, 197f.). As shown, transfers and sanctions would meet with little acceptance and thus would not provide a reliable basis. The guarantee that individuals would follow the rules of a society must stem from other sources than self-interest.

The following point emerges in connection with the stability problem: If Gauthier is concerned with the *functional* problem of how to keep a society stable, then he would also have to allow this problem to be studied by other disciplines. He would also have to concede that it depends on the findings of these disciplines as to whether a society whose members do *not* have certain dispositions can remain stable. *If* economics, for instance, manages to construct a system of institutions that does not collapse even if everyone actually acts like *straightforward maximizers*, then Gauthier would have to reconsider his position.

I do not intend to suggest here that designing such an institutional system would actually be successful. For the moment, I want to stress that Gauthier's thesis of the necessity of moral dispositions depends on the analysis of the stability problem and will, indeed, stand or fall by it. And this is a question, moreover, for the positive sciences. The following section will center on the issue of whether it is not in fact possible for a society of *straightforward maximizers* to also preserve its stability and persist over the long term.

Criticism: Can't Duty Be Understood as "Nothing More Than" (Longer-term) Interest?

The chief flaw of *Morals by Agreement* is the stance it takes on the issue of how individuals, when faced with dilemma structures, can be brought into successful compliance with norms that were once recognized as rational. Gauthier himself explicitly raises the issue of compliance: "The genuinely problematic element in a contractarian theory is not the introduction of the idea of morality, but the step from hypothetical agreement to actual moral constraint" (Gauthier 1986, 9).

As shown, the problem of dilemma structures is supposed to be resolved by the general internalization of moral dispositions. It remains uncertain, however, why the dilemmas would not reappear with the same intensity, even given the successful internalization of these dispositions. How can Gauthier discount the possibility that there might be individuals who only *pretend* to be morally disposed, but who do not actually cooperate with the others?[119] And if such secret defections can be expected, then it is doubtful whether those who are morally disposed would be able to maintain their dispositions. Gauthier admits that a CM who winds up in a population of SMs would also have to act like an SM. Yet he appears to assume that it would be sufficient if there were a large number of CMs already present (see Gauthier 1986, 182ff.).[120] How many would need to be present as cooperation partners? Gauthier does not give a figure, but the statement also cannot be found anywhere that *one* defector would be enough to overturn moral norms established through internalized dispositions. Still, it is precisely this logic that makes the prisoner's dilemma a central concern in modern societies.

The individual actor has so much power in a modern society, particularly under the conditions of globalization (as described in chapter 1), that she is in a position to destroy institutions. What's more, a *potential* defector is sufficient for causing others to begin preventative counter defections (see the section "Order ethics as an ethics of benefits and incentives"). This suggests that the mere *possibility* there could be an SM in a society would be enough to overturn an institution that is meant to be enforced in terms of the model of *Morals by Agreement*, that is, by means of internal dispositions. If we all act as *straightforward maximizers*, then the dispositions of the CMs are in grave danger. This also implies the following: if Gauthier really takes dilemma structures and the behavior of actors in such situations seriously, he must abort his attempt at a solution. At any rate, he offers contingent solutions, not systematic ones.

A solution to the implementation problem à la Hobbes, however, absolutely does not come into question for Gauthier. As we have seen, Gauthier considers the enforcement of moral standards through incentives and sanctions to be merely a political, and not a moral, solution. This begs the question of what a moral solution would have to look like. How can recognized rational norms be enforced without sanctions? Does *Morals by Agreement* present here an alternative that goes beyond the postulated dispositions?

In the last chapter ("The Liberal Individual"), there are outlines of such an alternative. Gauthier believes that "the liberal individual"—who represents his prototype—is not just an "economic man," but is morally affected and *voluntarily* enters into cooperative relationships with others (see Gauthier 1986, 346). This individual remains faithful to moral norms, while *simultaneously* maximizing his benefits. However, she cannot be aware of the essentially instrumental role of morality—of its ultimate role in maximizing benefits (ibid. 339). If this were to happen, then one would have to expect that morality would be undermined. Norms could no longer be adhered to that could be regarded as intrinsically valuable.

Gauthier therefore adds a further enforcement power, namely, education. The following remark is made more or less in passing, but its importance to the overall approach can hardly be overstated [121]:

> [A]n essentially just society must be strengthened through the development of the affections and interests of the young. (ibid. 351)

A moral solution appears to be invoked here that does not require sanctions and that one should fall back on if the society of liberal individuals is not functioning properly. [122] Yet even if education can be a key factor, one has to wonder whether *enforcement* will not, in the end, finally take place through sanctions. Aren't sanctions used in the course of educating young people? But perhaps Gauthier means education more in the sense of Habermas's unforced force of the better argument? (See the section "Society requires rational motivation for life forms capable of ideal role taking and constitutional patriotism (Jürgen Habermas)"; as we have seen, some remarks hint at this.) In this case, then, the earlier criticism of Gauthier would still be valid, as it applies equally to Habermas (see the section "Criticism: And what if a performative contradiction does not disturb me?"). Specifically, even though the implementation problem is indeed initially detected and/or raised (at least by Gauthier), its effects are ultimately underestimated. [123] The introduction of dispositions can only be a stopgap measure. Binmore further comments that Gauthier's dispositions reflect the invention of a nonexistent enforcement mechanism. [124] One could also say that a morality that only works because of the fact that its mechanism is not transparent establishes a taboo. It cannot have a future.

Besides neglecting the implementation problem, Gauthier makes the following second error: he commits nirvana fallacies. Improper analogies are thus identified in economics in which *idealized* arrangements or distributions are related to *actually existing* institutional arrangements or property distributions. The actually existing phenomena are thus determined to be inefficient from the outset. This means that the benchmarks that are used do not represent any feasible alternatives because they cannot be realized. These idealized benchmarks specifically do not have the status of realizable alternatives, as they are designed for other purposes. [125] If they are utilized within the context of an invalid nirvana fallacy, then consequential results are no longer possible. For if all actually existing phenomena only appear to be inefficient, a meaningful assessment cannot take place. Even if the objection is raised that actual arrangements can be assessed as inefficient in graduated steps, the desire would always remain to adjust even the least inefficient arrangements in terms of the ideal, whether or not this could be carried out with a reasonable effort. A nirvana fallacy accordingly usually leads to problems being structured in a way that is not suited to their solution and which typically favors and reinforces thinking in terms of mistaken dualisms.[126]

Gauthier uses such an ill-advised comparison in the arguments he makes to rebut the objection of Hobbes's *Foole* (see the section "Gauthier, Locke, and Nozick: The status of rights"). The *Foole* insists that compliance with the law can only be achieved if direct benefits are presented to those subjugated to the law. According to Gauthier, however, this is in reality a political, and not a moral solution, that involves the high costs of monitoring and enforcement (see Gauthier 1986, 164f.). It would be much cheaper and hence more beneficial for everyone if we were all to observe the laws voluntarily without the threat of sanctions. It goes without saying that a comparison is being made here to an extraneous alternative, for the structure of the prisoner's dilemma (see the section "Order ethics as an ethics of benefits and incentives") in fact stipulates the unenforceability of voluntary compliance. What sense does it make to hope that a prisoner's dilemma could be resolved without sanctions? To contemplate this, in my view, resembles a scientist or an engineer who might entertain the possibility that the construction of a skyscraper could indeed be cheaper if only the laws of gravity would change. In this case, the building would no longer be in danger of falling over, but could remain standing on its own. If it is not possible to assume that sanctions can be waived, then their establishment *is*—in a strict economic sense!—efficient. Interaction structures of the prisoner's-dilemma type, consequently, are to be included among the limiting conditions that must be considered in the design of institutional arrangements and sanctions. These constraints have to be observed in a way that is analogous to the natural laws, and the efficient solution is the one that is preferred under these limiting conditions in relation to the relevant alternatives. It cannot be helpful to already dismiss those conditions during the construction of the problem, for instance, by means of convenient postulates.

A second candidate for a nirvana fallacy is found in Gauthier's discussion of the initial endowment of the actors at the time of the original contract settlement. To distinguish certain parts of this endowment (by means of the *Lockean proviso* discussed earlier) as reflecting pre-contractual assets that cannot be impinged upon by the other actors, Gauthier constructs a so-called *base point*. This base point identifies a specific endowment of goods, namely, those that the individual actor would have access to if the others did not exist (see Gauthier, 1986, 204 and 209). It therefore encompasses Robinson's endowment. Each individual would have to recognize this base point as the fundamental endowment of everyone else before the contract settlement. Who, however, would ensure that the inviolability of this base point would be respected? Wouldn't institutions and sanctions have to be created? And even if she sees her own base point as just or fair, why wouldn't A still doubt the base point of B and try to take away part of B's initial endowment? And if B anticipates the behavior of A, wouldn't she already demand negotiations up front on the base point of A? Once again, then, an extraneous alternative is at issue, namely, the base point. We cannot assume that individuals will actually use this base point as a means of making comparisons. Just the same, this particular case is somewhat different than the case that is alluded to in the argument against Hobbes's *Foole*. Here, the concern is with a comparison that the *individuals* (usually) would not make themselves. In the previous case, the comparison was one that *theorists* could not meaningfully construct. Nonetheless, the feature they share is the comparison with an extraneous alternative.[127] By contrast, the only basis point that OE uses is the Hobbesian "Right to everything" (Hobbes, 1651/1991, 91), which everyone has in their natural state. In modern terms: everyone has the potential to defect.

A third criticism relates to Gauthier's understanding of economics. He obviously has a very limited view of the discipline.[128] This is reflected in the fact that he understands the market as an ideal of a state of "freedom from morality" (as suggested by the title of chapter IV) and makes the sweeping generalization that economics' role is to represent this ideal. As Gauthier sees it, economics recognizes the full market as the only ideal conception of human interactions and therefore associates with it the real-world demand of eliminating all possible (legal) restrictions on interactions (see Gauthier 1986, 83ff.). All these restrictions would prevent the "free play of forces" from doing its work and potentially bringing the private interests into perfect harmony. Here, Gauthier relies on Smith. The laissez-faire school (which goes back to Smith) confers on the state the right to encroach upon the freedom of the individual only if the market needs to be protected from coercion and fraud (ibid. 92). The market thus constitutes the *antithesis* to a prisoner's dilemma. Whereas the market perfectly harmonizes the various interests, the prisoner's dilemma inevitably fails in this regard (see ibid. 83).

Several issues should be separated out here for our analysis. First, it is doubtful whether Smith has been correctly interpreted. For in the overall conception of the *Wealth of Nations* there is strong, explicit evidence that he does not have in mind such an ideal market that is free of restrictions, but rather girds the market with a regulatory framework. Smith notes that the duties of the state include, for instance, the maintenance of *property rights*, the fostering of commercial and price freedom (see Smith 1776/1976, book I, 133ff., 69f.) and free trade (ibid. book IV, 107ff.) and the guarantee of education (ibid. book V, 282ff.).[129]

Second, there is a question as to whether one can impute the laissez-faire ideal to economics as a whole. Constitutional economics, for instance, specifically emphasizes the importance of a regulatory framework. Here, Gauthier's limited view of economics is especially noticeable, as he apparently only has certain neoclassical variants in mind.

Third, the systematic problem remains of whether the market—which is also to say the ideal of the full market—*must* be conceived of as a state of "freedom without morality." Gauthier resorts here to using drastic language: the market embodies moral anarchy (see ibid. 84). With reference to OE, Gauthier's statements may be interpreted as follows: in a market economy, morality definitely cannot be found in the behavior of the actors. The actors are subject to competitive pressures and thus continually find themselves in dilemma situations.[130] They are *not* capable of acting morally *against* the incentives that emerge from these situations. This does not mean that the market is free of morality in its entirety. Morality may be discovered again in another systematic space, namely, in the market conditions. Moral intuitions are integrated into these conditions by way of their institutionalized enforcement. Gauthier, by contrast, assumes that economics *neglects* the required conditions. From a phenomenalistic vantage point, he sees only the phenomenon of the market and thus, in a sense, just the tip of the iceberg. He does not reconstruct the market's underpinnings—the numerous requirements and conditions that support the market and the individuals acting within it.[131] For instance, the organization of an anti-trust division sets up moral norms because it is in the interest of everyone (even those who are worst off) that competition is ensured and monopolies are prevented.[132] It is true that competition—like any dilemma situation—may bring forth results that are not desired by any of the affected parties. The establishment of suitable conditions, however, can channel competition in a way that benefits everyone. The task of economics is to construct such conditions. Economics is therefore given a moral task, at least if one is able to assume that moral norms must also be *enforceable*. What's more, only economic analysis as an estimate of the impact of alternative rule systems can ensure enforceability under conditions of globalization.

OE explicitly anticipates the possibility that all actors will act as *straightforward maximizers*. Just the same, is it possible to identify a systematic location for Gauthier's underlying ideas, particularly with regard to the dispositions for cooperation that are necessary for the preservation of social stability?

Within the scope of OE, these dispositions can be ascribed a heuristic function. The search for new institutional arrangements in order to exploit new opportunities for cooperation and for the realization of new cooperation gains must be guided by ideas. Institutional reforms are partly based on ideas derived from existing (remnant) moral inventories in the society. Undoubtedly many of the social reforms of the nineteenth and twentieth century (pension, health, unemployment insurance) developed in response to moral criticism of conditions that were considered untenable.

It must be clearly pointed out, however, that such a heuristic under OE cannot, strictly speaking, be attributed to a moral surplus value that would be absolutely necessary for keeping a society stable. Rather—as described in the section "Order ethics as an ethics of benefits and incentives"—a heuristic is simply a *guideline* that makes it possible for members of a society to even notice new, additional opportunities for cooperation. Such a rule of thumb cannot be determined in advance and cannot be fixed. It must rather be modified according to the empirical conditions, and also especially the implementation conditions. Above all, though, a heuristic is frequently informed by the resources of an already existing moral tradition, although this is not necessarily always the case. It is not possible to specify in advance which norms are capable of being implemented or which are not. This is, instead, the task of (a mostly) economic analysis. Gauthier, conversely, tries to pin down dispositions for cooperation and existing human abilities and also determine their content. Substantively, however, he does not go beyond addressing everyday plausibilities.[133] Even more problematic is his formal definition of dispositions, which are supposedly *independent* of limiting conditions such as sanctions (see the section "Gauthier on justice and dispositions"). This, however, does not apply to a heuristic in the sense described above.

In this context, a possible accommodation between OE and *Morals by Agreement* might look like the following: Gauthier would first have to modify his substantive ideas of cooperative arrangements or at least make them more flexible. On the other hand, he would have to concede that dispositions can depend on empirical limiting conditions, which include incentives and sanctions. Only then can dilemma situations really be taken seriously, and only then can the control challenges facing modern societies even be tackled in a meaningful way.

At this point, a further fundamental difference becomes apparent between OE and Gauthier: where OE obviously has a broad understanding of ethics, Gauthier's view is quite restricted. Gauthier believes that if a person agrees to sanctions as an enforcement mechanism, then she also departs from the realm of ethics and, it would seem, morality.[134] Here, OE responds that enforcement is ultimately not possible without sanctions. Indeed, without at least informal sanctions, it has traditionally never been possible.

SOCIETY REQUIRES SHARED FEELINGS OF SYMPATHY AND SOLIDARITY (RICHARD RORTY)

Rorty has been a key figure in the philosophical discussion on both sides of the Atlantic for some time.[135] His earlier writings were mostly dedicated to the area of theoretical philosophy, epistemology, and philosophy of science. However, he has had considerable influence in Germany with regard to the relationships between theoretical and practical philosophy and the linkage of epistemological questions to the structures and the legitimation mechanisms of democratic societies. It has moreover become rather clear, perhaps given his numerous political statements, that Rorty can only be meaningfully understood against the backdrop of his social-philosophical theories.

Rorty's relevance to the subject of this book lies primarily in his (at least prima facie) critical posture in relation to many traditional and widely held philosophical viewpoints. This will be the subject of the first section ("Contingency and irony: Renouncing reason"). In the second section ("Solidarity: The source of shared experiences of suffering"), the foundations of Rorty's theories of social philosophy will then be introduced, according to which social integration primarily occurs on the basis of feelings of sympathy and solidarity (as a source of the experience of suffering). I will then finally criticize this viewpoint in the third section ("Criticism").

Contingency and Irony: Renouncing Reason

Rorty sees himself—and is often seen (cf. Malachowski 2002)—as a "renouncer" of many ideas from the well of the philosophical tradition. To be sure, many of these ideas have already been repeatedly discarded in the past, especially by Nietzsche, American pragmatism, and French poststructuralism. Nonetheless, Rorty (once again) summarizes the findings of multiple traditions in a thoroughly original way:

1. The concept of truth—crudely put—is resolved by "objectivistic" connotations. Truth is equated with successful problem solving.
2. "Reason" (in an emphatic sense), on the other hand, is primarily relativized as a problem-solving instrument to the point of its complete exclusion from having any determinative behavioral and social role.

Rorty explicitly targets analytical philosophy here, that for him represents the school which has assumed the mantle of the Enlightenment and devoted itself to the tradition of justification through reason.[136] Rorty (1989) believes this tradition to be at its end, understanding it as a liberal view to take the outcome of such disputes as true. Truth does not start out as something that is to be determined independently of such social "disputes" (more broadly understood: interactions). Instead, what is declared to be true is what in hindsight has worked or won out.

The second point is especially relevant for this book. Explicitly distancing himself from theorists like Rawls, Rorty intends to attenuate the reliance on reason in discussions within democratic societies. Reason should not be opposed to democratic decision making. Here, the role of practicality mentioned earlier comes to the fore, as indeed does the role of political philosophy as an essential discipline for philosophy in general. The notion of disposing with faculties like reason as a source of external evaluative criteria of democratic arrangements is also largely compatible with OE.

Rorty's central concept here is "contingency." He recognizes three types of contingency: the contingency of language, the contingency of the self, and the contingency of a liberal polity. The first two—the contingency of language and that of the self—can only be introduced here briefly.

With regard to language, Rorty interprets the evolution of philosophy since idealism as an increasing recognition of the "self-createdness" of truth by and for human beings. Truth is "made"—just as art is "made"—and should not be understood as an imitation of nature. The analytical philosophy of language since Wittgenstein also ultimately deconstructed language as a tool. It showed both its uses and its limitations. It also demonstrated that there is no one adequate language that can be determined to be better than all other languages for describing our world—hence, the fundamental thesis about the contingency of language. However, Rorty goes a step further by dispensing with the requisite clear goals of language identified in the analytical tradition (for instance: communication, justification, argumentation, explanation). If one follows Rorty, language is totally contingent: it is basically "spontaneous," developing without clear aims and objectives (and is thus analogous, implicitly not explicitly, to the unintended consequences of purposive behavior analyzed by economics).

The contingency of the self is related to psychology and morality. In this regard, Rorty calls upon Freud, among others. This understanding of the self as heteronomous, but in no way self-positing in the sense of idealist thought is nothing new. Nonetheless, Rorty particularly stresses Freud's anti-reductionist perspective. To the extent that Freud elevates narratives—and what is especially relevant to Rorty's analysis, narratives about cruelty—to the level of theory and devotes considerable space to them, he represents for Rorty the antipode of a Hobbesian (and thus also an ultimately economic) point of view. This latter approach is reductionist (see, for instance, Rorty 1989, 31): it reduces human beings (although Rorty does not say explicitly how) and does not (as I further interpret Rorty) seem to take the contingency of the self seriously. It rather once again attempts to attribute this self to a different constitutive element. Rorty, however, finds that it would be more appropriate to examine the complexity of the self and its narratives in a Freudian or related manner. This is the path that Rorty wants to take himself.

The contingency of a liberal polity is finally the decisive concept in this instance, for it suggests that calling upon shared values to stabilize a democratic society is futile (Rorty 1989, 51f. and 54ff.). Whoever argues in favor of a liberal polity today[137] can neither rely on truth, nor rationality, nor a sense of moral obligation. All of these "values" have become contingent and enervated. Rorty turns to, among others, Isaiah Berlin and his theory—roughly stated—of the necessary (recognition of and) education in contingency.[138] According to this theory, the continuation of liberal polities primarily depends on their members learning to recognize irresolvable interpersonal conflicts about fundamental values for what they are, and (possibly despite this) to specifically not allow their behavior in response to be determined by metaphysical beliefs suggesting the compatibility of these values.

Rorty's main interest is in a new, more appropriate self-description for modern societies. OE has this goal as well: it similarly finds that societies today suffer from inadequate (moral) categories, which are taken as the basis for discussing these societies. Just the same, OE argues that ethical categories need to be reoriented toward a justification of benefits and incentive mechanisms (see, for instance, Homann 2002). Rorty has another goal in mind: he believes that the self-description of a modern society should be informed by aesthetic and poetic sources rather than those linked to reason.[139] With regard to argumentation, what matters most is developing suggestive arguments and plausible metaphors. Along these lines, it should be possible to affect a verbally renewed form of society with artistic methods. I will discuss this in greater detail in the following section.

The goals of Rorty's conception are tolerance and stability: tolerance in reference to different values (see Rorty 1998) and stability despite different values. In this respect, Rorty again agrees with OE, which does not specify that stability can only be achieved with the right arguments, for the right reasons. This last point of view, which Rorty ascribes to Rawls,[140] is not understood by Rorty as being either necessary or possible. As I see it, Rorty can be understood as making a case for precisely the type of constitutional consensus as a basis of modern societies that Rawls rejects as insufficient. So long as the individuals adhere to the constitution's underlying principles, it is not the task of theory to determine how they can obtain this constitutional consensus or how they should behave in private. As Rorty writes:

> The closest we will come to joining these two quests is to see the aim of a just and free society as letting its citizens be as privatistic, "irrationalist," and aestheticist as they please so long as they do it on their own time—causing no harm to others and using no resources needed by those less advantaged. . . . The vocabulary of self-creation is necessarily private, unshared, unsuited to argument. (Rorty 1989, xiv)

Thus the individuals must respectively create themselves "anew" on the basis of their own beliefs—but they cannot disadvantage others in the process. OE describes it this way: I may not put others at a disadvantage precisely because I will otherwise not receive their consent. So far, Rorty's position appears consistent with OE. Nevertheless, the quote above contains several formulations that go beyond its parameters: What does Rorty mean by the requirement that only the time can be used that belongs to an individual herself and, above all, by the statement that no resources can be used that the less advantaged need. Need in what sense? Who decides this? It may be the case that this can be reformulated in reference to a conception of consent, in which those who are worse off do not give their consent when they are denied resources. This is consistent with Rawls's second principle of justice (see, for instance, Section "Rawls's theory of justice and its connection to order ethics").

Yet, in that case, one should do away with the concept of "need" entirely, for it contains too many subjectivistic connotations. What a person "needs" can vary, depending on utility and (opportunity) costs. Rorty's fundamental point is shared by OE nevertheless. The quote above is (also) directed at analytical moral philosophy—against those representatives of metaethics who believe, according to Rorty, that they can subject private vocabulary to (if not public then at least) philosophical analysis with the purpose of determining, and separating from each other, "rational" and "irrational"[141] modes of argument. Rorty argues that we cannot find a normative basis for modern societies along this path—at least nothing that is viable over the long term. In the language of OE: the implementation problem in these approaches is not found at the beginning, but at the end of the analysis (if it is taken into account at all).

Rorty could conclude that a normative justification of democracy must be grounded in (reciprocal) advantages. He does not do this, however. Instead, as already indicated, he wants to deliberately turn away from theoretical justifications in favor of practical ones. These practical justifications are based on narratives, especially those concerning the evolutionary history of liberal institutions (see, for instance, Rorty 1989, 68) and the people who in the past have acted on their behalf. One might even say they are based on the myth of liberalism. Myths like these certainly play a greater role in the democracy of the United States than, for instance, in (contemporary) Germany. The myths surrounding George Washington, Abraham Lincoln, or Martin Luther King are only a few examples. Rorty, however, not only relies on these kinds of narratives, but also, more generally, on the transmission of experiences of suffering that, in his view, can be shared and sympathized with (obviously as an anthropological fact) by everyone. This leads to the following considerations.

Solidarity: The Source of Shared Experiences of Suffering

Although the first two aspects of Rorty's theory—contingency and irony—do not present any problems from OE's perspective and are indeed very much welcomed, the third aspect—solidarity—seems much more problematic. One might also say that Rorty is correct in his critique of other social philosophical conceptions, but that his constructive dimension is noticeably lacking. In this section, I will first introduce this constructive dimension of Rorty's theory of solidarity, whereas his critique will be discussed in the section that follows ("Solidarity: The source of shared experiences of suffering").

In Rorty's view, modern societies are not integrated through reason (or reason-based justifications) or formal rules, but rather through feelings of solidarity (see, for instance, Rorty 1989, 91f., 93). Social cohesion in modern societies is thus only ensured when their members feel like they are in solidarity with others.[142] These feelings are supposed to be awakened, which can only occur when a given society continually "creates" and defines itself anew on the basis of myths, on the basis of common narratives.

Here, Rorty turns to shared and communicable experiences of suffering and feelings, to "sad and sentimental stories" (Rorty 1998, 172):

> Victims of cruelty, people who are suffering, do not have much in the way of language. That is why there is no such thing as the "voice of the oppressed" or "the language of the victims." The language the victims used once is not working anymore, and they are suffering too much to put new words together. So the job of putting their situation into language is going to have to be done for them by somebody else. The liberal novelist, poet, or journalist is good at that. The liberal theorist usually is not. (Rorty 1989, 94)

Rorty finds examples for what he has in mind in the works of Dickens, Orwell, or Nabokov.[143]

Especially crucial here is the notion—as already mentioned in the discussion on Freud (see the section "Contingency and irony: Renouncing reason")—that "self-creation narratives" should teach that cruelty is fundamentally bad, and for this purpose they should primarily draw upon historical experiences of cruelty.[144] Rorty's definition of a liberal person stems from the following perspective: a liberal is someone who fundamentally rejects cruelty (see Rorty 1989, xv).

At the risk of anticipating my later critique, I would like to already mention here that the rejection of cruelty may very well be suited to a conception of liberalism, but also that such a determination marginalizes essential aspects of a liberal position. Liberalism, in my view, is thus better defined as a position that has universal consent as its single normative criterion (and this again can be attributed to the pervasiveness of dilemma structures in modern societies).[145]

This approach, which is based on an interaction theory, does not appeal to Rorty. His own approach is more oriented toward the individual, which I will discuss in greater detail in the next section. Its payoff is finally realized in its emphasis on the aesthetic element in the process of communicating myths and thus feelings of solidarity. An aestheticized culture that has irony as a primary stylistic tool is, in his opinion, at least one essential key for social stability. Rorty thus, to a certain extent, shifts the burden within philosophy from its epistemological and metaphysical side (and justifications based on reason) to its aesthetics side.

This aestheticized culture is supposed to communicate secularized values. For Rorty, secularization is a value in itself, not something that *implies* values and social control through values. This brings us to my critique of Rorty, which is the focus of the following section.

Criticism

The primary weakness of Rorty's conception lies in the fact that it remains at the level of individual ethics. Despite his criticism of rational-ethical justifications, Rorty ultimately only exchanges one individual-ethical justification for another. The switch to an institutional or order-ethical paradigm does not take place. In contrast to some of the other approaches discussed here (see sections "Society needs shared values (material value-ethics)" and "Society requires a shared conception of humanity as a basis for virtues (Philippa Foot)"), the reasons are less due to Rorty's failure to recognize the implementation problem (which is reflected to some extent, for instance, in "the precedence of democracy over philosophy").[146] In my view, the reason has rather to do with Rorty's insufficient understanding of the factors that provide for a society's stability.

The desire to integrate a society through feelings of solidarity shows that the phenomenon of pluralism—especially under the conditions of globalization—is not taken seriously. Even if we could impute universality to feelings of solidarity, the essential difficulty would remain of universally determining the type of feelings of solidarity and their scope. Would this occur via the members of a given community (or communities) or a given society? These feelings would necessarily show varying intensities, scopes, and other characteristics depending on the society, and perhaps also depending on the local community.

Rorty could certainly wholly agree with this, while also offering the following response: the feelings of solidarity can vary, but they also keep the respective societies together in different ways. They are well adapted to the local conditions, and benefits and incentives are furthermore ultimately manifested in different ways. This, however, gives rise to the following reply: it is certainly true that feelings of solidarity must be manifested locally, yet the decisive consideration is how the rules are developed. Feelings of solidarity may have an impact if the prevailing conditions are "correct." Still, they may also have no impact at all, erode, or even bring about the opposite of the intended (moral) effects (Mafia effects)[147] if the rules reward it. And it is precisely this transition to a type of control by means of rules that Rorty cannot, or will not, commit to. He cannot bring himself to finally acknowledge that the reasons for (and causes of) a society's stability lie in its system of rules. Certainly, Rorty thoroughly addresses this topic,[148] yet it is also repeatedly rejected. He holds fast (normatively) to the view that if it is not a shared capacity for reason that can provide the basis for a modern society's development then it must be shared *feelings*. Be that as it may, this foundation is not convincing: it strongly smacks of immediate normative recourse that goes from the level of moral-philosophical postulates to that of behavioral (and not rule-directed) control. Such a position, however, cannot do justice to the problems of modern societies; it must finally deteriorate into a normativistic "appellitis" (see, for instance, Luhmann 1986). Rorty correctly rejects a justification of moral norms through reason in an emphatic sense. Then again, his alternative of doing away completely with justifications is only apparent. Why shouldn't the concept of justification be substantively redefined? A justification on the basis of reciprocal advantages—that is, on the basis of self-interest—would appear to me to offer a completely adequate substitute here.

Rorty not only cannot complete the transition to an institutional-ethical paradigm, but he also does not consider self-interest to be an engine of solidarity and stability. Rorty ultimately distrusts self-interest when it is freed from any commitment to (Western) values (see, for instance, Rorty 1989, 84ff.). Here, he argues in a way that is highly analogous to precisely those rationalist approaches (see, for instance, Rawls, chapter 4) he rejects.

On the whole, Rorty falls back on a variant of anthropological theories of modern societies. He finally appeals to that quality of human beings that is supposedly somehow calibrated to feelings of solidarity. Unlike the classical theories of this type, he calls less on certain psychic or physical characteristics, but rather ultimately on an aesthetic sense, especially with regard to those narratives and myths that communicate experiences of suffering. Rorty's moral surplus value thus consists in the shared feelings of sympathy and solidarity that are transmitted in this manner.

I find another difficulty on this point, however, for it is not clear just what the myths are supposed to do. Myths can be utilized for many different tasks—even for those that are nondemocratic (consider the Nazis' exploitation of myths). In my view, the extent to which democratic uses of myths can be distinguished from other types of uses is not made sufficiently clear.

This problem can also be attributed to the fact that Rorty's original premise does not systematically deal with the phenomenon of pluralism. Rorty rather begins by focusing on the increasing contingency of earlier rational certainties. One could say that those rationally grounded norms and discoveries could no longer be justified by reason. Rorty thus rejects their justification and the concept of justification in general. He does not do so in a definitive manner, however, because he fears that other norms and insights could be given equal status to the earlier ones. He appears to prefer that we decide about contingent norms on the basis of certain feelings. By the same token, it is repeatedly emphasized that these norms should finally reflect basic Western norms.

Rorty's approach could likely be reinterpreted and assessed positively within the framework of OE. Myths and narratives of experiences of suffering can take on a heuristic function by drawing attention to social problems and suggesting institutional reforms. Books such as Rachel Carson's *Silent Spring* and others have contributed significantly to the success of the eco-movement and thus in the end to the implementation of ecological standards. Narratives like these, though, cannot be used for example within the scope of OE to provide definite answers to social problems, but instead for working out processual and rule-based aspects.[149]

Depending on artistic products to meet social objectives remains a gamble, however, particularly when it is also done in the interest of promoting social enlightenment. The philosophy of art and music has repeatedly shown that works of art (like musical compositions) resist simple attempts to have them put to social use. This still does not imply a distrust of artists as "unreliable partners"; it does, however, reflect the recognition that works of art follow their own logic, for they treat different problems and have other target groups than scientific theories or practical proposals for reform.

NOTES

1. Hösle writes that he has cited the "relevant social sciences" (Hösle 1997, 18), and claims, unlike other philosophers, to integrate into his approach "the material insights of those social scientists regarding the functional laws of social systems" (ibid. 15). Nevertheless, there is virtually no reference to economics, except for perhaps a brief mention of New Political Economy (ibid. 754), which is acknowledged as having a bona fide theory that, just the same, describes what Hösle also bemoans: the pervasive egoism of bureaucrats, politicians, and the like.

2. Morality is the "final legitimate authority" (ibid. 115), and even criticism of morality can itself only be carried out by again invoking morality. The normative sphere is "not surpassable" (ibid. 116).

3. Hösle sees Luhmann as his main opponent, sharply rejecting the latter's insistence on the incompatibility of the codes of the subsystems' morality and economics and others (see also Hösle 1997, 218).

4. See also his article in *Der Spiegel* (Hösle 2001) on Nazi war criminals, who, in his opinion, exhibit a disability that resembles a physical defect: namely the inability to recognize the (objective) values.

5. Hösle presumably means here both system-theoretical approaches according to Luhmann as well as economic approaches.

6. "It seems vital to leave the formalism behind and develop a universalistic material ethics in which goods and values play a role" (Hösle 1997, 155f.).

7. Such an objective hierarchy, however, continues to exist as an ideal—with all its theoretical ramifications.

8. Hösle retains the term "natural law," as it has become part of common usage (ibid. 777). He refers to the natural law of Locke, among others. In each instance, rights preceding the social contract are provided.

9. Generally, Hösle has a strong tendency to discuss problems of the state and the economy in legal categories by means of balancing competing values and legally protected interests. However, he seems to reject the old legal maxim "volenti non fit injuria" (ibid. 791).

10. See also (ibid. 114): The economy must exist under legitimate purposes.

11. Hösle apparently is only aware of an either-or of so-called "higher" and "economic" activity: "But the dignity of mental or moral activity is found precisely in the fact that it is not primarily motivated by economic considerations" (ibid. 878). Therefore, intellectually productive individuals should also not fret about the success of those who orient themselves in terms of the "primitive needs of consumers" (ibid.).

12. This not infrequent assertion (e.g., by Foot, see the section "Society requires a shared conception of humanity as a basis for virtues (Philippa Foot)") is not supported by Hösle with empirical data, but postulated and supplemented with some specific demands. Private transport, for instance, is not justified by natural law, and must therefore be reduced if not ultimately completely abolished (ibid. 876). And even the taking of interest is under suspicion of being inadmissible according to natural law: although interest is still necessary at the moment, we may one day eventually return to outlawing interest, as Hösle's appears to hope (see ibid. 875).

13. In particular, even the government of devils contemplated by Kant could not be stable. See Kant (1976, vol. 8, 366) and the section "Historical perspectives: Precursors of order ethics." Hösle does not address the fact that Kant does not have in mind devils as such, but rather devils with *understanding*.

14. To be sure, Hösle writes at length about the conditions of modernity (ibid. 714ff.). However, he does not mention, as far as I can see, the pluralism of modernity and the related loss of opportunities for establishing *shared* orientations.

15. In a way similar to the anthropological foundation of the conceptions of Habermas (see the section "Society requires rational motivation for life forms capable of ideal role taking and constitutional patriotism (Jürgen Habermas)") and Rawls (see chapter 4).

16. See the section "Moral communication: Toward a semantics of benefits" of Brandom.

17. See, for example, the work of Sen on development theory (for an overview, see Sen 1999). Sen may be interpreted to mean that *benefits* must be created for the people affected by globalization—even if he himself sometimes interprets this differently than OE.

18. A philosophical tradition from antiquity deals with such problems under the concept of "phronesis."

19. This does not apply, however, to Neo-Aristotelians in the vein of J. Knight (1969/2003).

20. I pass over here conceptually complex questions and understand "community spirit," for the sake of simplicity, as a value.

21. For a discussion of Aristotle's virtue ethics, see Nussbaum 1988.

22. On Thomas Aquinas's conception of a virtue ethics, see for instance Nelson 1992.

23. For the current state of utilitarian theory, see, for example, Scarre 1996.

24. Besides those virtue-ethical approaches such as Foot's or Geach's, which grew out of language philosophy in the narrow sense, virtue ethics can also be found within the political philosophy of communitarianism (for an overview on communitarianism, see Avineri and DeShalit 1993). An exemplary representative is Alasdair MacIntyre (1984), who endorses a virtue-ethical approach precisely *without* a universal claim. MacIntyre refers back to Aristotle, whom he interprets in the following way: Aristotle closely linked the concept of virtue with that

of the citizen of a community. A person was then virtuous if he carefully heeded the (written and unwritten) laws of his community. In this way, Aristotle reconstructed the existing virtues from his social—that is, local—environment, and established them on the basis of a non-universalizable ethics. For example, for *specific* social classes (such as the poor) he allows for *specific* virtues that cannot in fact be obtained by the members of other classes. The poor, for instance, could not carry out all of the actions expected of a virtuous human being. They could not attain wisdom to the same extent as the wealthy, nor could they be as generous. However, according to Christian doctrine—at least according to MacIntyre—specific virtues could also not be obtained by the wealthy (it will not be investigated here whether this interpretation of the New Testament is correct, yet it is nonetheless questionable). Later on in the history of philosophy, however, a series of virtue ethics emerged making *universalizable* claims (see MacIntyre 1984, chapter 5), which were supposedly doomed to fail. Such approaches ignored that human beings always operate in social contexts that are influenced by tradition. I—which is to say every single individual—am "the bearer of a tradition, whether I like it or not, whether I recognize it or not" (MacIntyre 1984, 221). The individual cannot freely choose between different traditions. For this reason, an approach that aims to construct a universalizable basis for virtues should be immediately rejected.

MacIntyre accordingly does not make any claim regarding the universal validity of his own communitarian approach. He rather finds that virtues are only locally valid for certain communities. People who live together in a community are familiar with common traditions that may be repeatedly called upon. The continuity of these traditions is furthermore ensured insofar as the members of the community always bear them in mind. The communitarian approach largely proceeds from the traditions that have developed in certain sections of American society. Communitarian virtue ethics, which was hotly debated in the context of the liberalism-communitarian controversy of the 1980s and early 1990s, shares some of the same problems as Foot's approach, while adding a few more. In particular, it is not clear whether it makes sense, even in modern times, to assume such a strong bond between the individual and the community, as MacIntyre postulates (see this criticism, for example, in Gutmann 1985).

25. See also Foot 2002, 203f: from her standpoint, those who are "bad" are not so much the brazen—since they implicitly at least have standards, even if they do not adhere to them—but rather the amoral, because they are insincere. Among their representatives, she counts Nietzsche, Thrasymachus, and Gide. However, Foot's discussion of Nietzsche (cf. Foot 2001, chapter 7), which (unavoidably) makes references to National Socialism, ignores Nietzsche's philosophy. Foot unfortunately does not bother to arrive at a deeper understanding of *Zarathustra*, for instance.

26. I focus on these three arguments, which of course cannot do justice to the full implications of Foot's theory.

27. The critique is later taken up, for example, in Rawls 1971, Sen 1970b, and Williams 1973.

28. For the classical theory, see Mill 1863/1975 and Bentham 1789/1970. For variants from the twentieth century, see for instance Brandt 1967, Smart 1971, Birnbacher 1988/1995, and Singer 1979/2011.

29. This does not change, for instance, C. D. Broad's attempts to take greater account of the distribution of benefits in a utilitarian assessment. See also Lyons 1965.

30. Generally speaking, Foot represents a non-teleological theory of morality. She says for instance, in morals, good intentions count (see Foot 1997, 25).

31. See classically Arrow 1951 and Sen 1970b and Buchanan 1964/1979.

32. For the distinction between act and rule utilitarianism, see Smart 1971.

33. Foot admits to having never developed an appreciation for the contractualist perspective upon which OE rests (see Foot in 1997, 29). At most, the remark can be understood to mean that Foot is not completely sure whether ethics or moral philosophy is more fundamental than political philosophy, which the contractualist would also tend to represent (see ibid.).

34. She refers here to philosophers such as McDowell, who in his book *Mind and World* (McDowell 1994)—similar to Brandom (1994)—sees human nature's defining characteristic as the ability to act according to reasons: "because acting on reasons is a basic mode of operation in human beings" (Foot 2002, 202).

35. This is also further developed in Foot 2001 in the form of the concept of a "natural normativity." This book is intended to offer "a new beginning for moral philosophy."

36. This is indeed also found in a very similar form in Hösle (1997, 874).

37. Unlike some other critics of the *homo economicus*, Foot restricts her critique of egoism explicitly to *psychological* theories (see Foot 2002, 199f.).

38. Occasionally (following classical Axelrod 1984), the position is held that the prisoner's dilemma does not represent a systematic problem for societies, because prisoner's-dilemma games are seldom played in isolation, but mostly *iterated*. In these types of games, cooperation is in everyone's interest and therefore self-evident. This argument, however, overlooks the fact that iteration itself implies a form of sanctioning (as people meet each other again and can punish their collaborators), which is precisely what OE calls for.

39. See also the section "Historical perspectives: Precursors of order ethics."

40. See my discussion in the section "Moral communication: Toward a semantics of benefits."

41. On the problem of Thomistic ethics in the modern era, see for instance Nelson 1992.

42. She writes, on the other hand, that the four cardinal virtues also demand sacrifice. Under certain circumstances, one would have to "sacrifice everything for charity or justice" (Foot 1978, 3).

43. As an example, she remarks that the people of Leningrad during the siege by Nazi Germany hardly required a categorical imperative that was implemented through a rational motivation. The contingent fact that other citizens were also disposed to be loyal to their city would actually have been sufficient (see ibid. 167).

44. Her research program—namely, the study of human nature (see Foot 1978, 10)—would thus also not be sufficiently fertile for modern societies.

45. I use this term in the sense of Rawls's "freestanding conception": a conception, accordingly, is freestanding if does not rely on a comprehensive doctrine for its derivation. A freestanding virtue ethics would thus not depend (or at least not much) on the incentivized support of institutions.

46. This is discussed in political science, as for instance in Ostrom 1990. There, conditions are named under which individuals in dilemma situations organize themselves and are able to arrive at solutions—without this theory conflicting with constitutional economics or OE, as Ostrom's approach is valid only under the conditions it enumerates. These include, for instance, that the group may not be very large and must not only be familiar with anonymous communication. Both conditions are undoubtedly not fulfilled at the macro level of modern societies. Problems can still be solved in this way, however, in local contexts and small- to medium-level communities.

47. This interpretation of Kant is very problematic and at the least reductive; see for instance Homann 2002, chapters 8 and 9. I will have to pass over the details here, however. See also the section "Historical perspectives: Precursors of order ethics."

48. However, they attribute a weaker status to these preconditions than Kant does to the transcendental conditions. In particular, Habermas endorses only a weaker form of cognitivism: moral statements have an "analogous-truth" status (see Habermas 1983/1999a, 66).

49. See Habermas, 1981, vol. 2, chapter VI, clearly drawing on Husserl (1936/1996; see also Habermas 1990/1991) and Schütz (1979/1984).

50. Along with earlier precursors, the performative contradiction has a long tradition in analytic philosophy. See also classically Austin 1962.

51. See also Habermas 1981, vol. 1, chapter 1.

52. Hegel already argued in this manner in *Elements of the Philosophy of Right*, see Hegel 1969ff., vol. 7, § 75. See also the section "Modus vivendi, constitutional consensus and overlapping consensus" on Rawls.

53. A complete catalogue of these preconditions, which Habermas (1983/1999a, 87ff.) only cites examples of, apparently does not exist. Here, Habermas merely offers suggestions that come from Robert Alexy (1978).

54. This is how I interpret especially Habermas 1983/1999a, 88f.

55. Hösle (1997, 446) claims that a clear distinction between convincing and persuading is not found in all languages. For example, the Romance languages know only *one* word, namely

"persuasion." However, one can also point out that the Italian or French languages have the terms *convincere* or *convaincre*.

56. Habermas again refers here to Alexy (1978), whose suggestions he appears to accept without modification.

57. And thus also (for example) neither refutable nor falsifiable.

58. Rational motivation is similarly privileged in prominent manifestations of the theory of deliberative democracy. The key essay by Joshua Cohen (1989) also endorses an observance of norms and rules by means of rational motivation (and good reasons instead of preferences). Similarly, see also Elster (1983 and 1989) and—with a different theoretical background—Raz (1999).

59. See, for instance, Habermas 1983/1999a, 63, 72f., and 109 and similarly Habermas 1992, 30 (here: legitimacy vs. legality).

60. Similarly, it is stated in "Notes" that there is a "rationally motivating force grounded in reason," albeit only "weak" (Habermas 1991, 33). And in *Between Facts and Norms*: the normativity of discourse theory offers "only the weak force of rational motivation" (Habermas 1992, 5). Interestingly, Habermas attempts here to already locate rational motivation in Peirce's concept of communication community, resulting from the "cooperative search for truth on the part of scientific investigators" (Habermas 1992, 16). In the section "Criticism: And what if a performative contradiction does not disturb me?" I question this interpretation of Peirce.

61. Habermas obviously requires that arguments in all cultures generally proceed along similar lines. Every culture in any case would have to try to avoid any performative contradictions (this is how I interpret, for instance, Habermas 1983/1999a, 95).

62. As I see it, Habermas does not himself establish the parallels to Russell. And a difference between Habermas and Russell could be that (at least the late) Russell merely indicates that is necessary to start *somewhere*, but that this starting point can also be revised later. In Habermas, the starting point for ethical argument appears to be much more firmly anchored and hardly revisable.

63. Literally: "Modern rational law" (Habermas 1991, 87). However, Habermas himself points out that this argument is already contained in the (ethical, not only legal-theoretical) principle U as a precondition. It is not clear how the assertion can be made that this argument only emerges in legal theory.

64. See, for instance, Habermas (1983/1999a, 102): there he speaks of the "need to institutionalize discourses, trivial though it may be," suggesting that the importance of institutions was not yet fully recognized. In particular, these "attempts at institutionalization are subject in turn to normative conceptions and their goal, which springs *spontaneously* from our intuitive grasp of what argumentation is" (ibid., emphasis in original). Thus rational motivation is reinstated more or less on a meta level.

65. Economics does not appear to fall within the scope of his considerations.

66. Elsewhere, Habermas says rather similarly that the parties involved in the process of law making "are *not* allowed to take part *simply* in the role of actors *oriented to success*" (Habermas 1992, 32; my emphasis). This sentence also reveals the coexistence of strategic and communicative action: the subjects are granted a success orientation, but a moral surplus value must be added. See also similarly in Habermas (1992, 678): here, the law is dependent on a trait such as the "democratic morals" of the citizen and on precisely *more* than just the pursuit of individual interests.

67. See, for instance, the already cited passages in Habermas 1992, 297ff., and chapter 1.

68. A similar—not the same—observation is made by Rorty, "Habermas, and other metaphysicians . . . think that liberal political freedoms require some consensus about what is universally human" (1989, 144).

69. This is likely where Habermas (1998, 167) finds support for his conviction that populations should—and above all can—reward a *shift in consciousness* (here politicians are evidently meant).

70. Kohlberg (1981, 19ff.) means quite plainly (and not only in descriptive but also *normative* terms) that in every society *some* principles (such as "the value of human life is absolute" (ibid, 22) must have validity independently of contracts. Here, it becomes clear that he does not yet have at his disposal the idea that such principles can have two stages (in the sense of OE).

This makes it possible to explain in a theoretically consistent manner why different majorities are required for different types of rules or principles and why it can be unanimously decided to abandon a unanimity rule.

71. Rawls's theory of the individual, for instance, draws this conclusion. He attaches great importance to the fact that the intuitions of society's members are reflected in his conception of justice. See also the section "Reason vs. rationality."

72. In addition to Rawls (see chapter 4), this position is also represented by Thomas Nagel (1979, X), who privileges intuition over arguments.

73. An analogy is suggested here to Reichenbach's distinction between "context of discovery" and "context of justification" (see Reichenbach, 1938/1983, 3). As is well known, the strict separation of the two contexts has often been criticized (see, for instance, Urbach 1978 and already Lakatos 1970).

74. See Sternberger, 1979, 13ff. According to Sternberg (1990, 387), he first used the term in an article for the *Frankfurter Allgemeine Zeitung* from 27.01.1970. See later Sternberger 1982/1990 and (collectively) 1990.

75. Here, acceptable for Habermas means: constitutional patriotism is the only patriotism that "does not alienate us from the West" (Habermas 1986/1987, 50).

76. It is also emphasized in Habermas (1996, 118) that constitutional patriotism can form on the basis of citizens' interpretations. At the same time, it is noted that this attitude strikes some observers as *not* being sufficient to prevent a society's collapse.

77. See Habermas, "Innovations will not happen if the political elites cannot find any resonance with the *already transformed* value orientations of their electorates" (1998, 168; emphasis in original).

78. In passing, it is worth remarking that Helmut Dubiel (1992) differs with Habermas in taking another—in his view "minimalist"—position. In this case, democratic societies require *more* than constitutional patriotism for their cohesion, but also specifically the experience of having lived together through conflicts. Cohesion develops spontaneously by itself out of such experiences. Hirschman (1994) takes up this idea from Dubiel, yet distinguishes between two types of conflicts, namely, more-or-less conflicts and either-or conflicts. The former, in fact, lead to more cohesion. By contrast, the latter, whose number is increasing today, does not. Hirschman (1994, 304) concludes that, in today's world, the invocation of common sense merely hides the inability of theorists to devise adequate ways of viewing problems and problem solutions. In his view, we need political entrepreneurship, imagination, and the like—precisely what is referred to in this book as heuristics.

79. Homann (2002, 57 and 205). The corresponding passages in Habermas include, among others, Habermas (1991, 49) and Habermas (1992, 31).

80. This is also not made any clearer over the course of the nearly 700 pages of *Between Facts and Norms*. The work simply returns again and again to the issue of the (mutual) "complement" of morality and law (see, among others, ibid. 21, 41ff. 58, 151ff., 359ff., 541ff.).

81. See, for instance, the current discussion surrounding pragmatism in Weingartner, Schurz, and Dorn 1998.

82. As I see it, the role of criticism is not referred to systematically.

83. In a later work on Peirce (Habermas 1989/1991), Habermas certainly continues to emphasize that rational argument and "rationally motivated agreement" (ibid. 24) play a major role in Peirce. He admits, though, that the late Peirce at least relativizes the "compelling force of the better argument" (ibid. 31) in favor of the effect of a natural, evolutionary force.

84. See also similarly Liebhafsky 1993, 746: "Peirce's theory, then, is a theory of inquiry in which belief is challenged by doubt and in which the ensuing *struggle* between belief and doubt produces new belief and the continuum" (emphasis added).

85. Here, I follow especially Haskell (1984, 210ff.).

86. In the original: "So with all scientific research. Different minds may set out with the most antagonistic views, but the progress of investigation carries them by a force outside of themselves to one and the same conclusion" (Peirce 1878/1998, 5.407).

87. See Wible 1994a and Luetge 2004.

88. It has frequently been argued that the invisible hand referenced by Smith is simply a metaphysical metaphor, as was suggested, for instance, by Smith's contemporaries John Kells

Ingram and Cliffe Leslie (see Rothschild 2001, 118) and later by Marxist critics. This point of view, however, has been fiercely disputed, for instance, by Hayek (1978) and Arrow and Hahn (1971, 1). Emma Rothschild considers Smith's use of the metaphor to be ironic (see ibid., chapter 5), which is disputed; completely off the mark is Evensky 1993, who ascribes to Smith's thesis the notion that the invisible hand only works if the individuals involved are morally motivated. On the invisible hand in science and scientific theory, see Kitcher 1993 and Luetge 2004.

89. As already mentioned, Habermas criticizes the "late Peirce" (Habermas 1989/1991, 31) for relativizing the force of argument and consequently rational motivation in favor of an evolutionary perspective. This criticism, though, only concerns the late Peirce and in the rest of the article (see ibid, 14, 23, 24) Peirce continues to be taken as evidence of the strength of arguments. The analogies to the market mechanism drawn by Rescher and Haskell—in particular regarding the *positive* effects of an invisible hand in the shape of the price mechanism for the progress of knowledge—are not noted by Habermas even in this later work.

90. In my view, this also applies to Habermas's theory of law: there it says, among other things, that the law may indeed permit the individual to "*drop out of* communicative action" (Habermas 1992, 120, emphasis in original) and the refusal of illocutionary commitments (ibid.), but this would only ensure that a "privacy" is justified that itself has no moral quality. Habermas is *not* able to capture the moral quality of institutionalized morality—that is, order ethics—in this way.

91. This could apply to Buchanan's approach. This may also explain why Buchanan is sometimes completely ignored in philosophical discussions where his work would otherwise be quite relevant.

92. Directly deliberative coordination mechanisms are supposedly mechanisms where decisions are made in "open arenas" and individuals make decisions in light of the deliberations made by others. Such mechanisms, for instance, are then supposed to come into play when the involved parties are scattered in many different locations and various resources are needed. In such cases, such directly deliberative mechanisms are preferable to the market, in particular due to high information costs (see Sabel and Cohen 2001, 15). In any case, Sabel and Cohen's arguments in my view draw on specific examples that hardly go beyond everyday plausibilities (see, for instance, the "policy reason," ibid. 12). Also, the directly deliberative mechanisms necessarily "sit" on the underlying institutional structure of society (as I interpret ibid. part 4); without such a functioning underlying structure (in the sense of Rawls 1993, for example, 115f. and the 7th lecture) they won't take effect. Sabel and Cohen seem to be primarily interested in simply finding a little more room for arguments to be made *before* the decision.

93. Meier 1998, for instance, describes this on the example of ancient Athens.

94. Habermas appears to perform the motivation switch here that he has demanded himself. See Habermas 1992, 31.

95. Indeed, another proponent of the theory of deliberative democracy, C. Sunstein (2001) sees this precisely as a *problem* of the Internet and a threat to democracy. He fears that the Internet will result in the loss of both spontaneous and shared experiences (ibid. 8f.). Even if this were true, the question of countermeasures would remain. By and large, the measures discussed by Sunstein cannot be implemented in practice. His approach is also not sufficiently thought through in terms of the problem of implementation.

96. Dahl (1989, 252) discusses the opportunities of televoting made possible by television, which, of course, from today's vantage point lies far behind the capabilities of the Internet.

97. See also the section "Society requires (almost) nothing (Ken Binmore)" on Binmore.

98. This point is also emphasized by Vallentyne (1991b, 2). Fishkin (1988), by contrast, criticizes Gauthier for neglecting to exclude some preferences as immoral at the outset. Similarly, Gunnarsson (2000) criticizes Gauthier's approach as subjectivistic. He relies exclusively on benefits instead of reasons (see, for instance, ibid. 129ff and 138ff.). With regard to ethical actions, it would concern substantive reasons and their evaluation (see ibid. 260f.). A person's "pleasure" could not make an action—ethically—rational, because it does not always provide a rational result *in practice*. In fact, this is the case with prisoner's-dilemma situations. Gunnarsson is therefore correct insofar as these situations require that a moral theory *not only* builds on

the benefits of certain norms or rules, but rather also conceives of institutionally established incentives.

99. Just as natural scientific theories that are adapted to our everyday intuitions can fail us if they are applied to areas beyond the mesocosm. See Vollmer 1983.

100. Along these lines, see Gauthier 1986, 93 and 125.

101. Binmore (1994, 283f., fn. 36) criticized this as a conservative approach that assumes that (social) contracts have no role to play where markets operate successfully.

102. It should be noted that this determination is based on the *calculation self-interest*; it is not be confused with the direct restriction of self-interest described above in relation to path (a).

103. See also the later work Gauthier 1997b. Gauthier (1998) contrasts his own theory of justice as mutual advantage with Barry's (1995) approach, which defines justice as impartiality. Gauthier rejects this approach with what appear to be convincing arguments, because it a) fails with regard to the prisoner's dilemma (see Gauthier 1998, 128f.) and b) requires an implausible view of justice according to which people need to justify their actions to others (see ibid. 131). This view is a relic of the theory that purports that people want to justify their actions before God. See also my critique of Brandom in the section "Order ethics as an ethics of benefits and incentives."

104. See also Gauthier (1991b, 327). Here, it becomes even more plain in my opinion that dispositions are viewed as being *not* dependent on the behavior of others.

105. However, Gauthier still considers himself a contractarian. See, for instance, Gauthier 1997b.

106. Morris and Ripstein write: "Gauthier's solution is internal and dispositional, rather than external and coercive" (Morris and Ripstein 2001b, 6). They appear to view this, however, as an *advantage* of the approach. Gauthier himself even points out later: "But in *Morals by Agreement* I argue that just principles of interaction require a non-coercive baseline. The outcome of a coercively extracted agreement has no claim to be just" (Gauthier 1998, 123).

107. See the "Theory of Justice": "Justice is the first virtue of social institutions" (Rawls 1971, 3).

108. Gauthier (1994, 717ff.) remarks that it is rational for the individual to assign to herself certain "policies" to follow. This would be better than her having to newly calculate her actions on a case-by-case basis.

109. The term goes back to Locke's theory of appropriation, which stipulates that the appropriation of natural resources by other actors must leave behind plenty of other, at least equally good natural resources.

110. Gauthier is a renowned Hobbes scholar; see Gauthier (1969/2000). It is also certainly true (see Gauthier 1986, 268) that his own position is consistent with Hobbes's insofar as both emphasize the role of reciprocal behavioral restrictions. However, they conceive of both the justification as well as the enforcement of these behavioral restrictions in completely different ways. Gauthier by and large concedes this with regard to the justification (see ibid.), but apparently not with regard to enforcement.

111. Hobbes 1651/1991, 92; italics in original.

112. As I see it, psychological insights are only referred to in one place (Gauthier 1986, 187), and even there only secondarily.

113. "Were duty no more than interest, morals would be superfluous" (Gauthier 1986, 1).

114. In his recent writings (see, for example, Gauthier 1998), however, *constrained maximization* no longer appears to be as central.

115. For a similar approach, see Kitcher 1993b.

116. Although Gauthier himself—here in line with OE—stresses that one should view other actors as sources of mutual benefit (see Gauthier 1986, 222).

117. See also similarly Gauthier 1988, 184ff. and Gauthier 1991b, 330.

118. In this respect, Rawls represents a similar view. See chapter 4.

119. This issue is also raised by Sayre-McCord (1991).

120. He thus implicitly puts forward a critical-mass theorem.

121. This is confirmed in Gauthier 1997b, where the role of education is also emphasized (see Gauthier 1997b, 148).

122. Morris and Ripstein confirm this view when they refer to Gauthier's conception as "morals by socialization" (Morris and Ripstein 2001b, 6). They simultaneously confirm the action theoretical-anthropological-based dispositions concept, not the interaction-theoretical one.

123. Buchanan (1988/1991, 195) leans toward this view, as does Harman (1988), who doubts that rational actors will accept a distribution outcome based on a hypothetical contract. I do not find the hypothetical nature of the contract to be the problem, however, but rather the nature of the existing social structures.

124. See Binmore 1994, 26f. and 80.

125. See also Weber's theory of ideal types (see Weber 1922/1988).

126. Binmore (1994 83f.) undertakes a similar critique of Gauthier in regard to MRC.

127. Gauthier (1988, 177) subsequently qualified the importance of the "Lockean proviso," without evidently completely repudiating it as Hampton (1991) and Danielson (1991b) criticize him for precisely this later on.

128. See also the similar criticism from Binmore (1994, 179–182). In regard to economics, Gauthier was forced to respond to the accusations of Buchanan (1988/1991, 195), who found that Gauthier employs the rational actor as a realistic conception of humans. In his reply, however, Gauthier seems to accept this, arguing against Morris's (1988) critique of his conception of humans that the contractual argument is not based on anthropological (and nontuistic) roots, but on the prisoner's-dilemma structures of interactions. Gauthier 1988, 215.

129. On the functions of the state in general, see Smith 1776/1976, Book V, 213ff.

130. Here, it is possible to see another difference to OE. According to OE, the market *consists of* dilemma structures; it does not reflect the surmounting of them.

131. This is also the Binmore's view, who stresses that the decision to privilege the market over other distribution mechanisms is a decision that requires itself moral "input" (Binmore 1994, 64, fn. 78).

132. Hence the viewpoint already cited of Adam Smith (1776/1976).

133. For instance, the "just man" (Gauthier 1986, 328) would be affected emotionally and thus follow the dictates of fairness.

134. Gauthier appears to understand this somewhat differently in later works. See, for instance, Gauthier 1998.

135. I am indebted to Caroline Waldeck for her suggestions concerning this chapter.

136. See, for instance, Rorty 1989, xvf.

137. Rorty admits that the classical Enlightenment was completely fruitful and adequate for its time. Today, however, it would fail to serve a useful purpose.

138. See Berlin 1958/1969.

139. See also, for instance, his discussion on Kant in Rorty 1989.

140. This needs qualification. See chapter 4.

141. One might ask here whether Rorty must not also consequently demand solidarity with all creatures (and not just human beings). This kind of non-anthropocentric, but rather pathocentric position is endorsed by Peter Singer (1979/2011).

142. Along similar lines, see for example Rorty 1989, xvi, 189f., 192, 196.

143. On Rorty's interpretation of Nabokov, see Rorty 1989, chapter 7; on Orwell, chapter 8.

144. Similarly, see one of the few values of (liberal) critical rationalism formulated by Karl Popper, namely, "that cruelty is always 'bad'" (Popper 1961/2013, 501f.; see also Luetge 2001).

145. Here lies a difference to Buchanan, who contends that a liberal sees the individual as normative, as the ultimate source of values. On Buchanan, see the section "Society requires an ethic of work and an ethic of saving (James M. Buchanan)."

146. Nonetheless, Rorty subscribes to an evolutionary implementation theory that relies on evolution as the instrument that ultimately determines moral points of view. This is also indicated by his theory of truth, which identifies truth with successful problem solving (see Rorty 1998). The difficulty of such an evolutionary theory lies in the fact that it is not possible to say why we would choose to completely dispense with the fully present controlling possibilities of evolutionary processes.

147. On the Mafia, see the study by Gambetta (1993).

148. See, for instance, Rorty 1989, 84ff. Later, the point is also made that a modern society can make do with institutions and narratives (see ibid. 189f.), but not with institutions alone.

149. Examples may be cited here from the literature of science fiction, which thematizes the efforts of communication and cooperation and challenging conditions. For a more detailed discussion on this point, see the section "Discussion: Can't society also dispose with empathetic preferences?"

Chapter Four

Society Requires a Sense of Justice

A book on the normative foundations of modern societies under globalization cannot simply pass over some of the most important work, perhaps *the* most important work, on political philosophy since 1945. By this, I do not just mean John Rawls's *A Theory of Justice*, but his oeuvre as a whole. This is because one can only appreciate the full extent of Rawls's conception in the context of his later amendments to his undoubtedly groundbreaking book. With his later writings, the author was able to successfully rebut the increasingly vociferous criticisms of certain fundamental points that immediately followed the publication of the *A Theory of Justice*.[1] I will therefore primarily limit my discussion and reconstruction of the Rawlsian conception to the later work *Political Liberalism* (1993).

My objective here is to present the significance of Rawls's conception for order ethics. Rawls himself is primarily concerned with providing an adequate political theory for modern societies under the conditions of "reasonable pluralism." This theory is supposed to take account of the basic intuitions of the citizens of a democratic constitutional state and give the (institutionally) embodied traditions in such a state—like the United States—a coherent and consistent form.[2]

I am concerned on the other hand with the moral-philosophical question of what demands Rawls places on the citizens of this state. OE will again serve as a yardstick that equally relies on *institutions* as an essential instrument for shaping modern societies, a point where it agrees with Rawls.[3] I will first show that "justice as fairness" is largely compatible with OE. I will then argue, however, that a central element in Rawls's conception, the sense of justice, goes beyond OE's purview. This sense of justice is the moral surplus value that Rawls demands of the members of a modern society.

RAWLS'S THEORY OF JUSTICE
AND ITS CONNECTION TO ORDER ETHICS

Central to the conception of justice as fairness (abbreviated hereafter as JF)—especially in its later forms—is the notion that it is a political, not a metaphysical, conception.[4] The reason for it is as follows: JF—like OE—assumes that the pluralism of modernity is not a temporary but a permanent state. It cannot reasonably be expected that there will be a return to common goals or common religious or philosophical doctrines, except as a result of state oppression. On the other hand, a return to a pre-modern state cannot be *desirable*—that is, in the personal interest of everyone—because more difference is a key productive factor for modern societies. Only an authoritarian or totalitarian state can declare a binding comprehensive doctrine, although it is unlikely that such a state could remain permanently stable.

Given this constraint—this basic fact of modernity—a basis for living together in a state and a functioning social cooperation (see Rawls 1993, 299ff.) cannot be found in such doctrines or the values they propagate. On the contrary, this basis must rather avoid the conflicts between the different doctrines that are upheld in a society. Rawls calls these doctrines "comprehensive" because they not only relate to the political sphere, but ultimately to all areas of existence. Several comprehensive doctrines come into conflict quite easily with each other. The basis for a democratic constitutional state then cannot be determined by a comprehensive doctrine like one of these, but must rather be a political conception. "Political" is to be understood in the following sense:

1) The conception must be *freestanding*. For Rawls, this means that it should contain as few elements of comprehensive doctrines as possible (ibid., 9f.). It must be presentable to the citizens and by the citizens without such elements. By characterizing his conception as freestanding, Rawls responds to those criticisms of the *A Theory of Justice* accusing him of giving JF a problematic metaphysical justification.

Nonetheless, it can (and should) be possible to derive and justify JF on the basis of numerous diverse doctrines (ibid., 12ff.). At this point, Rawls's expectation comes to bear that JF will eventually be supported by an *overlapping consensus* reflecting the greatest number of doctrines possible. However, only an agreement between *reasonable* doctrines would be of consequence (see ibid., 58ff.). The intended meaning here of "reasonable" will be discussed in the section "Morality in Rawls's conception of justice as fairness."

OE can also be viewed as freestanding, since it does not rely on comprehensive doctrines. Moreover, it similarly endeavors to obtain the consent of a society's members. It cannot completely ignore, however, *prima facie* irrational doctrines (see also the section "Morality in Rawls's conception of justice as fairness").

> 2) Only the *basic* structure of a society can be judged by such a conception (see ibid., 12f.). Under the basic structure of a society, Rawls understands the essential institutions of a society, ascribing great importance to these for all the citizens of a state (see ibid., 11), and the way in which these institutions form a total system. This system encompasses the fundamental freedoms set out in the constitution like the freedom of conscience and expression, property laws, the economic system, and the structure of the family (see ibid., 257). These are the only areas that concern JF, and only they should be assessed according to JF's principles of justice.

This is also the precise goal of OE. OE does not claim that it can offer solutions to problems germane to individual or private spheres of society, but only to fundamental sociopolitical concerns.

> 3) The essence of this conception of justice lies in the *two* known principles that were already introduced in the *A Theory of Justice*. Since Rawls understands them slightly differently in *Political Liberalism*, their new formulation will be quoted here at length:
>
>> Each person has an equal claim to a fully adequate scheme of equal basic rights and liberties, which scheme is compatible with the same scheme for all; and in this scheme the equal political liberties, and only those liberties, are to be guaranteed their full value. (Ibid., 5)
>>
>> Social and economic inequalities are to satisfy two conditions: first, they are to be attached to positions and offices open to all under conditions of fair equality of opportunity; and, second, they are to be to the greatest benefit of the least advantaged members of society. (Ibid., 6)

The first principle—according to Rawls 1993, as well as Rawls 1971—is given priority over the second[5]: equality of treatment prevails. If there are any inequalities at all, then they must also favor the most disadvantaged members of society, that is, the poorest must profit from unequal distributions.

> 4) As is generally known, Rawls construes the *acceptance* of both these principles by society as a choice in the *original position* (see Rawls 1993, 22ff.). As Rawls repeatedly emphasizes (see, for instance, Rawls 1997, 203), this original position is only a means of depiction: it is neither a historical state, nor is it a philosophical idea that is prescribed for citizens' political reflections. The original position rath-

er links these deliberations to a coherent conception that appoints rational, that is, self-interested, parties when they discuss the substance of a future constitution. Rawls here has the deliberations of the American founding fathers in mind, who he occasionally quotes (see, for instance, Rawls 1993 lii f.). The original position in particular simulates the information constraints that actors like the founding fathers were necessarily subjected to. These constraints (the famous "veil of ignorance")[6] are critical in the choice of the principles of justice, because they establish a position in which the benefits to individual actors—arising due to their current circumstances in the society—do not matter. This situation, Rawls suggests, contains incidental benefits, whose impact on a choice in the original position would need to be neutralized. This relates to our moral intuitions, which JF aims to coherently summarize.[7]

Information barriers exist in the original position especially with regard to the following points (see ibid., 24ff.): stakeholders know nothing about their future position in society, their gender, or their abilities, and they do not know the comprehensive doctrines of the people with whom they will be living together. According to Rawls, given these informational constraints, rational actors in the original position will choose the two principles of JF.

For our purposes here, it is important that Rawls grants *rational autonomy* to the parties in the original position (see ibid., 72ff.). This means that no external evaluative criteria are given to the parties when they are to supposedly choose between alternative principles. All acknowledged principles in the original position are therefore *by definition* fair. Rawls suggests—at least if these statements are taken in isolation—that it is not possible to again verify the chosen principles with regard to an external (e.g., philosophical or ethical) standpoint.[8] As will be shown in the section "Morality in Rawls's conception of justice as fairness," Rawls qualifies these statements in other contexts.

If these elements of JF are taken together, the following main features give rise to a conception that strongly resembles OE. The citizens are not required to accept a certain morality—in the sense of a Rawlsian comprehensive doctrine—in order to preserve society. Everyone is allowed to subscribe to their own private, personal doctrine, as long as it is reasonable (more on this in the section "Morality in Rawls's conception of justice as fairness"), and they cannot be obliged to adhere to common objectives or a common orientation. Rawls presumes that such a society will remain stable. Functioning social cooperation and the social stability that results are for him central criteria for judging a conception of justice (see ibid., 231 and 66). Here, he differs from other political philosophers and moral philosophers (for instance, from Neo-Aristotelianism) who do not insist on stability, but instead hold the realization of certain (moral) values as the evaluative criterion. Rawls, however, chooses—with restrictions that will be discussed in the section "Morality in Rawls's conception of justice as fairness"—a functional justification that is consistent with OE. OE finds that moral values that do not contribute to social stability cannot only not be supported from a political and functional perspective, but also from the standpoint of ethics.[9]

Further congruence with OE is found with a direct requirement that JF places on citizens. They must, namely, also support the institutions that conform with the conception of JF. Without such willing and voluntary support, the society and the state will collapse (see Rawls 1993, 36ff.). Rawls emphasizes this when he remarks that JF itself is the shared ultimate goal of all citizens (see Rawls 1993, 202f.), even if there are no other shared goals. Social cooperation on the basis of JF, however, is in the interest of everyone, and must therefore be endorsed and supported by everyone through an adherence to the rules. At this point, however, it is necessary to already note a qualification, for, according to Rawls, citizens should *not only* support JF out of self-interest. In the following section, I will discuss how this might be interpreted.

So far, then, it may therefore be observed that JF resembles OE and (largely) only demands of citizens their support of and participation in democratic institutions.

MORALITY IN RAWLS'S CONCEPTION OF JUSTICE AS FAIRNESS

The aspect of JF that has been described up to now is in effect only half the story. As with other approaches already introduced within the scope of this book, Rawls does not accept an OE-type model unreservedly.

Rawls also believes that the citizens of a modern, democratic society must have greater demands placed on them than regulatory compliance and a commitment to reforming the rules. This "more" pertaining to demands consists primarily in the postulate that the citizens of a modern state would need to have two moral assets: on the one hand, a personal conception of the good (which is unproblematic in the sense intended here) and, on the other, a *sense of justice*.

The Sense of Justice

Rawls characterizes the sense of justice[10] as an essential ingredient of a well-ordered society[11] and defines it as "the capacity to understand, to apply, and normally to be moved by an effective desire to act *from (and not merely in accordance with)* the principles of justice."[12] In the phrase "to act from" lies the crucial point: in the construction of his theory, Rawls wants to completely avoid any implication that individuals only follow the rules *because* they believe they will benefit from it. The principles of justice according to Rawls (this interpretation is at any rate implied) must also be followed by the individuals when *no* personal benefits are apparent.

This is also suggested in a second, slightly dissimilar, Rawlsian definition of the sense of justice, according to which it is the ability "to *honour* fair terms of social cooperation" (my emphasis) that matters. Here, weight is placed on the words "to honour": fair rules can thus be respected by individuals, and in fact *independently* of how the incentives look. Rawls, in any case, does not speak in this context of a *formation* of incentives. To be sure, he identifies the rules that are to be followed as fair. This still does not say anything about how these rules are to be *sanctioned,* and especially not about whether contra-productive incentives might be devised as a specific kind of sanction, as in the prisoner's dilemma. If my interpretation is correct, Rawls would have to require rule compliance even if incentives of the prisoner's-dilemma type were to speak against it.[13]

This basic theme runs throughout Rawls's overall conception and is noticeable in several of his antagonistically constructed conceptual pairs: reason and rationality, *modus vivendi* and overlapping consensus, and constitutional consensus and overlapping consensus. In all three cases, the sense of justice plays a decisive role. On the one hand, unlike reasonable individuals, those who may only have rationality lack exactly this sense of justice. On the other hand, according to Rawls, an overlapping consensus only develops if the involved individuals are equipped with just such a sense of justice. These cases will be considered in turn in the following sections.

Reason vs. Rationality

Rawls distinguishes between the reasonable and the rational (see ibid., 47ff.). Purely rational actors, he contends, lack a "moral sensibility" (ibid., 51). They would have their own goals, which they would also prioritize, deciding which of these goals are most essential to them. Only purely rational actors could have a life plan in reference to which they would be able to align their goals. They would moreover not be completely self-interested, but also be able to develop an interest in others. It becomes clear, then, that more is at issue here than simply the popular opposition between amoral means-ends thinking, on the one hand, and the moralistic reflection about ends, on the other. Rawls's opposition is ultimately much more nuanced.

That being said, the essence of the reasonable actor is distinguished by four aspects (see ibid., 81f.):

a. *First,* the reasonable actor would be willing to propose consensual rules and comply with them, but *under the proviso that he could simultaneously rely on the rule compliance of the others.*

b. *Second*, the reasonable actor acknowledges the "burdens of judgment" (ibid., 54ff.). These burdens would indicate the boundaries inside of which one standpoint might be explained and justified in relation to others. A reasonable citizen recognizes that there are reasonable and legitimate differences of opinion that cannot be remedied by further argument since they are based on the dissimilar judgments of individuals. Such disputes could arise for a variety of reasons:

- empirical findings may be contradictory and complex;
- if several considerations are relevant, they could be weighted differently by individuals;
- concepts are often vague and allow room for interpretation;
- different people are affected by different experiences;
- when it comes to normative questions, arguments of equal strength are frequently found on both sides; and
- each social system—according to Isaiah Berlin (1958/1969)—can only allow for a limited number of values. Therefore, a selection must be made among the current values (see Rawls 1993, 57 and 197).

Rawls thus rejects discourse theory, among other things, because it is primarily concerned with bringing about social unity by means of the citizens' reconciliation through argument (see the section "Society requires rational motivation for life forms capable of ideal role taking and constitutional patriotism (Jürgen Habermas)"). The "unforced force of the better argument" is, according to Rawls, not actually sufficient for establishing a consensus through reason. Habermas supposedly misunderstands the burdens of judgment, which allow for reasonable disagreements, not only provisionally, but systematically.[14]

c. The *third* aspect of the reasonable actor implies that citizens of a democracy should not only in effect be normal and cooperative members of society, but that they should also *want* to be. Citizens want to be recognized as full members of society in order to strengthen their own sense of self-worth. No one, therefore, can be a citizen of a state who is not interested in also being recognized by the other citizens of that state.

d. *Fourth*, citizens finally have what Rawls refers to as "reasonable moral psychology" (ibid., 86). Here, the concern is with a theory of the individual that is "philosophical not psychological" (ibid., 86).[15] This theory does not claim to approximate a maximum correspondence to reality. Rather, it conceives of a specific model of the individual that only serves a particular purpose within JF, in the same way that the model of the *homo economicus* is only a construct that has a particular purpose (see the section "Order ethics as an ethics of benefits and incentives").[16] Within JF, philosophical moral psychology is designed in a way that makes the demands of Rawls's theory comprehensible to the citizens and motivates them to cooperate in a society defined by JF (see ibid., 86f.).

In particular, this theory of the individual implies that citizens:

- can develop conceptions of justice and fairness and also *want* to behave according to these conceptions;
- support the institutions they consider to be just, that is, cooperate if they can be sure that others will do the same (see a.);
- trust other individuals who are also cooperating and do not try to defect;
- cooperate more intensely and increasingly in more areas, the longer an already successful cooperation lasts; and
- increasingly strengthen and expand fundamental rights and freedoms, the longer these have already been recognized.

From these four aspects, an image of the reasonable citizen emerges that is contrasted with the merely rational actor. Rawls formulates this relationship again somewhat differently elsewhere. In not having a moral sensibility, rational individuals lack the most decisive of the two moral abilities, namely, the sense of justice. Without this ability, they would "fail to recognize the independent validity of the claims of others" (ibid., 52).[17] This "independent validation" clearly means that an individual A would not only accept the claims of the individuals B and C out of her own self-interest, but also because B and C are legitimate sources of claims in her eyes. A must acknowledge this fact regardless of her own self-interest. In the accompanying footnote (ibid. fn. 6), Rawls admits that even rational actors could acknowledge the claims of others (B and C), since they are made within the context of existing "loyalties and bonds" (ibid.). Yet this acknowledgment does not occur for the right reasons: it is only given *because* of these loyalties and bonds, not *because* B and C are considered to be legitimate sources of claims. The acknowledgment of claims as "independently valid" is thus obviously to be seen as analogous to "acting *from* principles of justice" (see the section "The sense of justice").

From the perspective of OE, it now must be investigated whether the construction of the reasonable citizen possibly has too many preconditions. The concern is whether claims are being made on the individual that cannot be made good on. Bearing this question in mind, the reasonable actor can be reconstructed in the following manner.

The *first* aspect—the willingness to propose and observe rules *under the condition* that others comply with the rules—seems unproblematic at the outset. If individual A proposes a rule R, this rule might be interpreted as an *investment* that could make A and the other members of a society, B and C, better off. If R were agreed upon, however, and A could be sure that B and C would comply to R, would A herself follow R? This depends on the *sense* in which A can depend on the others' rule compliance. If A is sure that the others will comply with rule R because it is subject to sanctions that would punish its infringement, A would then also have to *fear* these sanctions should she violate R. In this case, A would adhere to the rule out of her own self-interest.

If, however, R is *not* backed by sanctions, and if A expects the rule to be observed because she knows B and C, for example, and is confident that they would not break R because of their integrity, or, further, if A is able to presume that B and C are good, upstanding democratic citizens due to her reasonable moral psychology, then A has a clear incentive to *not* comply with R herself. This is the conclusion that necessarily results from the prisoner's-dilemma model. The very first aspect of the reasonable actor, therefore, is already highly problematic.

The *second* aspect, however—the recognition of the burdens of judgment and thus the rejection of social integration through reason—can only be welcomed from the standpoint of OE. The fact that reasons alone do not secure loyalty was already understood by Hobbes: "Covenants, without the Sword, are but Words, and of no strength to secure a man at all" (Hobbes, 1651/1991, 117).

The *third* aspect, conversely, is more problematic. Unless there are associated *benefits*—which is obviously not what Rawls has in mind—why is it necessary to suggest that citizens have an interest in their individual acknowledgment as full-fledged members of society? Can't there be stability in a society in which at least some of the citizens have no interest in being acknowledged by a society's other members?[18]

As indicated, the *fourth* aspect of reasonable moral psychology is finally Rawls's own construction for strategic-theoretical purposes and thus not being judged in isolation. Still, it is possible to also say something about moral psychology in connection with the points that have already been discussed. Each one of the individual points that make up the theory of the individual may be integrated into the framework of OE. Individuals can provide preliminary inputs (investments) to collaborations. They invest in the continuation of productive cooperation and support out of their own self-interest fundamental rights and institutions, whose effectiveness they have come to know over an extended period of time. Consequently, only Rawls's supplementary point is not required from the standpoint of OE. These investments in cooperation would have to occur for specific reasons with certain goals in mind, and not out of the self-interest of the involved parties.

Other aspects of the reasonable actor only further exacerbate this problematic. Rawls, for instance, underscores that the fair share of basic goods due to all citizens should not be understood in terms of benefit and rational advantage. Rather, this fair share is to be adapted to the needs of citizens as they are specified by the primary goods (ibid., 188). The society (apparently all citizens collectively) apportions this fair share to each individual. In return, citizens as *reasonable* persons—and this could not be accomplished by rational actors[19]—would "assume responsibility for their ends and . . . moderate the claims they make on their social institutions" (ibid., 189). This opens the door for numerous interpretations: Should the individual, for the sake of reason, dispense with a claim on an institution? Should he, for the sake of reason, dispense with his own claim, even when others do not? Or should he, for the sake of reason, give priority to his long-term over his short-term interests and preserve the institutions in question—in which he perhaps sets a good example for others—and not aid their destruction? Rawls does not address these issues.

A further aspect relates once again to the problem of stability. Rawls stresses that some "forms of judgment and conduct" (ibid., 194) are critical for lasting social cooperation. Here, he is thinking of virtues of fair social cooperation: civility, tolerance, reasonableness, and a sense of fairness (which is apparently not the same as a sense of justice[20]). These virtues are clearly understood as reasoning abilities that individuals would have to exhibit in order to maintain cooperation and democratic states. These reasoning abilities—understood as the ability to make reasonable investments, that is, as heuristics—present no problem for OE. Nevertheless, I see a certain risk in grounding the willingness to cooperate and stability on certain presupposed human characteristics. This has the effect of turning a blind eye to the conditions under which these characteristics themselves might show stability. The incentive problem that highlights the fact that certain incentive constellations cause these very characteristics to disappear or at least have no effect is lost sight of. When the incentive problem is taken into account, stability becomes a question of incentives, not a question of the existence of certain human characteristics.

In Rawls's depiction of agreement in the original position, one remark throws a particularly interesting light on the problem of the reasonable actor. Rawls asserts that to clarify a problem through reason is like clarifying it by "solving the agreement problem posed by the original position" (ibid., 274). This could be taken to mean that reason serves in laying the groundwork for universal consensus. Reason would then have the task of conceiving what a problem solution would have to look like to ensure that all stakeholders—upon being relocated to the original position—could find agreement. If this interpretation is correct, then a new opportunity is presented for comprehending the Rawlsian conception in terms of its compatibility with OE. In this case, reason would fulfill its purposes as a heuristic, that is, it would (simply) serve the conceptual development of new ideas for mutually productive collaborations. As recommendations for rule reform, these would then need to be introduced to the public political debate. In view of the hypothesis under discussion here, such a heuristic role for reason would not go beyond OE's theoretical framework, which only presupposes self-interested actors and assumes that the stability of modern society is sufficiently ensured by self-interested compliance to and further development of the rules.

The crucial question, however, is whether Rawls—when interpreted consistently and properly—would require that an individual *resist* incentives on the basis of her reason in case of doubt. In view of the four aspects of the reasonable conception discussed here from JF, this requirement appears at any rate to be a logical result of Rawls's conception. This is suggested in particular by the discussion of point 1 (reciprocal compliance, even without sanctions). Everyone should cooperate, but only if the others do as well. Yet nothing is said about how this reciprocity is to be guaranteed and controlled. Rawls seems to demand that individuals—as reasonable actors—behave in a fair and cooperative manner even without such a guarantee and hence also in resistance to incentives. Reason supposedly makes this possible. This interpretation is supported again by an additional passage in a completely different location, specifically in the description of the hierarchy of fundamental freedoms. Here, Rawls writes: "at each stage the reasonable frames and subordinates the rational" (ibid., 339). This "subordinates the rational" suggests that incentives that could have an impact on a rational individual cannot, or *cannot be allowed to,* get through to a "reasonable being." This demand—if my analysis is correct—is found in the logic of the Rawlsian approach.

Modus Vivendi, Constitutional Consensus, and Overlapping Consensus

Rawls emphasizes that his conception should be sustained by a broad consensus of reasonable comprehensive doctrines, and not just by a *modus vivendi*. He describes the *modus vivendi* as a contract between parties with conflicting objectives. Both have an interest in this contract and adhere to it *because* it serves their own interest.[21] However, both would be willing to break the contract if the circumstances changed and their own interests could be better pursued at the expense of the other. According to Rawls, this situation cannot provide a basis for social unity. A consensus that is only based on "self or group interests" or is simply the "outcome of political bargaining" (Rawls 1993, 147) must be considered inherently unstable. A consensus, in other words, depends on the external conditions remaining the same. If they do change, the consensus of *modus vivendi* breaks down, as does the social unity along with it.

This argument is key for Rawls. As already mentioned in the section "Rawls's theory of justice and its connection to order ethics," he assumes that a society collapses when its conception of justice and its democratic system are not "willingly and freely supported by at least a substantial majority of its politically active citizens" (ibid., 38). Of course, this common conception is only supposed to exist in the political realm as a shared notion of political *justice*. Be that as it may, in Rawls's view, social collapse cannot be prevented by the observance and development of *rules*.[22]

Given this instability, social unity needs to rest on a stronger foundation.[23] For this purpose, Rawls conceived of the overlapping consensus of reasonable comprehensive doctrines. This consensus implies that individuals should not only agree to a political conception—the conception of justice JF—out of their own self–interest or an interest to observe the rules of this contract. They *must* also be able to find agreement on the basis of their own personal comprehensive doctrine. Rawls discusses in detail how representatives of different comprehensive doctrines could consent to a single *political* conception and a series of *political* values (fundamental freedoms and rights) and hence ascribe to them a certain precedence over their own doctrines (see ibid., 134ff.).

He *first* points to the fact that political values are highly relevant to all members of society. They determine the general scaffolding of social life, the *basic structure* which—as already mentioned (see the section "Rawls's theory of justice and its connection to order ethics")—plays a central role in JF. Rawls stresses *secondly* that—as history shows—when comprehensive doctrines are *reasonable*, they always allow room for interpretation, making the further development of such doctrines possible. This applies, for instance, to the Christian and Islamic doctrines. Both were able to evolve over time and adapt to changing conditions. He points out in particular that theologians and philosophers have succeeded time and again in reconciling religious (or also philosophical) values, on the one hand, and political values, on the other. Such compatibility must be possible because, as Rawls notes (ibid., 154ff.), the political conception JF says nothing about the truth of comprehensive doctrines.

It neither maintains that these doctrines are true, nor that they are false. The supporters of these doctrines are not even required to accept JF as true. They would merely have to concede that, in their society, there exists not only their own reasonable comprehensive doctrine, but others as well.

It is of primary importance for our purposes to understand how overlapping consensus and *modus vivendi* are different. At least three points are worth noting in this regard:

a. First, as already explained, an overlapping consensus does not depend on changing circumstances and thus has greater stability (see ibid., 146f.).
b. Second, an overlapping consensus encompasses conceptions of the individual, society, and principles of justice and therefore has broader reach than a *modus vivendi*, extending namely into the realm of morality.[24] Moral reasons should tip the scales in the approval of JF, and these moral reasons should moreover be developed on the basis of the indicated conceptions.[25]
c. The third point is the most important for the matter at hand. Rawls emphasizes—and this supposedly follows from point b), the moral nature of the overlapping consensus—that such a consensus may not exhaust itself in a creating kind of *convergence point*, where the conflicting interests in society would meet and agree "on accepting certain authorities, *or on complying with certain institutional arrangements*" (ibid., 147, emphasis added). Here, what Rawls has in mind comes into sharp focus: the idea of a society whose members believe that their only duty is to obey the rules of this society should be rejected. For this reason, Rawls is unlikely to find OE adequate as a model for modern societies. Even OE's demand of a commitment to reform the rules would not satisfy him. Rawls insists that the citizens not only adhere to and modify the rules, but that they must also observe (and modify) the rules for the *right reasons*. Otherwise, the stability of a society would be at risk.

It should be noted that what is at issue here is not a *functional* argument, for reason should be in the service of stability. This is not the only argument in favor of reason, but an important one. If it could also be shown that stability would be possible even *without* an overlapping consensus, then this functional argument could at least be omitted. I will return to this point in the section "Modus vivendi, constitutional consensus, and overlapping consensus."

The third pair of terms, conversely, is the overlapping consensus and constitutional consensus and is one stage beyond the *modus vivendi*. Where in the latter instance, the citizens only follow the rules due to their own *self-interest* and a compromise between competing interests, in the case of the constitutional consensus there is agreement with regard to some of the values of political liberalism, namely, the political process and especially some basic rights and freedoms (see Rawls 1993, 159). Rawls clearly believes that this agreement should ensure greater stability than the *modus vivendi*. Constitutional consensus develops from the *modus vivendi* in the following manner:

To begin with, the liberal principles of justice of JF must have been accepted as the result of a compromise and already been followed, by and large, for a certain period of time. Citizens come to realize—as I understand it—that these principles are beneficial to them. Then, the prevailing comprehensive doctrines—in which room has been built in for interpretation—change over the course of time so that the following three conditions can be put into place for the constitutional consensus:

a. First, the fundamental rights are defined and removed from the short-term political agenda.[26] The fundamental rights can therefore no longer be further negotiated by shifting political majorities.
b. Second, a transition must be gone through from a purely factual acceptance of the principles to their *justified* acceptance. Citizens need to arrive at reasons for their principles that seem generally acceptable. Argument plays an important role here.[27]
c. Once these first two conditions have been met, then the institutions that have formed as a result of the principles of justice promote the long-term virtues of cooperation among the citizens. These virtues include, for example, the capacity for social cooperation and compromise. Evidently what is not intended here is the sense of justice, which above all requires a conception of justice, and—by virtue of this conception—a capacity to "act *from* principles of justice" (see the section "The sense of justice"). The virtues of cooperation, nonetheless, still do not contain such an explicitly formulated conception of justice.

When these conditions are met, a constitutional consensus can then be established. The constitutional consensus is still too narrow, however, and needs to be converted into an overlapping consensus. The crucial development here lies in the fact that groups would form on the basis of a constitutional consensus with their own political doctrines and subsequently enter into public discussions with other groups that would likewise have their own political doctrines. As a result, doctrines that were previously group-specific would be subject to public scrutiny and have to prove their worth in argumentative contests with their rivals. Yet in order to conduct this contest non-violently and to allow groups to convince others of the validity of their respective doctrines, the various groups need to develop a political conception of justice. They would have to consider which arguments would appear most cogent to the other groups.[28] This would cause questions of justice to be discussed in increasingly nuanced ways, which, in turn, would lead to the development of "conceptual resources to guide how the constitution should be amended and interpreted" (ibid., 165). The constitutional consensus, by contrast, still does not say anything about this. Moreover, a point would have to be reached as a result of these stronger arguments in which the fundamental rights and freedoms would garner universal consent. During the course of public discussion, the political groups would largely recognize that a shared foundation for this discussion is needed in order to avoid conflicts. This foundation would provide the basis for the fundamental rights and freedoms (following JF) insofar as it removes them from the political discussion.

This development would conclude with all political groups (with reasonable doctrines) supplying arguments from within their own doctrines that would permit them to agree to JF. Rawls stresses, however, that this development would not be inevitable: the role of "different social and economic interests" (ibid., 167) would still need to be considered:[29]

In the course of the public discussion on conceptions of justice many diverse liberal conceptions could emerge that would be acceptable (and also reasonable) in the sense of JF. The differences between them are partly—but not only—attributable to interest conflicts between the groups endorsing these conceptions. Although it is Rawls's hope that these conceptions might be brought together in an overlapping consensus, it is also conceivable that these conflicts might not in fact be overcome. This could be the case for two reasons: on the one hand, if the conceptions are supported by "deeply conflicting political and economic interests" (ibid.) and, on the other, if these oppositional interests cannot be reconciled through a suitable constitution. In such cases, it would not be possible to arrive at an overlapping consensus (ibid., 168). This may be interpreted to mean that a consensus can only be established when the interests of the parties involved are reconciled, in the sense that a suitable constitution must be able to offer improvements to the respective situations of everyone. A consensus—more precisely an overlapping consensus, not necessarily a constitutional consensus—can thus break down because the interests that support it turn out to be overly conflicted. According to Rawls, it should not be expected that this disagreement can be overcome through an additional (moral) requirement (of a moral surplus). Instead, it can only occur through constitutional rules. But where does this leave the higher "dignity" of the overlapping consensus in relation to the constitutional consensus and the *modus vivendi*? A balancing of interests is already possible—and necessary—within the framework of this lower consensus stage. Is simply the passage of time, therefore, the decisive additional ingredient? In that case, a constitutional consensus would have to evolve into an overlapping consensus after a certain duration, and an overlapping consensus would consequently be nothing more than a long-standing constitutional consensus.

Although not a *sufficient* condition for an overlapping consensus, Rawls in any case likely means that the overcoming of interest conflicts is indeed a *necessary* condition. For the *modus vivendi*, as well as the constitutional consensus, this condition would supposedly be both necessary and sufficient. This seems to be a reasonable interpretation. In Rawls's view, the overlapping consensus cannot develop without both of the lower levels. In comparison to these levels, however, it should provide *and also* require a certain "surplus." "Provide" in the sense that an overlapping consensus will offer more stability than a constitutional consensus, precisely because it is not only based on interests. "Require" in the sense that an overlapping consensus cannot develop if the citizens are continually only concerned with their own interests. They would need to develop what has already been discussed: a sense of justice.

Rawls's conception of overlapping consensus—like his conception of the reasonable actor—makes clear that JF demands more of citizens than an adherence to the rules. As we have seen, Rawls states this explicitly in his rejection of a *modus vivendi* as a basis for a democratic society. The core argument is that compliance with institutions does not by itself yet lead to a society or social unity. A *modus vivendi* is inherently unstable because it quickly runs the danger of being revoked by the stakeholders when there is a change to the external conditions. Rawls maintains that a lasting, stable democratic society could not develop on this basis. One would need a "surplus." That is to say, a consensus has a broader reach than a constitutional consensus,[30] along with a certain attitude or capacity—that is, a moral surplus value—on the part of the citizens. This would be the sense of justice.

From the standpoint of OE, this could be interpreted as follows: the overlapping consensus provides a heuristic that gives the members of society a starting point for determining the direction in which the constitution might be developed. This is compatible with OE, which indeed not only requires adherence to the rules by citizens, but also their development (or at least recommends that this would be in their own interest, since stability is not possible without development; see the section "On the relationship of order ethics and individual-oriented approaches"). OE permits individuals and groups to invest in this development because they hope to gain a long-term advantage from doing so. No moral surplus value is required for this. The individuals do not need to have a sense of justice or, what is perhaps even more significant, they do not have to be equipped with the *same* or with a similar functioning sense of justice.

This interpretation fits well with the fact that Rawls uses an argument in the comparison between constitutional consensus and overlapping consensus that can be seamlessly integrated into the framework of OE. He establishes the necessity of the overlapping consensus with a *functional* argument, namely that of conflict avoidance. Still, there are at least certain types of conflicts that can in turn prevent an overlapping consensus. Does this reflect some kind of vicious circle? Is it possible that precisely those conflicts that are supposed to be avoided stand in the way of an overlapping consensus? Put differently: Could it be the case that an overlapping consensus does not actually solve these conflicts, but only appears to? It is not clear whether Rawls has a specific idea of how intense the conflict would have to be in order to prevent an overlapping consensus. Does an interest-based constitutional conflict like the one surrounding the preservation of slavery have to be at issue? Or could smaller conflicts—like the construction of certain streets—also be enough to undo an agreement? Rawls would probably respond that such delineations are not concerns of philosophical reflection, but can only be clarified in practice. Nonetheless, it is important in my view for statements about the stability of an overlapping consensus to present a theory of conflicts. This should at least speak to the question of what *types* of conflicts this consensus must be able to *avoid*. It would then be easier to decide whether a consensus merely represents a constitutional consensus or a consensus that is already overlapping.

Table 4.1 once again summarizes the three stages of social agreements, the respective capacities required in each instance and the corresponding demands that, according to Rawls, are to be placed on individuals.

Table 4.1. The three stages of social arrangements according to Rawls

Type of Agreement	Content: Depth and Breadth	The Citizens' Required Capacities
Modus Vivendi	Simple contractual compromise about (some) basic rights; JF is de facto accepted	Self-interest
Constitutional Consensus	Fundamental rights are laid down; acceptance of JF is *justified*	Self-interest; virtues of cooperation (developed gradually)
Overlapping Consensus	Fundamental rights are laid down; acceptance of JF is *justified*; political groups shape their own conceptions of justice; a direction is predetermined for the development of the constitution	Sense of justice; conceptions of the individual and the society; no deeply conflicting interests!

An interpretation of the overlapping consensus as a heuristic could have the added advantage that an independent sense of justice would not necessarily have to be required. For the purposes of OE, it would be sufficient to assume that there are self-interested citizens without a moral surplus value. I will discuss this point further in the following section. I would like to already point out here, however, that such a reinterpretation is not compatible in every respect with Rawls's account of JF.

Can the Concept of Justice as Fairness Possibly Be Based on Interests Alone?

In the following, I will discuss how overlapping consensus and constitutional consensus or *modus vivendi*, on the one hand, and the Rawlsian sense of justice and its related oppositions of reason and rationality, on the other, can be interpreted in terms of OE.[31]

The *overlapping consensus* could be understood to contain an additional heuristic to the constitutional consensus, which indicates the direction in which the rules should be changed.[32] If, however, as Rawls repeatedly emphasizes, this direction must meet the interests of everyone concerned, then the overlapping consensus could be developed without difficulty within the framework of the justification of justice by way of interests. Indeed, rule reform can only be *enforced* if the parties involved are able to agree to it or if it results from constitutional rules that can generally be agreed to. I can thus see no conflict between an interest-based justification of morality and the conception of an overlapping consensus. This is certainly true if both actually pursue the same goal—if both the justification of interests and the overlapping consensus were finally conceived to solve the same problem. In the case of Rawls, I can only see this problem arising from the fact that the stability of a society should be systematically ensured in the long run. Rawls stresses this in many places—in *A Theory of Justice, Political Liberalism* and in later works.[33] This means that Rawls—as evidenced by his own statements—is not finally interested in an ultimate goal such as the realization of morality "in itself" or a goal that lies beyond all interests. The task at hand is much more practical in nature: the long-term preservation of a stable society. As I see it, the assertion that this goal is in the *long-term* interest of every citizen, and indeed must be, hardly needs justification. Interaction structures of the prisoner's-dilemma type can no doubt systematically undermine the maintenance of stability. This is why, as in OE, an institutional framework is established, which, again, is in the interest of everyone. Its establishment in the democratic process, though, may require better *information* about the functioning of modern societies and market economies. Still, the incentives for establishing this framework can finally only go back to its benefits for everyone and to (everyone's) interests.[34] All members of society must be able to hold on to the promise of benefiting from a rule form, otherwise they won't agree to it. And given the structure of modern societies, they will also ruin the benefits to others, or at least diminish them significantly.

I do not deny that a group A, for instance, might attempt to convince a group B of the long-term benefits of a reform that have yet to be recognized by B. *Nevertheless*, even in such an argument process the arguments used by A finally have to speak to the greater satisfaction of the *interests* of B. A will not be able to convince B with other kinds of arguments (see my discussion of the semantics of incentives in the section "Moral communication: Toward a semantics of benefits"). One might therefore say that the possible advantages of a rule reform first need to be reciprocally *communicated* by the members of the society. Yet this communication can only be meaningfully constructed on the basis of benefits, not on the basis of values. The latter are ultimately independent of the interlocutors' self-interest and even advanced in *opposition to it*.

The *sense of justice* could be interpreted in terms of OE as follows: it is useful for the betterment of all citizens that the members of a society have this sense. It could be in the interest of all citizens that everyone acts "*from* principles of justice," assuming that "*from* principles of justice" means that everyone adheres to the rules because they know that they thereby *invest* in the establishment and maintenance of still-functioning norms. Rule observance and compliance are accordingly not only linked to costs, but may also be understood as investments for the sake of future returns.

This idea has been expanded on by Suchanek (2001). Suchanek emphasizes that we, as members of modern societies, continually and systematically invest in the reliable expectations that the rules are supposed to provide. When each individual follows rules, she implicitly relates her behavior to the hope that others will behave similarly. In this way, the general atmosphere favoring rule compliance improves and thus supports a level of trust that finally fosters new and productive collaborations.

This is *one* way to interpret Rawlsian thought within the framework of ethics using economic methods. The question, however, which cannot be answered conclusively here, is the extent to which social stability can build on the mechanism of *individual* investment. Don't prisoner's-dilemma structures also again come into play?[35] Won't productive investments also be threatened by exploitation and preventive counter defections? And even if this is not the case (or is so only to a limited degree), how much of a difference can they make?

These questions may have answers. In concluding, however, I only want to point out that there are clues in Rawls's work that suggest that the moral surplus value he envisages (largely) serves a *purpose*, is functional, and can be interpreted in terms of OE. When Rawls writes—correctly or not—that the purely political and procedural constitutional consensus is too narrow because it is not sufficient for avoiding conflicts (see ibid., 166), a functional justification is obviously being made. An overlapping consensus is not assumed for its own sake. This observation is supported by the assertion discussed earlier, whereby an overlapping consensus might be prevented by deeply conflicting interests. Similar support for this is found in the remark that justice as fairness will have a "serious problem" (ibid., 252) if the mutual reinforcement of the sense of justice and democratic institutions does not function. But here also ultimately lie the *strengths* of Rawls's conception, for it opens up a space of possibilities that can be filled by other disciplines, empirical evidence, and the social "reality." The fact that there will remain some complications along the way can be accepted for the time being. Reforms are, indeed, not prohibited.

NOTES

1. It will not be possible here to pursue the following: a) the debate on communitariansm (see, for instance, Pogge 1989, Kukathas and Pettit 1990, Kymlicka 1989), because I find that it has become increasingly less relevant for newer discussions on Rawls; and b) the debate on utilitarianism, which alone would require a book of similar scope (see Hare 1974/1978, Hart 1974/1978, Sen and Williams 1982).

2. See, for instance, Rawls 1993, xxxii, 8f.

3. Consider one of the basic principles of the *A Theory of Justice*: "Justice is the first virtue of social institutions" (Rawls 1971, 3).

4. Rawls first explicitly and systematically formulated this idea in Rawls 1985.

5. According to Rawls 1993, the first principle is part of the constitution agreed to by all citizens and sets fair rules and constitutional barriers. The second principle, however, is *not* part of the constitution, but rather part of a subordinate legislative level (see ibid., 337). For details on an attempt to experimentally test the choice of the principles in the *original position*—which is, however, fraught with some methodological difficulties—see Frohlich, Oppenheimer, and Eavey 1987.

6. Rawls 1993, 70; see Rawls 1971, 12 and 136ff.

7. See already Rawls 1971, 21f.

8. Because of these and similar statements, Alejandro (1998, chapter 8, esp. 179) finds that Rawls justifies the status quo too much. The parties involved are expected—more or less by committing a normativistic fallacy—to comply with the given rules and circumstances. This seems to be a misunderstanding: Rawls merely acknowledges the significance of the problem of norm enforcement, which is indeed for a political philosopher unavoidable.

9. Copp (1996) holds this condition of stability for a theory of justice to be inappropriate: the fact that a particular theory of justice might not be able to ensure stability is no argument against this theory. Rather, it is due to human psychology that justice is fragile even under the best of conditions (see Copp, 1996, 204). In my view, Copp's argument completely misses the mark. It would mean that the enforcement problem in theories could largely not be considered, since concerns like "human psychology" could always come up in the enforcement process. Such a position reflects an "all-or-nothing" type argument: obviously no theory can anticipate all the *individual problems* that go along with the enforcement process. But a theory can be judged in terms of how it more or less deals with the *general* problem of its own enforcement.

10. The sense of justice probably appears in Rawls's work for the first time in the essay "The Sense of Justice" (Rawls 1963). Here, Rawls draws on Rousseau's *Émile* (1762/1979), where the author already stresses a sense of justice that is not only developed through the *understanding*, but is due to a *sentiment* of the heart enlightened by reason (see Rawls 1963, 281). In the following, the formulations remain more general than in Rawls 1993: the ability to acquire a sense of justice is determined more formally in a theory of justice (ibid. 305) as a fundamental aspect of the moral personality and helps Rawls to distinguish between utilitarian and aristocratic ethics (ibid. 304f.). Rousseau (1762/1964, 47) states in the original that "le sentiment du juste et de l'injuste fût inné dans le coeur de l'homme."

11. Rawls emphasizes that it is not the parties that exercise the sense of justice in the original position, but only the fully autonomous citizens of a well-ordered society (see ibid., 320f.). A society is called well-ordered if a) it acknowledges the two fundamental principles of justice, b) its basic structure is consistent with these principles of justice, and c) its citizens have a normally effective sense of justice so that they generally follow the rules of the basic institutions (see ibid., 35). On the sense of justice, see fundamentally Rawls 1993, 80f. and 252; for criticism, see also Binmore (1998, 256).

12. Alexy (1997, 293f.) further divides the sense of justice into a sense of compliance and a sense of judgment. This is to be welcomed, since in this way the importance of *compliance* to the rules becomes clearer. Bittner (1997, 51), on the other hand, distinguishes between a common and a particular sense of justice. He responds to Rawls with the objection that no *common* sense of justice could be generated from fundamental political dissent, while, at the same time, no *particular* sense of justice could be especially strong.

13. Rawls indeed writes (see Rawls 1993 315f.) that the assumption of a predisposition toward a sense of justice is "purely formal" (ibid. 315). This, however, *veils* the role of the sense of justice, since Rawls understands "purely formal" to mean that the adherence to selected principles in this manner—assuming the institutions of society comply with the principles of fairness and are known—is guaranteed. See also Rawls 1993, 35; the citizens then generally follow the rules of the basic institutions of their society, *because* they have a normally effective sense of justice.

14. Habermas also underestimates these systematic differences of opinion in his remarks on Rawls (see Habermas, 1997): he correctly sees that Rawls vacillates between reason and self-interest as the basis of his conception (along these lines, see ibid. 183 and 189). In this matter, Habermas is quite consistent (see Habermas 1996, 49ff., where the discussion concerns the "conflicting justification programs" (ibid. 83) in Rawls). Yet his discourse-theoretical solution relies on an even stronger (and therefore even more problematic) assumption, namely, that of practical reason (see Habermas 1997, 177), with whose help actors are able to fulfill discursively redeemed validity claims (ibid. 186). On the Habermas-Rawls controversy, see also McCarthy 1996.

15. See also Rawls 1975, in which he stresses that moral philosophy is *not subordinate* to the philosophy of mind or epistemology. For the presentation of their problem, moral philosophy could, and would have to, tailor its own categories.

16. Hence, the demand (for example, in S. Brennan and Noggle 2000) also would not amount to anything. Rawls's moral psychology would have to be augmented with the recent findings of developmental psychology.

17. See analogously already Rawls 1971, 436 ff.

18. According to Rorty, a just and free society allows its citizens to be "as privatistic, 'irrationalist,' and aestheticist as they please so long as they do it on their own time—causing no harm to others and using no resources needed by those less advantaged" (Rorty 1989, xiv). See also the section "Contingency and irony: Renouncing reason."

19. This is my interpretation of Rawls 1993, 187–190, and especially 189.

20. The sense of *fairness* is clearly still not an independent moral capacity or a moral value, and thus a weaker requirement than the sense of justice.

21. A *modus vivendi* is thus not just a cease-fire (as opposed to a peace treaty), but a "simple" (barter) contract.

22. Habermas particularly stresses this point in his dispute with Rawls (see Habermas 1997, 188f.). Habermas finds himself in agreement with Rawls that the stability of a society requires the moral validity of its own defined conception of justice in a (neither religious nor metaphysical, but) reasonable sense. By contrast, Hershovitz (2000), citing James Madison (!)—argues affirmatively for grounding stability on an institutional system of "checks and balances," even if this may sound more cynical than Rawls's conception.

23. Dauenhauer (2000) denies the very possibility of this step: given the historicity of the political situation, there could not be *more* than one *modus vivendi*. In any case, one must distinguish between responsible and irresponsible *modi vivendi*.

24. Evidently Pogge (1989) has this in mind. Even before the *Law of Peoples*, Pogge wanted to expand Rawls's ideas about the nation–state, explaining global injustices by the fact that only a *modus vivendi* had been reached so far at the global level (see Pogge 1989, § 19).

25. An interesting analogy can been drawn here to Hegel's *Philosophy of Right*. In § 270, it says that the citizens should "belong to a church—a church is all that can be said" (Hegel 1969ff., vol. 7, 420), "since religion is an integrating factor in the state" (ibid.).

26. This corresponds to Brennan's and Buchanan's ideas about rules such as restrictions on the federal budget, which eliminate it from the short-term calculus of politicians (see Brennan and Buchanan 1980). Buchanan—similar to Baier (1989)—would call for nothing more than a constitutional consensus. In contrast to Buchanan, however, Baier (1989, 790) assigns a greater role to values.

27. Rawls could draw here from previous work done in discourse ethics (see the section "Society requires rational motivation for life forms capable of ideal role taking and constitutional patriotism (Jürgen Habermas)"), which, however, would probably have to be conceived differently.

28. To illustrate this, Rawls draws on the discussions surrounding the U.S. constitution after the Civil War (see Rawls 1993, 165).

29. It is noteworthy that Rawls at this point addresses different "economic interests," whereas he otherwise tends to speak of political and conceptual differences between actors and people. It is only in the elaboration of his conception that Rawls appears to have become increasingly aware of the role of interests. However, the term *economic* here is clearly intended in the sense of a narrow understanding of the field of economics. See, for instance, Rawls 1979, which is very much in keeping with classical welfare theory.

30. Mills (2000) disagrees with this—as I do—and, moreover, in two ways: the overlapping consensus is neither necessary, for there could be social stability without it, nor is it possible since too many people would have to be excluded from this consensus as "unreasonable."

31. Whether such an integration would meet with Rawls's approval is something that can only be speculated on (rather negatively).

32. Pogge (1989) also takes this heuristic train of thought in Rawls's work seriously, when he examines the effectiveness of concrete institutional reform proposals (see Pogge 1989, 6 and parts II and III). Nevertheless, he is not successful in making such proposals for reform himself, in my view because of his approach's lack of economic foundations. This is something that he also admits to (see Pogge 1989, 8).

33. Including in his *Law of Peoples*, although several new aspects are also brought to bear here; see chapter 1.

34. Rawls seems to deny this when he says that the implementation of arrangements could also result in losers (see Rawls 1993, 83f.). This remark is in response to Barry (1989, 186ff.), who insists that there should be a strict delineation between the idea of reciprocity and the idea of mutual benefits—which Rawls accepts. With regard to an early interpretation of Rawls in Hobbes's interest-based sense, see Buchanan 1976.

35. This type of situation (although based on the social system of science) is discussed in Luetge 2004. There, incentives are sometimes not enough for creating a general atmosphere that is safe for intellectual property and that would prevent plagiarism. Instead, a supplementary institutional solution must be found.

Chapter Five

Society Requires Incentives and Rules

SOCIETY NEEDS AN ETHIC OF WORK AND AN ETHIC OF SAVING (JAMES M. BUCHANAN)

It might appear surprising at first to find Buchanan's conception of constitutional economics among the approaches that are under discussion here. After all, like OE, constitutional economics requires nothing more of society's members than an adherence to the rules and an ongoing commitment to discovering ways of modifying these rules so that they are beneficial to everyone.

Generally speaking, the significance of rules in constitutional economics can hardly be overestimated (see Brennan and Buchanan 1985). Even with regard to the vulnerabilities of Buchanan's original conception, arguments for the importance of rules are by no means dismissed. Instead, they have been improved and refined. In the following, I will first examine Buchanan's "orthodox" perspective in order to then look at the developments in Buchanan's thought that are especially evident in his later work. In several of his later writings, one finds explicit statements according to which a type of "moral" behavior is required that goes beyond an adherence to the rules (and a commitment to modifying them).

Buchanan's Original Conception

The groundwork for Buchanan's conception of constitutional economics or constitutional social theory was established by *The Calculus of Consent* (Buchanan and Tullock 1962) and *The Limits of Liberty* (Buchanan 1975), and later especially fleshed out in *The Reason of Rules* (Brennan and Buchanan 1985). The discussion that follows will focus on the questions that emerge in the latter work. It will be shown that Buchanan's (and Brennan's) original conception does not make any additional demands of society's members beyond an adherence to the rules and a commitment to rule reform.

There are two building blocks to constitutional social theory that prevent this approach (at least in its initial form) from representing a variant of individual-oriented approaches (see the section "Moral communication: Toward a semantics of benefits"). The approach also (implicitly) reflects an order ethics that can be developed out of it (see Homann 2002 and Luetge 2012), even if Buchanan and Brennan do not undertake this themselves:

1. Constitutional social theory is based on the underlying behavioral assumptions of economics, to which I will return in the section "Morality in Buchanan's later work." At this point, it is important to note that the assumption of self-interested actors by no means suggests that "actually existing" human beings direct their activity exclusively according to their own self-interest.
2. Buchanan rejects the objectivistic approach of welfare theory according to which one could establish a collective welfare function for groups or entire societies and hence determine "the good" for them externally. This concerns a non-cognitivistic, subjectivistic approach that resists the temptation to identify a moral surplus value that is thought to be necessary for social stability.

Morality in Buchanan's Later Work

In Brennan and Buchanan (1985), the first steps of a development can be found that extends throughout Buchanan's later work. As indicated, the book generally underscores the significance of rules. There is little discussion of morality. Nonetheless, the relevance of morality is alluded to in two places:

On the one hand, Brennan and Buchanan cite the example of the football player who not only receives a fifteen-yard penalty for a committed foul—as prescribed by the rules—but is also additionally penalized with "moral opprobrium" (Brennan and Buchanan 1985, chapter 7). This moral opprobrium can be understood in two different ways. It either pertains to a punishment, which can be added to the fifteen-yard penalty. In this case, a fifteen-yard penalty and opprobrium are to be largely understood in terms of the same system of cost calculation. One could also convert the moral opprobrium into a rule-based punishment in which the player would receive a punishment for his inappropriate conduct. On the other hand, according to a different understanding of "moral opprobrium," the fifteen-yard penalty and opprobrium are not to be thought of in terms of the *same* system of cost calculation. They are rather incommensurable magnitudes. In this case, the opprobrium would stem from an alternative sanctions mechanism to the one pertaining to rule-based punishments and cannot be calculated in terms of the fifteen-yard penalty or added to it.

This second understanding of moral opprobrium appears to be more consistent with Brennan's and Buchanan's aims. The example of the football player is accordingly used as evidence that an individual who accepts her punishment for violating a rule still does not act justly by doing so (see ibid.). According to Brennan and Buchanan, she first acts justly when she follows the rules and hence keeps her promise to the other players. The "sense of justice" (ibid.)[1] can be utilized here to prevent rule violations and would thus need to be strengthened—both through moral sanctions and moral opprobrium. Thus morality is used here along with rules as an alternative sanctions mechanism. Just the same, morality is merely understood in this instance as a complement to the rules and is not given conceptual priority.

Brennan's and Buchanan's second application of a "surplus-related" concept still does not impart it with a decisive function. In the book's final section, a "civic religion"[2] is called for. In brief, the intended civic religion is supposed to foster a new public appreciation for rules and especially to bring about a turning away from a belief in the state's ability to control society. Rules, consequently, are primarily seen as limitations on the role of the state. This appeal is above all directed at the academic community: it should abstain from offering policy recommendations (for new, additional rules) and instead uphold the Enlightenment's attitude of skepticism toward the state. Here, too, as in the case of the football player, it is still not possible to speak of a fundamental role for this concept, even if the introduction of such an appeal at the end of the book hints that a civic religion is especially important to the authors.[3]

The role of morality in Buchanan does not become clear until several works published after the late 1980s.[4] In 1989, a contribution appeared in *Essays on the Political Economy* (Buchanan 1989) with the title "On the Work Ethic." The essay was further revised in 1991 (Buchanan 1991) and assumed its final form in 1994 in *Ethics and Economic Progress* (Buchanan 1994).[5] In this latter work, Buchanan steps outside of the framework of his previous conception of a constitutional economics and goes beyond the requirements of rule compliance and a commitment to continuing to develop the rules. Buchanan suggests three types of behavior to the members of a society (in particular American society).[6]

1) We should all work harder.

Buchanan finds that the traditional work ethic has been lost that is especially important for the economic strength of a country—chiefly since the civil rights movements of the 1970s—and needs to be revived. His justification for this is economic in nature: all of the members of a society A with a functioning work ethic are much better off than the members of a society B who lack such an ethic. In Buchanan's view, an increased amount of (life-) time dedicated to work, and not leisure, corresponds to increased opportunities for the members of A to become more specialized. The greater the degree of specialization in a society, the more everyone can profit from it. Here, Buchanan draws on Smith's (1976/1990, 9ff.) classical argument in favor of the division of labor, which benefits everyone. Everyone has the opportunity to specialize in the kind of work she does best, while being relieved from those tasks in which she is less productive. The further this specialization progresses, the greater the advantages that accrue to all citizens. Because more work leads to more specialization, an internalized work ethic that encourages more work has universal utility.

2) We should all save more.

As he has contended in several works (see Brennan and Buchanan 1980 as well as Buchanan 1989), Buchanan believes that the *governmental* budgets have wasted too much money and burdened future generations with too much debt. Yet here he also means that individuals must (again) adopt an "ethic of saving." This ethic, on the one hand, has been undermined by Keynesian theory, which casts doubt on the economic value of saving.[7] On the other hand, he further notes, the modern welfare state has clearly disincentivized the need for individuals to save for their own future.

Buchanan points out that his analysis is strictly economic (see Buchanan 1964/1979). He stresses that we should save more in order to increase our own utility.[8] At the same time, we would also increase the utility for all other members of society. This utility increase would result from the fact that, through savings, we would boost the total amount of available capital in a society for making investments. Analogous to the argument in favor of a work ethic, the market would thus expand, leading to a higher degree of specialization. Again, this would benefit everyone.

This is why, according to Buchanan, it is very important to (re-)internalize this "savings ethic," for it would elevate economic productivity. All the same, institutional reforms to the political legal framework can supposedly provide a viable alternative to the internalization of a savings ethic—apparently in contrast to the case of the work ethic (see number 1). A correction to the incentives emerging out of this framework is apparently easier to undertake and is already in fact effectively accomplished in the form of tax-law reforms. The savings ethic is thus less critical than the work ethic, which cannot be as easily substituted by changes to institutional incentives (see Buchanan 1994, 58).

3) We should all pay the preacher.

This third demand relates, at the most basic level, to what Buchanan understands to be the relationship between rules and morality. He emphasizes that moral norms have an economic value (hence the subtitle of the chapter 3: "Economic Origins of Ethical Constraints"). Buchanan wants to explain with economic methods how such norms came about. At the same time, he also wants to distinguish himself from earlier explanatory approaches from economics (see Buchanan 1994, 61). Many such approaches exist. They all have in common that they represent moral norms as beneficial (for individuals, groups, or societies) and reconstruct the evolutionary process of their origin, whereby the unfavorable norms were "eliminated." Beyond this, however, the approaches proceed in different ways.

According to the so-called "economics of self-control," which is endorsed by Howard Rachlin (2000), Ted O'Donoghue, Matthew Rabin (1999), and others, moral norms evolved because they proved to be advantageous for the way individuals led their lives. For such an explanation, the actions of others do not play a role. Whoever relies on it must also maintain that precisely those norms prevail that prove to be beneficial for the compliant individual independent of how others behave. If a command like "always be honest!" wins out, this must then mean that the honest members of society—always or at least in general—have profited from being honest. When confronted with prisoner's-dilemma type situations, this approach must either assert that such situations can be resolved through one-sided cooperative behavior (I always cooperate, whether you do or not) or admit that no moral norms could surface evolutionarily that would cause individuals to wind up in such situations by observing them. Neither of these answers is satisfactory, however. On the one hand, one-sided cooperation cannot result from prisoner's dilemmas, which indeed is precisely the point.[9] One-sided cooperation would either be exploited or could not prevail evolutionarily, or else the anticipation of this exploitation would already cause "preventative counter defections" (Homann 2002, 98 and 115) and thus a departure from norm compliance. The "economics of self-control" therefore cannot successfully deal with situations in which my behavior is inextricably linked to the behavior of others.

An alternative approach takes into account the behavior of others and attempts to construe behavioral limitations as the result of contractual negotiations (bargaining).[10] Accordingly, those behavioral limitations prevail that all participants can agree to. This means that every individual limits her behavior when everyone else does the same. Behavioral limitations must therefore offer reciprocal advantages; they must allow everyone to benefit. This argument is consistent with Buchanan's own about the justification of *political-legal* rules (see the section "Buchanan's original conception").

However, he does not locate the origin of morality in a limitation of *individual* behavior that is derived from contracts.

Buchanan (1994, 66 ff.) instead finds that the point of morality is rooted more in the interest of the individual to limit the behavior *of others*.[11] Actor A has an interest in actor B being convinced by moral arguments that she should give him (Actor A) something without repayment. In such an example, A might have a dollar and B an apple. In a normal exchange, A would receive the apple for his dollar. That said, it would be better for him if he could acquire the apple for free, supposing that B could be convinced that she should give A the apple for moral reasons. Consequently, A is prepared to invest in the development and transmission of moral norms to the amount of no more than one dollar. A thus effectively invests in the attempt to "reprogram" in the behavior of B (and beyond that possibly the behavior of other actors) for his own benefit.[12]

Buchanan (ibid. 70) understands the possibility of such reprogramming as an opportunity for A to change his fellow actors' order of preferences. He thus stands here in opposition to many areas of economics. Generally speaking, preferences are taken to be fixed in economics. Behavioral changes are attributed to modifications in the limiting conditions, not to changes in preferences (see Homann 2002, chapter 4). On this issue, Buchanan recognizes economics as imposing an undue constraint on itself. He writes:

> Ordinary sense observation suggests that the economists' stance in this respect is violative of reality. At best, the economists' model can be defended only and some principle of methodological reductionism. Persons do not simply emerge full-blown with well-defined preference orderings over all potential alternatives for choice. (Buchanan 1994, 76)

Buchanan, in other words, draws on empirical evidence and concludes that—empirically speaking—preferences are entirely changeable. Preferences can be influenced by the social environment and the culture in which an actor lives. In his view, the economic model is not realistic enough. It is much more reductionist, as it perceives human beings in a way that conflicts with real life. Buchanan, consequently, grasps the postulate of fixed preferences ontologically and as a statement about the world. I will return to this aspect of Buchanan's thought—which accords with many critics of economics—in greater detail in the section "Discussion."

Buchanan introduces the possibility that preferences can be changed with a specific aim in mind: it should be possible in this way to resolve certain interaction problems, although only—or at least principally—in cases in which those solutions based on exchange or negotiations are not an option. Supposing, once again, that A has a dollar and B has an apple, and, further, that neither is able to unilaterally convince the other that giving away his or her possession is a moral thing to do (as in the prisoner's dilemma, this one-sided solution would be the most beneficial for each individual). Each actor wants to acquire the possession of the other. It would therefore be of most benefit to them if they were to exchange their items rather than holding on to them. If, however, no exchange is possible between A and B, then the most beneficial solution for both could instead also be reached through morality. Here, they must be convinced that they are *obligated* to give up their possession without being compensated. They would therefore both have an interest in investing in morality, even if neither succeeded in obtaining a one-sided advantage through moral argument. The investment in the spread of morality is thus also in fact productive when a mutually beneficial alternative to institutionalized exchange is required.

This means that the significance of morality can and must decline in proportion to the degree that exchange and negotiations are available as alternatives to solving interaction problems.[13] Limitations on behavior through moral norms, however, remain relevant for situations in which solutions through exchange are burdened by high transaction costs. At this point, Buchanan (1994, 71) interestingly indicates above all situations affecting many actors, where behavioral interdependence is especially pronounced. Exchange solutions in this case would be "highly complex and difficult to enforce" (ibid.). As examples, Buchanan cites precisely those two types of situations in which the work ethic and savings ethic are supposed to provide an answer. Each form of morality is supposed to be beneficial for all participants. At the same time, however, a "formal contract of exchange" (ibid. 72) is burdened by prohibitively high transaction costs. Political-legal solutions would not be able to safeguard the inherent "dormant" reciprocal benefits (see ibid. 73). This leaves, according to Buchanan (ibid.), only the internalization of an ethic in order to reap these benefits. As is emphasized once again, the particular advantage of an ethic would lie "in the elementary fact that ethics are not contractual" (ibid.). Everyone would do better if the others worked more or saved more, yet no one could be coerced to work or save by means of a contract. The advantage of this situation rests in the fact that no contract would thus be *required*. It would not be necessary to wait for a formal contract settlement that is associated with high transaction costs.

Instead, it is important that the individuals themselves recognize the interdependence of their actions. Then the incentives related to acting in terms of a "Puritan Ethic" would emerge more or less naturally. I will return to the question of whether solutions arrived at through the internalization of an ethics can—as Buchanan apparently suggests—circumvent the logic of the prisoner's dilemma.

It is important to note that, in Buchanan's view, not every morality is productive and worthy of investment. There is rather an entire series of systems of norms that are unproductive and make all participants worse off.[14]

Among these (see Buchanan 1994, 79) are demands for "pure" altruism, where one, for instance, gives away her possessions to the poor and stops working "to take the time and smell the flowers" (ibid.) or supports coercive governmental measures for protecting the environment. Buchanan finds that only those *Puritan* norms and values are productive that benefit and create values for all members of a society. Besides the work ethic and the savings ethic, traditional demands are also to be counted:

- to be honest in negotiations
- to keep promises
- to tell the truth
- to respect people and property
- to exercise sober judgment
- to be tolerant

All of these demands largely correspond to those norms that comprise the classical "ethic of the honest businessman" (cf. Locke/Woiceshyn 1995 and Sahlman et al. 1999) in the traditional approaches of business ethics. Its economic significance lies in the reputational effects: whoever is able to convincingly maintain such an ethic improves her image and can hope to ultimately improve her bottom line. The common reproach regarding deception out of purely "commercial" interests has no place here, therefore. Such a positive image can only be acquired over time. A company that only thinks short term and does not make a deliberate effort to adhere to a system of values will sooner or later harm its image and, as a consequence, its revenues.[15]

An economic interpretation of this ethic, and consequently also an interpretation in the sense of OE, does not therefore present any difficulties—*as long as* what matters is the self-interested adherence to these demands for the sake of preserving one's own reputation. This is entirely consistent with OE. Accordingly, OE and Buchanan are in agreement with regard to the *result*.

The outlined justification of ethics, however, would correspond to those approaches in a) (economics of self-control) and b) (contractarian morals), which Buchanan specifically does not propagate. His concern is not with imposing restrictions on one's *own* behavior out of self-interest. The caring for the behavior of others or "preaching"—whose economic importance Buchanan intends to demonstrate—is thus not addressed yet. His argument is that everyone should engage in preaching the *right* values out of self-interest because everyone would be better off. It is beneficial for the members of a society to spread *certain* moral behavioral limitations, specifically those that stem from puritanical ethics. In addition, everyone would have an interest in the other members adhering to these limitations.

Buchanan appears to recognize that he runs the risk with his three demands of being labeled a moralizer. He therefore quickly tries to explain (see Buchanan 1984, 28) that all three demands are in everyone's interest. There is a similarity here between his demands and constitutional rules. They are both functionally equivalent. Buchanan remarks unambiguously in a footnote:

> Ethical constraints or rules, as means of correcting or internalizing relevant externalities, are, of course, alternatives to possible legal-political constraints. (Buchanan 1994, 28, fn. 2)

This means that externalities—effects on others—cannot simply be corrected if the game rules that are mandatory for everyone and the institutions have been changed. Moral norms can also impart such a correction. It should be noted here that Buchanan goes beyond his position in Brennan and Buchanan (1985); while morality there simply makes available *supplementary* sanctions mechanisms above and beyond political legal rules, in Buchanan (1994) it obtains a largely "freestanding"[16] role. Thus Buchanan (ibid. 28) holds it to be very unlikely that the externality of the choice between work and leisure can be remedied by politics (and law). This problem can *only* be solved by morality. Hence it is not by any means to be taken as a supplement, but rather as a *substitute* for the rules.

DISCUSSION

I intend to criticize Buchanan's undertaking in two respects. First, I maintain that

a. to the extent that it concerns a *normative* project, it is not clear why the problems of implementing moral norms—which Buchanan himself recognizes with regard to other spheres of society—should not also take effect here. If this criticism is right, then the ethic of work and the ethic of saving could also not achieve what they're supposed to. The pending problems could instead only be solved through institutional reforms of a political-legal type.
b. to the extent that it concerns a purely *descriptive* project, Buchanan's analytical approach is highly problematic. Morality is treated as an empirical fact that should be figured into economic analyses in order to make them more "realistic."

To follow up on this point, I will discuss an issue that is critical within the scope of this book, namely, whether Buchanan actually calls for a moral surplus value with the demands that have been presented here or whether these demands can be interpreted in such a way that they may be integrated into OE. By way of concluding, I will finally propose a constructive interpretation.

First, with regard to point a): Buchanan's original conception presumes (with supporting arguments) that a society's political-legal rules can have a decisive influence on an individual's behavior. Such rules have control effects, and problems of a political and social nature can only be solved through the reform of these rules. The key argument asserts that rules *simultaneously* change the limiting conditions for all participants. Moral appeals thus have no impact because the situation would not change *simultaneously* for all participants, even given the precondition that everyone would choose to heed this appeal in principle. The individual who initially provides an advance payment is open to exploitation. Moreover, because she anticipates this himself, she reacts with a preventative counter defection. The type of behavior that is in the interest of everyone does not take place. This is why interaction problems of the prisoner's-dilemma type can only be resolved through rule changes. The participating individuals would then no longer be susceptible to exploitation and they would also have no incentive to engage in preventative counter defections.

Buchanan emphasizes this logic as a critical point in his original conception. Yet it apparently is not supposed to apply to the ethic of work and the ethic of saving. Is this plausible? If actor A *one-sidedly* begins to work harder or to save more, actor B would then feel herself to be relieved of this obligation. As in every prisoner's-dilemma situation, it would be best for B if everyone else worked harder but she did not have to herself and could still reap the rewards of this work that accrue to everyone.[17] It is not clear *prima facie* how the situation for which the ethic of work is intended to provide an answer can be distinguished from the following situations:

- for a business owner, it would be best if everyone else invested in measures to protect the environment, but also if she did not have to herself.
- for a beachgoer, it would be best if everyone else made an effort to keep the beach clean, but also if she did not have to herself.
- for a prisoner in the classical PD situation, it would be best if his fellow prisoners cooperated and made denials, but he defected and confessed to the shared crime.

If these observations are correct—for example, if an interaction problem of the prisoner's-dilemma type presents itself even in cases of an ethic of work and an ethic of saving—then it is not clear why the solution by means of morality and ethics, which does not take hold in the cited cases, should suddenly bear fruit. The expectation should rather be that such an ethic would also end up being an ineffective appeal. I will return to the question of whether Buchanan actually makes a moral appeal to the individual actors to cultivate a certain kind of behavior or whether his demands might in fact be interpreted differently.

With regard to point b): a second serious difficulty with Buchanan's conception is epistemological in nature, specifically with regard to his analysis of the behavior of individuals. It is obvious in (at least) two places that his theoretical reconstruction of types of behavior is overly phenomenological (in the sense indicated in the section "Moral communication: toward a semantics of benefits"). On the one hand, Buchanan assumes that preferences in actuality change. According to the evidence of this that is cited in the section "Morality in Buchanan's later work," it is supposedly demonstrated through "ordinary sense observation" that economists use an unrealistic model for human beings (one that is "violative of reality"). According to the findings of such (everyday) observations, human beings are in fact not like the theory suggests. In particular, they lack any kind of well-defined ordering of preferences.

Conversely, Buchanan writes:

> We may start from the premise that individual behavior is morally-ethically constrained. We do not behave opportunistically in each and every encounter; we do not act in accordance with some "as-if" cost-benefit reckoning, as might be made against the formal legal structure of rewards and penalties. Many of us do not steal, even if we should be certain that there is no possibility of discovery, apprehension, and punishment. (Buchanan 1994, 63)

Here, too, Buchanan apparently means to say that human beings—viewed empirically—are not what economic theory presents them to be.[18] Instead, in reality, individuals comply with moral norms, even if they do not benefit from doing so. Many, in fact, do not make any cost-benefit analysis, but rather ignore incentives—indeed apparently systematically—in their behavioral choices.

This critique corresponds with the commonly accepted views of many critics of economics such as, among others, those of Sen (1977; 1999), Elster (1989), or Hirschman (1984).[19] Without going into all the precise details of a response from the side of economics, I would only like to point out here that economics is *not* allowed to perceive the rational actor as a representative image of the human being.[20] The *homo economicus* is merely a theoretical construction, a model that cannot be directly confirmed by empirical evidence. This model is utilized for a specific problem and can only be sensibly and properly applied to this problem. Other models are better suited to other problems.

The particular problem of economics lies in its explanation and determination of the conditions and outcomes of interactions on the basis of individual calculations relating to advantages and disadvantages. Economics involves explanations *for the purpose of* making determinations. In need of explanation are all social phenomena such as the rate of unemployment, the rate of inflation, the rate of divorce, or the relationship between empirically and theoretically oriented economists.[21] The advantage/disadvantage calculation of the involved individuals is introduced as the explanans for this explanation. Determinative recommendations are finally given on the basis of the particular explanation, which are aimed at policy making and the public. These determinative recommendations are suggestions for modifying existing political-legal rules or for reforms to or the elimination of institutions.

The model of the *homo economicus* is only suited for this type of problem. It is either less applicable, or not applicable at all, for questions that

- do not deal with social or collective phenomena (like the rate of inflation), but instead concern individual phenomena. Generally speaking, these involve psychological (though not necessarily socio-psychological) questions that examine individual cases, or more precisely: the cognitive processes of individuals. For these questions, psychology is able to make do *without* the precondition of self-interested behavior. In this framework, the model proposed by Herbert A. Simon (1983) and Jon Elster (1987; 1989) that is augmented with psychological findings can be used.
- do not deal with issues relating to institutional design, like most psychological, but above all sociological studies. Sociological systems theory, for instance, presents first and foremost a *description*; it develops a *semantics* for modern societies (see Luhmann 1997). Just the same, it does not pursue the objective of *designing* institutions. In particular, the expectation is not placed on sociology from the side of politics (and the public) to provide such institutional recommendations. Sociologists therefore can and must utilize alternative models of actors like the *homo sociologicus*, in which self-interest is not necessarily a constitutive feature.

In both of these types of cases, which are aimed at other theoretical *and/or* different practical problems, other analytical constructions are needed and used than the *homo economicus*. This does not mean, however, that one can conclude that the human being as *homo sapiens* is one way or another. To decide upon one representative image of the human being from the diverse constructions of the various disciplines would be misguided. Such a decision is neither necessary nor possible. It can only be said that an analytical tool is either appropriate or not for a particular problem when it is viewed in terms of the problem at hand. Such tools or mental instruments also cannot be directly checked empirically, but are selected in terms of their effectiveness. The effectiveness of a construct, in turn, can be measured according to the degree that it allows for a situation to be restructured in relation to the original problem in the respective discipline. With regard to economics, this means that the recommendations gleaned from an economic explanation must also be implementable. The *homo economicus* is thus only to be viewed as an effective construction when it helps to structure situations in a way that yields institutional recommendations that will benefit everyone. If it does *not* do this systematically or over the long run, then the *homo economicus* must be abandoned.[22]

Against the backdrop of these observations, Buchanan's discussion of the deficiency of realism in economics is deeply problematic. People do not simply have well-ordered or not well-ordered preferences. This is not something that can be proven to be a *factum brutum* as a result of "ordinary sense observation." Instead, within the scope of economics, well-ordered preferences are ascribed a theoretical foundation, specifically for the purpose of making institutional determinations. Buchanan's rejection of this preliminary theoretical judgment remains at the level of phenomenalism, as described in the section "Moral communication: Toward a semantics of benefits," and is therefore irrelevant for scientific theories. The same can be said about Buchanan's assertion that many people observe moral norms without making cost-benefit analyses. This claim can also only be interpreted as a phenomenological statement, as a statement based in everyday speech. An economic analysis would necessarily problematize this statement.

Economics can provide economic reasons for why it is beneficial to actors to observe moral norms when there is no expectation of immediate punishment or reward. Studies like these have been and continue to be conducted.[23] As a result, Buchanan's assertion that economic theory does not allow room for moral behavior (in this sense) cannot be supported. It does in fact permit moral behavior, albeit under certain constraints.

If there are no external incentives of a political-legal variety that run counter to actor A's compliance with norm X, and if incentives instead promote an adherence to X, it would then be surprising if A were to not follow X. This does not present a problem for economic theory, which would not assert that X would not be followed under any circumstances. Buchanan admits this himself, but he also insists that economics would not allow for X to be followed if there is no prospect of punishment for violating it. In actual fact, only a certain version of economics would not permit this, specifically the kind that narrowly anticipates the calculation of benefits *in every individual case.*[24] However, if not just the costs and benefits of *individual* cases can be calculated, but also the costs and benefits of *rules* that are applicable in *numerous* cases, then it is certainly conceivable that an actor would decide to follow a norm without having to fear any sanctions for breaking a rule. Of course it is true that "many of us do not steal." The economic reasons for this can be multiple. First of all, A might not be 100 percent sure that she will not be caught. In this case, even a small chance of being discovered, tied with the possibility of a very negative outcome (especially reputational damage) can deter someone, for instance, from committing a theft or riding public transportation without paying the fare. On the other hand, and this is more germane to the present context, it is generally much more cost-effective to remember a rule and to (more or less) follow it blindly than to have to make a new calculation in every individual case. If A had to make a new calculation every time she took the train or went to a store as to whether it would make sense to steal or dodge a fare, she would then have to utilize considerable intellectual resources that could be applied elsewhere. Thus, at least insofar as it postulates the individual's cost-benefit calculations with regard to rules and not individual cases, economic theory certainly allows for moral norms to be followed, even in cases in which their violation in individual cases would not entail any disadvantages.

I now come to the question of whether Buchanan actually makes demands of the members of a society that go beyond OE. There are at any rate statements in several places that point to a different kind of *intention*. He thus stresses that his aim is purely descriptive: he simply wants to provide an economic *analysis of the origin* of moral norms. As a result, he has no normative objective in mind. He does not want to prescribe to anyone what they should do. Nonetheless, economic analysis demonstrates that everyone is better off when a society can draw upon active, internalized norms in the sense of a Puritan ethic. He explicitly states:

> But let me emphasize once again that these arguments are presented as exercises in economic explanation and not as ethical discourse. . . . And also note that my argument does not address prescriptive issues concerning how any particular person "should" or "ought" to behave. The argument says nothing at all about whether or not an individual should work harder, save more, tell the truth, or keep promises. The argument says only that the individual, any individual, will be "better off," in terms of economic well-being, if others work harder, save more, keep promises, and so on. (Buchanan 1994, 80)

This quote suggests that an economic *explanation* of morality is at issue here.[25] Yet there is still more to be said on this point:

1. If the aim is to only provide an explanation, it remains unclear what the scope of this explanation should be. For example, it could relate only to the evolution of moral norms in the past, especially in premodern society. This is not implausible, but then it would be irrelevant for the conditions of a modern society.
2. Buchanan actually provides *more* than only an explanation. At the very least, he also presents *recommendations of an instrumental variety* that suggest to actors that they should behave in manner A *if* they want to reach objective B: "*if* you want to be better off, *then* you

should work more and save more." This, then, reflects a hypothetical imperative that rests on a (descriptive) scientific analysis.

If Buchanan's goal is to present hypothetical recommendations, then he would also have to discuss how these recommendations could be implemented on a political-legal level with respect to prisoner's-dilemma structures. According to Buchanan's original conception, these problems can only be solved if recommendations are made with regard to the configuration of rules and institutions. Buchanan, however, does not address this possibility. That is, he does not offer any recommendations for how his three demands might actually be implemented. He rather only gives an economic analysis of the effects of moral norms, whereby it is in everyone's interest to adhere to the demands to, for example, "work more" and "save more" and do something to contribute to their proliferation ("pay the preacher").

The possibility thus presents itself that Buchanan's goal is in fact to just make moral appeals. This is consistent, on the one hand, with his view—as cited and shown (to have already been largely put forward in Brennan and Buchanan (1985)—that "ethical constraints" represent an alternative to rules when it comes to correcting externalities. On the other hand, it principally accords with Buchanan's thesis (noted in the section "Morality in Buchanan's later work") that there could be interaction problems that can only be solved through morality, because solutions through contracts and alterations to incentives are too costly, that is, "highly complex and difficult to enforce."[26] Consequently, a mutually beneficial solution can only be arrived at through the internalization of an ethics that does not depend on a contract (or for that matter quid pro quo reciprocity).

The following observation thus seems to inform Buchanan's three demands:

> Externalities of the "too-low-savings-rate" or "too-low-work-rate" type cannot be remedied by political-legal rules. It therefore also does not make sense to devise related recommendations for reforming these rules. Be that as it may, as an economist I can still try to convince all those involved that it is in their self-interest to behave this way or another.

This might be interpreted as an attempt to enlighten the public about actual relationships, which is entirely compatible with OE.[27] *However*: if Buchanan's behavioral recommendations cannot be immediately implemented by individuals—because their behavior might be exploited (due to the logic of interactions)—then such a "scientific enlightenment" hardly differs from a political stump speech or a moral sermon. The situation would be different if this enlightenment entered into the political decision-making process about rules. But Buchanan—as has been repeatedly emphasized—specifically does *not* have this in mind. He rather recognizes here the opportunity for a (non-contractarian) morality. Beyond the demand for an adherence to the rules and rule reform, a Puritan work ethic and an ethic of saving (which is in everyone's self-interest[28]) is required in order to address a problem that cannot be solved by means of rules.

A constructive interpretation of Buchanan's moral surplus value might look as follows: first, the purely phenomenalistic approach to the phenomenon of morality and adherence to it should be abandoned. The adherence or non-adherence to moral norms would need to be construed economically as the result of the calculation of rational actors. This would mean that norm compliance can generally only be expected when the (political-legal) incentives in particular do not counteract this compliance.

On the other hand, the either-or situation—which Buchanan however does not make entirely clear—of morality *or* rules as an instrument of social control should be disposed with. Morality can never completely *replace* the controlling effects of political-legal rules. If necessary, morality can be given a temporary residual controlling effect,[29] which nonetheless can only have an impact in a few areas and under certain conditions:

- In some areas, a functioning ethic still exits.[30] In such cases, it may be worth already starting to make attempts to preventatively stabilize this ethic, that is, *before* erosion has set in.
- In areas with deficient rules, morality can be applied as a method of control on a *trial or alternative* basis.
- Under certain precisely defined conditions, actors can erect functioning social systems through self-organization. Among these conditions, Ostrom (1990) cites above all a moderate number of the affected actors (up to approximately 15,000, see ibid. 237 and XVI-IIff.) and a functioning background structure of institutions. Against this background, morality (even in Buchanan's sense) can assume a residual control, especially in firms that do not exceed the magnitudes that are postulated by Ostrom.

Still, this residual controlling effect will inevitably be thwarted without appropriate incentives. Morality necessarily erodes as soon as incentives are arrayed against it. And when this erosion has taken place, control through incentives is only possible on the political-legal level. Once morality has been bankrupted, it can no longer be "reactivated," or only done so at the cost of its real impotence in the face of the problems of modern societies and especially under conditions of globalization. Luhmann formulated this classical response in reference to ecological problems:

> Society is a highly complex structured system. Wouldn't morality necessarily have a trivializing effect when confronted with such complex structures? How

can one seriously believe that a new morality could be implemented in environmentally appropriate behavior, without colliding at every turn with other demands? Legal norms, after all, are not intended to protect against the unreasonable expectations that others hold to be rational and moral. (Luhmann 1985, 18; translated by C. R.).

Individual actors *may* indeed continue to find it advantageous to invest in "preaching"; it is also possible that this *could be* beneficial for the entire society. However, the political-legal incentives that apply equally to everyone remain in place, and, given such incentives, a solution that is beneficial for everyone could fall through. Strictly speaking, then, what *could be* beneficial *is not* necessarily actually beneficial. Or put it more succinctly: a lot may be expected, but not everything can be implemented.

SOCIETY REQUIRES (ALMOST) NOTHING (KEN BINMORE)

In his two volume *Game Theory and the Social Contract*, Binmore 1994 (vol. 1: "Playing Fair") and 1998 (vol. 2: "Just Playing") put forward an elaborate contract theory that explicitly draws on game-theoretical but also sociobiological concepts.[31] Binmore wants to revive liberalism, which he believes has been inadequately represented, especially in Anglo-Saxon countries.[32] Toward this end, he embraces the English tradition of the Whigs. He perceives himself as a torchbearer of Whig traditions (Binmore 1994, section 1.1) and designates Hume as his most important intellectual forebear (Binmore 1998, section 4.10.3 and xxiii). From Hume, Binmore adopts three key theoretical elements:

a. the empirical approach, which he above all understands as a demand to observe the existing social conditions of philosophical projects and to categorically reject those projects that turn out to be systematically untenable,
b. the idea of *mechanism design*, that is, the requirement of designing social institutions in a way that makes them incentive-compatible (see Binmore 1998, section 4.10.3), and
c. a skeptical attitude toward authorities.[33]

At first, it seems paradoxical that Binmore would design a contract theory that, of all theorists, relies on Hume, who is frequently recognized as an opponent of contract theory. However, Hume is thoroughly understood by several authors (see, for instance, Mackie 1980 and Gauthier 1979) as a contract theorist. In their view, Hume merely criticizes those social contract theories[34] that postulate an actual, historical agreement. In fact, Hume has nothing critical to say about a contract theory that only emphasizes an agreement's *construction*.[35]

This is also Binmore's position. Like all modern contract theorists since Rawls, he views the general agreement to be only a hypothesis or a construction.[36] The distinction to Rawls, but also to the approach of Harsanyi (1977), lies in Binmore's naturalistic point of view: very similar to the naturalistic research program of, for example, Shimony (1993), Binmore wants to do away with any of the kind of metaphysical remnants in his theory that he identifies in the earlier contract theories of his predecessors such as Rawls or Harsanyi. In the following, the Binmore's naturalistic approach will first be introduced (see the section "Binmore's naturalistic contract theory"). I will then examine his critique of other socio-philosophical conceptions, which can be summed up in the phrase: no *commitments*! (see the section "No commitments!") Finally, I will discuss the concept of empathy, which represents Binmore's necessary surplus value for a functioning modern society. Here, I will emphasize, however, that this predisposition clearly differs in its theoretical status from the moral surplus values identified in the other conceptions introduced in this book (see the section "Empathetic preferences"). Nonetheless, I will conclude by raising the question as to whether a society could perhaps make do *without* "empathetic preferences" (see the section "Discussion: Can't society also dispose with empathetic preferences?").

BINMORE'S NATURALISTIC CONTRACT THEORY

According to Wolfgang Kersting (1994, 54 ff.), every contract theory requires three central elements: 1) the construction of the circumstances of the contract settlement (typically the original condition); 2) a conception of the actors' rationality; and 3) a conception of the justification of the contract argument. All three of these elements can be found in Binmore. The first two will be discussed in the following subsections, "Binmore's original position" and "Binmores conception of rationality." In anticipation of this discussion, I would now like to begin by taking a close look at the justification of the contract argument.

As indicated above, Binmore draws upon Hume's moral philosophy. According to Hume, society is held together by *conventions*. It is able to function because of long-cherished and continually practiced (and mostly unwritten) rules.[37] Binmore seizes on this argument and expands it into a full-blown contract theory: a "system of coordinating conventions" (Binmore 1994, 6) may in his view be equated with a "social contract," and the law consists in nothing more than "well-codified conventions" (ibid. 33). Hume's conventions are rules that the members of the society give to themselves through consensus. They can be unwritten, but also fully codified. They can be reformed and improved upon, whereby such improvements are only possible through "mutual consent" (ibid. 7).

The upshot of Binmore's contract theory lies in that it is inherently naturalistic, and that it is also justified naturalistically.[38] For Binmore, a naturalistic conception demands the rejection of all authorities legitimated by metaphysics. The stability of society—which is also a primary objective for Binmore—is legitimated in his view by the vast majority of socio-philosophical approaches by means of authorities that ultimately exhibit a metaphysical character. Among those authors who argue in this way, Binmore includes, for example, Rawls,[39] Harsanyi, Gauthier, and Nozick. They all share the opinion that it is possible for actors to make so-called *commitments* or pledges in social interactions whose observance is not ensured through sanctions and incentives. Binmore's critique of this stance is examined in detail in the section "No commitments!" For the moment, it is important to note how Binmore positions his own naturalism in relation to the indicated authors (see Binmore 1994, 11). A naturalistic conception:

1. does not pose questions like "What does X really mean?"
2. formulates only hypothetical, not categorical, imperatives; a final justification of morality is thus excluded, and
3. demands above all that only implementable and enforceable solutions be seen as capable of justification.

This third point is incorporated by Binmore in his definition of a "fair social contract" (ibid. 41), which he formulates as follows: as a game theorist, Binmore strongly differentiates between two "games"—the "Game of Life" and the "Game of Morals" (see Binmore 1994, 25ff., 42, and 335f.). The Game of Life determines the valid framework for the actors in their social relationships, whether they are of a physical or psychic nature (see ibid. 25). The actors cannot change the conditions of this framework, but must instead take account of them as external factors in the calculus of their decision making. By contrast, the Game of Morals is conceived as a situation that can be renewed at any time. The actors can also voluntarily enter into the Game of Morals and change its outcome (the Game of Morals will be discussed in more detail in the section "Binmore's original position"). In the Game of Morals, the social contract that is considered fair under existing conditions is (re-) defined. However, here is the crucial point: when the actors "play" the Game of Morals, only those solutions may be considered as candidates for a fair social contract that are themselves *equilibria in the Game of Life*. No other possible solutions are achievable by the actors because they are not enforceable. This viewpoint will be elaborated upon in the following.

Binmore equates the concept of equilibrium in the game of life with the game-theoretical concept of the Nash equilibrium.[40] A Nash equilibrium is defined as a situation in which the strategy of each player consists in the optimal reaction to the strategies of every other player. In particular, no player in the Nash equilibrium can improve her position by means of an alternative strategy. This means that Nash equilibria represent *stable* social arrangements. All other arrangements are inherently unstable because actors can try to improve their situation and thus not consent to the arrangement. In a "one-shot" prisoner's dilemma, for instance, the only possible Nash equilibrium is represented by the mutual defection of all players. In other games, such as the "Battle of the Sexes,"[41] there are multiple Nash equilibria. Binmore stresses that the Game of Life also shows evidence of *many* equilibria. In this way, his approach is distinguished in particular from conservative theories, which tend to posit a single, unchanging equilibrium. Interestingly, Binmore criticizes one such conservative approach, which might be accused of excessive or naïve realism, for *not being realistic enough*. Realism hence means recognizing the *large number of possible equilibria* (see ibid. 289, fn. 44 and Binmore 2001).[42]

In contrast to the Game of Life, which represents a limiting condition that must be acknowledged, the Game of Morals reflects a tool, or more precisely, a coordination instrument. Binmore suggests that it aids in the selection of one possible equilibrium out of the many *possible* equilibria, which is then labeled as a fair social contract. Before we can discuss the definition of a fair social contract, however, the Game of Morals must be fleshed out more fully. It concerns a fictional and invented game (see Binmore 1994, 41f.) which—as in Rawls (see chapter 4)—connotes an instrument that helps to test whether a social institution will be perceived by the affected actors as just. In addition, it helps the actors to consider what institutional reforms might look like. The Game of Morals can be utilized by every actor at *any time*, that is, any actor can decide at *any time* that the existing social contract is no longer just. Here, Binmore clearly distinguishes himself from those approaches that presuppose a *one-time* contract settlement, which binds the contracting parties and their descendants indefinitely (see also the section "Binmore's original position"). The actors will therefore always turn to the Game of Morals whenever it is in their interest to do so (see the section "Binmore's conception of rationality").

In contrast to the Game of Life, the Game of Morals offers additional features that do not exist "in real life." A (game-theoretical) solution in the Game of Morals—that is, a situation that is desired by all affected actors that may even include reciprocal improvements—is not enforceable simply because it is deemed to be *desirable*. Instead, it makes more sense to only consider those solutions from the Game of Morals that also represent equilibria in the Game of Life, and that effectively pass the "reality test." For example, in the section "No commitments!" within the scope of the fictional Game of Morals, I discussed the entirely plausible assumption of *commit-*

ments, which are supposed to bind the actors *without* sanctions. Yet such an assumption does *not* make sense to Binmore, since no fair and enforceable social contracts can be identified with its help. At this point, the following definition may be provided (see ibid. 41):

> a fair social contract is an equilibrium in the Game of Life in which all participants use strategies that would offer no incentive to anyone in the [hypothetical] Game of Morals to utilize the construction of the *original position* (see ibid. 41 and also Binmore 1998, 424).[43]

This leads to the following conclusion: on the one hand, only an *enforceable* contract (equilibrium) is also fair; on the other hand, all those affected must be able to expect *advantages* from the—existing or new—contract, for otherwise they would have to start the Game of Morals from the beginning to change their circumstances. Such a new turn at the game would be understood as a new negotiation of the social contract.

Finally, it should be noted that Binmore's naturalism does *not* commit the naturalistic fallacy. There are no prescriptive statements that have been derived from purely descriptive, for example, evolutionary, theoretical statements. First, a naturalistic basis is simply supposed to provide the "empirical basis" (ibid. 139) for the ethically relevant facts. However, a decision would still have to be made on this basis. Second, Binmore (1994, 11, fn. 6 and 2004) stresses that he is merely looking for *hypothetical* imperatives that will allow recommendations to be made of the type "A should do X if A wants to achieve Y." And finally, third, the discussion toward the end of the two-volume work (see Binmore 1998, 505f.) seems to suggest that Whig liberalism makes *proposals* to persuade and to get people to participate, and whose acceptance cannot be prejudiced by individuals. This does not mean that the issue of implementation is not thought about or taken into account in the conception. When Binmore stresses the necessity of considering only equilibria in the Game of Life, this is precisely what he has in mind.

Binmore's Original Position

I will now examine Binmore's construction of the circumstances of the contract settlement in more detail, especially in contrast to Rawls's approach (see chapter 4). What matters most here is that while Binmore formally uses Rawls's concept of the "original position" (ibid. 13; cursive in original), he provides it with different content. Binmore uses the term "original position" in order to distinguish his approach from conceptions that assume the existence of a *one-time* contract settlement and do not allow for any renegotiations. In this respect, he agrees with Rawls. However, he also criticizes Rawls on another point, namely, that he effectively eliminates the state of nature (see ibid. 14). To Rawls's way of thinking, the actors in the contract settlement select the two basic principles of a fair social order *because* these principles best conform to their moral intuitions (see chapter 4). They therefore do not select them because they want to self-interestedly flee from a threatening state of nature, that is, anarchy.

Binmore rejects this line of reasoning. To him,[44] it does not make sense to do away with the state of nature as a potentially anarchistic threat. The state of nature, rather, must always be conceived of as the status quo.[45] For Binmore, the status quo is the situation that needs improvement—it is the situation that the actors, as individuals or as members of groups, are unsatisfied with and that motivates them to play the Game of Morals. This status quo[46] can lead to many possible new social contracts, among which *some* would represent improvements for all participants. The *original position* would be used to help these participants imagine which of the *achievable* new social contracts they could agree to. This would also entail the assumption on their part that they do not know their social positions under the conditions of the new contract. Whereas Rawls justifies (see the section "The sense of justice") his corresponding "veil of ignorance"[47] with essentially *a priori* observations, and later with the sense of justice (within certain Western-type societies), Binmore (1994, 336ff.) argues differently. The veil of ignorance—which we would use in everyday judgments—would have to be applied in a more tenuous form, indeed as tenuously as possible precisely so that it can fulfil its purpose. This should be understood *descriptively*, for this is how the veil "works" in all of us, although we also have access to *empathetic preferences*.[48] Binmore (1998, chapter II) develops this basic assumption in a formal model that addresses informational limitations (on the basis of probabilities), possible (achievable) social contracts, and a "realistic" modeling of the negotiation process.

So far, a more fundamental question remains unanswered: Where does the *original position* come from? Binmore wants to avoid justifying its use on metaphysical grounds. But, then, why should individuals call upon it?

Like Rawls, Binmore assumes that the *original position* is a reconstruction of tools, or rather mental apparatuses, that human beings always use. However, in contrast to Rawls, he aims to identify the evolutionary or sociobiological history of its genesis. Binmore (1994, 145) takes it as a given that the *original position* emerged in the early history of humankind—in the "social mesocosm"[49] of the small group. More specifically, the norms that regulated the distribution of food in the horde of prehistoric man were capable of being construed economically, and indeed as a means of insurance. Not every prehistoric human could expect to have success hunting every day. Moreover, the elderly and children wanted to be taken care of. In order to avoid continual distribution conflicts between those who benefited from serendipity and those who happened to be consistently less well-off, the individuals recognized at some point that they should create a kind of insurance system that would allow the temporarily undersupplied to partake in the nourishment acquired by the others.[50]

This led to norms developing into *food-sharing norms*, which reflected a form of experience that had crystalized out these distribution conflicts. Of course, these norms were not permanent, but were also renegotiated. The original position, according to Binmore, gradually developed over time out of the experiences gained in these negotiations (*bargaining*) (see Binmore 1998, sections 2.5.4 and 4.6.2). Supposedly, they were not primarily passed on through *cultural* mechanisms, that is, through instruction and transfer, but instead through *genetic fixation* (see, for instance, Binmore 1998, 212f.). Within the framework of the sociobiological concept of gene-culture co-evolution (see, for example, Lumsden and Wilson 1981), genetic fixation is explained in terms of a type of cultural practice P, whereby a group G_1 that used P was superior to groups G_2 and G_3 and could thus reproduce and spread out more successfully at the latters' expense.

Afterward, the original position was liberated from its original, narrow use and applied rather haphazardly to new social contexts (see Binmore 1998, 210 and section 4.6.1). This proved successful in some of these contexts (i.e., it led to an improvement of the participants' circumstances), while in others it was less successful. Today, the focus is on transferring the use of this fairness mental apparatus from small group contexts to large modern societies (see ibid. 211 and section 4.10.1).

Binmore even contends that *evolution* equipped us with the mental apparatus of the *original position*. This phenomenon, though, is contingent. Binmore emphasizes that if other mental apparatuses had been "washed up" to shore by evolution (Binmore 1994, 145), he would have to justify his conception differently. In order to preserve the stability of a modern society, it makes sense to draw upon these available mechanisms to create fairer and generally more acceptable institutional arrangements. Thus the mechanism for determining fairness is identical in the modern and premodern time periods. Just the same, it is applied in different ways: in the modern era, only those *institutions* that have been established for anonymous social contexts may be evaluated with the help of the *original position*; in contrast, this mental apparatus was "invented" in the premodern era to assess norms in face-to-face relationships. Binmore maintains that this transfer and extension of the scope of a human being's moral equipment reflects "The Expanding Circle" (1981) that Peter Singer identifies and explicitly demands, if in a different manner.[51] Binmore sees this extension occurring with the help of our *empathetic preferences*, which stayed with us in the transition to modernity and may be functionally utilized in new ways. This will be the subject of the section "Empathetic preferences."

The fact that Binmore ascribes great importance to an evolutionary justification is also indicated in his argument for the role of the Nash equilibrium, which he also wants to justify in evolutionary terms (see Binmore 1994, 158).[52]

Binmore's Conception of Rationality

Given that Binmore argues from a game-theoretical position, it is not surprising that he adopts the game-theoretical standard rationality of Bayes's theorem as his conception of rationality, which also corresponds to the rationality of neoclassical economics.[53] Drawing on its classical torchbearer Savage (1951), who in turn invokes Hobbes, Binmore characterizes this conception of rationality in the following way (see Binmore 1994, 307 ff.):

According to Hobbes (1640/2008), human beings can be described with regard to four dimensions, namely

- strength of body
- experience
- reason
- passion (or feeling)

Each of these elements is formally integrated into Bayes's decision-making theorem. In Savage's (1951) view, actor A, who is confronted with a decision-making problem, has

- a large number of possible physical *behavioral options* (his bodily power),
- *beliefs* (convictions based on his experience),
- *decision-making rules or principles*, which in this case are those of Bayes's theorem (his understanding), and
- *preferences* (his motivating interests).

The most important point here is that beliefs are distinguished from preferences (see Binmore 1994, 304). If one understands Bayes's theorem as a *normative* theory, then rational actors *should* not let their "subjective" preferences influence their beliefs about the "objective" world and about the prevailing limiting conditions in this world.

Binmore's acceptance of Bayes's rationality is relevant for this book here for two reasons.

First, it is interesting to note the way in which Binmore justifies the use of neoclassical rationality—frequently criticized as reductionistic—in moral contexts. As we have already seen, he largely works with evolutionary arguments: neoclassical rationality is supposedly chosen on the basis of evolutionary processes (see Binmore 1994, 27). Nonetheless, Binmore clearly distinguishes between the *homo economicus* and the *homo sapiens* (see ibid. 20, 43, 57 f.)[54]: the fact that the *homo sapiens* (as a "human being" who we get to know in the real world) is not to be equated with the *homo economicus* appears to be indicated in particular by the *homo sapiens*' ability to come up with narratives about his motives and motivations, which can even (apparently) refute the theory of his self-interestedness. However, Binmore emphasizes (ibid. 20f.) that we *cannot* even gain sufficient clarity about our underlying motives and that one could further construe the invention of narratives themselves as being motivated by self-interest.

For example, it is not difficult to ascribe inherent ("hardwired") "ethical propensities" (ibid. 22) to the *homo sapiens*. However, these ethical propensities must be methodologically integrated into an economic or game-theoretical reconstruction for explaining their genesis and especially their stability under competitive conditions with regard to their use for their particular bearers. Binmore (1994, 20) explains it this way: many authors believe that consciousness determines behavior. A statement such as this, however, comes from everyday thinking (in my formulation: it is "phenomenalistic"; see the section "Moral communication: Toward a semantics of benefits") and is unproblematic for subjective experience. The crucial question concerns why a phenomenon like consciousness survives in social interactions and in competition (see Binmore 1994, 20). Phenomenalistic theory can only respond by saying that human beings come into the world with a consciousness that is hardwired. This does not explain much, however. It is not necessary to introduce the competition of the capitalistic marketplace. Already in the earliest stages in human history, evolution rewarded and permitted those phenomena to survive that were useful to their bearers. Consciousness could only survive because it was advantageous as a coordination instrument under the prevailing limiting conditions in early human history and those that persisted over the long term.

Second, it is important in the current context that Binmore rejects the maximin principle as an underlying principle of rationality that is endorsed by Rawls.[55] Binmore (1994, section 4.6) concurs with Rawls's fundamental intuition that utilitarianism should be discarded.[56] Rawls's mistake is that he engages in this discussion on the wrong level: it is not the conception of rationality that needs to be abandoned,[57] but rather other, less critical assumptions. To this end, Binmore reconstructs Rawls's essential three arguments in favor of maximin and then attempts to invalidate them one by one.

According to Rawls, the maximin principle results from the balancing of deliberations.[58] Just as with principles in the natural sciences, it can be derived from the weighing of the deliberations of rational actors and thus refutes Bayesian theory. Binmore, however, sees this problem in an entirely different light: Rawls mistakenly looks for errors in Bayesian rationality. In doing so, however, he once again neglects the issue of enforcement, for the decisive point is why actors in fact also *adhere* to well-founded principles. Rawls solves this problem with his assumption concerning *commitments*—an assumption, however, that is not convincing to Binmore (see also in the following section "No commitments!"). His solution, accordingly, is only apparent. The Bayesian rationality theory, Binmore suggests, can instead also remain in the deliberations balance (this will be discussed in more detail in the section "No commitments!").

Rawls's argument in favor of the maximin principle assumes that human beings tend to avoid risk. Binmore disagrees with this. To be sure, evolution favored risk-averse behavior under certain conditions, as in the cases of the subsistence economies of isolated villages or in certain petit bourgeois contexts that necessitated the individual's painstaking adherence to rules in order to avoid being shut out of a community (see Binmore 1994, 325). In general, however, risk-averse behavior does *not* imply special selection criteria. The basic theoretical argument to support this is as follows: risk-averse actors have less room to maneuver than risk-neutral (or even risk-happy) actors because they are less willing to live without the benefits of a potential cooperation (see ibid. 326; see also Binmore 1998, chapter 1). Still, in order to assume a strong position, the willingness to do without such benefits must be credibly indicated in negotiations.

A further methodological argument comes alongside this evolutionary argument: even if one can assume the presence of risk-averse actors, the premise of risk aversion must be incorporated into the *utility function*, not the decision-making rule (see Binmore 1994, 324). This is because the individual actor must *first* ensure in the negotiations in the *original position* that he has adequately assessed the utility to his fellow actors, possibly in consideration of maximin preferences. *Afterward*, however, he would have to proceed on the basis of use maximization in the conventional sense, for otherwise he would not be able to make any conclusions at all.

Rawls maintains that the maximin principle is the only suitable decision-making rule behind the veil of ignorance. This veil—in Binmore's reconstruction of Rawls[59]—masks both the participants' identity as well as the status quo with regard to the quantity of possible natural states (see Binmore 1994, 330 F.). If the assumption can be made that this quantity of possible natural states is sufficiently large, the decision-making problem of the negotiating partners would then concern a so-called "'large world' decision problem" (ibid. 331), which is characterized by a very large range of potential outcomes and causalities of various complexity. With regard to a large world problem, it can be expected that the actors actually behave in a cautious, that is, risk-averse manner in the sense of maximin—just as human beings would in isolated villages who are especially vulnerable to the forces of nature (see the example given in b).

Binmore does not find the assumption of a large world problem to be plausible. He agrees with Rawls—albeit for different reasons—that the negotiating partners cannot know anything about their respective *identities* in the *original position*. Yet it does not make sense to *completely* deny them of having knowledge of the status quo. If one were to make this assumption, the risk would be run that the actors would negotiate about principles of justice that would also have to be valid in exceptional circumstances. In other words, if they were to actually assume the presence of a large quantity of possible states of nature, without however knowing anything about what "the world will look like tomorrow," then the agreed-upon principles of justice would have to also apply to *extreme* situations. As a result, even situations resembling the so-called "Plank of Carneades" would have to be dealt with according to the standard version of justice. This is not only implausible (principles never apply to all possible cases), but it also contradicts Rawls's own conception: he actually desires to provide a conception of justice for *normal cases*, for modern society with all of its requisite functioning institutions (see Rawls 1971 and 1993).

In concluding, Binmore stresses that while he rejects the maximin principle, he also finally arrives at similar findings to Rawls. He in fact derives the rules of a just society with the help of Bayesian theory. Just the same, these rules are closely related to those of "justice as fairness," especially in their egalitarian and anti-utilitarian implications (see Binmore 1998, section 4.6.9, and 2001). Consequently, Binmore does not improve Rawls's result, but only his *justification*, and ultimately hints at the better chance of implementation of his naturalistic, non-metaphysical conception. It simply would not be possible to continue any longer on the basis of metaphysical preconditions in a pluralistic society.[60] "[J]ust saying yes" (Binmore 1994, 72) is rather the only criterion for fair rules that could still have validity.[61]

NO COMMITMENTS!

Binmore locates the most important distinction between his conception and most other preceding contract theoretical approaches in the fact that his conception does not require the settlers of the contract to entertain binding *commitments*. He defines a *commitment* as an "action in the present the binds the person who makes it irrevocably in the future" (Binmore 1994, 161). A *commitment*, therefore, is a *binding unilateral pledge* (see ibid.), that is, a promise in which the one-time agreement to it cannot be nullified. Also, as I understand it, it cannot be or must not be secured through sanctions.[62] A *commitment* is thus *not* to be equated with a rule R—in Buchanan's sense, for example—which A follows because she expects that R promises more advantages even if R is disadvantageous for A in an individual case. If a *commitment* corresponded to a rule in this sense, the differences between Binmore's naturalism and Brandon's non-naturalistic position would disappear.

The primary difficulty in the assumption of *commitments* lies in the construction of a credible enforcement mechanism (see ibid. 162). It is not easy to either put a *commitment* into effect or to convince others that a *commitment* has been put into effect. Here, one can build on threatening sanctions such as the status of (usually financial) "hostages." For example, a company that has made a *commitment* to protecting the environment can make this *commitment* more believable by setting aside a large financial sum (e.g., at a bank). The company stipulates in the contract that this money will be used if the *commitment* is ever infringed upon. Binmore notes that *commitments* are usually secured with more subtle methods, especially via reputational mechanisms.

On the analytical level, it is important that such *commitments* are built into the construction of the game (along with a credible enforcement mechanism) and not presented to actors as game-related moves *afterward* (see ibid. 162). Binmore expresses an idea here that appears in OE as the distinction between game-related moves and game rules: in the game-related *moves*, neither morality nor *commitments* can appear; if the game is in fact being played, then they both need to be dealt with already at the level of the game *rules*.

The problem of *commitments* can also be elucidated on the example of the prisoner's dilemma.

Binmore (with regard to the case of the prisoner's dilemma) considers those theorists that recognize the possibility that actors can make *commitments* to be "circle-squarers." Authors like these try to conceive cooperation in the prisoner's dilemma as being rational for the participants, something Binmore considers to be as unproductive as the attempt to square a circle. The conditions of the prisoner's dilemma in fact make cooperation impossible, and any actor who makes concessions in advance regarding cooperation would only be taken advantage of by the others.

Cooperation is a strategy in the prisoner's dilemma that is dominated by other strategies. To choose it as a strategy in the prisoner's dilemma would be suicidal. A game theorist would thus much rather offer the maximum: "Never use a strongly dominated strategy!" (ibid. 149).

This very maxim is nevertheless dismissed by many authors and considered irrational.[63] While Binmore contends that these views go back to Kant (see ibid., section 2.4.1), this opinion stems from a limited interpretation of Kant's writings and has been refuted by alternative readings. In the following, therefore, I will not reproduce Binmore's *historically oriented* Kant interpretation, but instead *systematically* examine the position he criticizes.

Binmore suggests that authors who conceive of the possibility of binding *commitments* in the prisoner's dilemma do not in fact want to play the prisoner's dilemma game, but rather a mere coordination game—the "dodo game." That is, under the conditions of a prisoner's dilemma, they act *as if* the prisoner's dilemma game were not being played at all, but instead an entirely different game.

In such an approach, the critical factor is the *invention* of a—according to Binmore (ibid. 27)—*nonexistent enforcement mechanism*. Some kind of mechanism—whether external social surveillance under premodern conditions or self-control through incentives under modern conditions—must be the aim of any ethical conception.

The assumption of *commitments*, however, tries to solve the problem of enforcement or implementation by taking a shortcut. This move in effect avoids the intervening step of dealing with the "inferior" problems concerning the incentive compatibility of institutions that serve to provide the members of a society with incentives.[64]

If it were possible to enter into binding, one-sided promises, a slaveholder, for instance, would be able to argue that his slave is bound to him because of a promise (see Binmore 1994, 36ff.). Nonetheless, as Hume already recognized,[65] verbalizing words or writing them down does not yet imply a binding promise![66] Only reciprocity, and nothing else, is binding, which is also to say, only those mutual advantages that are first made available in a suitable form by means of institutional incentives.

Institutions not only bind or prohibit, but they also *make possible* precisely what the proponents of *commitments*, according to Binmore, shy away from: the establishment of greater freedom, the possibility that everyone will be able to do what they want to an even greater degree. As Binmore puts it: "*Nor is it correct to say that anarchy will necessarily result if everybody 'just' does what he wants*" (Binmore 1994, 30; my emphasis). To let everyone do what they want does not necessarily lead to anarchy, *assuming*, that is, that there are binding contracts. These contracts, moreover, may only bind participants if they are *self-policing* (Binmore 1994, 30; see also Binmore 1998, section 4.6.2), and, lastly, only those arrangements are self-policing that are in equilibrium (see Binmore 1994, 36).

Binmore identifies the following contemporary authors as allowing room for the possibility of *commitments*.

Rawls (1971)[67] asserts that the agreements made in the *original position* are already binding due to the fact that *they are agreements*. Rawls explicitly rejects the view that contracts are binding because of sanctions. In Rawls 1993, he also strictly separates—as shown in chapter 4—between a *modus vivendi*, on the one hand, and an overarching consensus, on the other. With regard to the former, the participants only pursue it out of self-interest as a temporary alternative. The latter, however, involves a higher degree of dignity. The participants uphold it because of their fundamental beliefs (also apparently in contradiction to incentives) and because it is the only long-term guarantee for social stability (at least in *combination with* economic incentives).

Gauthier (1986)—as the section "Society requires internalized dispositions for cooperation (David Gauthier)" shows—makes the assumption that "constrained maximizers" (CMs) will win out against "straightforward maximizers" (SMs). He presumes that CMs have a disposition that allows them to behave in a certain way that is always independent of existing incentives. Binmore (1994, 80) does not accept this. Rational agents would not freely comply with *constraints*, whether in the form of dispositions or in some other form. Even if one could posit that dispositions actually *formed* due to evolution, this does not mean that they would also have to remain *stable* for the same reason. Two questions are conflated here that need to be distinguished. The problem of original rights emerges in Gauthier in a similar fashion: he endorses here a Lockean position that posits the existence of pre-contractual rights, to which he attaches a binding effect that goes beyond benefits and incentives (see also the section "Gauthier, Locke, and Nozick: The status of rights"). Binmore (1994, 38), however, emphasizes that all such rights are artificial. They first need to be reconstructed using contractual arguments like the *original position* and also ultimately be based on self-interested negotiations.

Harsanyi utilizes the concept of *commitments* insofar as he situates the negotiations of the contract settlers in the *original position* behind an especially thick the veil of ignorance. In Binmore's words, the negotiations occur "in some Kantian limbo outside space and time" (Binmore 1998, 431). Behind this veil, participants are supposed to assume that everyone involved has similar preferences. Binmore characterizes the corresponding assumptions as the "Harsanyi doctrine" (see Binmore 1994, 61 and the section "Rawls's theory of justice and its connection to order ethics"). The participants supposedly continue to be bound—that is, *committed*—to the agreements made under these conditions, even afterward, that is, after the veil has been "lifted." It is precisely this assumption, however, that Binmore criticizes in following Hume: it is not words that bind, but only (reciprocal) advantages.

EMPATHETIC PREFERENCES

While Binmore objects to Harsanyi's assumption about *commitments*, he nonetheless adopts another concept from him, although in different form. Harsanyi believes that actors have "extended sympathy preferences" (see Harsanyi 1977). This means—roughly speaking—that such actors *put themselves in the shoes of others*, and are only then able to follow the moral precept of the Golden Rule. Binmore refers to this concept of Harsanyi, yet prefers the term "empathetic preferences" (see, in particular, Binmore 1994, 28, 58ff. as well as section 4.3.1 and Binmore 1998, section 2.5.4). The intuitive idea here is that the *homo economicus* must be able to anticipate other actors' behavior in order to better adjust to it.

Using the concepts of empathetic preferences, Binmore wants to highlight the distinction between the classical concept of "sympathy" in Smith and Hume, on the one hand, and his own modern concept, on the other. This delineation provides the easiest way to clearly define empathetic preferences.[68]

According to Binmore (1994, 286), a sympathy-based preference is revealed when it is possible to conclude from the behavior of actor A that she has put herself in actor B's situation in such a way that she *adopts* B's preferences. A thus takes on the role of B in its entirety.

By contrast, an empathetic preference is exhibited when it is possible to conclude from the behavior of actor A that she has put herself into actor B's shoes, while also *retaining* her own preferences (see ibid. 288). A clearly differentiates between her own utility function and B's. This point is especially important for Binmore (see also ibid. 59 and 288). Here, despite A's decision to put herself in B's shoes, she is still able to compare her own preferences with those of B or to *evaluate* or *criticize* these preferences from her own vantage point.[69] Binmore offers the following illustrative example: Adam can say that he would rather be Eve, who eats from the apple, than himself (Adam), who wears a fig leaf (see ibid. 290).

Binmore identifies a decisive human quality in the fundamental disposition toward empathy[70] (and precisely *not* sympathy),[71] finding it to be a critical aspect of an individual's "humanity" (see ibid. 289). This capacity was already routinely utilized far back in the days of our tribal history. Binmore indeed speculates (see ibid. 288 and the section "Morality in Rawls's conception of justice as fairness") that it was even mainly responsible for the size of the human brain and human achievement. The disposition toward empathy proved to be so useful for the survival of its bearers that the evolution of larger brains could only be helpful.

As a result of optimized cooperation, the disposition toward empathy not only allowed individuals, but also their communities, to gain an advantage in competition with other communities.[72] Even if one were to view the members of these communities in the reconstruction as *homines oeconomici*, empathetic preferences would still appear to be advantageous, for, as already emphasized in the section "Binmore's naturalistic contract theory," the Game of Life allows for several, indeed numerous, states of equilibrium. Empathy was highly useful for choosing among these equilibria: the individual actors were able to coordinate their behavior more easily and, when they were able to put themselves into the shoes of their respective cooperative partners, to therefore arrive more quickly at a universally acceptable solution (see ibid. 57 and 289ff.).

Irrespective of how the disposition toward empathy might actually have developed, the question remains as to how it could *persist* under modern conditions and continue to be *useful*.[73] Binmore (1994, 58ff.) argues that this disposition is able to survive because empathetic preferences represent an input for the coordination mechanism of the *original position*. It is precisely the actors in modern societies who need at least *some kind* of input in order to be able to take advantage of the benefits of the *original position*. Without empathetic preferences—or a functional equivalent—they would not be able to ponder just how their fellow actors might perceive the advantages of, for instance, an institutional reform.

Empathetic preferences play a critical role in the diverse time horizons within which, according to Binmore, (1994, 63 FF.), the preferences of the members of a society change.[74] There are three different horizons that may be considered.

An individual must make numerous decisions in a *short-term* time horizon. Within this framework, both his personal and his empathetic preferences have been established and cannot be altered. This means the individual empathizes with his fellow actors in a way that is prescribed by his fixed empathetic preferences and, with the help of these preferences, plays the Game of Morals (see ibid. 86). In this way, she complies with familiar conventions and rules that encapsulate lengthy economic calculations. Moral considerations of fairness (for Binmore) no longer play any role in the *moves* of the game.[75] Morality lies in the *conventions* that are taken for granted. As a consequence, even though morality no longer plays a role on the level of behavior or the *moves* of the game, considerations of fairness are nonetheless especially decisive within the framework of the respective valid social contract. Binmore suggests that this should be a comfort to everyone who sees morality as having largely no impact. Morality makes a crucial contribution at least in the *short term* (see Binmore 1998, Section 4.6.8), for most decisions are made in a short-term time horizon (see Binmore 1994, 89).

Over the *long term*, all preferences change—both personal and empathetic preferences. The individual adapts to new situations and new constraints, but even these constraints are themselves susceptible to change over the long run. The long-term time horizon concerns "big decisions" (ibid. 65) in which fairness considerations play a significant role to the extent that they can help in establishing new social contracts or modifying current ones.

On the one hand, empathetic preferences are variable. It is particularly interesting—and Binmore demonstrates this with game theoretical analyses (see ibid. 88)—that the social contracts that are settled as a result of fairness considerations are designed long-term (but also already medium-term, see c), as if the participating parties had conducted strictly self-interested negotiations, that is, "bargaining" processes, from the very beginning. Hence the entire "moral" content of the social contracts (in an individual ethical sense) erodes over long periods.

On the other hand, all the personal preferences are also formed through the social contracts. The individuals adapt themselves and their desires to what is useful for everyone, namely, the outcome of the social contract that has been agreed to by everyone because of the reciprocal advantages.[76] With Binmore, one could also say that the only forum for moral discussions is the market that promises mutual advantages (see ibid. 89), and over the long term no morality can remain stable that is directed against these (mutual) interests. However, morality can—as a rational behavioral constraint—serve to cushion the blow of *short-term* discomforts for the affected.

The *medium-term* time horizon, however, is especially important: while, according to Binmore, the individuals' personalities do not change within this time frame, their empathetic preferences do. Over the medium-term, social evolution brings empathetic preferences into a so-called "entity equilibrium,"[77] in which all actors have *similar* empathetic preferences. As in the long-term time horizon, in this equilibrium the moral substance disappears from the Game of Morals, which helps in the "settlement" of social contracts. The outcome of the fairness considerations in the Game of Morals is identical with the "Nash bargaining equilibrium" (see ibid. 88 and originally Nash 1950 and 1951), that is, the actors would arrive at the same result if they were to explicitly negotiate their individual interests from the start.

In any event, this is not how it looks for the actors. Because of the prevailing semantics, they have the impression that they are still able to rely on moral considerations (in the traditional sense) in the Game of Morals. They do not realize that even their moral considerations are controlled by their interests.[78] Binmore (1994, 133 and 1998, 182) recognizes the corresponding mechanisms as being at least partially "hardwired." In his view, evolution anchored the disposition toward empathy in our genes (see also ibid. 241 and 337). The advantages of this disposition that developed through gene-culture co-evolution (see the section "Binmore's original position") are so considerable that it would have been too risky to make their realization dependent on relatively tentative cultural practices. Just the same, empathy is supposedly not genetically determined in every respect. Binmore (1904, 65ff.) refers to Dawkins (1976) concept of "meme" in order to also avoid analyzing genetically fixed behavioral patterns with similar, that is, Darwinian methods. These behavioral patterns would also be subject to differentiated reproduction, that is, only the most fit memes would survive.

What distinguishes the medium term from the long term is the fact that the players' personal preferences must still be taken to be fixed in advance. Within this framework, evolution does not yet have enough time to also leave the formation of personal preferences to the market.

Binmore establishes the role of empathetic preferences in society with the differentiation of these three horizons. They serve in the coordination—or more precisely: the reform—of existing social contracts and the settlement of new ones. In the process of such reforms, the participants play the game of morals, requiring at the same time empathetic preferences or a functional equivalent as input. Binmore also characterizes empathetic preferences as morality (or least a significant portion of them; see ibid. 241). In my view, he did not make a preliminary decision regarding a moral surplus value that would be a precondition for the functioning of a society. As I will explain in the following, empathetic preferences are better classified in other categories and have a different theoretical locus than the moral surplus values assumed by the other approaches discussed in this book.

DISCUSSION: CAN'T SOCIETY ALSO DISPOSE WITH EMPATHETIC PREFERENCES?

Binmore recognizes empathetic preferences as being essential for the functioning of a society. These preferences might then be seen as a functional equivalent for Rawls's sense of justice, Habermas's rational motivation or Gauthier's dispositions for cooperation. To my mind, however, there are good reasons for placing the predisposition toward empathy in a different category.

First, upon closer examination it becomes clear that empathetic preferences have fewer implications for their bearers' behavior than the capacities that are assumed by the other authors. For instance, one frequently has the impression that Rawls and Habermas (taking their work together for a moment) already knew in advance how the citizens of their imagined societies would behave, or at least which rules they *should* give themselves. This is true to an even greater extent for the approaches in the area of value and virtue ethics. In these approaches, for example, there are frequently signs of an antipathy toward economic conceptions, or those that rely on self-interest constitutively for their implementation.[79] These signs are even clearer in Habermas, especially when looking at his mostly short-range political statements (see, for instance, Habermas 1987 or 2001).

Binmore's writings, however, do not give this impression. On the one hand, his political statements are directed against both "right" and "left" orientations (see, for instance, Binmore 1994, 6). This point should be taken seriously.[80] Even his Whig liberalism cannot be equated with the current platforms of liberal parties.

On the other hand, empathetic preferences have a special quality. The assumption that actors in modern societies have a predisposition toward empathy still does not say anything about the specific design of rules and institutions.[81] If A tries to put himself in the shoes of his fellow actor B, A's evaluation of B is obviously crucial. If A finds B to be mostly unreliable or to be someone who is interested in a short-term profit, then A will adjust her behavior accordingly and thus—*ceterus paribus*—undertake, for instance, a preventative counter defection (see Homann 2002, 98 and 115). Conversely, if A perceives B to be reliable and there are no reverse incentives for A's defection, then A will tend toward cooperation. This is an open process whose outcome cannot be anticipated by theorists.

Second, beyond the openness of empathy-equilibrium processes, the following trait of the predisposition toward empathy appears to me to be even more significant: *it is not exploitable*, even and especially if one recognizes, with Binmore, that it is a (possibly genetically anchored) *differentia specifica* of humans.

By this, I intend to say the following: if A imposes behavioral restrictions on herself when confronted with a prisoner's-dilemma type situation—for instance, due to a rational motivation or sense of justice—then she runs the risk of being exploited by actor B. This is assuming that B acts exactly like A by accepting similar restrictions (due to sanctions or alternative means). However, if A has empathetic preferences in similar kinds of situations, the danger of exploitation is not automatic, especially if B chooses to *not* behave in the same way as A. For example, let us assume in the classical prisoner's-dilemma situation in which there are two prisoners that one of the two (A) has a sense of justice. If the other prisoner (B) knows this, yet does not permit himself the luxury of having a sense of justice, then he can easily take advantage of A by making a confession. On the other hand, if A can merely avail herself of empathetic preferences, this only means that A would be able to anticipate how B will react to A's particular actions. A could then also use this knowledge, for instance, to exploit B. At any rate, B would not be able to gain a one-sided advantage from the knowledge of A's empathetic preferences. B would accordingly have to expect that A would be able to successfully put herself in his shoes and comprehend B's deliberations. Since the predisposition toward empathy is not exploitable, it should therefore not be placed in the same category as the other candidates for moral surplus values that have been discussed so far.[82]

I am not able to accept, however, Binmore's thesis that empathetic preferences are *essential* for the functioning of modern societies. I completely agree with him that such preferences play a fundamental role in making life *easier* for society's members. When I'm able to successfully empathize with my cooperation partner, I am undoubtedly able to put our cooperation on the more solid footing. If I cannot do this, however, cooperation, in my view, *can* nonetheless remain stable with her, as could a society that will be formed by one of us. *It all depends*.

The act of putting yourself in someone else's shoes is no end in itself. According to Binmore, it instead serves in the solution of a certain problem, namely, the problem of coordination or compromise with other actors who do not (generally) live in the same society. Should this problem not be solvable with the help of empathy, then other functional equivalents might be available. As Binmore says, the actors require *some kind* of input when using the original position. Evidently, he intends to suggest that there is no other input as *well suited* as empathetic preferences (see Binmore 94, 60). Even if one concedes this position, in my view there are still alternate (at least rudimentary) possibilities for using other devices to bring about the coordination effect that is normally generated by empathetic preferences.

Pursuing this point further, it makes sense to look for illustrative cases in which there is a collision of cultures. After all, it is culture, according to Binmore (1984, 63 and fn. 75), that generally determines the precise manifestation of empathetic preferences. In such cases, it would be necessary to examine whether cooperation was possible and, if so, how this cooperation first began and how it was able to remain stable later.

This first raises the *methodological* question as to the "areas" from which these cases might be taken. On the one hand, those historically verified instances are certainly worth examining of people coming together for the first time from completely different cultural milieus and with divergent empathetic preferences. Cases like these are especially interesting when the individuals are forced to come to terms with each other for an extended period of time. One can turn to the ethnological reports that describe these kinds of encounters.

On the other hand, I also consider it legitimate to make use of appropriate literary descriptions and constructions. It has always been literature's particular prerogative to enter into the mind-set of other cultural milieus (those that actually exist or are imagined). Some literary authors might even be called experts in empathy. But neither their expertise, nor their work is an end in itself. Literature creates social orders and polities that can serve as a heuristic in the design of institutional control systems. This is especially true for the creation of rules for *situations* that emerge in a new way and were previously unknown to us. Literature provides us with a simulation of such situations and a means of testing out potentially appropriate solutions.

In this respect, I would suggest that science fiction literature has a special role to play:[83] It reflects the one genre in all of literature that is specifically concerned with imagining situations in which cultures (with disparate [in Binmore's terminology] empathetic preferences) collide for the first time. Even if the possibility that human beings will encounter aliens in the foreseeable future is rather remote, these kinds of literary explorations are still instructive in my opinion.[84] They emphasize the importance of thinking in terms of *constitutions*, which are initially presented as thought experiments or simulations, but whose findings offer new possibilities for the further development of actual control systems.

By thinking in terms of constitutions, situations can be simulated that may serve as (order-) heuristics, yielding—via functional analogies—recommendations for institutions in politics and society. Especially in an era of dramatically expanding globalization in which the Internet has made available entirely new technical (and also social) possibilities, ideas—which is to say: heuristics—are the most important resource for a society that wants to actively exploit and influence the opportunities of these developments and does not wish to remain a passive imitator of other more engaged societies. It is therefore recommended that the members of the society invest in the production of such heuristics.

With regard to the focus of this book, a typology of order-heuristics might look as follows.

a) Situations in which empathy and cooperation only function under great difficulty

First of all, it is possible to refer here to ethnology, which has long provided evidence for the diversity of values among human cultures. Second, behavioral research has shown how similar primates are to us in many respects and that the effect of empathy is also an important factor in this instance. Third, there is also the *topos* of artificial life in science fiction writing—even if the actual state of research on artificial intelligence is undoubtedly far behind what has been imagined by literary futurists. In the films *Terminator 2* (1991) and *A.I.* (2001), artificial life forms are portrayed that are physically identical to us, that would fight each other for human recognition, and that sometimes react more humanly than humans.

b) Situations in which empathy is nearly impossible and cooperation is still possible, though with difficulty

In his novel *The Robots of Dawn* (1983), I. Asimov describes how the criminal detective Elijah Bailey is sent from Earth to another planet (Aurora) in order to solve a murder. Auroran society is much more advanced than the one on Earth; the technology there makes it possible for human beings to almost completely avoid personal interactions. Aurora is thus a highly evolved, but "calcified" society with rigid rituals, lacking in spontaneity and new influences. In the present context, the following is especially noteworthy: when Bailey finds himself on Aurora, he is unable to put himself in the shoes of the planet's inhabitants. He remains a complete stranger in a strange world. Nonetheless, he is successful in explaining to at least some Aurorans of the benefits of his ideas, and in gradually convincing them of the need for a change.

Another example is offered by the film *Star Trek: First Contact* (1996), which portrays the first encounter between human beings and aliens (in the year 2063). Due to different physiological, psychological, and social conditions, neither side is able to empathize with the other. Nonetheless, a functioning form of communication and cooperation develops, because they can communicate to each other about benefits (such as with regard to the development of technologies).

In the film *2001* (1968), the intelligent computer HAL does not cooperate in the end with its human counterparts, who ultimately decide to pull the plug on the computer because it wants to kill them. Nevertheless, in the course of being turned off—which resembles "death"—Hal succeeds in eliciting sympathy (at least among the audience) because the viewers are able to empathize with the process of dying.

c) Situations in which neither empathy nor cooperation is possible

In his novel *Solaris* (1961, filmed in 1972 and 2002), Stanislaw Lem depicts the efforts of various generations of astronauts to communicate with an ocean on a distant planet that has been identified as a life form. The attempt to empathize with the ocean fails, specifically, because it lacks certain basic physiological preconditions. A rudimentary communicative exchange does not develop even once: numerous theories are made about the ocean, yet after all attempts have failed at communication, the only alternative for the humans is to finally leave the planet.

Lem portrays an entirely similar situation in *The Invincible* (1964). In this instance, astronauts do not confront an individual life form, but instead 1 billion small flying creatures that are capable of forming a collective intelligence. Here, too, communication does not develop between the clearly intelligent life forms.

In the film *Independence Day* (1996), a race of rapacious aliens that has plundered one planet after another finally lands on Earth to destroy humanity. While communication with the aliens does in fact prove successful, cooperation is not in the cards: the invaders, who view themselves to be far superior technologically, *cannot* be plausibly convinced of the benefits of working together.[85]

This typology of situations is not meant to serve as ironclad *evidence*. Nonetheless, it might serve to indicate that the predisposition toward empathy is not necessary for stable cooperation in every case. Cooperation is actually conceivable even where empathetic preferences do not play a role. Other instances might be imagined, however, in which cooperation necessarily fails because of the various preconditions of the interaction partners.

To conclude, I would like to nevertheless emphasize the following: the predisposition toward empathy appears (as I will make clear in the following conclusion) to be the most suitable candidate for an acceptable minimal precondition on a personal level for the stability of modern societies under conditions of globalization.

NOTES

1. The relationship to Rawls "sense of justice" is obvious. See chapter 4.
2. Ibid. 197.
3. It is interesting to note that the term "morality" only appears in chapter 7, which was drafted by G. Brennan, as moral opprobrium, whereas in chapter 9, which was drafted by J. M. Buchanan, Buchanan only speaks of a civic religion.
4. In the following, I use the term "moral norms" where Buchanan writes "ethical rules."
5. I refer solely here to the final form in Buchanan 1994.
6. It is not clear here whether one can speak of moral appeals. I will return later to the fact that Buchanan himself only desires to provide an economic explanation of the origin of moral norms. Nonetheless, it is difficult to not recognize an appeal in the chosen expression "We should. . . ."
7. See Buchanan 1994, 39ff., as well as Buchanan and Wagner 1987.
8. Buchanan differentiates his concern from the question of intergenerational justice (see Buchanan 1994, 42ff.). The case at hand relates to the individual benefits to the individual who has been encouraged to save, not to the utility to future generations.
9. Examples of the vast body of literature include Rapoport and Chammah 1965, Hardin 1982, Axelrod 1984, and Poundstone 1992.
10. A prominent exponent of this approach is Gauthier. See the section "Society requires internalized dispositions for cooperation (David Gauthier)."
11. One can also say more emphatically: Morality is that which I desire from others.
12. As a result, he (Buchanan 1994, 75) also stresses that so-called "meddlesome preferences" (see Blau 1975, following Sen 1970a) are not at issue. The individual only has an interest in the behavior of others when it affects his own interests. In contrast, the individuals recognized by Sen interfere with others' behavior when it does not relate to their own interests.
13. One potential illustration (which Buchanan, however, does not mention) might be found in the realm of environmental politics. The more market economic principles are utilized for solving ecological problems, the less it makes sense to invest in spreading an "ecological ethic" that would require industrial societies to impose restrictions on themselves, zero growth, and so on.
14. "Subsets of ethical precepts or principles are 'better' than others, if we use 'better' in terms of welfare as ultimately measured by the individuals' own preferences" (Buchanan 1994, 1).
15. A single negative incident that becomes known can be enough to destroy a positive image that has been built up over many years. See the related statement from R. Haas (1994, 509), then CEO of Levi's.
16. In reference to Rawls's concept of "freestanding view," see the section "Society needs a sense of justice (John Rawls)."
17. Of course, she would still be able to realize those advantages of her own work that only benefit her. Buchanan can thus assert that I simultaneously benefit myself and act in the interest of everyone else when I save more or work more. Yet this would be easy to disprove. Some rules can create counterproductive incentives and cancel out the benefits of more work (such as through high, progressive taxation).
18. More precisely: as Buchanan maintains that economic theory maintains.
19. This viewpoint was rarely represented in Buchanan's previous writings, but indeed in several places in Brennan and Buchanan (1985).
20. I say "should not" because no reflective conception of economics would commit this error. It is true, however, that some economists have committed this error and continue to do

so. One example is George J. Stigler, who explicitly refers to a representative image of human beings. See also Binmore 1994, 19.

21. See the writings of Stigler 1991 and Grubel and Boland 1986.

22. Although I am unable to follow this train of thought in detail, I would nevertheless like to emphasize that I see no conflict in the position elucidated here with a (hypothetical) realism. Realism does indeed allow for the construction of varying analytical tools to illuminate diverse aspects of reality and to treat different kinds of questions (see the section "Derivation of order ethics"). Realism also makes it possible to temporarily remove such analytical tools from the process of empirical verification. See Lakatos 1970. I do not share the position of radical constructivism (for a critique of this approach, see Vollmer 1990).

23. There is a large body of literature on this. See Axelrod 1984.

24. For example Gauthier's SMs (see the section "Society requires internalized dispositions for cooperation (David Gauthier)").

25. This would correspond with Buchanan's call to economists (in the conclusion of *Ethics and Economic Progress*), where the reader, after learning that "institutions matter," is now also told that "ethics also matter" (Buchanan 1994, 145). This call, however, can also be interpreted normatively.

26. The parallels to Gauthier will be noted here, who sees political solutions as being too "costly." See the section "Gauthier, Locke, and Nozick: The status of rights."

27. Buchanan also points in this direction: "[E]fforts to elaborate our understanding of the economic interdependencies among our separate savings choices can proceed in tandem with practical steps toward reform in the incentive structures" (1994, 59). See similarly also Buchanan (ibid. 125).

28. It should be underscored that Buchanan's economic approach differs from most of the other approaches that have been discussed here such as that of discourse ethics or Rawls's. The latter does not justify the respective moral surplus value in terms of self-interest. Buchanan has thus taken an additional step in this respect. His problem, however, is that he (obviously only for the cases discussed here) does not propose any implementation through rule reform.

29. Which even Luhmann (1989, 378) acknowledges.

30. For instance, long-term policy making is even more common in Asian countries than in Europe, which has economic consequences. For associated empirical data, see already Hofstede and Bond 1988.

31. Sugden (2001, F213) recognizes the significance of Binmore's work as residing in its synthesis of two previously existing syntheses, one being a synthesis between a mostly economically oriented "bargaining theory" and political philosophy and one being a synthesis between general game theory and evolutionary biology.

32. Dore (1997, 237) is in complete agreement: Binmore's approach provides, for the first time, a liberal alternative to utilitarianism.

33. Binmore believes that we still live today in neo-feudal structures (Binmore 1998, 504).

34. He is in agreement here with Nietzsche (*Genealogy of Morals*, Nietzsche 1980, vol. 5; 2nd critique, section 17).

35. "This, however, hinders not, but that philosophers may, if they please, extend their reasoning to the suppos'd *state of nature*; provided they allow it to be a mere philosophical fiction, which never had, and never cou'd have any reality" (Hume 1739–1740/1978, book III, part 2, 493; emphasis in original).

36. And as such, it is criticized because of its the fundamental justification of coercion by generally libertarian-based positions (see Kliemt 2001).

37. Hume consequently criticizes the contract theories of his era because—in contrast to his own "realistic" theory—they assume contract settlements that have no historical basis. As already indicated, this criticism generally does not apply to modern versions of contract theory.

38. As I have already elaborated on the concept and definition of naturalism—especially with regard to the social sciences (and the humanities; see the section "The problem's outline" and Luetge 2004a)—I will only examine here the relevant aspects of Binmore's notion of naturalism.

39. Dore (1997, 235) is not able to identify in Rawls any allegiance to the external commitments. I concur with Binmore, however, in not agreeing with this. Rawls firmly subscribes to

the notion of external authorities in Rawls 1993. See the section "Society needs a sense of justice (John Rawls)."

40. See Nash 1950 and 1951, as well as Binmore 1994, section 2.2.2.

41. Binmore 1994, 117, and also 119. See also the section "Categories of order ethics."

42. Binmore adds that the powerful rarely have realistic views with respect to possible equilibria and do not see enough of a payoff in improvement opportunities (even those that are in their own self-interest; see Binmore 1994, 289, fn. 44).

43. "A fair social contract is simply an equilibrium in the game of life that calls for the use of strategies which, if used in the game of morals, would leave no player in the game of morals with an incentive to appeal to the device of the original position" (Binmore 1994, 41).

44. Nor does it make sense to the Rawls commentator Wolff (1977).

45. This, for instance, is exactly what Alejandro (1998, chapter 8) argues against, criticizing Rawls for making too strong a case in favor of the status quo.

46. Like Buchanan (see the section "Society requires an ethic of work and an ethic of saving (James M. Buchanan)"), Binmore stresses that we always need to start with the status quo in making institutional improvements.

47. Rawls 1993, 90; see Rawls 1971, 12 and 136ff.

48. Dore (1997) is thus correct when he says that Binmore is "Rawlsian," which the latter also to a certain extent admits (see Binmore 1998, 433). Nonetheless, Binmore provides other justifications for Rawls's theses and consequently, in my view, distinguishes himself much more strongly from Rawls than Dore is willing to acknowledge.

49. On the concept of mesocosm, see Vollmer 1983.

50. I have strongly abridged the economic reconstruction. Binmore also portrays the possible situations in the small group on the basis of a theoretical model. See Binmore 1998, chapters 2 and 3.

51. As a utilitarian, Singer would not exactly welcome Binmore's extension of the circle by including the evaluations of institutions. Instead, he would demand that individuals themselves expand their moral intuitions into larger circles. See Singer 1993.

52. In agreement with large parts of game theory, see, for instance, Eichberger 1993 as well as Dixit and Nalebuff 1991.

53. See Binmore 1994, 13, 15, 18 and sections 4.2.1 and 4.5; see also Binmore 1998, 429, 437. Binmore (1994, 304 ff.) adheres to the original, purely formalistic Bayes's theorem and distinguishes his position from what he calls "Bayesianismists" (ibid. 305), who further interpret Bayes's probability theorem as a basis for rational learning processes. Binmore finds this to be an over-interpretation that ascribes too much substantive significance to a formalism. He also rejects their inductivistic approach regarding the "updating of prior probabilities" (ibid.).

54. Thus Binmore is completely aware of the methodological status of the assumption of rationality. His view of naturalism, therefore, does not mean that theorists should base their—methodologically unreflected—conclusions on empirical data about the preferences or functional uses of human beings. In this respect, Binmore, in my view, is fundamentally misunderstood in Sugden's rather harsh critique (Sugden 2001; see ibid. F219, F222, F229, F241).

55. The maximin principle says that, when faced with a choice under conditions of uncertainty, rational people select those alternatives that maximize their payout in a worst-case scenario. For Rawls, this means in particular the actors who settle a social contract under the veil of ignorance choose precisely those kinds of institutional arrangements for future society that will benefit them the most should they find themselves on the bottom rung of the social ladder. For Rawls, both principles of justice are of "those a person would choose for the design of a society in which his enemy is to assign him his place" (Rawls 1971, 152).

56. See the classical example according to which the poor may become increasingly poor and the rich increasingly rich if this increases the overall benefit (see Binmore 1994, section 4.6).

57. Binmore contends that the maximin principle hardly has any place within game theory. Instead, the conception that is generally recognized there is the orthodox conception of rationality. Binmore does not actually see this fact as an argument, but rather as a heuristic indicator.

58. Rawls defines the balancing of deliberations as a condition in which all judgments on all generally valid levels find agreement after due consideration. See in particular Rawls 1993, 73 and Rawls 1971, 44f.

59. Binmore (ibid.) summarizes the original four Rawlsian veils into one (see Rawls 1971, 195ff.).

60. See, for instance, Binmore 1994, 169, 208, 334 and 1998, xxii and 288.

61. Binmore uses the formulation "just saying yes" in different ways, including to elucidate the distinction between explicit and implicit agreements. I primarily understand this formulation as a concise summation of his naturalistic conception, which elevates the consent of individuals to the only (naturalistic) normative criterion.

62. Certainly, several of the theories of other conceptions critiqued in this book could be attributed to this assumption. The question examined in the present context concerning the moral surplus that is required of individuals is closely related to the question of how commitments can be adhered to. This adherence is usually attributed to the special capabilities of the human species or rational beings. See also the following chapter 4.

63. The effort is moreover made to provide empirical evidence of this (see also, for instance, the Binmore critique from Holler 2000, 202). The methodological foundation of this evidence, however, is strongly disputed by Binmore.

64. One could also say: the assumption of commitments ignores morality's historically organic development. Morality cannot simply be postulated, but demands a negotiation over benefits and a determination of incentives. This further implies that moral improvements frequently only emerge gradually in history. For example, the abolition of slavery is a cultural achievement; just the same, it was also generally accepted over long stretches of Western history.

65. "The observance of promises is itself one of the most considerable parts of justice; and we are not surely bound to keep our word because we have given our word to keep it" (Hume 1751/1975, appendix III).

66. This also applies to Searle's (1964) famous attempt to refute the naturalistic fallacy. This attempt fails because of Searle's mistaken belief that saying the words "I promise" already implies the actual making of a promise (see Binmore 1994, 37 and fn. 38 as well as Hare 1964).

67. In his interpretation of Rawls, Binmore primarily draws on Rawls 1971, because he finds that Rawls waters down the conception too much in his later writings. In my opinion, the idea of commitments may still be found in Rawls 1993, even if in somewhat different form. See the section "Society needs a sense of justice (John Rawls)."

68. It is clear from this definition, which accords with the thinking of most economists, that a preference for Binmore is revealed by the actors' behavior and cannot be discovered by other means (e.g., through psychological examinations). See Binmore 1994, 51 and 104 and also with regard to the problems of the theory of revealed preferences see, for instance, Kreps 1988, chapter 2.

69. This plays a significant role in my own approach indicated in the section "Discussion: Can't society also dispose with empathetic preferences?" to the extent that the non-exploitability of these empathetic preferences is already contained in it.

70. The fundamental disposition toward empathy, according to Binmore, should be distinguished from "empathetic preferences." Empathetic preferences are preferences that an actor reveals in a specific case in relation to one or more different actors. These can and will vary from actor to actor and from case to case.

71. Elster (1989), however, maintains that "love and duty"—that is, precisely what Binmore understands under the term *sympathy*—constitutes the "cement of society." Binmore (1994, 24) pointedly responds that modern societies do not need cement; they moreover rather resemble a dry stone wall in which each stone is kept in place by every other stone, that is, through reciprocity. Greed and fear, in turn, are sufficient for maintaining this reciprocity.

> Modern society is like a dry stone wall. Its stones do not need cement. Each stone is held in place by its neighbours, and it, in turn, holds its neighbours in place. The mechanism is *reciprocity*. . . . Greed and fear will suffice as motivations; greed for

the fruits of cooperation, and fear of the consequences of not reciprocating the cooperative overtures of others. (Ibid., emphasis in original)

72. Binmore (1994, 63 and fn. 75) assumes that actors with similar cultural backgrounds have similar empathetic preferences.

73. Particularly under conditions of globalization, which, however, Binmore does not explicitly state.

74. Here, Binmore discusses the alteration of preferences, something that is generally not "permitted" in economics, since preferences are seen as fixed for methodological reasons (see, for instance, Stigler and Becker 1977). Binmore (1994, 63) is entirely aware of this problematic; however he justifies his decision to discuss cultural preferences at this point with the observation that the concern is not with an economic scenario. In my view, this would need to be construed as follows: Binmore here is working on a different kind of problem. At issue is not the explanation of the actors' behavior independent of changes to institutional constraints, but rather the question about the functional role the disposition toward empathy might play in an evolutionary scenario. For this particular problem, Binmore's approach seems methodologically sound.

75. The idea that morality is inherent to the game rules is not something that Binmore himself clearly indicates; this is, rather, my own (rational) reconstruction.

76. Binmore (1994, 90) formulates it this way: the autonomy of the citizens in selecting their own goals erodes over the long term. A discussion, however, on the concept of autonomy would be required, which would take us too far afield. See, on the other hand, Kant's concept of "heautonomy" (self-legislation; Kant 1976 FF., volume 10, 39 and 95; first 1790).

77. Ibid. 65. See also Binmore 1994, Section 1.2.7, 1.3, 290ff. and on utility comparison, 1998, 440ff.

78. In OE, this observation may be understood as follows: morality is not only explanans, but also explanandum (see Homann 2002, 255). The evolutionary process of morality must also be accounted for.

79. Thus in Rawls's case the strict separation between modus vivendi, constitutional consensus, and overarching consensus. See the section "Modus vivendi, constitutional consensus, and overlapping consensus."

80. To be sure, it is also not possible to accuse the other authors discussed here of a systematic political partisanship.

81. Here one may find a general weakness to Binmore's approach. As Dore (1997, 236f.) also points out, Binmore relies exclusively on evolutionary game theory. Although I find this to be entirely relevant for modern societies, it is not possible to make any more progress in designing institutions without the help of additional branches of economics or other social sciences.

82. It is possible to see empathetic preferences as a functional equivalent to Hobbes's concept of forum internum. See the section "Gauthier, Locke, and Nozick: The status of rights."

83. Rowlands 2003 focuses on the subject of philosophy in science fiction films. He offers an introduction to philosophical subjects like personal identity, free will, and the mind-body problem with reference to movies like *Terminator*, *The Matrix*, *Total Recall*, and *Minority Report*.

84. Associated arguments can also be integrated into the framework of the derivation of OE (see the section "Derivation of order ethics"): the space travelers who land on the planet might find a society of aliens there and not only have to deal with internal problems but also with the possibility of communicating and cooperating with the natives.

85. Here, the reader is directed to the discussion of the semantics of benefits in the section "Moral communication: Toward a semantics of benefits."

Chapter Six

Conclusion

Normativity ex nihilo?

SUMMARY AND GENERAL FINDINGS

So far, the conclusion of this book is largely negative: none of the moral surplus values examined in chapters 3 to 5 is able to withstand critical scrutiny. These moral surplus values either cannot be realistically expected to be socially effective and/or they are not absolutely necessary for the functioning of modern societies. This conclusion will be elucidated here once again in three steps:

The first step will summarize the fundamental *methodological* viewpoints of the discussed authors to ethical questions, specifically, with respect to the following question: Can an ethical approach be developed (i.e., *intuitional* approaches) at all *on the basis* of the available moral intuitions in a society or can (perhaps even: must) it also be constructed *in opposition to* such intuitions (i.e., *anti-intuitional* approaches)? Table 6.1 presents an overview.[1]

Table 6.1. Intuitional and anti-intuitional approaches

Intuitional Approaches	Anti-intuitional Approaches
Hösle	Gauthier (see the section "Gauthier's point of departure for a functional justification of morality")
Foot	
Habermas (see the section "Basic principles: The principle of universalization as a rule of argumentation," no. 2)	Buchanan[iii]
Rawls (see the section "Rawls's theory of justice and its connection to order ethics,")	
Rorty[i]	Order ethics
Binmore[ii]	

[i] Rorty's narratives embody the corresponding basic intuitions.
[ii] Binmore indeed refers to intuitions, but in a special way: the original position belongs to the evolutionarily formed intuitions that are used in the controlling of modern societies—although not necessarily in the same way they were used in premodern societies. See the section "Binmore's original position."
[iii] Buchanan actually favors certain attitudes, namely, the ethic of work and the ethic of saving. However, he opposes other common intuitions that contradict this ethics.

The second step again represents the actual results of the efforts from the previous chapters. The following moral surplus values were reconstructed in chapters 3 to 5.

Table 6.2. Overview of moral surplus values

Author	Moral Surplus Value
Hösle	Shared objective values
Foot	Shared image of humanity as a basis for virtues
Habermas	Rational motivation; life forms capable of ideal role taking; constitutional patriotism
Rawls	Sense of justice
Gauthier	Dispositions
Rorty	Shared feelings of sympathy and solidarity
Buchanan	Work ethic; ethic of saving
Binmore	(Predisposition toward empathy)
Order Ethics	—

This list is not to be simply understood as a disconnected sequence. An initial tentative structure may be recognized in the moral surplus values in the following way:

1. The first group of approaches attempts to secure the stability of modern societies by means of anthropological capacities and qualities or (put differently) by means of capacities of the individual that are independent of social structures and the incentives that originate from them. In this instance, the approaches include

   - Hösle, who demands a basic value orientation of the individual
   - Foot, who demands an individual focus on virtues
   - Habermas, who demands that the actors be rationally motivated without a systematic consideration of incentives
   - Gauthier, who requires rigid dispositions that are independent of situational incentives
   - Rorty, who stresses the need for sympathy-inducing narratives to be equally independent of situations

2. In my view, the approach from Rawls is unique. The sense of justice may indeed be understood as an anthropological trait. Nonetheless, it must be acknowledged (see the section "Can the concept of justice as fairness possibly be based on interests alone?") that Rawls, unlike the approaches under 1), remains—implicitly and to some extent explicitly—*open* to the kind of conceptual changes that could be necessary as a result of the practical testing of his approach.
3. The third group, finally, puts incentives and rules front and center, if with different points of emphasis:

   - Buchanan generally relies on society giving itself its own rules to preserve its stability. The ethic of work and the ethic of saving are in fact cited as moral surplus values, yet they are explicitly understood as investments, which in the end are not opposed to incentives (see the section "Society requires an ethic of work and an ethic of saving (James M. Buchanan)").
   - Binmore ultimately does not explicitly rely on rules or institutions for the implementation of ethical norms, but rather on a certain type of preferences, namely, empathetic preferences. However:

     a. On the one hand, the *critical difference* between Binmore's empathetic preferences and the surplus values of the other approaches lies in the fact that empathetic preferences are *not* systematically *exploitable*, and are therefore unproblematic. They are supposed to serve the aims of the *investment*, not the aims of victims. As a result, they are *not* conceived as a "breakthrough" or as a way of surmounting the economic logic of advantages.

b. On the other hand, the implementation of norms *through rules* (in the sense of OE) is compatible with Binmore's approach. Indeed, such an implementation continues to consistently carry out this approach, as I have already described (see the section "Discussion: Can't society also dispose with empathetic preferences?").

- OE attempts to do without moral surplus values.

In a third step, the reconstructed moral surplus values can now be linked up again to the problems of the respective authors. Sensible and productive interpretations of surplus values first emerge in context and relative to the respective issues. The following table provides an overview—in admittedly oversimplified form—of the specific questions focused on by the authors discussed in chapters 3 to 5.[2]

Table 6.3. Overview of the presented problems

Author	Problem: To Provide a Theory That
Hösle	takes account of the reality of objective values
Foot	identifies a role for virtues in modern societies
Habermas	corresponds to the actors' intuitions (also from 1992), reconstructs institutions as not only strategically, but also "communicatively" justified
Rawls	provides citizens with a tool for examining their ethical convictions
Gauthier	aims to find a justification for ethical norms on the basis of the weakest possible preconditions
Rorty	acknowledges the literary social impact of literary and artistic products
Buchanan	serves in the rational examination and formation of institutions (whereby there can be different types of auxiliary control possibilities)
Binmore	serves in the rational examination and formation of institutions on the basis of evolutionarily developed mental apparatuses
Order Ethics	serves in the rational examination and formation of formal institutions as well as the rational examination and heuristical guidance of informal institutions

As worked out in detail in the respective subsections of chapters 3 to 5, one sees again here that the presentations of the problem differ considerably. Two main thrusts can be recognized, however. Where the first group of authors (Buchanan, Binmore) is more focused on the formation of institutions and hence the public discussion about such formation recommendations, the second group (Habermas, Rawls) is rather interested in providing a perspective that is easier to comprehend from the standpoint of the actors in a modern society and is more consistent with their intuitions. This is especially relevant for the order-ethics approach under discussion here insofar as a productive integration of the approaches of the second group tends to be possible with the help of this kind of breakdown.[3] There is less risk that these approaches will be prematurely excluded from the discussion. On the other hand, it is also easier to recognize the theoretical advances of the institutionally oriented approaches of the first group and to give them their due in the ethical discussion.

Now that the moral surplus values—along with their respective theoretical positions—have been presented once again, the essential findings that have emerged out of the foregoing chapters of this book can be summarized.

The arguments from the individual chapters underscore the following: normativity that rests on anthropological capacities or traits is not very systematically productive. Those approaches that rely on the fact that humans have certain characteristics lead to one of two possible dead ends: they either cannot assume from a systematic standpoint that the moral surplus values they postulate will remain permanently *stable* under the conditions of modern societies or globalization (see chapter 1), and/or the surplus values are not absolutely *required* for the stability of modern societies. The claim is not being made here that all *conceivable* anthropological capacities or traits have been discussed. A representative number was merely selected among those that are being widely discussed today. It is therefore possible that other moral surplus values might be cited that are not susceptible to the arguments introduced in this book. However, any theorist who presents such a moral surplus value has the burden of showing that it is systematically distinct from those that have been treated here.

Another argument that speaks against the fruitfulness of anthropologically grounded normativity is that there are pronounced human qualities that contradict those that are presented in chapters 3 to 5. Adam Smith thus describes a human being as an animal with "the certain propensity to truck, barter, and exchange one thing for another. . . . It is common to all men, and to be found in no other race of animals."[4] Without getting into a detailed discussion[5] of the theoretical basis of this observation, it may be noted that this characterization resembles the one from Binmore most.[6] For Binmore, in order to negotiate and trade effectively, it is useful for an individual to put herself in the shoes of the other party. A prior sense of obligation to "moral" ideas—that is, *commitments* or the like—is not a necessary precondition for negotiations, however.[7]

Minimal Requirements of Order Ethics

If none of the moral surplus values that have been examined are actually viable, then it is necessary to raise the question about alternatives. To begin with: it is possible that in the premodern era surplus values of the type described ensured social stability in combination with informal control systems and face-to-face control mechanisms, that is, by means of different kinds of incentives, yet incentives nonetheless. However, a return to this supposedly golden age is for all intents and purposes impossible. Once a moral surplus value—in the sense of the "moral basis" of an economic system—has eroded, there is no way to restore it systematically.[8] Even more to the point: a modern society that wants to productively exploit a division of labor and competition must change over to a control system based on rules. The advantages of the modern world cannot be appropriated with premodern control systems. (This does not exclude the possibility that even informal control systems can [once again] take effect in limited spheres, especially in those where an externally predetermined, rule-based framework exists.)

Just what would an alternative control system look like? While it can only be hinted at here, it would involve the individual disciplines taking on tasks that they have already largely assumed responsibility for, even if they are generally unaware of an overall conceptual outline.

An alternative control mechanism consistent with order ethics does not draw upon anthropological findings, features, or surplus values for its support, but is rather based on *situations*. The precise rules and kinds of control systems that are required for an interaction I depend purely on I's situational limiting conditions. It might pertain to an interaction occurring in terms of (still) functioning informal controls, whereby the partners are able to more or less recognize in each other the same or at least similar normative backgrounds. Interactions like this will continue to exist as they always have. In this case, one can assume the presence of a basic level of trust that facilitates the particular interaction. Still, cases like these are the exception rather than the rule in modern societies, especially under conditions of globalization (see chapter 1). Interactions are taking place with surprising frequency between actors with highly distinct cultures and social and normative backgrounds.[9] These actors are not able to draw upon moral surplus values, but instead may only submit themselves to universally accepted rules—or devise their own rules, assuming that no suitable rules exist.[10] At any rate, the *consent of the participating actors* is the ultimate normative criterion that can still be applied. Binmore, accordingly, speaks of "just saying yes" (Binmore 1994, 72, see the section "Binmore's naturalistic contract theory"). I find this formulation too strong, however: "saying yes" appears to reflect an *explicit* consensus and rely too much on argumentation (even with "good reasons," see the section "Moral communication: Toward a semantics of benefits"), whereas an implicit consensus—in juridical terms: implied conduct—can be entirely sufficient.

What capacities or qualities are necessary for this alternative form of control? Is it possible to identify something like a final weak scaffolding, which is based on—not anthropological, but—mostly situational or interactional qualities?

In view of the concepts examined in this book and the arguments introduced so far, only the predisposition toward empathy would come into question. Of course, several possible theoretical situational types were indicated in the section "Discussion: Can't society also dispose with empathetic preferences?" in which this capacity could no longer be jointly anticipated by the interaction partners. These kinds of situations are by no means to be ruled out in cases of intercultural dialogue. It is worth making the attempt—especially in an "ad fonts" *philosophical* work—to identify weaker preconditions than the predisposition toward empathy. In my view, three such minimal preconditions can be identified that would have to be present—even in situations where moral surplus values and related concepts are either wholly missing or precluded—in order to ensure regulatory control and thus sufficient stability in a modern society under conditions of globalization.

1) Sociality

Although it may appear obvious, it nevertheless needs to be stated that *interactions* belong to a society. Robinson alone does not constitute a society. This corresponds to the classical understanding of the *zoon politikon* (see chapter 2).

2) Capacity for communication

A precondition for 1) is that the interaction partners are able to communicate with each other *in some form* (although it is presented here separately to emphasize a different point).[11] This communication does not have to consist in an elaborate form of sense-making, as with complex or refined speech. A basic form of communication is nonetheless required that allows for agreement or refusal to be indicated, for instance.

3) Capacity for investment

It is not enough that human beings are able to communicate with each other. From the perspective of the approach discussed here, an additional precondition must be met: human beings must be able to invest in the future. Individuals who are always exclusively interested in maximizing their own *momentary* utility are not capable of forming a stable society. This is not surprising for an economic approach, even if it does not work with *bounded rationality*, *extended sympathy preferences*, or related concepts. Every shared enterprise requires an investment in the future.[12] This capacity—which does not merely concern social stability or collective morality, but in principle every form of behavior and cooperation—requires thought and deliberate planning. In the philosophical tradition, it is treated as the concept of *animal rationale*.[13]

The form in which this capacity for investment is manifested or characterized in different individuals, groups, or even societies can vary greatly. What matters most here is the semantic aspect (see the section "Moral communication: Toward a semantics of benefits"): it makes a considerable difference whether an *individual* perceives an action to be a sacrifice (e.g., for the benefit of the common good, no matter what the justification might be) or an investment. It makes a difference, moreover, whether a corporation views a project to be a sacrifice (e.g., that is required on the grounds of a putative "social" or "societal responsibility") or an investment. And lastly, it makes a difference whether a *political measure* is declared to be a sacrifice or an investment.

If one speaks in terms of a *sacrifice* in each of the three cases, then some kind of moral surplus value would have to be required of the respective actors. According to the arguments that have been made so far, however, this alternative bears little fruit. On the other hand, if one speaks in terms of an *investment*, then it is possible to make do with much weaker preconditions, namely, with those that have been indicated here. The self-interest of the actors is sufficient for ensuring the implementation of the project or the political measure. In addition, in my view, this already points to a notable theoretical advantage of order ethics—at least if one understands the implementation problem to be the central difficulty of modern ethics.

Taken together, these three preconditions provide the cornerstones for a modern society whose stability can neither be secured through moral surplus values, nor needs to be in this form. The actors must simply be able to communicate and to invest. Given that these preconditions appear to be so weak, one can speak here of a normativity *ex nihilo*.[14]

I do *not* intend to suggest that these preconditions are or must be the only preconditions for a functioning modern society. My central argument is rather that the moral surplus values that have been proposed so far either cannot remain stable and/or are not necessary for a functioning modern society. I therefore recommend that an attempt should be made to attenuate the preconditions for modern societies, specifically with the three—very weak—preconditions described here.[15]

Moral Surplus Values and Interest Predication

The three indicated preconditions have an additional significant advantage over the moral surplus values that have been addressed in this book: they do not demand or expect that individuals transgress the logic of benefits and incentives.

The basic outlines of this logic were worked out in the section "Order ethics as an ethics of benefits and incentives." The primary concern is with the economic behavioral model that was defended against certain standard objections in the section "Derivation of order ethics." The null hypothesis that is presented there—according to which social stability can only be achieved through the self-interest of the actors—must now be qualified in the following respects:

1. Generally speaking, the assertion of this null hypothesis remains: under interaction conditions that are largely characterized by globalization, pluralism, and competition, the actors cannot be expected to make a sacrifice in a way that disregards their own interests. On the other hand, this also means that self-interest proves to be a reliable "partner" when controlling society through rules and incentives. The only minimal requirement here is that the actors be able to invest in the future.
2. Despite the self-interested agreement to the rules, another problem arises, however, within the scope of regulatory and incentive control: the risk of subsequent opportunistic behavior. This problem cannot be responded to by (political) regulatory control alone; instead, precautionary measures must also be taken on other levels (via associations, companies, or other organizations) against ex post opportunism. The participating parties must establish and signal the presence of a credible degree of self-commitment (see the section "Derivation of order ethics").
3. First and foremost, however, the null hypothesis is to be defined (and not merely supplemented) by the capacity for empathy. Actors who not only generally invest in the future, but can also put themselves in the shoes of their fellow actors, increase the stability of their society—and indeed without at the same time necessarily running the risk of their own exploitation. The capacity for empathy can thus be understood as an exploitation-resistant capacity whose development in a society is in the self-interest of every member and (as discussed in the section "Society requires (almost) nothing (Ken Binmore)") is also desirable from an ethical standpoint.

These three points, then, produce the more refined model of an order ethics. From a philosophical point of view, the most critical aspect of the findings is that the actors do not have to constantly maintain their behavioral pattern in opposition to contradictory incentives. A normative theory that demands such a "transgression" from the actors fundamentally endangers its own efficacy. The moral surplus values described in chapters 3 to 5 require the transgression of the logic of benefits and incentives that is criticized here in the following way:

1. Hösle explicitly requires that shared objective values be predetermined for individuals in their actions. In particular, ethics should dominate "economics."
2. Foot argues that individuals should be consistently oriented toward virtues in their actions. Foot opposes moral relativism that denies the possibility of absolute moral concepts and wants to precisely avoid an orientation toward self-interest and benefits.
3. Habermas expressly positions rational motivation against a "mere" strategic interest. The danger of a performative contradiction can motivate actors to act against incentives. On the other hand, Habermas tries to provide an evolutionary-psychological explanation for the existence of life forms that are capable of ideal role taking, that is, of assuming others' preferences irrespective of incentives. Although Habermas ascribes a greater role to the law as a controlling instrument, the proviso remains that the individual must be able to change her motivation from strategic to communicative action.
4. Rawls has also designed a dualistic theory: purely rational actors—as opposed to reasonable actors—lack the faculty of a sense of justice. The overarching consensus, which demands that individuals not act strictly according to their own interests, but according to a sense of justice, is contrasted with the *modus vivendi*, which is only based on interests. When in doubt, individuals must also be able to act against existing incentives—despite the fact Rawls does not recognize this as a long-term *investment*.
5. Gauthier, on the other hand, who explicitly aims to derive morality from self-interest, requires that actors be able to maintain their rigid dispositions even when confronted with existing incentives. Gauthier argues that a *constrained maximizer*, who accordingly is guided by a moral upbringing, can and must be able to break away from incentives, even and especially in the case of a prisoner's-dilemma type situation.
6. Rorty actually dispenses with shared values as an opportunity for integration in modern societies. Instead, he demands that actors develop feelings of solidarity and sympathy, which, in his view, are most con-

stitutive of a stable society. Conversely, Rorty distrusts the channeling of individual interests by means of institutions as a stabilization factor.
7. Buchanan demands that the members of modern societies work more, save more, and above all invest more in morality. While such an investment is actually conceived in terms of economic categories, the extent to which these investments can be systematically maintained if they are constantly undercut by incentives is nevertheless not clear.
8. Binmore, as already stressed, does not endorse any kind of moral surplus value. The predisposition toward empathy precisely does not require any transgression of the benefit-incentive logic, but rather alerts individuals to the possibility of better calculating their utility in their interactions. This predisposition is thus neither exploitable, nor subject to the risk of systematic erosion.

Moral surplus values, therefore, are not able to build on the logic of benefits and incentives. It is certainly true that this logic—as discussed in the section "Derivation of order ethics"—allows room for "moral" behavior as regards the openness of contracts. Nonetheless, even this behavior must be construed with the same logic: contracts can only lead to fruitful collaborations if the participating parties can continually expect greater *advantages* over time to result from limitation placed on their behavior than from other relevant behavioral patterns. In addition, such cooperation can only remain permanently stable if the participating parties succeed in establishing *incentives* and sanctions for preventing opportunistic types of behavior. As a result, the concept of open contracts is not directed against the logic of benefits and incentives, but is precisely the extension of this logic that is needed under conditions of globalization for enabling flexible behavior in response to unclear and heterogeneous limiting conditions.

Approaches 1)—6), and to some degree even 7), do not construe "moral" behavior in these categories, however. They demand that the actors behave "morally" even in *opposition* to incentives. Consequently they must, on the one hand, systematically overextend the actors. On the other hand, these approaches are also not able to take advantage of the existing pluralism and social heterogeneities. They shrink in the face of these challenges, adopting a merely defensive posture: the surplus values should first be secured before there can be any discussion concerning differences. These kinds of approaches cannot provide any normative foundation for modern societies under the conditions of globalization.

This is not only true for the conceptions of the examined authors, but also more generally for certain *types of argumentation* that are not systematically viable in modern societies under conditions of globalization:

- the benefits of education are not sufficient for ensuring social stability.

- postulating additional motivations beyond self-interestedness also does not lead to more stability since the interaction structures remain in place.
- the effort to strengthen shared values or virtues is a laudable undertaking that nevertheless has no impact on interaction structures.
- the argument that says modern societies subvert their own preconditions over the long term is not tenable given that modern societies do not systematically depend on individual capacities such as moral surplus values.
- and lastly: even the ostensibly economic argument that maintains that doing away with institutions would save on costs is not supportable. It bypasses the problematic of implementability in relation to dilemmatic interaction structures.

Generally speaking, any argument that is ultimately based on a concept of human nature in the broadest sense must be rejected.

Can the Intuitions behind the Moral Surplus Values Be Made Fruitful in Other Ways?

Despite all my criticism in this book of the attempts to postulate moral surplus values, I have also consistently tried to develop fruitful and constructive interpretations—if not of the surplus values themselves, then at least of the intuitions behind them. These efforts, which began in chapter 2, are summarized here once again in the following table. The deliberations of numerous proponents of a moral surplus value (Habermas, Rawls, Gauthier, Rorty) may be understood as providing with their surplus values improved heuristics for the discourse[16] about modern societies.

Hösle and Foot highlight secondary aspects in the definition of moral actions. Buchanan attempts on the basis of economic calculations to find an auxiliary location for an ethics alongside regulatory control. Finally, Binmore makes an appeal for a precondition that is not susceptible to the same dangers as other surplus values.

Behind all of these approaches, there seems to be a shared intuition: not everything can be left to rule-based control. All of the authors, including Buchanan and Binmore, want to retain supplemental mechanisms for the control of modern societies. To paraphrase Luhmann, they obviously do not want to rely *exclusively* on systems whose autonomous operation could lead to unacceptable outcomes. Is it possible they fear a kind of (not necessarily technological) determinism—a sort of primitive social technology?

There is no doubt that not only unstable, but also (comparatively) stable, systems can foster conditions that are unacceptable to those who are subjected to them. This possibility has been demonstrated by a long-standing philosophical tradition (e.g., Horkheimer/Adorno 1947, Arendt 1951). Nonetheless, assuming a functioning regulatory system is already in place, doesn't

Table 6.4. From the dogmatic to the heuristic: Constructive interpretations of surplus values

Author	Moral surplus value	Constructive interpretation
Hösle	Shared objective values	A moral action is not entirely definable theoretically; residual problems can only be solved in practice, and here values can serve as heuristics.
Foot	Shared conception of humanity as a basis for virtues	Moral judgments are not motivating in themselves; the significance of the problem of implementation in ethics must be emphasized.
Habermas	Rational motivation; life forms that are capable of ideal role taking; constitutional patriotism	Discourses provide heuristics for the reform of rules; the conception is compatible with the intuitions of the citizens of a democracy.
Rawls	Sense of justice	The overarching consensus contains a heuristic for the reform of rules; the sense of justice indicates that we (should) constantly invest in rules.
Gauthier	Dispositions	Dispositions may fulfill a heuristic function for the reform of rules.
Rorty	Shared feelings of sympathy and solidarity	Myths and narratives of experiences of suffering can disclose process-like aspects and thus have heuristic relevance.
Buchanan	Ethic of work; ethic of saving	An ethic of work and of saving can possibly assume subsidiary auxiliary control functions.
Binmore	(Predisposition toward empathy)[i]	The predisposition toward empathy has a different status and is not exploitable; it therefore does not require reinterpretation.

[i] Not to be understood as a moral surplus value in the strict sense.

this (again invoking Luhmann) ultimately concern matters of *fine-tuning* or "auxiliary control"? If the background incentives that are determined by rules thwart the (moral) intentions of the participants, then the only long-term solution is to modify these incentives. If the background incentives do *not* thwart their intentions, then there remains a great deal of room to maneuver. It is not possible to determine ahead of time what behavioral possibilities will be seized upon by the individuals, for example, whether they will be motivated by a moral surplus value and thus—in the sense of my interpretation—invest in the effort to modify and further develop the rules. This could very well occur, and it might even be possible to posit a statistical probability p that a quantity x of society's members will decide to make such an investment (at least provisionally). But once again: certain overriding background incentives would be necessary here, otherwise the willingness to invest would quickly erode.

If the intuition behind the moral surplus values can be interpreted as a desire for auxiliary control, a theoretical problem still remains concerning semantics. (Here, I take up again the discussion in the section "Moral communication: Toward a semantics of benefits.") Clearly, an investment in regulatory change—in whatever form—must have a public impact. However, if a semantics (and a rhetoric) is used in the public discussion that draws stark distinctions between incentives and rational motivation, values and interests, following rules "for their own sake" and an interest-based rule compliance—that aims to discredit self-interest and thus ignores background incentives—then the full force of this book's critique would once again apply. In a case like this, resorting to auxiliary control effects would not be possible.

By the same token, if semantics can be reoriented toward concepts like "investing," "reciprocal self-interest," "reciprocal benefits," "cooperation," or "win-win situations," then a productive interpretation of surplus values is possible. Many traditional demands such as an orientation toward other criteria besides success, noneconomic criteria, and so on, might be thought about differently. In this case, postulated, endorsed, and recommended as being in the (long-term) interest of the individual would be enduring *investments*.

NOTES

1. Anti-intuitional approaches are generally not widely accepted in contemporary ethics. An additional proponent, for instance, would be Bernard Williams (1973).

2. To be clear, the aim here is not to characterize the only or the only possible problem that is being presented by each of the respective authors. This would require a much more detailed analysis. Instead, the goal is merely to present a relevant overview of the various interpretive methods and objectives of a narrow sub-area, specifically, the problem that concerns us here.

3. This was done in the respective concluding sections "Society needs shared values (material value-ethics)" to "Society requires (almost) nothing (Ken Binmore)."

4. Smith 1776/1976, book I, 17.

5. Here, one might take up the discussion on Smith's anthropology, in particular his notion of sympathy; it is not possible, however, to pursue this in any detail in this context. See also Binmore 1998, and the section "No commitments!"

6. This is because Smith's notion of "sympathy" may be interpreted as "empathy" in the sense intended by Binmore. See, accordingly, Binmore 1998, and the section "No commitments!"

7. This is not to say that such commitments are necessarily detrimental to negotiations.

8. In this instance, it is only possible to refer to the findings of economics and other social sciences showing that this alternative is not available for incentive-related and political-societal reasons. See, for instance, the writings from Buchanan (1975), Brennan and Buchanan (1985), Olson (1965; 1982), Binmore (1994; 1998), and Luhmann (especially 1997). See also my arguments in the section "Morality in Buchanan's later work," no. 5.

9. Theoretically extreme cases—which nevertheless allow much to be learned with regard to actual cases—are discussed in the section "Discussion: Can't society also dispose with

empathetic preferences?" in reference to the interaction models found in science fiction literature.

10. I note here the growing number of cases in which it is not the rules that are determined by state actors, but rather by nonstate actors (e.g., corporations), that assume an essential controlling function.

11. In Lem's "Solaris" (1961/1970), this kind of communication fails. See the section "Discussion: Can't society also dispose with empathetic preferences?"

12. It is therefore highly unproductive from a theoretical standpoint to construe the homo economicus as someone who cannot invest in the future.

13. The capacity to invest—that is, to engage in long-term thinking that goes beyond one's own particular generation—might be recognized in terms of what the Western tradition understands under the concept of "reason." This, however, would have to be the subject of a much more comprehensive analysis.

14. They are weaker than the "minimum content of natural law" put forward by H. L. A. Hart (1961, 189f.), who chiefly assumes a "limited altruism" (ibid. 190) that is not treated here.

15. A brief comment on methodology: this kind of approach, which—as already discussed in the section "The problem's outline"—can be characterized as naturalistic, dispenses with strong preconditions for methodological reasons, not necessarily due to an ontological requirement to economize. Furthermore, I would also like to point out once again that the naturalistic approach does not have to focus on individual psychological or neuro-scientific factors in matters of practical philosophy, but can and should, with the help of the social sciences, also take account of social and situational factors.

16. On the interaction between discourse and (self-interested rational) decision making, see Aaken, List, and Luetge (2004).

Outlook

Under the conditions of globalization, we are increasingly no longer able to restrictively formulate the preconditions for social stability or to overly rely on shared individual qualities. Examples of this can be found in

- the discussion in many countries about the image of the family, for instance with regard to the question of how childcare should be regulated,
- the discussion about religious instruction with regard to non-Christian denominations as well as the replacement of religion as a subject with a teaching of general ethics,
- the discussion about increased immigration (which has long been recorded in statistics on population and pension trends),
- the issue of cross-border legislation in the Internet,
- and many more.

These are only a few examples of how globalization can cause many cherished intellectual and cultural habits to disappear. No state—and no federation of states—is able to systematically anticipate the shared individual capacities or qualities of its citizens. Not only are their personal backgrounds too diverse, but the forms of interactions in which they find themselves have the effect of obscuring these backgrounds in specific actions and causing a shift toward self-interest as the dominant motivation. This shift toward self-interestedness, however, should not merely provide an occasion for protesting the unfortunate state of the world, the decline of values or the loss of virtue. Instead, it should be viewed as an opportunity to set out on a journey—without hypocrisy, national bigotry or a moralistic prism that distorts a true appreciation of actual problems—toward a world that will likely be more profoundly different than anything that has been imagined so far.

Bibliography

Aaken, Anne van, Christian List, and Christoph Luetge, eds. 2004. *Deliberation and Decision: Economics, Constitutional Theory, and Deliberative Democracy*. Aldershot and Burlington: Ashgate.
Ackerman, Bruce A. 1980. *Social Justice in the Liberal State*. New Haven: Yale University Press.
Alcock, John. 2001. *The Triumph of Sociobiology*. Oxford: Oxford University Press.
Alejandro, Robert. 1998. *The Limits of Rawlsian Justice*. Baltimore: Johns Hopkins University Press.
Alexy, Robert. 1978. "Eine Theorie des praktischen Diskurses." In *Normenbegründung, Normendurchsetzung: Materialien zur Normendiskussion*, edited by Willi Oelmüller, 22–58. Paderborn: Schöningh.
———. 1997. "Theorie der Grundfreiheiten." In Philosophische Gesellschaft Bad Homburg and Wilfried Hinsch 1997, 263–303.
Apel, Karl-Otto. 1984. *Transformation der Philosophie*. 2 Bde., 3rd ed. Frankfurt/M.: Suhrkamp.
———. 1988. *Diskurs und Verantwortung*. Frankfurt/M.: Suhrkamp.
———. 1990/1996. "Diskursethik als Verantwortungsethik. Eine postmetaphysische Transformation der Ethik Kants." In *Ethik und Befreiung*, edited by Raul Fornet-Betancourt, 10–40. Aachen: Augustinus-Buchhandlung, 1990. Reprinted in *Kant in der Diskussion der Moderne*, edited by Gerhard Schönrich and Yasushi Kato, 326–359. Frankfurt/M.: Suhrkamp, 1996.
———. 1997. "Institutionsethik oder Diskursethik als Verantwortungsethik? Das Problem der institutionalen Implementation moralischer Normen im Falle des Systems der Marktwirtschaft." In *Zur Relevanz der Diskursethik: Anwendungsprobleme der Diskursethik in Wirtschaft und Politik*, edited by Jean-Paul Harpes and Wolfgang Kuhlmann, 167–209. Münster: LIT.
Arendt, Hannah. 1951. *The Origins of Totalitarianism*. 1st ed. New York: Harcourt, Brace, and Company.
Armstrong, David M. 1983. *What Is a Law of Nature?* Cambridge: Cambridge University Press.
Arrow, Kenneth J. 1951. *Social Choice and Individual Values*. New York: Wiley.
Arrow, Kenneth J. and Frank H. Hahn. 1971. *General Competitive Analysis*. San Francisco: Holden-Day.
Asimov, Isaac. 1983. *The Robots of Dawn*. Garden City, NY: Doubleday.
Austin, John L. 1962. *How to Do Things with Words*. Cambridge, MA: Harvard University Press.

Avineri, Shlomo and Avner De-Shalit, eds. 1992. *Communitarianism and Individualism*. Oxford: Oxford University Press.
Axelrod, Robert M. 1984. *The Evolution of Cooperation*. New York: Basic Books.
Baier, Kurt. 1989. "Justice and the Aims of Political Philosophy." *Ethics* 99: 771–790.
Baines, Harold V. and James R. Ursah, eds. 2009. *Globalization: Understanding, Management, and Effects*. New York: Nova Science Publishers.
Barad, Judith and Ed Robertson. 2000. *The Ethics of Star Trek*. New York: Harper Collins.
Barry, Brian. 1989. *Theories of Justice*. London: Harvester Wheatsheaf.
———. 1995. *Justice as Impartiality*. Oxford: Clarendon.
Beitz, Charles R. 2000. "Rawls's Law of Peoples." *Ethics* 110: 669–696.
Benhabib, Seyla. 1994. "Deliberative Democracy." *Constellations* 1: 30–51.
Benjamin, Walter. 1936/1970. *Das Kunstwerk im Zeitalter seiner technischen Reproduzierbarkeit: drei Studien zur Kunstsoziologie*. 4th ed. Frankfurt/M.: Suhrkamp (engl.: *The Work of Art in the Age of Its Technological Reproducibility, and Other Writings on Media*. Cambridge, MA: Harvard University Press, 2008).
Bentham, Jeremy. 1789/1970. *An Introduction to the Principles of Morals and Legislation*. Edited by H. L. A. Hart. London: T. Payne and Son, 1970. In Bentham 1968ff.
———. 1968ff. *The Collected Works*. Edited by J. H. Burns. London: Athlone Press.
Berlin, Isaiah. 1958/1969. "Two Concepts of Liberty." In *Four Essays on Liberty*, 118–172. Oxford: Oxford University Press.
Bhagwati, Jagdish N. 2004. *In Defense of Globalization*. New York: Oxford University Press.
Binmore, Ken. 1994. *Game Theory and the Social Contract: Vol. 1: Playing Fair*. Cambridge, MA, London: MIT Press.
———. 1998. *Game Theory and the Social Contract: Vol. 2: Just Playing*. Cambridge, MA, London: MIT Press.
———. 2001. "Natural Justice and Political Stability." *Journal of Institutional and Theoretical Economics* 157: 133–151.
———. 2004. "Natural Justice." In Luetge and Vollmer 2004, 128–150.
Birnbacher, Dieter. 1988/1995. *Verantwortung für zukünftige Generationen*. Erg. Ausg. Stuttgart: Reclam.
———. 1995. *Tun und Unterlassen*. Stuttgart: Reclam.
Bischof, Norbert. 1985. *Das Rätsel Ödipus: die biologischen Wurzeln des Urkonfliktes von Intimität und Autonomie*. München: Piper.
Bittner, Rüdiger. 1997. "Die Hoffnung auf politischen Konsens." In Philosophische Gesellschaft Bad Homburg and Wilfried Hinsch 1997, 39–51.
Blau, Julian H. 1975. "Liberal Values and Independence." *Review of Economic Studies* 42: 395–402.
Blumer, Herbert. 1969/1986. *Symbolic Interactionism: Perspective and Method*. Paperback print. Berkeley: University of California Press.
Böckenförde, Ernst-Wolfgang. 1967/1991. "Die Entstehung des Staates als Vorgang der Säkularisation." In *Recht, Staat, Freiheit: Studien zur Rechtsphilosophie, Staatstheorie und Verfassungsgeschichte*, 92–114. Frankfurt/M.: Suhrkamp.
Böhm, Franz. 1961. "Demokratie und ökonomische Macht." In *Kartelle und Monopole im modernen Recht: Beiträge zum übernationalen und nationalen europäischen und amerikanischen Recht*, 2 Bde., edited by Institut für ausländisches und internationales Wirtschaftsrecht, Bd. 1, 3–24. Karlsruhe: Müller.
Bohnet, Iris, Bruno S. Frey, and Steffen Huck. 2001. "More Order with Less Law: On Contract Enforcement, Trust, and Crowding." *American Political Science Review* 95, No. 1: 131–144.
Boyd, Richard. 1981. "Scientific Realism and Naturalistic Epistemology." In *PSA 1980*, vol. II, edited by Peter Asquith and Ronald Giere, 613–62. East Lansing, MI: Philosophy of Science Association.
———. 1983. "On the Current Status of Scientific Realism." *Erkenntnis* 19: 45–90.
Brandt, Richard B. 1959. *Ethical Theory: The Problems of Normative and Critical Ethics*. Englewood Cliffs: Prentice-Hall.

———. 1967. "Some Merits of One Form of Rule-Utilitarianism." *University of Colorado Studies* 3: 39–65.
Brandom, Robert. 1994. *Making It Explicit: Reasoning, Representing, and Discursive Commitment.* Cambridge, MA: Harvard University Press.
———. 2000. *Articulating Reasons: An Introduction to Inferentialism.* Cambridge, MA: Harvard University Press.
———. 2001. "What Do Expressions of Preference Express?" In Morris and Ripstein 2001a, 11–36.
———. 2002. "Geist als Verantwortung: Im Gespräch mit dem Philosophen Robert Brandom" *Neue Zürcher Zeitung*, 17.8.2002.
Brennan, Geoffrey and James M. Buchanan. 1980. *The Power to Tax: Analytical Foundations of a Fiscal Constitution.* Cambridge: Cambridge University Press.
———. 1985. *The Reason of Rules: Constitutional Political Economy.* Cambridge: Cambridge University Press.
Brennan, Samantha and Robert Noggle. 2000. "Rawls's Neglected Childhood: Reflections on the Original Position, Stability, and the Child's Sense of Justice." In Davion and Wolf 2000, 46–72.
Broome, John. 1997. "Reason and Motivation." *Proceedings of the Aristotelian Society*, Supplementary Vol. 71: 131–46.
———. 2000. "Normative Requirements." In Dancy 2000a, 78–99.
Brown, Michael E., Steven E. Miller, and Sean M. Lynn-Jones, eds. 1996. *Debating the Democratic Peace.* Cambridge, MA: MIT Press.
Buchanan, Allen. 2000a. "Rawls's Law of Peoples: Rules for a Vanished Westphalian World." *Ethics* 110: 697–721.
———. 2000b. "Justice, Legitimacy, and Human Rights." In Davion and Wolf 2000, 73–89.
Buchanan, James M. 1964/1979. "What Should Economists Do?" In *What Should Economists Do?* 17–37. Indianapolis: Liberty Press.
———. 1965. "Ethical Rules, Expected Values, and Large Numbers." *Ethics* 76: 1–13.
———. 1972. "Rawls on Justice as Fairness." Public Choice 13: 123–28.
———. 1975. *The Limits of Liberty: Between Anarchy and Leviathan.* Chicago: University of Chicago Press.
———. 1976. "A Hobbsian Interpretation of the Rawlsian Difference Principle." Kyklos 29, H. 1: 5–25.
———. 1988/1991. "The Gauthier Enterprise." In Paul 1988, 75–94, reprinted in Buchanan 1991, 195–213.
———. 1989. *Essays on the Political Economy.* Honolulu: University of Hawaii Press.
———. 1990. "The Domain of Constitutional Economics." *Constitutional Political Economy* 1: 1–18.
———. 1991. *The Economics and the Ethics of Constitutional Order.* Ann Arbor: University of Michigan Press.
———. 1994. *Ethics and Economic Progress.* Norman: University of Oklahoma Press.
———. 1995. "Individual Rights, Emergent Social States, and Behavioral Feasibility." *Rationality and Society* 7: 141–150.
Buchanan, James M. and Gordon Tullock. 1962. *The Calculus of Consent: Logical Foundations of Constitutional Democracy.* Ann Arbor: University of Michigan Press.
Buchanan, James M. and Richard E. Wagner. 1987. "The Political Biases of Keynesian Economics." In James M. Buchanan, *Economics: Between Predictive Science and Moral Philosophy*, 389–408. College Station: Texas A & M University Press.
Chu, C. Y. Cyrus and Wen-fang Liu. 2001. "A Dynamic Characterization of Rawls's Maximin Principle: Theory and Implications." *Constitutional Political Economy* 12: 255–272.
Cohen, Joshua. 1989. "Deliberation and Democratic Legitimacy." In *The Good Polity*, edited by Alan Hamlin and Philip Pettit. Oxford: Blackwell.
Copp, David. 1991. "Contractarianism and Moral Skepticism." In Vallentyne 1991a, 196–228.
———. 1996. "Pluralism and Stability in Liberal Theory." *The Journal of Political Philosophy* 4, H. 3: 191–206.

Crisp, Roger and Dale Jamieson. 2000. "Egalitarianism and a Global Resources Tax: Pogge on Rawls." In Davion and Wolf, 2000, 90–101.
Dahl, Robert A. 1989. *Democracy and Its Critics*. New Haven: Yale University Press.
Dancy, Jonathan, ed. 2000a. *Normativity*. Oxford: Blackwell.
———. 2000b. Editor's Introduction to Dancy 2000a, vii–xv.
Daniels, Norman, ed. 1974/1978. *Reading Rawls: Critical Studies on Rawls'* A Theory of Justice. Oxford: Blackwell.
———. 2000. "Reflective Equilibrium and Justice as Political." In Davion and Wolf 2000, 127–154.
Danielson, Peter. 1991a. "Closing the Compliance Dilemma: How It's Rational to Be Moral in a Lamarckian World." In Vallentyne 1991a, 291–322.
———. 1991b. "The Lockean Provison:" In Vallentyne 1991a, 99–111.
Dauenhauer, Bernard P. 2000. "A Good Word for a Modus Vivendi." In Davion and Wolf 2000, 204–220.
Dawkins, Richard. 1976. *The Selfish Gene*. Oxford: Oxford University Press.
Davion, Victoria and Clark Wolf, eds. 2000. *The Idea of a Political Liberalism: Essays on Rawls*. Lanham: Rowman & Littlefield.
Demsetz, Harold. 1969. "Information and Efficiency: Another Viewpoint," *Journal of Law and Economics* 12: 1–22.
Denzau, Arthur T. and Douglass C. North. 1994. "Shared Mental Models: Ideologies and Institutions." *Kyklos* 47: 3–31.
Dixit, Avinash K. and Barry Nalebuff. 1991. *Thinking Strategically: The Competitive Edge in Business, Politics, and Everyday Life*. New York: W.W. Norton.
Dore, Mohammed. 1997. "On Playing Fair: Professor Binmore on Game Theory and the Social Contract." *Theory and Decision* 43: 219–239.
Doyle, Michael. 1983. "Kant, Liberal Legacies, and Foreign Affairs," *Philosophy and Public Affairs* 12: 205–235 and 323–353.
Dubiel, Helmut. 1992. "Konsens oder Konflikt? Die normative Integration des demokratischen Staates." In *Staat und Demokratie in Europa*, edited by Beate Kohler-Koch, 130–137. Opladen: Leske und Budrich.
Eichberger, Jürgen. 1993. *Game Theory for Economists*. San Diego: Academic Press.
Elster, Jon. 1983. *Sour Grapes: Studies in the Subversion of Rationality*. Cambridge: Cambridge University Press.
———. 1989. *The Cement of Society: A Study of Social Order*. Cambridge: Cambridge University Press.
Evensky, Jerry. 1993. "Ethics and the Invisible Hand." *Journal of Economic Perspectives* 7, H. 2: 197–205.
Finkelstein, Claire. 2001. "Rational Temptation." In Morris and Ripstein 2001a, 56–80.
Fishkin, James S. 1988. "Bargaining, Justice, and Justification: Towards Reconstruction." In Paul 1988, 46–64.
Förster, Eckart. 1992. "'Was darf ich hoffen?' Zum Problem der Vereinbarkeit von theoretischer und praktischer Vernunft bei Immanuel Kant." *Zeitschrift für philosophische Forschung* 46: 168–185.
———. 2000. *Kant's Final Synthesis: An Essay on the Opus Postumum*. Cambridge, MA: Harvard University Press.
Foot, Philippa. 1978. *Virtues and Vices and Other Essays in Moral Philosophy*. Oxford: Basil Blackwell.
———. 1985. "Morality, Action and Outcome." In *Morality and Objectivity*. London: Routledge.
———. 1997. *Die Wirklichkeit des Guten: moralphilosophische Aufsätze*. Edited by Ursula Wolf. Frankfurt/M.: Fischer.
———. 2001. *Natural Goodness*. Oxford: Clarendon.
———. 2002. *Moral Dilemmas and Other Topics in Moral Philosophy*. Oxford: Clarendon.
Forst, Rainer. 1994. *Kontexte der Gerechtigkeit: Politische Philosophie jenseits von Liberalismus und Kommunitarismus*. Frankfurt/M.: Suhrkamp.
Frankena, William K. 1939. "The Naturalistic Fallacy." *Mind* 48: 464–477.

Frohlich, Norman, Joe A. Oppenheimer, and Cheryl L. Eavey. 1987. "Laboratory Results on Rawls's Distributive Justice." *British Journal of Political Science*, January 1987: 1–21.
Gadenne, Volker. 1996. "Rationale Heuristik und Falsifikation." In *Rationalität und Kritik*, edited by Volker Gadenne and Hans J. Wendel, 57–78. Tübingen: Mohr.
Gambetta, Diego. 1993. *The Sicilian Mafia: The Business of Private Protection*. Cambridge, MA: Harvard University Press.
Gauthier, David. 1969/2000. *The Logic of Leviathan: The Moral and Political Theory of Thomas Hobbes*. Reprint. Oxford: Clarendon.
———. 1979. "David Hume: Contractarian." *Philosophical Review* 88: 3–38.
———. 1986. *Morals by Agreement*. Oxford: Clarendon.
———. 1988. "Morality, Rational Choice, and Semantic Representation: A Reply to My Critics." In Paul et al. 1988, 173–221.
———. 1991a. "Why Contractarianism?" In Vallentyne 1991a, 15–30.
———. 1991b. "Rational Constraint: Some Last Words." In Vallentyne 1991a, 323–330.
———. 1994. "Assure and Threaten." *Ethics* 104: 690–721.
———. 1997a. "Resolute Choice and Rational Deliberation: A Critique and a Defense." *Nous* 31: 1–25.
———. 1997b. "Political Contractarianism." *Journal of Political Philosophy* 5, no. 2: 132–148.
———. 1998. "Mutual Advantage and Impartiality." In *Impartiality, Neutrality and Justice: Rereading Brian Barry's Justice as Impartiality*, edited by Paul Kelly, 120–136. Edinburgh: Edinburgh University Press.
Geach, Peter T. 1977. *The Virtues*. Cambridge: Cambridge University Press.
Gewirth, Alan. 1978. *Reason and Morality*. Chicago: University of Chicago Press.
Gibbard, Allan. 1990. *Wise Choices, Apt Feelings: A Theory of Normative Judgement*. Oxford: Clarendon.
Giere, Ronald N. 1999. "Using Models to Represent Reality." In *Model-Based Reasoning in Scientific Discovery*, edited by Lorenzo Magnani, Nancy J. Nersessian, and Paul Thagard, 41–57. New York: Kluwer Academic/Plenum Publishers.
Giunti, Marco. 1988. "Hattiangadi's Theory of Scientific Problems and the Structure of Standard Epistemologies." *British Journal for the Philosophy of Science* 39: 421–439.
Goethe, Johann Wolfgang von. 1991. *Sämtliche Werke nach Epochen seines Schaffens*. Münchner Ausgabe. München: Hanser.
Gregory, Chris. 2000. *Star Trek: Parallel Narratives*. Basingstoke: Macmillan.
Grossman, Sanford J. and Oliver D. Hart. 1986. "The Cost and Benefits of Ownership: A Theory of Vertical and Lateral Integration." *Journal of Political Economy* 94: 691–719.
Grubel, Herbert G. and Lawrence A. Boland. 1986. "On the Efficient Use of Mathematics in Economics: Some Theory, Facts and Results of an Opinion Survey." *Kyklos* 39: 419–442.
Guéhenno, Jean-Marie. 1993. *La fin de la démocratie*. Paris: Flammarion.
Gunnarsson, Logi. 2000. *Making Moral Sense: Beyond Habermas and Gauthier*. Cambridge: Cambridge University Press.
Gutmann, Amy. 1985. "Communitarian Critics of Liberalism." *Philosophy & Public Affairs* 14: 308–322.
Haas, Robert D. 1994. "Ethics: A Global Business Challenge. Character and Courage." *Vital Speeches of the Day* 60: 506–509.
Habermas, Jürgen. 1973. "Wahrheitstheorien." In *Wirklichkeit und Reflexion: Walter Schulz zum 60. Geburtstag*, edited by Helmut Fahrenbach, 211–265. Pfullingen: Neske.
———. 1981. *Theorie des kommunikativen Handelns*. 2 Bde. Frankfurt/M.: Suhrkamp (engl.: *The Theory of Communicative Action*, 2 vols. Boston: Beacon Press, 1984/1987).
———. 1983/1999a. "Diskursethik: Notizen zu einem Begründungsprogramm." In *Moralbewußtsein und kommunikatives Handeln*, 53–125. Frankfurt/M.: Suhrkamp (engl.: Moral Consciousness and Communicative Action. Cambridge, MA: MIT Press 1990).
———. 1983/1999b. "Moralbewußtsein und kommunikatives Handeln." In *Moralbewußtsein und kommunikatives Handeln*, 127–206. Frankfurt/M.: Suhrkamp. (engl.: *Moral Consciousness and Communicative Action*. Cambridge, MA: MIT Press, 1990).
———. 1986/1987. "Eine Art Schadensabwicklung: die apologetischen Tendenzen in der deutschen Zeitgeschichtsschreibung." *DIE ZEIT*, 11.7.1986. Reprinted in *Streit ums Geschichts-*

bild: Die "Historiker-Debatte". Darstellung, Dokumentation, Kritik, edited by Reinhard Kühnl, 42–50. Köln: Pahl-Rugenstein, 1987.

———. 1987. *Eine Art Schadensabwicklung*. Frankfurt/M.: Suhrkamp (engl.: *The New Conservatism*. Cambridge, MA: MIT Press, 1991).

———. 1988/1991. "Lawrence Kohlberg und der Neoaristotelismus." In Habermas 1991: 77–99.

———. 1989/1991. "Charles S. Peirce über Kommunikation." In *Texte und Kontexte*, 9–33. Frankfurt/M.: Suhrkamp.

McCloskey, Deirdre. 2006. *The Bourgeois Virtues. Ethics for an Age of Commerce*. Chicago: University of Chicago Press.

———. (2010). *Bourgeois Dignity. Why Economics Can't Explain the Modern World*. Chicago: University of Chicago Press.

———. 1990/1991. "Edmund Husserl über Lebenswelt, Philosophie und Wissenschaft." In *Texte und Kontexte*, 34–48. Frankfurt/M.: Suhrkamp.

———. 1991. *Erläuterungen zur Diskursethik*. Frankfurt/M.: Suhrkamp (engl.: *Justification and Application: Remarks on Discourse Ethics*. Cambridge, MA: MIT Press, 1993).

———. 1992. *Faktizität und Geltung: Beiträge zur Diskurstheorie des Rechts und des demokratischen Rechtsstaats*. Frankfurt/M.: Suhrkamp (engl.: *Between Facts and Norms: Contributions to a Discourse Theory of Law and Democracy*. Cambridge, MA: MIT Press, 1996).

———. 1996. *Die Einbeziehung des Anderen: Studien zur politischen Theorie*. Frankfurt/M.: Suhrkamp (engl.: *The Inclusion of the Other: Studies in Political Theory*. Cambridge, MA: MIT Press, 2000).

———. 1997. "Versöhnung durch öffentlichen Vernunftgebrauch." In Philosophische Gesellschaft Bad Homburg and Wilfried Hinsch 1997, 169–195.

———. 1998. *Die postnationale Konstellation*. Frankfurt/M.: Suhrkamp (engl.: *The Postnational Constellation*. Cambridge: Polity Press, 2000).

———. 1999. *Wahrheit und Rechtfertigung: philosophische Aufsätze*. Frankfurt/M.: Suhrkamp (engl.: *Truth and Justification*. Cambridge, MA: MIT Press, 2003).

Hampton, Jean. 1986. *Hobbes and the Social Contract Tradition*. Cambridge: Cambridge University Press.

———. 1991a. "Two Faces of Contractarian Thought." In Vallentyne 1991a, 31–55.

———. 1991b. "Equalizing Concessions in the Pursuit of Justice: A Discussion of Gauthier's Bargaining Solution." In Vallentyne 1991a, 149–161.

———. 1997. *Political Philosophy*. Boulder: Westview Press.

Hardin, Russell. 1982. *Collective Action*. Baltimore: Johns Hopkins University Press.

Hare, Richard M. 1964. "The Promising Game." *Revue Internationale de Philosophie* 70: 398–412.

———. 1974/1978. "Rawls' Theory of Justice." In Daniels 1974/1978, 81–107.

Harman, Gilbert. 1988. "Rationality in Agreement: A Commentary on Gauthier's Morals by Agreement." In Paul 1988, 1–16.

Harsanyi, John C. 1976. *Essays on Ethics, Social Behavior, and Scientific Explanation*. Dordrecht: Reidel.

———. 1977. *Rational Behavior and Bargaining Equilibrium in Games and Social Situations*. Cambridge University Press: Cambridge.

Hart, Herbert Lionel Adolphus. 1961. *The Concept of Law*. Oxford: Oxford University Press.

———. 1967. "Social Solidarity and the Enforcement of Morality." *University of Chicago Law Review* 35: 1–13.

———. 1974/1978. "Rawls on Liberty and Its Priority." In Daniels 1974/1978, 230–252.

Hart, Oliver D. 1987. "Incomplete Contracts." In *The New Palgrave: A Dictionary of Economics*, edited by John Eatwell et al., Bd. 2, 752–759. London/Basingstoke: Macmillan.

Hartmann, Nicolai. 1935. *Ethik*. Berlin: de Gruyter.

Haskell, Thomas L. 1984. "Professionalism versus Capitalism: R.H. Tawney, Emile Durkheim, and C.S. Peirce on the Disinterestedness of Professional Communities." In *The Authority of Experts: Studies in History and Theory*, edited by Thomas L. Haskell, 180–225. Bloomington: Indiana University Press.

Hattiangadi, Jagdish N. 1978–1979. "The Structure of Problems, Part I + II." *Philosophy of the Social Sciences* 8: 345–365 and 9: 49–76.
Hayek, Friedrich August von. 1978. "Competition as a Discovery Procedure." In *F. A. v. Hayek: New Studies in Philosophy, Politics and Economics*. Chicago: University of Chicago Press.
———. 1973–1979. *Law, Legislation, and Liberty*. 3 vols. Chicago: University of Chicago Press.
Hegel, Georg Wilhelm Friedrich. 1969ff. *Werke in zwanzig Bänden*. Frankfurt/M.: Suhrkamp.
Hershovitz, Scott. 2000. "A Mere Modus Vivendi?" In Davion and Wolf 2000, 221–230.
Hirschman, Albert O. 1984. "Against Parsimony: Three Easy Ways of Complicating Some Categories of Economic Discourse." *American Economic Review*, Papers and Proceedings, 74: 89–96.
———. 1994. "Wieviel Gemeinsinn braucht die liberale Gesellschaft?" *Leviathan* 22: 293–304.
Hobbes, Thomas. 1640/2008. *The Elements of Law, Natural and Politic*. Oxford: Oxford University Press.
———. 1651/1991. *Leviathan*. Edited by Richard Tuck. Cambridge: Cambridge University Press.
Höffe, Otfried. 1987. *Politische Gerechtigkeit: Grundlegung einer kritischen Philosophie von Recht und Staat*. Frankfurt/M.: Suhrkamp.
———. 1988. *Den Staat braucht selbst ein Volk von Teufeln: philosophische Versuche zur Rechts-und Staatsethik*. Stuttgart: Reclam.
———. ed. 1998. *John Rawls: eine Theorie der Gerechtigkeit*. Berlin: Akademie-Verlag.
———. 1999/2002. *Demokratie im Zeitalter der Globalisierung*. New ed. München: Beck.
Hösle, Vittorio. 1997. *Moral und Politik: Grundlagen einer Politischen Ethik für das 21. Jahrhundert*. München: Beck.
———. 2001. "Die Irrtümer der Denker—was Intellektuelle mit der NS-Ideologie verband." *Der Spiegel* Nr. 29, 16.7.2001.
Hofstede, Geert and Michael H. Bond. 1988. "The Confucius Connection: From Cultural Roots to Economic Growth." *Organisational Dynamics* 16, Spring 1988: 5–21.
Holler, Manfred J. 2000. Review of *Game Theory and the Social Contract Vol. 2: Just Playing*, by Ken Binmore. *Journal of Economics* 71: 200–204.
Homann, Karl. 1988. *Rationalität und Demokratie*. Tübingen: Mohr.
———. 2002. *Vorteile und Anreize: zur Grundlegung einer Ethik der Zukunft*. Edited by Christoph Luetge. Tübingen: Mohr Siebeck.
———. 2003. *Anreize und Moral: Gesellschaftstheorie—Ethik—Anwendungen*. Edited by Christoph Luetge, Philosophie und Ökonomik Bd. 1. Münster: LIT.
———. 2007. "Globalisation from a Business Ethics Point of View." In Homann, Koslowski, and Luetge 2007, 3–9.
Homann, Karl, Peter Koslowski, and Christoph Luetge, eds. 2007. *Globalisation and Business Ethics*. Aldershot and Burlington: Ashgate.
Homann, Karl and Christoph Luetge. 2004/2013. *Einführung in die Wirtschaftsethik*. 3rd edition. Münster: LIT.
Horkheimer, Max and Theodor W. Adorno. 1947/1971. *Dialektik der Aufklärung*. Frankfurt/M: Fischer (engl.: *Dialectic of Enlightenment*. Stanford: Stanford University Press, 2002).
Hume, David. 1739–1740/1978. *A Treatise of Human Nature*. 2nd ed. Oxford: Clarendon.
———. 1748/1975. "An Enquiry Concerning Human Understanding." In *Hume's Enquiries*, edited by L. A. Selby-Bigge and P. H. Nidditch. Oxford: Oxford University Press.
———. 1748/1987. "Of the Original Contract." In *Essays. Moral, Political and Literary*, edited by Eugene Miller, rev. ed. Indianapolis: Liberty Classics.
———. 1751/1975. "An Enquiry Concerning the Principles of Morals." In *Hume's Enquiries*, edited by L. A. Selby-Bigge and P. H. Nidditch. Oxford: Oxford University Press.
Husserl, Edmund. 1936/1996. *Die Krisis der europäischen Wissenschaften und die transzendentale Phänomenologie: eine Einleitung in die phänomenologische Philosophie*. Edited by Elisabeth Ströker. 3rd ed. Hamburg: Meiner.
Jonas, Hans. 1979. *Das Prinzip Verantwortung: Versuch einer Ethik für die technologische Zivilisation*. Frankfurt/M.: Insel.

Kant, Immanuel. 1976ff. *Werkausgabe*. Edited by Wilhelm Weischedel, 12 vols. Frankfurt/M.: Suhrkamp.
Kavka, Gregory S. 1986. *Hobbesian Moral and Political Theory*. Princeton: Princeton University Press.
Kersting, Wolfgang. 1994. *Die politische Philosophie des Gesellschaftsvertrags*. Darmstadt: Wissenschaftliche Buchgesellschaft.
Kitcher, Philip. 1993a. *The Advancement of Science: Science without Legend, Objectivity without Illusions*. New York: Oxford University Press.
———. 1993b. "The Evolution of Human Altruism." *Journal of Philosophy* 90: 497–516.
———. 2001. *Science, Truth, and Democracy*. New York: Oxford University Press.
Kliemt, Hartmut. 2001. "Natural Justice and Political Stability: Comment." *Journal of Institutional and Theoretical Economics* 157 (2001): 155–161.
Kohlberg, Lawrence. 1981. *The Philosophy of Moral Development: Moral Stages and the Idea of Justice. Essays on Moral Development, Vol. 1*. San Francisco: Harper & Row.
———. 1984. *The Psychology of Moral Development: The Nature and Validity of Moral Stages. Essays on Moral Development, Vol. 2*. San Francisco: Harper & Row.
Kreps, David M. 1988. *Notes on the Theory of Choice*. Boulder: Westview Press.
Krings, Hermann. 1991. "Norm und Praxis: zum Problem der Vermittlung moralischer Gebote." *Herder Korrespondenz* 45: 228–233.
Kripke, Saul A. 1982. *Wittgenstein on Rules and Private Language*. Cambridge, MA: Harvard University Press.
Kukathas, Chandran and Philip Pettit. 1990. *Rawls: A Theory of Justice and Its Critics*. Cambridge: Polity Press.
Kuhn, Thomas S. 1977. *The Essential Tension: Selected Studies in Scientific Tradition and Change*. Chicago: University of Chicago Press.
Kymlicka, Will. 1989. *Liberalism, Community, and Culture*. Oxford: Clarendon.
Lakatos, Imre. 1970. "Falsification and the Methodology of Scientific Research Programmes." In *Criticism and the Growth of Knowledge*, edited by Imre Lakatos and Alan Musgrave, 91–196. Cambridge: Cambridge University Press.
Laudan, Larry. 1977. *Progress and Its Problems*. Berkeley: University of California Press.
———. 1987. "Progress or Rationality? The Prospects for Normative Naturalism." *American Philosophical Quarterly* 24: 19–31.
———. 1990. "Normative Naturalism." *Philosophy of Science* 57: 44–59.
Lem, Stanislaw. 1961/1970. *Solaris*. London: Walker.
Liebhafsky, E. E. 1993. "The Influence of Charles Sanders Peirce on Institutional Economics." *Journal of Economic Issues* 27, No. 3: 741–754.
Lerner, Daniel. 1958/1964. *The Passing of Traditional Society: Modernizing the Middle East*. New York: Free Press.
Locke, Edwin A. and Jaana Woiceshyn. 1995. "Why businessmen should be honest: The argument from rational egoism." *Journal of Organizational Behavior*, Vol. 16: 405–414.
Luetge, Christoph. 2001. "Popper als Ethiker." *Allgemeine Zeitschrift für Philosophie* 26, H. 2: 149–162.
———. 2004a. "Ordnungsethik—naturalistisch konzipiert." In Luetge and Vollmer 2004, 117–127.
———. 2004b. "Economics in Philosophy of Science: Can the Dismal Science Contribute Anything Interesting?" *Synthese* 140 (3): 279–305.
———. 2005. "'Wirtschaftsethik.'" In *Historisches Wörterbuch der Philosophie*, Bd. 12, Sp. 853–855. Basel: Schwabe.
———. 2006. "An Economic Rationale for a Work and Savings Ethic? J. Buchanan's Late Works and Business Ethics." *Journal of Business Ethics* 66: 43–51.
———. 2007. "Social Glue under Conditions of Globalisation: Philosophers on Essential Normative Resources." In Homann, Koslowski, and Luetge 2007, 191–201.
———. 2008. "Public Reason and Order Ethics: A Critical Assessment." In *Public Reason and Applied Ethics: The Ways of Practical Reason in a Pluralist Society*, edited by Adela Cortina, Domingo García-Marzá, and Jesus Conill, 177–188. Aldershot and Burlington: Ashgate.

———. 2012. "Economic Ethics." In *Encyclopedia of Applied Ethics*. Oxford: Elsevier.
———. ed. 2013. *Handbook of the Philosophical Foundations of Business Ethics*. 3 vols. Heidelberg/New York: Springer.
Luetge, Christoph and Gerhard Vollmer, eds. 2004. *Fakten statt Normen? Zur Rolle einzelwissenschaftlicher Argumente in einer naturalistischen Ethik*. Baden-Baden: Nomos.
Luetge, Christoph, Hannes Rusch, and Matthias Uhl, eds. 2014. *Experimental Ethics*. Basingstoke: Palgrave Macmillan.
Luetge, Christoph and Johanna Jauernig, eds. 2014. *Business Ethics and Risk Management*. Heidelberg: Springer.
Luhmann, Niklas. 1985. *Kann die moderne Gesellschaft sich auf ökologische Gefährdungen einstellen? Rede zur 35. Jahresfeier der Rheinisch-Westfälischen Akademie der Wissenschaften am 15. Mai 1985*. Opladen: Westdeutscher Verlag.
———. 1986. *Ökologische Kommunikation: kann die moderne Gesellschaft sich auf ökologische Gefährdungen einstellen?* Opladen: Westdeutscher Verlag.
———. 1989. "Ethik als Reflexionstheorie der Moral." In *Gesellschaftsstruktur und Semantik*, Bd. 3, 358–447. Frankfurt/M.: Suhrkamp.
———. 1997. *Die Gesellschaft der Gesellschaft*. 2 Bde. Frankfurt/M.: Suhrkamp.
Lumsden, Charles J. and Edward O. Wilson. 1981. *Genes, Mind, and Culture: The Coevolutionary Process*. Cambridge, MA: Harvard University Press.
Lyons, David. 1965. *Forms and Limits of Utilitarianism*. Oxford: Clarendon.
Maass, Harald. 2001. "Ha Bei Ma Si: Jürgen Habermas in Peking." *Frankfurter Rundschau*, 18.04.2001.
MacIntyre, Alasdair. 1984. *After Virtue: A Study in Moral Theory*. Indiana: University of Notre Dame Press.
Mackie, John L. 1980. *Hume's Moral Theory*. London: Routledge and Kegan Paul.
Malachowski, Alan R. 2002. *Richard Rorty*. Princeton: Princeton University Press.
McCarthy, Thomas. 1996. "Kantianischer Konstruktivismus und Rekonstruktivismus: Rawls and Habermas im Dialog." *Deutsche Zeitschrift für Philosophie* 44: 931–950.
McClennen, Edward F. 2001. "The Strategy of Cooperation." In Morris and Ripstein 2001a, 189–208.
McDowell, John. 1994. *Mind and World*. Cambridge, MA: Harvard University Press.
Mead, George H. 1934. "Fragments on Ethics. Supplementary Essay IV." In *Mind, Self, and Society: From the Standpoint of a Social Behaviorist*, edited by Charles W. Morris. Chicago: University of Chicago Press.
Meier, Christian. 1998. *Athens: A Portrait of the City in Its Golden Age*. New York: Metropolitan.
Mill, John Stuart. 1863/1975. *Utilitarismus*. Stuttgart: Reclam.
Mills, Claudia. 2000. "'Not a Mere Modus Vivendi': The Bases for Allegiance to the Just State." In Davion and Wolf 2000, 190–203.
Morris, Christopher W. 1988. "The Relation between Self-Interest and Justice in Contractarian Ethics." In Paul 1988, 119–153.
Morris, Christopher W. and Arthur Ripstein, eds. 2001a. *Practical Rationality and Preference: Essays for David Gauthier*. Cambridge: Cambridge University Press.
———. 2001b. "Practical Reason and Preference." In Morris and Ripstein 2001a, 1–10.
Nagel, Thomas. 1979. *Mortal Questions*. Cambridge: Cambridge University Press.
Nash, John. 1950. "Equilibrium Points in N-Person Games." *Proceedings of the National Academy of Sciences* 36: 48–49.
———. 1951. "The Bargaining Problem." *Econometrica* 18: 155–162.
Nelson, Daniel M. 1992. *The Priority of Prudence: Virtue and Natural Law in Thomas Aquinas and the Implications for Modern Ethics*. University Park, Pa.: Pennsylvania State University Press.
Nida-Rümelin, Julian. 2002. *Ethische Essays*. Frankfurt/M.: Suhrkamp.
Nietzsche, Friedrich. 1980. *Sämtliche Werke: kritische Studienausgabe in 15 Bänden*, edited by Giorgio Colli and Mazzino Montinari. München: dtv.
Nozick, Robert. 1974. *Anarchy, State, and Utopia*. New York: Basic Books.

Nussbaum, Martha. 1988. "Non-Relative Virtues: An Aristotelian Approach." *Midwest Studies in Philosophy* 13.1: 32–53.
O'Donoghue, Ted and Matthew Rabin. 1999. "Addiction and Self-Control." In *Addiction: Entries and Exits*, edited by Jon Elster, 169–206. New York: Russell Sage Foundation.
Olson, Mancur. 1965. *The Logic of Collective Action*. Cambridge, MA: Harvard University Press.
———. 1982. *The Rise and Decline of Nations*. New Haven: Yale University Press.
Ostrom, Elinor. 1990. *Governing the Commons: The Evolution of Institutions for Collective Action*. Cambridge: Cambridge University Press.
Paul, Ellen Frankel, ed. 1988. "Gauthier's New Social Contract." *Social Philosophy and Policy* 5, No. 2, Social Philosophy and Policy Center.
Peirce, Charles S. 1877/1998. "The Fixation of Belief." In *Collected Papers of Charles Sanders Peirce, Bd. 5: Pragmatism and Pragmaticism*, edited by Charles Hartshorne and Paul Weiss, 223–247 (5.358–5.387). Bristol: Thoemmes.
———. 1878/1998. "How to Make Our Ideas Clear." In *Collected Papers of Charles Sanders Peirce, Bd. 5: Pragmatism and Pragmaticism*, edited by Charles Hartshorne and Paul Weiss, Bristol: Thoemmes, 248–271 (5.388–5.410).
———. 1879/1998. "Economy of Research: Original Paper." In *Collected Papers of Charles Sanders Peirce, Bd. 7: Science and Philosophy*, edited by Arthur W. Burks, 76–83 (7.139–7.157). Bristol: Thoemmes.
———. 1893/1998. "Evolutionary Love." In *Collected Papers of Charles Sanders Peirce, Bd. 6: Scientific Metaphysics*, edited by by Charles Hartshorne and Paul Weiss, 190–215 (6.287–6.317). Bristol: Thoemmes.
———. 1902/1998. "Economy of Research: Later Reflections." In *Collected Papers of Charles Sanders Peirce, Bd. 7: Science and Philosophy*, edited by Arthur W. Burks, 84–88 (7.158–7.161). Bristol: Thoemmes.
Philosophische Gesellschaft Bad Homburg and Wilfried Hinsch, eds. 1997. *Zur Idee des politischen Liberalismus: John Rawls in der Diskussion*. Frankfurt/M.: Suhrkamp.
Pogge, Thomas W. 1989. *Realizing Rawls*. Ithaca, NY: Cornell University Press.
———. 1994. "An Egalitarian Law of Peoples." *Philosophy and Public Affairs* 23, no. 3: 195–224.
Popper, Karl R. 1934/1994. *Logik der Forschung*. 10th edition. Tübingen: Mohr.
———. 1945/1950. *The Open Society and Its Enemies*. Princeton, NJ: Priceton University Press.
———. 1961/2013. "Facts, Standards, and Truth: A Further Criticism of Relativism." In *The Open Society and Its Enemies*, 485-510. Princeton, NJ: Priceton University Press.
———. 1963/1969. *Conjectures and Refutations: The Growth of Scientific Knowledge*. London: Routledge.
———. 1994/1999. *All Life Is Problem Solving*. London/New York: Routledge.
Posner, Richard A. 1973/2007. *Economic Analysis of Law*. New York: Aspen Publishers.
Poundstone, William. 1992. *Prisoner's Dilemma: John von Neumann, Game Theory, and the Puzzle of the Bomb*. New York: Doubleday.
Quine, Willard Van Orman. 1995. "Naturalism; Or, Living Within One's Means." *Dialectica* 49: 251–61.
Rachlin, Howard. 2000. *The Science of Self-Control*. Cambridge, MA: Harvard University Press.
Railton, Peter. 2000. "Normative Force and Normative Freedom: Hume and Kant, but Not Hume versus Kant." In Dancy 2000a, 1–33.
Rapoport, Anatol and Albert M Chammah. 1965. *Prisoner's Dilemma: A Study in Conflict and Cooperation*. Ann Arbor: University of Michigan Press.
Rawls, John. 1963. "The Sense of Justice." *Philosophical Review* 72, no. 3: 281–305.
———. 1971. *A Theory of Justice*. Cambridge, MA: Harvard University Press.
———. 1975. "The Independence of Moral Theory." *Proceedings and Addresses of the American Philosophical Association* 48 (November 1975): 5–22.
———. 1979. "Economic Systems." In *Ethical Theory and Business*, edited by Tom L. Beauchamp and Norman E. Bowie, 57–63. Englewood Cliffs, NJ: Prentice-Hall.

———. 1985. "Justice as Fairness: Political Not Metaphysical." *Philosophy and Public Affairs* 14: 223–251.

———. 1992. *Die Idee des politischen Liberalismus: Aufsätze 1978–1989*. Edited by Wilfried Hinsch. Frankfurt/M.: Suhrkamp.

———. 1993. *Political Liberalism*. New York: Columbia University Press.

———. 1993/1996. "Das Völkerrecht." In *Die Idee der Menschenrechte*, edited by Stephen Shute and Susan Hurley, 53–103. Frankfurt/M.: Fischer.

———. 1997. "Erwiderung auf Habermas." In Philosophische Gesellschaft Bad Homburg and Wilfried Hinsch 1997, 196–262.

———. 1999. *The Law of Peoples*. Cambridge, MA: Havard University Press.

Raz, Joseph. 1999. *Engaging Reason: On the Theory of Value and Action*. Oxford: Oxford University Press.

———. 2000. "Explaining Normativity: On Rationality and the Justification of Reason." In Dancy 2000a, 34–59.

Razin, Assaf and Efraim Sadka, eds. 2008. *The Economics of Globalization*. Cambridge: Cambridge University Press.

Reichenbach, Hans. 1938/1983. *Erfahrung und Prognose*. Braunschweig/Wiesbaden: Vieweg.

Rescher, Nicholas. 1976. "Peirce and the Economy of Research." *Philosophy of Science* 43: 71–98.

———. 1978. *Peirce's Philosophy of Science: Critical Studies in His Theory of Induction and Scientific Method*. Notre Dame: University of Notre Dame Press.

———. 2002. *Fairness*. New Brunswick: Transaction Publishers.

———. 2005–2006. *Collected Papers*. 14 Bd. Frankfurt/M.: Ontos Verlag.

Rodrik, Dani. 2011. *The Globalization Paradox: Democracy and the Future of the World Economy*. New York: Norton & Company.

Rogers, Graham A. J., ed. 1995. *Leviathan: Contemporary Responses to the Political Theory of Thomas Hobbes*. Bristol: Thoemmes.

Rorty, Richard. 1989. *Contingency, Irony, and Solidarity*. Cambridge: Cambridge University Press.

———. 1998. *Truth and Progress: Philosophical Papers III*. Cambridge: Cambridge University Press.

Rosenberg, Alexander. 1996. "A Field Guide to Recent Species of Naturalism." *British Journal for the Philosophy of Science* 47: 1–29.

Rothschild, EmMA 2001. *Economic Sentiments: Adam Smith, Condorcet, and the Enlightenment*. Cambridge, MA: Harvard Univ. Press.

Rousseau, Jean-Jacques. 1762/1964. *Emile ou de l'éducation*. Paris: Garnier.

———. 1762/1977. *The Social Contract*. London: Penguin Classics.

Rowlands, Mark. 2003. *The Philosopher at the End of the Universe*. London: Ebury Press.

Russell, Bertrand. 1946/2004. *A History of Western Philosophy*. New ed. London: Routledge.

Russett, Bruce M. and John R. Oneal. 2001. *Triangulating Peace: Democracy, Interdependence, and International Organizations*. New York: Norton.

Sabel, Charles F. and Joshua Cohen. 2001. "Directly Deliberative Polyarchy." http://www.law.columbia.edu/sabel/papers/DDP.html.

Sahlman, William A., et al. 1999. *The Entrepreneurial Venture*. Boston, MA: Harvard Business School Press.

Savage, Leonard J. 1954. *The Foundations of Statistics*. New York: Wiley.

Sayre-McCord, Geoffrey. 1991. "Deception and Reasons to Be Moral." In Vallentyne 1991a, 181–195.

Scarre, Geoffrey. 1996. *Utilitarianism*. London: Routledge.

Scheler, Max. 1916/1980. *Der Formalismus in der Ethik und die materiale Wertethik: neuer Versuch der Grundlegung eines ethischen Personalismus*. 6th ed. Bern: Francke.

———. 1928/1988. *Die Stellung des Menschen im Kosmos*. 11th ed. Bonn: Bouvier.

Schütz, Alfred. 1979/1984. *Strukturen der Lebenswelt*. 2 Bde. Edited by Thomas Luckmann. Frankfurt/M.: Suhrkamp.

Searle, John. 1964. "How to Derive 'Ought' from 'Is.'" *The Philosophical Review* 73, no. 1: 43–58.

Segerstrale, Ullica. 2000. *Defenders of the Truth: The Sociobiology Debate*. Oxford: Oxford University Press.
Selten, Reinhard. 1990. "Bounded Rationality." *Journal of Institutional and Theoretical Economics* 146: 649–658.
Sen, Amartya. 1970a. "The Impossibility of a Paretian Liberal." *Journal of Political Economy* 78: 152–157.
———. 1970b. *Collective Choice and Social Welfare*. San Francisco: Holden-Day.
———. 1974. "Choice, Orderings and Morality." In *Practical Reason*, edited by Stephan Körner, 54–67. Oxford: Blackwell.
———. 1977. "Rational Fools: A Critique of the Behavioral Foundations of Economic Theory." *Philosophy and Public Affairs* 6: 317–344.
———. 1987. *On Ethics and Economics*. Oxford: Blackwell.
———. 1999. *Development as Freedom*. New York: Anchor Books.
Sen, Amartya and Bernard Williams, eds. 1982. *Utilitarianism and Beyond*. Cambridge: Cambridge University Press.
Shimony, Abner. 1993. *The Search for a Naturalistic World View*. 2 vols. Cambridge: Cambridge University Press.
Simon, Herbert A. 1983. *Reason in Human Affairs*. Stanford University Press.
Singer, Peter. 1979/2011. *Practical Ethics*. 3. ed. Cambridge: Cambridge University Press.
———. 1981. *The Expanding Circle: Ethics and Sociobiology*. Oxford: Clarendon.
———. 1993. *How Are We to Live? Ethics in an Age of Self-Interest*. Melbourne: Text.
Smart, J. J. C. 1971. "Extreme and Restricted Utilitarianism." In *Studies in Utilitarianism*, edited by Thomas K. Hearn, 251–264. New York: Appleton-Century-Crofts.
———. 1961/1973. "An Outline of a System of Utilitarian Ethics." In Smart and Williams. 1973, 1–74.
Smart, J. J. C. and Bernard Williams. 1973. *Utilitarianism: For and Against*. Cambridge: Cambridge University Press.
Smith, Adam. 1776/1976. *The Wealth of Nations*. Chicago: University of Chicago Press.
Smith, Holly. 1991. "Deriving Morality from Rationality." In Vallentyne 1991a, 229–253.
Snare, Francis. 1991. *Morals, Motivation, and Convention: Hume's Influential Doctrines*. Cambridge: Cambridge University Press.
Sober, Elliott. 1991. *Core Questions in Philosophy: A Text with Readings*. New York: Macmillan.
Sorensen, Roy A. 1992. *Thought Experiments*. New York: Oxford University Press.
Spinoza, Baruch de. 1670–1677/1951. *A Theologico-Political Treatise. A Political Treatise*. New York: Dover.
Sternberger, Dolf. 1979. "Verfassungspatriotismus." *Frankfurter Allgemeine Zeitung*, 23.05.1979.
———. 1982/1990. "Verfassungspatriotismus: Rede bei der 25-Jahr-Feier der 'Akademie für Politische Bildung'." Reprinted in Sternberger 1990, 17–31.
———. 1990. "Verfassungspatriotismus." In *Schriften*, Bd. X. Frankfurt/M.: Insel.
Stevenson, Charles Leslie. 1944/1976. *Ethics and Language*. New Haven: Yale University Press.
Stigler, George J. 1981. "Economics or Ethics?" In *The Tanner Lectures on Human Values*, edited by Sterling McMurrin, vol. 2, 144–191. Salt Lake City: University of Utah Press.
———. 1991. "The Direction of Economic Research." In *Economics, Culture and Education: Essays in Honour of Mark Blaug*, edited by G. K. Shaw, 37–52. Aldershot: Elgar.
Stigler, George J. and Gary S. Becker. 1977. "De Gustibus Non Est Disputandum." *American Economic Review* 67: 76–90.
Stiglitz, Joseph E. 2002. *Globalization and Its Discontents*. New York: Norton.
Stirner, Max. 1845/1972. *Der Einzige und sein Eigentum. Mit einem Nachwort*, edited by Ahlrich Meyer. Stuttgart: Reclam.
Suchanek, Andreas. 1994. *Ökonomischer Ansatz und theoretische Integration*. Tübingen: Mohr.
———. 2001. *Ökonomische Ethik*. Tübingen: Mohr Siebeck (UTB).

Sugden, Robert. 2001. "Ken Binmore's Evolutionary Social Theory." *The Economic Journal* 111: F213–F243.
Sunstein, Cass. 2001. *Republic.com*. Princeton: Princeton University Press.
Swanton, Christine. 2003. *Virtue Ethics: A Pluralistic View*. Oxford: Oxford University Press.
Urbach, Peter. 1978. "The Objective Promise of a Research Programme." In *Progress and Rationality in Science*, edited by Gerard Radnitzky and Gunnar Andersson, 99–113. Dordrecht: Reidel.
Vallentyne, Peter. 1991a. *Contractarianism and Rational Choice*. Cambridge: Cambridge University Press.
———. 1991b. "Gauthier's Three Projects" In Vallentyne 1991a, 1–11.
Vollmer, Gerhard. 1993. "Gelöste, ungelöste und unlösbare Probleme: zu den Bedingungen wissenschaftlichen Fortschritts." In *Wissenschaftstheorie im Einsatz: Beiträge zu einer selbstkritischen Wissenschaftsphilosophie*, 183–210. Stuttgart: Hirzel.
———. 1995. "Was ist Naturalismus?" In *Auf der Suche nach der Ordnung: Beiträge zu einem naturalistischen Welt- und Menschenbild*, 21–42. Stuttgart: Hirzel.
Weber, Max. 1922/1988. *Gesammelte Aufsätze zur Wissenschaftslehre*. Edited by Johannes Winckelmann, 7th ed. Tübingen: Mohr.
Weingartner, Paul, Gerhard Schurz, and Georg Dorn, eds. 1998. *The Role of Pragmatics in Contemporary Philosophy: Proceedings of the 20th International Wittgenstein Symposium, 10–16 August 1997*. Wien: Hölder-Pichler-Tempsky.
Weizsäcker, Carl Christian von. 1999. *Logik der Globalisierung*. Göttingen: Vandenhoeck und Ruprecht.
Wellmer, Albrecht. 1986. *Ethik und Dialog: Elemente des moralischen Urteils bei Kant und in der Diskursethik*. Frankfurt/M.: Suhrkamp.
Wible, James R. 1994a. "Rescher's Economic Philosophy of Science." *Journal of Economic Methodology* 1: 314–323.
———. 1994b. "Charles Sanders Peirce's Economy of Research." *Journal of Economic Methodology* 1: 135–160.
———. 1997. *The Economics of Science: Methodology and Epistemology as If Economics Really Mattered*. London: Routledge.
Williams, Bernard. 1973. "A Critique of Utilitarianism." In Smart and Williams 1973, 77–150.
Wittgenstein, Ludwig. 1953/1984. "Philosophische Untersuchungen." In *Schriften*, Bd. 1. Frankfurt/M.: Suhrkamp.
———. 1965/1989. "Vortrag über Ethik." In *Vortrag über Ethik und andere kleine Schriften*, edited by Joachim Schulte, 9–19. Frankfurt/M.: Suhrkamp.
Wolff, Robert P. 1977. *Understanding Rawls: A Reconstruction and Critique of A Theory of Justice*. Princeton: Princeton University Press.
Wright, Georg Henrik von. 1963. *The Varieties of Goodness*. London: Routledge & Paul.
Zedillo, Ernesto, ed. 2008. *The Future of Globalization: Explorations in Light of Recent Turbulence*. London: Routledge.

Index

absolute concept, 78, 218
Ackerman, Bruce, 33–36
action and rule, distinction between, 29–33
act utilitarianism. *See* utilitarianism
Adorno, Theodor W., 220
aesthetics, 23, 63, 128, 131, 132
agreement, 26, 40, 43, 53, 54, 61, 85, 86, 108, 119, 144, 152, 155, 159, 181–182, 191, 193, 217
altruism, 29–33, 37, 172
Altruism Game, 51
anarchy, 28, 34, 111, 115, 124, 186
analytic (language) philosophy, 102, 126, 127, 129
Anglo-Saxon moral philosophy, 77–78
antagonism, 58, 89, 103, 107, 148
anthropology, 3, 7, 18, 22, 70, 71, 75, 132, 211, 213, 214–215
anti-trust division, 124
Apel, Karl-Otto, 85, 90, 92
appeal, 26, 29–33, 38–41, 55, 70, 76, 83, 132, 167, 174, 179
Aquinas, Thomas, 77, 78, 81
arbitrariness, 44, 79, 86
Arendt, Hannah, 220
Aristotle, 47, 63, 70, 76, 77, 80, 81, 83, 134n24, 147
Armstrong, David M., 23
Arrow, Kenneth, 79
Asimov, Isaac, 201
Assurance Game, 53

auxiliary control, 220–222

balance of power, 11, 86
bargaining, 55, 154, 169, 187, 196, 197; initial position for, 114
base point, 122
Battle of the Sexes, 50, 184
Bayes' theorem/rationality, 188, 189–190, 191
behavioral ethics, 43
behavioral limitations, 117, 169, 172, 197, 199
Berlin, Isaiah, 127, 149
Bernini, 44
binding unilateral pledge, 183, 191
biology, 23, 44, 70, 72
Binmore, Ken, 28, 36, 41, 44, 48, 54, 59, 63, 77, 121, 181–198, 202
Blumer, Herbert, 85
Bounded rationality, 36, 216
Brandom, Robert, 45, 46, 56, 57–58, 66n50
Brennan, Geoffrey, 29–33, 37, 41, 165–167, 168, 173, 179
Broome, John, 56
Buchanan, James M., ix, 3, 20n38, 29–33, 36, 37, 41, 48, 63, 79, 113, 165–181, 191, 210, 211, 213, 219, 220
business ethics, 47, 54, 172

capabilities, 1, 18, 29. *See also* qualities
capitalism, 104, 189

cardinal virtues, 4, 29–33, 80, 83
Carson, Rachel, 133
categorical imperative, 74, 85, 136n43, 183
China, 107
Chu, C. Y. Cyrus, 36
citizenship, 1, 4, 6–7, 7, 10, 17, 18, 59, 63, 94, 99–100, 105, 147, 149–150, 152, 158, 159, 161
civil war, 73
coercion, 6, 13, 14, 53, 63, 72, 95, 106, 107, 111, 112, 118, 123
cognitivism, 90, 92, 96, 166
Cohen, Joshua, 106
collective phenomena, 79, 152, 166, 176, 202, 216
commitment, 7, 10–11, 45, 54, 62, 118, 147, 155, 165, 166, 167, 183, 184, 189, 191–194, 214, 217
communication: ability for, x, 215, 216; of benefits, 55, 56, 58, 62, 107, 161, 202; of values and preferences, 74, 127, 131; without domination, 107
communicative community, 102–103, 108, 137n60
communicative action, 89, 91, 94, 97, 101, 218
communicative rationality, 89, 91, 106
communitarianism, 134n24–135n25
community spirit, 4, 76
compensation, 40, 43, 50, 117, 171
competition, 7, 29–33, 73, 103, 104, 124, 189, 195, 214, 217
compliance, 4, 21, 27, 57, 61, 83, 84, 92, 93, 94, 98, 115–117, 119, 122, 147, 148, 150, 153, 158, 161, 167, 169, 177, 180, 222
confederation, 12, 17
conflict of interest, 26, 74, 83, 92, 109–110, 111, 157, 161
consciousness (conscience), 24, 39, 44, 45, 47, 83, 85, 96, 188
consensus. *See* consent
consent, 3, 6, 27, 35, 39, 41, 46, 62, 63, 78–79, 85–86, 88, 100, 101, 102–103, 104, 105, 113, 116, 128, 130, 144, 148, 149, 152, 153–161, 182–183, 193, 214–215, 218, 222; actual freedom of, 3
consequentialism, 29–33, 56, 121

constitutional consensus, 128, 155–160, 161
constitutional economics, 123, 165–166
constitutional patriotism, 76, 99–100, 211, 222
constraints, 8, 9, 23, 36, 37, 41, 115, 117, 119, 122, 146, 170, 173, 175, 177, 179, 194, 196, 197
constructivism, 43, 44, 64n4, 204n22
consumption, 75
contingency, 37, 126–130, 133, 187
contractarianism, 29–33, 41, 78, 117, 119, 172, 180. *See also* social contract theory
convention, 36, 96, 182, 190, 196
convergence point, 155
coordination, 41, 52, 53, 85, 86, 94, 105, 111–112, 182, 184, 189, 195–196, 198, 200
Coordination Game, 52, 192
Corporate Citizenship., 41
Corporate Social Responsibility (CSR). *See* Corporate Citizenship
corporation, 41, 43
corporatism, 13
corruption, 29–33
cost-benefit calculation, 46, 96, 98, 166, 175, 177–178, 180, 183, 196, 219, 220
courage. *See* cardinal virtues
covenant, 151
crowding out, 29–33
cultural background, 36, 88, 91, 100, 101, 200
cultural relativism, 91

Dahl, Robert A., 108
Dancy, Jonathan, 21
Darwinism, 197
Dawkins, Richard, 197
decision making, 13, 71–72, 109, 179, 183, 185, 188, 190, 196
deconstruction, 127
defection, 34, 49, 79, 80, 92, 117, 119–120, 122, 150, 161, 169, 174, 184, 199
deliberative democracy, 63, 101, 106, 137n58, 139n92, 139n95
democracy, 1, 3, 5, 7, 9, 41, 63, 73, 105, 108, 126, 129, 131, 149, 154, 158; economic theory of, 104

Demsetz, Harold, 40
Denzau, Arthur T., 36
deontology, 29–33
development policy, 7, 41
developmental psychology. *See* Kohlberg, Lawrence
dialogue, 85, 215
dichotomy. *See* antagonism
Dickens, Charles, 130
difference principle, 4, 16, 17
dignity, 73, 74, 85, 157
dilemma structure, 34, 39, 48, 52, 54, 95, 98, 109, 115, 119–120, 124, 125, 130, 220. *See also* prisoner's dilemma
discourse ethics, 84–108
discourse principle D, 86, 87
discursive rationality, 105
distributive justice, 14, 15–16
division of labor, 47
duty, 12, 13, 27, 78, 92, 109, 116, 119, 123, 155

ecology, 7, 133, 180–181, 203n13
economics, 8, 16, 24, 29, 38, 41, 44, 47, 55, 61, 70, 73, 74, 75, 79, 97, 99, 111–112, 123–124, 165–166, 167–169, 170, 172, 175, 177–179; neoclassical theory of, 111, 188
economic ethics, 29, 55, 58
economic rationality, 36, 37, 107, 109, 216
education, 38, 63, 121, 123, 127, 219
egalitarianism, 15, 191
Elster, Jon, 175, 176
empathy, 88, 182, 201–202, 215, 217, 219, 222
empathetic preferences, 29, 186, 187, 194–200, 211–212, 215
empirical conditions, 75, 76, 125, 181
empirical science, 23, 25, 43, 97
enforcement, 9, 13, 19n1, 35, 42, 46, 53, 55, 72, 94, 95, 98–99, 116, 120–122, 124, 125, 160, 171, 183–185, 189, 192, 193
Enlightenment, 25, 28, 126, 133, 167, 179
entrepreneurship, 40, 138n78
epistemology, 23, 38, 44, 45, 91, 98, 125, 131, 175
equilibrium, 53, 73, 183–185, 187, 193, 195, 197, 199

ethics of the honest businessman, 172
evolution, 3, 23, 41, 45, 74, 101, 106, 117, 129, 169, 178, 186–188, 189, 190, 194, 195, 197, 218
exploitation, 25, 29–33, 54, 80, 114, 117, 161, 169, 174, 179, 199, 211, 217, 219, 222
extended sympathy preferences, 194, 216
external sanctions, 56, 57, 96. *See also* normative sanctions
externalities, 173, 179

face-to-face society, 29–33, 39, 48, 81, 187, 214
fairness, 3, 12, 16, 43, 115, 146, 148, 152–153, 183, 184–185, 187, 196
family, 80, 145, 225
final justification. *See* Apel, Karl-Otto
final opinion. *See* Peirce, Charles S.
Foot, Philippa, 77–83, 210–211, 213, 218, 220, 222
Förster, Eckart, 27
free riding, 6, 26, 80, 81. *See also* defection
freedom, 12, 14, 28, 72, 73, 80, 115, 123–124, 145, 150, 154, 155, 157, 193. *See also* Liberty
Freud, Sigmund, 127, 130
Friedman, Milton, 41
functional justification, 26, 72, 73, 107, 108–111, 147

Gadenne, Volker, 47
Game of Chicken, 49
Game of Life, 183–185, 195
Game of Morals, 183–185, 186, 196, 197–198
game theory, 28, 48, 56, 81, 112, 181, 183, 188, 189. *See also* Altruism Game; Coordination Game; Game of Chicken; prisoner's dilemma; Stag-Hunt Game
Gauthier, David, 81, 108–125, 181, 183, 194, 198, 210–211, 211, 213, 218, 220, 222
Geach, Peter, 77
German idealism, 28
Germany, 67n59, 68n80, 99, 125
Giunti, Marco, 38
globalization, ix, x, 2, 2–3, 9, 14, 17, 17–18, 21, 22, 35, 43, 76, 120, 124,

131, 143, 180, 201, 203, 214, 215, 219, 225
global social contract, 5–6
golden mean, 76
golden rule, 194
good reasons, 13, 56, 57, 82, 92, 215
governance, 1, 5, 28, 59–60, 72
greed, 104, 206n71
growth, 16, 73, 74, 106

Habermas, Jürgen, 55, 58, 62, 76, 82, 84–108, 111, 118, 121, 198, 210–211, 211, 213, 218, 220, 222
happiness, 63, 73, 78, 80, 183, 194
Hare, Richard, 80
Harsanyi, John C., 182
Hart, H. L. A., 19n2, 223n14
Hartmann, Nicolai, 69
Haskell, Thomas, 103, 104
Hattiangadi, Jagdish N., 38
Hayek, Friedrich August von, 29–33, 38, 67n58, 138n88
heuristic, 23, 29, 46–47, 58–59, 61, 62, 76, 77, 81–83, 98, 105–108, 115, 133, 152, 153, 158, 159, 160, 200–201, 213, 220, 222
Hegel, Georg Wilhelm Friedrich, 72, 136n52, 163n25
Hirschman, Albert, 64n3, 76, 138n78, 175
Historikerstreit, 100
Hitler, Adolf, 70
Hobbes, Thomas, 24, 25, 27, 28, 48, 63, 64n10–64n11, 67n54, 70, 71, 113, 114–115, 116, 117, 120, 122–123, 127, 140n110, 151, 188, 207n82
Höffe, Otfried, ix, 2–8, 8, 9, 12, 16, 18, 22
Homann, Karl, 24, 29, 38, 48, 59, 76, 78, 81, 128, 166, 169, 170, 199
Horkheimer, Max, 220
Hösle, Vittorio, 69–76, 80, 210–211, 211, 213, 218, 220, 222
homo economicus, 38, 43, 44, 46, 67n54, 112, 117, 150, 175, 176–177, 188–189, 195
homo sapiens, 44, 67n70, 176, 188–189
homo sociologicus, 176
Hume, David, 25–27, 63, 66n48–66n50, 81, 91, 181, 182, 193, 194, 195, 204n35, 206n65

human rights. *See* rights
human nature, 25, 27, 67n54, 70–71, 72, 77, 80–81, 135n34, 136n44, 220
hypothetical imperative, 82–85, 179, 183, 185. *See also* Kant, Immanuel

ideal speech situation, 86
ideal communication community. *See* communication community
ideal role taking, 88, 95–99, 211, 222
idealization, 94, 102, 111, 121, 123–124
immigration, 225
impartiality, 5, 86, 87, 140n103
implementation: of ecological standards, 133, 181; of norms, 18, 29, 29–33, 34, 48, 54, 55, 64n1, 76, 79, 81, 83, 93, 94, 96, 98, 101–102, 120, 173, 179, 191, 211–212; of laws, 7, 34, 66n52, 115–119, 216; of moral demands, 39, 62, 72, 74, 81, 82, 84, 107, 110; problem, 20n29, 34, 64n1, 73, 82, 83, 101, 115–119, 120, 121, 129, 139n95, 193, 222
incentives, 16, 22–23, 25, 28, 29, 29–33, 39, 41, 43, 57, 60, 98, 125, 148, 165–202, 211, 219; compatibility with, 29–33, 55, 57, 60, 61, 76, 98, 98–99, 106, 107, 151, 174, 181, 193; economic, 56, 94, 96, 177; infringement of, 39, 60, 61, 92, 124, 218, 218–219; neutralization of, 82, 91, 95, 97, 102; repudiation of, 81, 89, 91, 175, 194, 211; structure of, 39, 56, 152, 153, 160, 180, 181, 217, 222
incomplete contract. *See* open contract
individual-oriented approach, 24, 59–63, 83, 131, 166, 211
individual ethics, 38–39, 46, 59, 60, 66n41, 67n56, 131
inequality, 9, 12, 16, 145
in foro interno/externo, 115
informal institution, 29, 42, 43, 81, 91, 213
institution, 6, 8, 10, 17, 28, 29, 29–33, 36, 37, 39, 41, 43, 55, 61, 72, 73, 94–95, 113, 124, 143, 145, 176, 213
institutionalization of discourse, 93, 94, 124, 137n64
interaction, 29–33, 39, 41–42, 83, 85, 88, 109, 183, 214

interdisciplinarity, 81, 97, 102
internalized disposition, 95, 113, 116, 118–120, 194
International Monetary Fund (IMF), 14
internet, 105, 107–108, 139n95, 201, 225
intrinsic motivation, 70, 96, 118. *See also* rational motivation
intuition, 60, 72, 81, 85, 86, 97–99, 106, 107, 110, 209–210, 213, 220–222
investment, x, 29–33, 40, 57, 150, 151–152, 161, 171, 211, 212, 215–216, 217, 219–222
invisible hand, 104, 138n88
irony, 130, 131

Jonas, Hans, 69
juridification, 29
justice: as virtue. *See* cardinal virtues: as fairness (JF), 143–144, 144–145, 146–147, 150, 153, 154, 155, 157, 158, 159; conception of, 10, 11, 13, 131, 144–145, 147–148, 150, 154, 156, 191; principles of, 3, 3–4, 11–12, 112–113, 150, 155–156, 191; sense of, 4, 6, 10, 17, 18, 58, 147–148, 161, 211, 218, 222
justification, 29–33, 33, 34, 41, 55, 55–29, 56, 62, 82, 83, 88, 108, 129, 131, 132, 159, 160. *See also* functional justification
just-war theory, 14–15, 69

Kant, Immanuel, 3, 5, 9, 27–28, 63, 69, 71, 81, 82, 85, 92, 134n13, 136n47–136n48, 192, 194, 207n76
Kazanistan, 13–14
Kersting, Wolfgang, 182
Keynes, John Maynard, 168
King, Martin Luther, 129
Kitcher, Philip, 43–44
Kohlberg, Lawrence, 93, 96–97, 102, 137n70

language game, 78
laissez-faire, 123
Lakatos, Imre, 138n73, 204n22
Laudan, Larry, 38
law: economic reconstruction of, 95; formal, 42. *See also* informal institution; international, 5, 7; natural, 72–73, 114, 115, 122, 134n13; of peoples, 8–14, 16, 17; rational, 72, 137n63
legal theory, 3, 93–94, 94, 95, 107
legality, 4, 94
legitimacy, 3, 71, 94, 96, 126
Lem, Stanislaw, 202
Leviathan, 6, 24, 64n11
liberalism, 8–9, 10, 12–14, 15, 76, 120, 127, 129, 130; Whig, 181, 185, 198; political, 16, 143, 155
liberty, 3, 13, 28, 145
lifeworld, 85, 87, 105
Lincoln, Abraham, 129
linguistics, 46, 56, 78, 94
Liu, Wen-Fang, 36
Locke, Edwin A., 172
Locke, John, 28, 66n50, 114, 140n109, 194
Lockean proviso, 114, 115, 122
long term, 12, 14, 18, 29–33, 36, 40, 41, 43, 56, 57, 67n54, 79, 80, 106, 119, 152, 156, 158, 160, 196–197, 222
Luetge, Christoph, 24, 29, 44, 45, 48, 59, 106, 164n35, 166, 204n38
Luhmann, Niklas, 64n2, 132, 133n3, 176, 180–181, 220, 222
Lumsden, Charles J., 187
Lyons, David, 78

Maass, Harald, 107
Machiavelli, 70
MacIntyre, Alasdair, 134n24
Mackie, John L., 181
Mafia, 131
Malachowski, Alan R., 126
Mandeville, Bernard, 104
market failure, 7, 111, 112
market forces, 3, 29–33, 73, 101, 123, 189
market mechanism, 103, 104, 139n89, 139n92
market society, 101, 103, 110, 160
material value ethics. *See* value ethics
mathematics, 25
maximin principle, 36, 65n33, 189–190, 191, 205n55
McDowell, John, 56, 135n34
Mead, George H., 85, 88
mechanism design, 181
medium term, 196, 197

mental models, 36
metaphysics, 16, 23, 25, 28, 55, 104, 127, 131, 144, 182, 183, 186, 191
Michelangelo, 44
minimax relative concession (MRC), 113, 115, 118
modern society, 1, 21, 22, 29–33, 34, 47, 48, 53, 58, 59, 62, 64n2, 74, 77, 80, 95, 101, 106, 131–132, 144, 176, 178, 187, 199, 206n71, 214, 216
modern conditions, 22, 75, 83, 98, 99, 110, 193
modus vivendi, 11, 148, 153–159, 193, 218
morality, 25, 27, 29, 47, 58, 60, 70, 82, 96, 109–111, 124, 167, 196, 219; erosion of, 60, 112, 180
moral: appeal. *See* appeal: code, 22, 36, 133n3; mesocosmos, 98, 110, 186; judgment, 81–82, 222; motivation; motivation; opprobrium, 166–167, 203n3; point of view, 8, 96; relativism, 78, 91, 173; resources, 59–60, 61; surplus (values), ix, x, 22, 40, 58–59, 60, 62, 69, 158, 198, 210–212, 213, 214, 216–217, 219, 220, 222
motivation, 6, 27, 29–33, 36, 38, 46, 56, 58, 81–82, 88–90, 94–95
motivation switch, 29–33, 101, 139n94
mutual advantage, 26, 29–33, 41, 62, 140n103, 171, 193, 197
mutual agreement. *See* consensus

Nabokov, Vladimir, 130
Nash (bargaining) equilibrium, 183–184, 187, 197
naturalism, 23, 24, 44–46, 46, 182, 183, 185, 205n54, 206n61, 223n15
natural sciences, 23, 46, 47, 75, 189
naturalistic fallacy, 24, 64n8, 185, 206n66
Neo-Aristotelianism. *See* Aristotle
neo-institutionalism, 5
neuroscience, 45–46, 223n15
Nida-Rümelin, Julian, 56–57, 67n75
Nietzsche, Friedrich, 126, 135n25, 204n34
nirvana fallacy, 40, 121, 122
non-cognitivism. *See* cognitivism
norm sensitivity, 57
normativity, 23, 24, 27, 45, 58, 64n1, 71, 84–85, 88, 137n60, 213–72, 216

North, Douglass C., 36
Nozick, Robert, 114, 183
null hypothesis, 21, 24, 36, 60, 217
Nussbaum, Martha, 77

O'Donoghue, Ted, 169
objective value, 69, 70, 72, 75, 77, 80, 211, 213, 218, 222
open contracts, 29, 39, 41, 41–43, 59, 60, 66n45, 219
opportunism, 43, 175, 217, 219
opportunity cost, 58, 129
optimal state, 78, 79
order ethics (OE), ix, 22–48, 55–63, 211, 212–213, 214–216
original consent, 113
original contract, 26, 114, 122
original position, 8, 11, 33, 35, 36, 41, 43, 114, 145–146, 152, 185–187, 190, 193–194, 196, 200, 210
original state, 11, 14
Orwell, George, 130
Ostrom, Elinor, 136n46, 180
Other-Regarding Game. *See* Altruism Game
outlaw state, 9, 12, 14–15, 20n21
overlapping consensus, 100, 144, 148, 154, 155, 156–160, 161

parametric rationality, 109, 112
Pareto improvement. *See* Pareto superiority
Pareto inferiority, 53
Pareto superiority, 40, 40–41, 43, 50, 53, 54, 66n44
passions, 25, 26, 27, 188
paternalism, 15
Peirce, Charles S., 102, 103–105, 137n60, 139n89
performative contradiction, 85, 86, 87, 90, 95, 101–105, 218
phenomenalism, 28, 60–61, 61, 81, 91, 124, 177, 180, 189
philosophy, 2, 8, 23–24, 45, 60, 63, 73; of language, 55, 77, 78, 85, 86, 90, 102, 105, 127; of mind, 23, 44, 45; of science, 23, 37, 44, 45, 98, 125. *See also* social philosophy
physics, 23, 46

pluralism, 1, 10, 16, 17, 18, 21, 35, 39, 76, 131, 133, 144, 217, 219
politics, 2, 7, 70, 173, 176
Pogge, Thomas, 15, 163n24, 164n32
Popper, Karl, 1, 37–39, 81
positive sum games, 29–33
positivism, 44
Posner, Richard A., 95
poststructuralism, 126
practical philosophy, 25, 45, 63, 125, 223n15
pragmatism, 59, 61, 76, 82, 83, 102, 126
pragmatic presupposition, 86
preferences, 38, 39, 86, 98, 175, 177, 188, 194–198, 211, 218. *See also* empathetic preferences
pre-modern society, 1, 48, 74, 76, 81, 83, 106. *See also* face-to-face society
preventive counterdefection, 79, 92, 117, 120, 161, 169, 174, 199
price mechanism, 104, 123, 139n89
prima philosophia, 23
principle of contingency, 37, 65n34, 127, 130, 133
prisoner's dilemma, 25, 26, 29–33, 39, 48–49, 50, 52, 53, 57, 73, 78, 80, 83, 91, 92, 93, 109, 110, 111–112, 112, 116, 120, 122, 123, 136n38, 139n98, 140n103, 148, 160, 161, 169, 171, 174, 179, 184, 192–193, 199, 218
problem solving, 37–38, 41, 47, 76, 81, 101, 109, 126, 171, 174
productive cooperation, 34, 117, 151, 222
progress, 15, 37, 46, 71, 73, 104
protectionism, 14, 74
psychic cost, 57
psychology, 44, 60, 80, 85, 93, 96, 97–98, 98–99, 102, 127, 149, 151, 176
public good, 79
public spirit, 4, 7
punishment, 26, 57–58, 117, 150, 166–167, 175, 177
Puritanism, 171, 172, 178, 180

Quine, William Orman van, 23

Rabin, Matthew, 169
Rachlin, Howard, 169

rationality, 16, 36–37; trap, 54. *See also* communicative rationality; discursive rationality; economic rationality; parametric rationality; strategic rationality
rational autonomy, 146
rational choice, 110, 111, 113
rational motivation, 55, 58, 82, 88–95, 96–97, 100, 102, 103, 104, 105, 107, 199, 211, 218, 222
Rawls, John, ix, 1, 2, 8–18, 35, 36, 37, 41, 58, 62, 100, 110, 113, 114, 126, 128, 143–164n35, 185–186, 189–191, 193, 210–211, 211, 213, 218
realism, 43–44, 64n4, 81, 177, 184, 204n22, 220, 222
redistribution, 29–33
reductionism, 56, 127, 170
regulation, 28, 29, 99, 107, 123, 217, 222
relevant alternative, 40, 122
religion, 13, 73–74, 167, 225
republicanism, 101
reputation, 104, 172, 178, 192
Rescher, Nicholas, 103, 104, 139n89
resource allocation, 34
revolution, 41
rights: global, 6, 7; human, 7, 12, 13, 15, 34, 78, 107; natural, 73; property, 13, 123, 145, 164n35; to war. *See* just-war theory
rivalry, 103, 156. *See also* competition
Rorty, Richard, 10, 63, 125–133, 211, 213, 222
Rosenberg, Alexander, 23
Rousseau, Jean-Jacques, 65n17, 162n10
Rucellai, Giovanni, 29–33
rule, 29–33, 39, 40, 41, 46, 58, 59, 60; adherence, 24, 61–62, 63, 88, 118, 147, 150–151, 155, 158, 161, 165, 166, 179, 180, 189, 190; breaking, 26, 29–33, 114, 151, 153, 177; reform, 63, 147, 150, 153, 155; implementation, 34, 211–212; utilitarianism. *See* utilitarianism
Russell, Bertrand, 91, 137n62

Sabel, Charles F., 106, 139n92
sacrifice, 29–33, 136n42, 216, 217
Sahlman, William A., 172

Savage, Leonard J., 188
sanction, 25, 39, 56, 57, 61, 89, 94, 95, 96, 116, 118–119, 120, 121, 122, 125, 150–151, 177, 183, 185, 191–192, 193, 199; informal, 48, 81, 125; normative, 56, 57, 167; recognition due to, 96–97. *See also* informal institution
Scheler, Max, 69, 70
Schiller, Friedrich, 92
science fiction, 33, 35, 65n32, 142n149, 200, 201
scientific method, 23, 38, 97
self-control, 169, 172, 193
self-interest, ix, 21, 24, 25, 26, 27, 29–33, 34, 35, 37, 43, 55, 61, 63, 71, 75, 76, 103, 104, 106–107, 111, 112–113, 132, 159, 166, 172, 176, 189, 217, 222
self-positing, 27–28, 127
selfishness, 26, 66n48
semantics of benefits, 55, 56, 58, 216, 222
Sen, Amartya, 51, 53, 67n54, 79, 134n17, 175
separation: of powers, 4; of church and state, 13
Shakespeare, 43
shared goal, 13, 147
shared norm, 80, 83, 85
shared value, 69, 127, 132, 154, 211, 218, 220, 222
short term, 29–33, 40, 41, 79, 80, 118, 152, 156, 172, 196, 197, 199
Shimony, Abner, 23, 182
signaling, 43, 55, 217
Simon, Herbert A., 36, 176
simplicity, 37, 43, 57
Singer, Peter, 141n141, 187, 205n51
skepticism, 90–114, 92, 101, 102, 167, 181
Smith, Adam, 26, 29–33, 55, 62, 63, 64n15, 70, 104, 123, 138n88, 168, 195, 213, 222n5–222n6
sociality, x, 215
social capital, 57, 58, 67n76–68n77
social contract(theory), 3, 5–6, 10, 11, 22, 26, 27, 33, 35, 36, 37, 41, 72, 78, 96, 113–114, 115, 117, 119, 122, 181, 181–185, 186, 191, 196–197, 198. *See also* global social contract
social integration, 94, 100, 101, 130, 151

social order, 36, 38, 39, 46, 95, 106, 145, 180, 186, 211
social philosophy, 25, 29, 59, 125, 126, 130, 182, 183
social psychology, 2, 85, 176
social sciences, 23, 24, 29, 38, 39, 46, 60, 61, 63, 70, 71, 75, 81, 82, 106, 133n1
social stability, ix, x, 1, 11, 16, 18, 21, 22, 24, 25, 28, 38, 40, 59, 63, 88, 95, 106, 115, 118–119, 124, 131, 132, 146–147, 151, 152, 154, 158, 161, 166, 183, 187, 189, 193, 211, 215, 216, 217, 219–220, 225
social structure. *See* social order
social trap, 91
society: liberal, 8–9, 10, 12–14, 15, 76, 121, 127; modern, x, 1, 4, 22, 29–33, 34, 35, 38, 40, 41, 47–48, 51, 53, 58, 59, 62, 64n2, 74, 76–77, 81, 84, 88, 98, 101, 106–107, 110, 118, 128, 130, 144, 160, 187, 214, 216; pluralistic. *See* pluralism; normative foundations of, 1, 2, 143, 219
sociobiology, 22, 181, 187
sociology, 2, 44, 106, 176
solidarity, 29–33, 94, 110, 130, 131, 131–132, 211, 218, 222
South Africa, 41
speech-act theory, 89–90, 91
Spinoza, Benedict de, 27, 63
Stag-Hunt Game, 54
Sternberger, Dolf, 99
Stirner, Max, 28
strategic rationality, 89, 91, 101, 105, 109, 111, 112, 137n66, 211, 218
Strawson, Peter, 85, 90
Suchanek, Andreas, 38, 161
sufficiency, 74
Swanton, Christine, 77
symbolic interactionism, 85
sympathy, 25, 26, 129, 132, 194–195, 206n71, 211, 216, 218, 222, 222n5
systemic rationality, 101, 105

tabula rasa, 38
temperance. *See* cardinal virtues
thought experiment, 24, 33–37, 38, 39
tit-for-that strategy, 117
tolerance, 4, 11, 12, 20n29, 128, 152, 172

Toulmin, Stephen, 85
transcendental idealism, 16, 45, 85, 136n48
trust, 43, 67n67, 73, 150, 161, 214
truth (claims), 90, 102, 126, 127, 141n146, 172, 178
two-tier set of rules and actions, 59, 64n1, 113

ultimate criterion, 80, 214
United Nations (UN), 6, 12
uncertainty, 41, 43, 75, 205n55
universal values, 69, 71–72
universalization principle U, 87–88, 90, 137n63
unlimited community. *See* Peirce, Charles S.
utility, 71; function, 190, 195; maximization, 79, 113, 189–190, 205n55, 216; constrained maximization of (CM), 116–117, 119–120, 194; straightforward maximization of (SM), 114, 116–117, 117, 119, 119–120, 124, 194
utilitarianism, 77, 78–79, 189, 191, 205n51

value ethics, 62, 69, 71, 72, 73, 75, 77, 198
veil of ignorance, 11, 37, 41, 146, 186, 190, 194, 205n55

veil of uncertainty, 41
virtues, 4, 6, 7, 8, 27, 77, 82, 83, 152, 156, 159, 211, 213, 218, 220, 222, 225; civic, 4, 7, 8, 18
virtue ethics, 62, 77–80, 81, 82, 134n24, 198
Vollmer, Gerhard, 23, 38, 98, 110

Washington, George, 129
weakness of will, 56, 92
wealth, 15, 69, 71, 134n24
Weber, Max, 75
welfare economics, 79, 164n29, 166, 203n14
welfare state, 3, 74
Wellmer, Albrecht, 92
Whig (liberalism), 181, 185, 198
Wilson, Edward O., 187
win-win situation, 29–33, 41, 222
wisdom. *See* cardinal virtues
Wittgenstein, Ludwig, 78
Woiceshyn, Jaana, 172
world republic, 3, 5, 5–6, 7, 8, 9, 18
world state. *See* world republic
work ethic, 167–168, 168, 171, 211
Wright, Georg Henrik von, 77

zero-sum games, 1, 29–33, 203n13

About the Author

Christoph Luetge conducts research in the field of business ethics. In his work, he analyzes the adequacy of ethical categories in modern competitive economies and large-scale societies. His approach of order ethics emphasizes the importance of the framework for ethical behavior. He is one of the first ethicists to apply the method of laboratory experiments to problems of business ethics.